CHRISTIANITY

IN

TALMUD AND MIDRASH

CHRISTIANITY

IN

TALMUD AND MIDRASH

BY

R. TRAVERS HERFORD, B.A.

Wipf and Stock Publishers
EUGENE, OREGON

Wipf and Stock Publishers
199 West 8th Avenue, Suite 3
Eugene, Oregon 97401

Christianity in Talmud and Midrash
By Herford, R. Travers
ISBN: 1-59244-193-9
Publication date: March, 2003
Previously published by Williams & Norgate, January, 1903 .

PREFACE

THE great host of books which have been written upon the early history of Christianity have, amidst all their differences, one characteristic in common. They are almost entirely based upon the study of Christian documents. This of course is natural, and no investigation which should neglect those documents would lead to results of any value. But the field of inquiry is not exhausted when the Christian literature has been thoroughly explored. There is a Jewish literature which also needs to be examined. Considering that, historically, Christianity is an outgrowth from Judaism, and that the Judaism with which the origin of Christianity was contemporary was the Judaism not of the prophets but of the Rabbis, it is obvious that the Rabbinical literature must also be consulted if a thorough investigation into the origin of Christianity is to be made. The necessity of examining the Rabbinical literature is of course denied by no scholar who has written on early Christian history, but such examination cannot be said to have been as yet thoroughly carried out. For the most part a few references are given to passages in the Mishnah and the Gemaras, or a line

or two translated. Few readers have at hand the
means of verifying these references; and thus even
the careful and accurate scholarship of writers like
Keim and Schürer does not prove very helpful, since
their readers cannot go to the sources which are
pointed out. And even Keim and Schürer indicate
but a small proportion of the material which is available in the Rabbinical literature. Edersheim does
know that literature as none but a Jew can know it,
and makes abundant reference to it; but the value
of his work as a historical study is much diminished
by a strong theological bias, apart from the fact
already mentioned, that it is usually impossible for
the reader to verify the quotations. No blame of
course attaches to these and many other scholars,
who have made incidental reference to the Rabbinical
literature, for the incompleteness and scantiness of
such reference. It can hardly be said to come within
the scope of any of the works referred to above to
give in full the Rabbinical material to which reference
is made.

It is the object of this book to try and present
that material with some approach to completeness,
in order to put within the reach of scholars who have
not access to the Rabbinical literature the full text
of the passages bearing on the subject, together with
translation and commentary. It is hoped that this
may be the means of supplying a want that as yet
remains unsatisfied, viz., of a work that shall let the
Christian scholar know *what the Rabbinical literature
really does contain bearing on the origin and early
history of Christianity.* It would be rash to say that
the collection of passages contained in this book is

exhaustive; in a great wilderness like the Talmud
and the Midrashim one can never be sure that some
passage of interest and importance has not been overlooked. But I believe it will be found that the chief
material available for the purpose has been gathered
together; and though it should not be quite complete, it will yet suffice to throw light upon several
points of interest. Even if the reader should be
of opinion that, after all, the Rabbinical literature
does not add much to what is known of Christian
history from other sources, he may at least reflect
that now he does know what that Rabbinical
literature contains.

The period covered by the passages cited extends
to the middle of the fourth century A.D., *i.e.*, roughly
speaking, the period for which the Talmud is available. No reference whatever will be made to mediæval polemics between Jews and Christians. My object
is to put before the reader all that I can find which
illustrates the relation between Jews and Christians
during the first four centuries of the common era,
and to do this solely from the Jewish side. I shall
make no attempt whatever to present the case from
Christian documents, because this has already been
thoroughly done. Further, I wish to write solely
from the point of view of historical scholarship,
with no bias towards either of the two great
religions whose representatives are mentioned in the
passages dealt with. My only aim is to present facts,
in the shape of statements contained in ancient
Jewish writings, and to extract from those statements whatever information they may afford bearing
on the historical problem of the early history of

Christianity. As a Christian who has for several years found his chief and absorbing intellectual interest in the study of the Rabbinical literature—so far as other and more pressing claims on his time would allow—I offer this book as a contribution to Christian scholarship, and I trust that the great Jewish scholars, whose works have been of so much help to me, will not frown on my small incursion into their domain.

I have only to add an expression of cordial thanks to the Rev. S. Alfred Steinthal for his kindness in reading the proofs.

Stand, Manchester,
October 1903.

TABLE OF CONTENTS

xi

LIST OF ABBREVIATIONS

M.   = Mishnah; thus, **M. Gitt. ix. 10** means Mishnah, treatise Gittin, chapter ix., section 10.

T.   = Tosephta; thus, **T. Sanh. viii. 7** means Tosephta, treatise Sanhedrin, chapter viii., section 7.

O.T. = Old Testament.

N.T. = New Testament.

R.   = Rabbi, or Rab; thus, **R. Jehoshua** means Rabbi Jehoshua.

Passages from the Rabbinical literature are cited by the leaf and the page, or the leaf and the column, following the name of the treatise. Passages from the Jerusalem Talmud are distinguished by the letter **j** before the name of the treatise, those from the Babylonian Talmud by the letter **b** similarly placed; thus j. Ḥag. means Jerusalem Talmud, treatise Ḥagigah; b. B. Mez. means Babylonian Talmud, treatise Baba Mezia.

The names of the several treatises, which are the same for Mishnah, Tosephta, and both Talmuds, also the names of the Midrashim, are abbreviated as follows:—

Ab.	Aboth.	Jom.	Joma.
A. d. R. N.	{ Aboth de Rabbi Nathan.	Kall.	Kallah.
		Kil.	Kilaim.
A. Zar.	Abhodah Zarah.	Keth.	Kethuboth.
Bamm. r.	{ Bammidbar Rabbah.	Kidd.	Kiddushin.
		Meg.	Megillah.
Bechor.	Bechoroth.	Menaḥ.	Menaḥoth.
Ber.	Berachoth.	M. Qat.	Moed Qatan.
Ber. r.	Bereshith Rabbah.	Nedar.	Nedarim.
Bicc.	Biccurim.	Nidd.	Niddah.
B. Q.	Baba Qama.	Par.	Parah.
B. Mez.	Baba Mezia.	Pesaḥ.	Pesaḥim.
B. Bathr.	Baba Bathra.	Qoh. r.	Qoheleth Rabbah.
Debar. r.	Debarim Rabbah.	R. ha-Sh.	Rosh ha-Shanah.
Dem.	Demai.	Sanh.	Sanhedrin.
Der. er. z.	Derech Eretz Zuta.	Shabb.	Shabbath.
Ech. r.	Echah Rabbah.	Shebhu.	Shebhuoth.
Erach.	Erachin.	Shem. r.	Shemoth Rabbah.
Erub.	Erubhin.	Sh. ha-Sh. r.	{ Shir ha-Shirim Rabbah.
Esth. r.	Esther Rabbah.		
Ḥag.	Ḥagigah.	Soph.	Sopherim.
Hor.	Horaioth.	Sot.	Sotah.
Ḥull.	Ḥullin.	Succ.	Succah.
Jad.	Jadaim.	Taan.	Taanith.
Jeb.	Jebamoth.	Vajiq. r.	Vajiqra Rabbah.

LIST OF CHIEF WORKS AND EDITIONS REFERRED TO

Mishnab. Amsterdam, 1685.

Talmud Jerushalmi. Krotoschin, 1866.

Talmud Babli. Wilna, 1880–85.

Ḥesronoth ha-Shas. No date.

Rabbinowicz, R. Diqduqē Sopherim, Variae Lectiones in Mishnam et Talm. Babylonicum, 1867–1886.

Tosephta. Ed. Zuckermandel, 1881.

Siphri. Ed. Friedmann, 1864.

Siphra. Ed. Weiss, 1862.

Mechilta. Ed. Friedmann, 1870.

Pesiqta de R. Kahana. Ed. Buber, 1868.

Pesiqta Rabbathi. Ed. Friedmann, 1880.

Tanḥuma. Ed. Buber, 1885.

Midrash Rabboth. Wilna, 1887.

Jalqut Shimoni. Warsaw, 1875.

Frankel, Z. Darkē ha-Mishnah, 1859.

    ,,   Mebo ha-jerushalmi, 1870.

Levy, J. Neuhebräisches Wörterbuch, 1876–1889.

    ,,   Chaldäisches Wörterbuch, 1867.

Sepher ha-Aruch. Basel, 1599.

Hamburger, J. Realencyclopädie für Bibel u. Talmud, 1870–1901.

Zunz, L. Gottesdienstliche Vorträge der Juden, 1832.

Jost, J. M. Geschichte des Judenthums, 1857.

Grätz, H. Geschichte der Juden.

Weiss, J. H. Geschichte der Jüdischen Tradition, 1871.

Weber, F. System der Altsynagogale Palestinensische Theologie, 1880.

Bacher, W. Agada der Tannaiten, 1884–90.

    ,,   Agada der Babylonischen Amoräer, 1878.

    ,,   Agada der Palestinensischen Amoräer, 1892–1899.

Laible H. Jesus Christus im Talmud. Berlin, 1891.

Friedländer. Der vorchristliche jüdische Gnosticismus. Göttingen, 1898.

Christianity in Talmud and Midrash

INTRODUCTION

THE passages from the Talmud and other Rabbinical works which will be considered in the following pages are excerpts from a literature of enormous extent, in which the intellectual energy of the Jewish nation during many centuries found ample and varied expression. To give a detailed account of this literature would lead me far from my main subject, and would, moreover, need a considerable volume for its full description. All that seems necessary here is to give in a few words a general account of the Rabbinical literature, so that the reader may be able to judge of the kind of evidence furnished by the passages which will be quoted, from some knowledge of their origin.

The details of date, authorship and contents of the several writings may be found in works of reference accessible to scholars, such as Zunz' " Gottesdienstliche Vorträge der Juden," Hamburger's " Real-Encyklopädie für Bibel und Talmud," or, for English readers, the " Introduction to Hebrew Literature " of Etheridge, a work of considerable value, in spite of the strong theological bias of the writer.

In an often quoted passage (Aboth, i. 1 *sq.*) the Talmud declares that "Moses received Torah[1] from Sinai and delivered it to Joshua, and Joshua to the Elders, and the Elders to the prophets, and the prophets delivered it to the men of the Great Synagogue. Simeon the Just was of the remnants of the Great Synagogue . . . . Antigonos of Socho received from Simeon the Just . . . . Josē ben Joezer of Zereda, and Josē ben Joḥanan of Jerusalem received from them."[2] Then follow the names of successive pairs of teachers down to Hillel and Shammai, who were contemporary with the beginning of the Christian era; and after these are mentioned singly the leading Rabbis of the first two centuries. The treatise, 'Pirqē Abōth,' as its title indicates, is a collection of 'Sayings' by these 'Fathers' of Israel. Now, whatever may be thought of the historical accuracy of the statement just quoted, it expresses clearly enough the view which the great founders of the Rabbinical literature held concerning their own work. It gives the keynote of the whole of that literature; it indicates the foundation on which it was built, and the method which its builders one

---

[1] Torah, literally 'Teaching.' The usual translation 'Law' is too narrow in its meaning. Torah denotes the whole of what, according to Jewish belief, was divinely revealed to man. As the Pentateuch contained the record of that revelation, the Torah denotes the whole contents of the Pentateuch, whether narrative or precept ; and further, it includes not merely the written contents of the Pentateuch, but also the unwritten Tradition, the so-called Oral Law, which finally took shape in the Talmud.

[2] There is a gap between Antigonos and the first Pair, as is pointed out by Strack in his edition of the Pirqē Abōth, 1882, p. 9. The Pairs of teachers are technically known as Zūgōth (זוּגוֹת).

and all adopted. The foundation is the Decalogue, and the method is Tradition.

The foundation is the Decalogue. More exactly, it is the famous declaration, *Hear, O Israel, the Lord our God, the Lord is One ; and thou shalt love the Lord thy God with all thy heart, and with all thy soul, and with all thy might* (Deut. vi. 4, 5), a declaration enshrined in the Jewish liturgy as the very soul of Judaism.[1] The Rabbinical literature is an attempt to furnish a complete answer to the question, " How shall a man love the Lord his God with all his heart and soul and might?" And even those Rabbinical writings which seem to have least reference to this main subject are dependent on it to this extent, that they would not have been written unless there had been in the minds of their authors the consciousness of this great fundamental principle.

The links in the chain of development are easily distinguished, according to the Rabbinical theory. Upon the Decalogue (of which the Shema' is the summary) rests the Pentateuch. The Ten Commandments were expanded into greater detail ; and the historical and legendary parts, as we should call them, were included, or rather were expressly written with the same object as the legal parts, viz., for instruction in the right conduct of life. Moses was regarded as the author of the whole, unless with the exception of the last eight verses of Deut. (b. B. Bathr. 14^b).[2]

Upon the Pentateuch rested the whole of the

---

[1] It is known as the *Shema'*, from its first word in Hebrew. The Shema', as recited, includes some other texts.

[2] See the Talmudic theory of the authorship of Scripture in Traditio Rabbinorum Veterrima de Librorum V. Test^ti ordine atq. origine illustrata a Gustavo Arminio Marx. Theol. licentiato. Lipsiæ, 1884.

other scriptures, according to the Rabbinical theory. That is to say, they were to be interpreted in conformity with the Pentateuch, or rather with the Torah, or Teaching, of which the Pentateuch was the written expression. The Rabbis held that the Torah, or teaching, which Moses was commissioned to give to Israel, was partly written and partly oral. It is the written Torah which is found in the Pentateuch, and developed in the other scriptures. The oral Teaching was said to have been handed down, from one generation to another, as the key to the interpretation of the written Teaching. That the Pentateuch was regarded as the standard to which the other scriptures must conform is shown by the well-known discussion as to whether the books of Ezekiel and Ecclesiastes were to be included in the Canon. The reason alleged against them was that they contradicted the Torah ; and it was only after this contradiction had been explained away that they were recognised as canonical (b. Shabb. 13^b, 30^b). What may be the value of this statement for the critical history of the O.T. Canon is a question which does not arise here.

The Rabbinical theory thus regarded the O.T. scriptures as a body of instructions based upon the Torah of Moses ; and when it is said, in the passage above referred to, that the prophets delivered the Torah to the Men of the Great Synagogue, this probably means that the Rabbis traced their own system to Ezra and Nehemiah, and thus could regard it as the continuation of the Teaching handed down by the Prophets from Moses himself. It is certain that they did thus regard it, even to the extent of believing that the whole of the Oral Law was given

to Moses, and by him handed down along with the
written Torah. The question here again is not as to
the historical facts of the development of the Rabbinism out of the O.T., but only of the view which the
Rabbis themselves held of the connexion between
them. And that view was, that after the time of the
men of the Great Synagogue, those whose names are
recorded as teachers taught by word of mouth the
Torah as it was now written, together with such
interpretation of it—not written, but handed down—
as would serve to apply it to cases not distinctly
provided for in the scriptures. It was, as always, the
Torah of Moses that was taught and expounded; and
the object was, as always, to teach men how they
ought to "Love the Lord their God with all their
heart and soul and strength and might." Historically,
we distinguish between the prophetical and the legal
elements in the contents of the O.T. The Rabbis
made no such distinction. In their religious instruction they distinguished between 'halachah' (precept)
and 'haggadah' (edification), terms which will be more
fully explained below. For the purposes of 'halachah'
they interpreted the whole of Scripture from the legal
standpoint; and, in like manner, for the purposes of
'haggadah' they interpreted the whole of Scripture
from the didactic standpoint, in neither case making
any difference between the several books of the O.T.,
as legal, historical or prophetic.

On the legal side, the task to which Rabbinism,
from the days of Ezra to the closing of the Talmud,
devoted itself with all its strength and ingenuity and
patience, was to develop a set of rules for the right
conduct of life, a code of laws, wherein the original

teaching of Moses should be applied to every conceivable event, act and duty of daily life. Historically, the founder of Jewish Legalism was Ezra, to whose mind was ever present the supreme necessity of guarding the national religion from those corruptions and laxities which had brought about the exile, and who saw no better protection against the recurrence of such a danger than an authoritative code, which should state—either in speech or writing—the divine commands which the Jewish people were to obey. If by the " Men of the Great Synagogue " we are to understand Ezra and those who worked on his lines, with him and after him, then we can understand the saying ascribed to that ancient assembly, " Make a hedge for the Torah " (Aboth, i. 1). The Torah is the divine teaching given to Moses and handed down by him; and the hedge is the Legalism, the outward form of law and precept, in which henceforth it was to be preserved. The Talmud indicates its view of the work of Ezra, and also of the connexion between his work and that of the Rabbis by saying (b. Succ. 27ª) : " In the beginning, when the Torah was forgotten, Ezra went up from Babylon and founded it ; again it was forgotten and Hillel the Babylonian¹ went up and founded it ; again it was forgotten and Rabbi Hija and his sons went up and founded it." In other

---

¹ Hillel was no doubt the founder of Rabbinism in the stricter sense, for he introduced the exegetical rules on which the Rabbinical casuistry is founded. But Ezra is the true founder of that Legalism, of which Talmudic Rabbinism is the logical result. To compare Hillel with Jesus on the ground of their gentleness is to ignore the fact that Hillel did more than anyone else had done to organise that Tradition of the Elders which Jesus denounced. In their conception of the *form* of religion, Jesus and Hillel stood at opposite poles of thought.

words, both the Legalism of Ezra, and the Rabbinism of which Hillel was the first representative, are the outward form of the Torah, the divine teaching given to Moses; and in every detail, every minutest precept which Rabbinical ingenuity developed, there is assumed as the ground of all the primal religious duty, "Thou shalt love the Lord thy God with all thy heart and soul and might."

Whether the form of definite precept and precise rule is the best adapted to promote the living of a righteous life is not here the question. Right or wrong, better or worse, it is the form which the Rabbis chose for the expression of their conception of the religious life. And the whole system of Rabbinism is misjudged, unless it be carefully and constantly borne in mind that it is all an expansion of the idea of human service of God, under the form of precept. What is usually called 'empty formalism,' 'solemn trifling' and the like, deserves a nobler name; for it is—whether mistaken or not—an honest effort to apply the principle of service of God to the smallest details and acts of life. That, in practice, such a conception of religious life might lead to hypocrisy and formalism is undeniable, and the Talmud itself is perfectly well aware of the fact. But that it necessarily leads to hypocrisy, that it is impossible on such lines to develop a true religious life, the whole history of Judaism from the time of Hillel downwards is the emphatic denial. The great Rabbis whose work is preserved in the Talmud were not hypocrites or mere formalists, but men who fully realised the religious meaning of what was expressed in the form of legal precept and apparently trivial

regulation. They were under no mistake as to what
it all meant; and the heroism which has marked the
Jewish people through all the tragic history of
eighteen Christian centuries has found its divine in-
spiration in the Torah as the Rabbis interpreted it.
To them it was the word of God, in all its fulness
and depth; and no Jew who thoroughly entered into
the spirit of the Rabbinical conception of religious
life ever felt the Torah a burden, or himself bound
as by galling fetters. Paul doubtless spoke out of
the depths of his own experience; but he does not
represent the mind of the great leaders of Rabbinism.
And the system of thought and practice which bears
that name is unfairly judged if it is condemned on the
witness of its most determined enemies. Judged on
its own merits, and by the lives and words of its own
exponents and defenders, it is a consistent and logical
endeavour to work out a complete guide to the living
of a perfect life, and whatever verdict may be passed
upon that endeavour, the right word is not failure.

The foundation, then, of Rabbinism is the precept,
*Thou shalt love the Lord thy God with all thy
heart and all thy soul and all thy might.* The
method is tradition. This is indicated by the names
which the Rabbis themselves gave to the mass of
religious precept which they taught, viz., Massōreth
(מסורת), and less frequently Qăbbālā.[1] The same fact

[1] Massōreth, or Massōrah, from מסר to hand over, deliver; more fully,
מ' הזקנים, παράδοσις τῶν πρεσβυτέρων (Mark vii. 5). Qăbbālā, from קבל to
receive, cp. Mark, *ib.* 4, ἃ παρέλαβον κρατεῖν, *which they have received
to hold.* The term Massorah is also used in a special sense to designate the
apparatus criticus devised by the Jewish Grammarians for the fixing of the
text of Scripture. The term Qabbala likewise has a specialised meaning
when used to denote the system of Theosophy or secret doctrine, set forth
in the books 'Jetzirah' and 'Zohar.'

is shown by the formula to be found on every page
of the Talmud, in which a precept is expressed,
" Rabbi A. says, in the name of Rabbi B," or, " Rabbi
A. says that Rabbi B. says that Rabbi C. says, etc."
Some authority must confirm the dictum of every
teacher, the authority, viz., of some previous teacher,
or else the authority of the Torah interpreted according to some recognised rule. No teacher could base
his teaching merely on his own authority; and the
fact that Jesus did this, was no doubt one of the
grievances against him on the part of the Jews.
*Ye have heard that it was said to them of old time
. . . . but I say unto you,* etc. (Matt. v. 21, 22),
implies the disavowal of the Rabbinical method ; and
the statement (Matt. vii. 28, 29) that Jesus *taught
them as one having authority and not as their scribes,*
was certainly cause sufficient that the people should
be *astonished at his teaching,* and that the scribes
should be incensed and alarmed.

The question naturally arises here, How could new
teaching find a place where, in theory, nothing was
valid unless it had been handed down ? That new
teaching did find a place is evident, if only from the
fact that the modest volume of the O.T. was expanded into the enormous bulk of the Talmud, to say
nothing of the Midrash; while, on the other hand,
the principle of receiving only what rested on the
authority of tradition was jealously upheld and
resolutely enforced. For want of a clear understanding
of the relation between the new and the old in
Rabbinism, that system has been condemned as a
rigid formalism, crushing with the dead weight of
antiquity the living forces of the soul, and preventing

all growth and expansion of thought. It is doubtless true that *the letter killeth but the spirit giveth
life;* but the truth of that great saying is not the
condemnation of Rabbinism, any more than it is of
Christianity; and it might have been spoken with no
less right by Aqiba than by Paul, for the one, no less
than the other, was an originator within the lines of
his own form of religious thought.

The answer to the question, ' How could new teaching find a place in a system based exclusively on
tradition '? admits of a simple statement. The Torah
as given to Moses, and by him handed down, was
regarded as containing the whole of divine truth, not
merely so much as might at any given time have
been discerned, but all that in all future ages might
be brought to light. This divine truth was partly
explicit, partly implicit. That which was explicit
was stated in Scripture, more particularly in the
Mosaic laws, and also in that oral tradition which
furnished the interpretation and application of the
Scripture. That which was implicit was the further,
as yet undiscovered, meaning contained in the Torah.
And the whole task of Rabbinism was to render that
explicit which had been implicit, to discover and un-
fold more and more of the divine truth contained in
the Torah, so as to make it available for the perfecting
of the religious life. When, therefore, a Rabbi taught
some new application of a religious precept, what
was new was the application; the precept was old.[1]
He was not adding to the Torah, but showing

---

[1] This is clearly stated in the Talmud (j. Ḥag. i. 8. 76ᶜ): "Even that
which an acute disciple shall teach in the presence of his Rabbi has already
been said to Moses on Sinai."

for the first time some hitherto unknown contents of it. The sum total of Torah was unaltered; but part of it had been transformed from implicit to explicit. Thus a new teaching could not but rest upon Tradition, because it was merely the unfolding into greater clearness of meaning what the Torah had all along contained. And it was only new, in so far as such and such a Rabbi had been the first to declare that development of the original principle. Rabbinism never did, because it never could, reach the logical end of its own method; but the complicated and minute legislation embodied in the Talmud, is, on the Rabbinical theory, merely the unfolding of what was contained in the original Torah —rendered explicit instead of implicit. Thus it appears that even in that department of the Rabbinical system where the principle of Tradition was most strictly maintained, there was ample room for the expansion and adaptation of the original principle to the varying needs of practical religious life. In other departments, perhaps rather the other chief department of the Rabbinical system, there was little or no attempt at restraint upon individual liberty of teaching. These two departments, or main divisions of Rabbinical teaching, are called respectively *Halachah* and *Haggadah* (or Agada, as it is often, though perhaps less correctly, given).[1] The distinction between these two has often been explained; but a few words upon them here may serve to bring out a fact which has not always been duly recognised. *Hălāchāh* (from הלך to go) denotes that which is

---

[1] See an article by W. Bacher, " On the origin of the word Haggada (Agada)," in the *Jewish Quarterly Review*, 1892, p. 406 fol.

recognised as a valid and therefore binding law of
religious practice. The connexion between this, its
undoubted meaning, and that of the root from which
it is derived, is uncertain, and has been variously
explained. The etymological question need not de-
tain us here. *Halachah* is therefore that system of
rule and precept to which the religious life of the Jew
must conform. The several rules and precepts, indi-
vidually, are called *Hălāchōth* (plural of Halachah).
The Torah of Moses was, first and foremost, Halachah ; what it taught was, above all things, how a
man should love the Lord his God with all his heart
and soul and might ; in other words, how he should
serve God most perfectly (see above, p. 7). The
task of Rabbinism was to ascertain and determine
Halachah, in its fullest extent, to discover the whole
of what divine wisdom had decreed for the guidance
of man. And it was in regard to Halachah that the
principle of Tradition was most rigorously upheld,
because it was above all things essential that Halachah, the law of right conduct binding on every
Israelite, should be accurately defined and based
upon ample authority.

The other main division of Rabbinical teaching,
known as Haggadah, differed from Halachah both in
its object and its method. Haggadah denotes illustrative teaching ; and it includes all that can help to
build up religious character otherwise than by the
discipline of positive command. It includes theological speculation in its widest range, also ethical
instruction and exhortation ; and its object is to
throw all the light of past thought and experience
upon the present duty. It is thus the necessary

accompaniment of Halachah; both have the same general purpose, viz., to teach a true service of God; but the one proceeds by way of direct command, and rests upon divine authority, the other by way of exhortation and explanation, with no other authority than the wisdom and knowledge of the individual teacher. This is said without forgetting the fact that the great teachers of Haggadah were looked upon with the deepest reverence, and their teaching received with great deference. Moreover, the Haggadah was considered to be contained in the Scripture, and to be deducible thence by regular rules of inference. But nevertheless it is true that the teaching and development of Haggadah was under no such strict restraint as was required for Halachah. And Haggadah served as the outlet for the creative imagination of the Rabbinical mind, which could find no scope in the severe logic of Halachah. The teacher of Haggadah gave free rein to his thought; his object was edification, and he made use of everything —history, legend, anecdote, fable, parable, speculation upon every subject from the most sublime to the most trivial—which might serve to teach some religious lesson, and thereby develop religious character. The Haggadist made no scruple of altering not merely the narrative but the text of Scripture, for the sake of drawing out a religious or moral lesson; and where Scripture was silent, the Haggadist freely invented incidents and traits of character in regard to Scripture personages, not stopping short of the Almighty Himself. Frequent appeal is made to the example of non-biblical Fathers in Israel, and it is to the Haggadah that we owe nearly all our information as to the personal character and life-history of the Rabbis. Anecdotes and historical reminiscences abound in the Haggadah, which is the chief reason why to non-Jewish readers the Haggadah is so much more interesting than the dry and difficult Halachah. It is hard for any one but a Jew to realise the direct personal concern, and therefore intense interest, of Halachic discussions ; while in the Haggadah, the human interest never fails, nor the charm—at least for those who have sufficient sympathy and insight to enter into a form of thought widely different from their own.

Having thus briefly indicated what is meant by Halachah and Haggadah, and before going on to describe their mutual relation in the Rabbinical literature, I pause for a moment to draw a comparison, or rather a contrast, between the development of Rabbinical and Christian thought. The contrast is certainly a sharp one, yet there is a considerable likeness. Both have a Tradition of the Elders, and rest a part of their teaching upon authority presumed to be divine. This has been already shown in regard to Rabbinism. In regard to Christianity the same fact appears in connexion with dogmatic theology. What is of faith is taught on the authority of creeds or decrees of councils, or the writings of the Church Fathers, or of Scripture as expounded by competent and accredited interpreters. The Roman Catholic Church definitely places Tradition among the sources of the teaching which she gives ; and if Protestantism repudiates Tradition to take her stand upon the Bible only, she nevertheless admits the authority of ancient expositions of Scripture and definitions of faith. Both Rabbinism and historical Christianity alike recognise that to set forth the contents of the word of God is the supreme object of religious thought; and they have jealously guarded the Torah, or the True Faith, from the interference of unauthorised exponents. The verbal expression is different in the two cases, as the matter of thought is different; but in both the liberty of individual opinion was confined within strict and definite limits, and to overstep those limits was in each case heresy.

In like manner both Rabbinism and Christianity have a department of religious teaching where no restraint is put upon the freedom of the individual to hold and teach his own opinions, whatever they might be. In Rabbinism this is Haggadah; in Christianity it is all that helps to the right conduct of life, moral teaching, encouragement to good works, and the like. There is in regard to these subjects nothing to prevent the Christian teacher from teaching out of his own heart and conscience whatever seems good and right. And while the great Christian teachers, in this department, are deeply reverenced, and their teaching received with the deference due to their wisdom and experience, there is no such authority attaching to their words as there is in the case of those who have helped to define the Faith. Their teaching is " not to establish any doctrine, but for example of life and instruction of manners," and no heresy is implied by divergence of opinion.

While there is thus a considerable likeness between Rabbinical Judaism and historical Christianity, in regard to both principle and method, the contrast between them is the more striking from the fact that each system applies restriction to what the other leaves free, and each allows liberty where the other imposes restraint. Rabbinism prescribes what a man shall *do*, and defines his service of God in precise rules, while it leaves him perfectly unfettered in regard to what he shall *believe*. Such a thing as a doctrinal creed is foreign to Rabbinism— Maimonides notwithstanding. Historical Christianity prescribes what a man shall *believe*, and defines the True Faith in precise creeds; while it leaves him perfectly unfettered in regard to what he should *do*—unfettered, that is, except by his own conscience. Christianity never set up a moral creed; she did not make sin a heresy, but heresy a sin. To sum up this comparison in a single sentence, while historical Christianity is based on the conception of ortho*doxy*, Rabbinism rests on the conception of what I venture to call ortho*praxy*. The one insists on Faith, and gives liberty of Works; the other insists on Works, and gives liberty of Faith.

It would be interesting and instructive to pursue this line of thought still further, and endeavour to form an estimate of the comparative value of the two contrasted systems as theories of religious life. I refrain from doing so, however, as my purpose in making the comparison has been sufficiently attained if I have succeeded in explaining and illustrating the answer of Rabbinism to the two great questions of Duty and Belief. That answer is given in the Halachah and Haggadah respectively; and I go on to show how these two elements are combined and distinguished in the Rabbinical literature. For this purpose I will briefly refer to the chief representative works of that literature.

Pre-eminent among them all stands the Talmud; and after what has been already said, it will not be difficult to explain the general nature of this colossal work. Bearing in mind that the main task of Rabbinism was to ascertain and define Halachah, it will be evident that in the course of years, and by the labours of many contemporary and successive Rabbis, a large number of decisions upon questions of Halachah gradually accumulated. Some of these, dating from far-off antiquity, were undisputed; others were subjected to keen examination and scrutiny before being pronounced to be really Halachah. But, while many decisions were rejected, for want of a sufficient basis of authority, the number of those that were accepted increased with every generation of teachers. More than once, during the first two centuries of our era, attempts were made to codify and arrange the growing mass of Halachah, the confusion of which was increased by the fact that the whole was carried in the memory alone, not put down in writing. The work of codification, attempted by Aqiba and others, was finally completed by Rabbi Jehudah ha-Qadosh (the Holy), usually known as Rabbi *par excellence;* and the collection which he formed is known as the Mishnah. The date of its completion is usually given as 220 A.D., or thereabouts. Mishnah denotes both 'teaching' and 'repetition'; and the work so called professed to be the repetition, in enlarged form, of the Torah of Moses. The Mishnah is a collection of

2

Halachoth—presumably of all the Halachoth whose validity was recognised so far as known to the compiler; and it deals with every department of practical conduct. Under six main divisions ('Sĕdārīm,' or orders), and sixty - three treatises ('Massichtōth'), the duties of the faithful Israelite are set forth, as positive or negative commands. But the Mishnah contains Haggadah as well as Halachah. Along with the precepts, and the discussions in which they were defined, there are illustrative and explanatory notes, historical and personal reminiscences, designed to show the purpose or explain the meaning of some decision. These are Haggadah; and they occur in the midst of Halachah, with not the slightest mark to distinguish the one from the other. The amount of Haggadah in the Mishnah, however, is not great compared with that of Halachah. And, in consequence, while the Mishnah is easier to read than the Gemara in point of language, it is far less interesting owing to the scantiness of the human element provided in the Haggadah.

As above stated, the Mishnah was completed somewhere about the year 220 A.D.; and though at first it only existed as oral teaching, it appears to have been very soon written down. From henceforth it was the standard collection of Halachoth, though other collections existed of which mention will be presently made. As the standard collection of Halachoth, it naturally became in its turn the subject of study, since many of its precepts were of uncertain meaning. To mention only one reason for this, the destruction of the Temple, and

the consequent cessation of all the ritual and ceremonial of worship, reduced the precepts connected
therewith to a branch of archæology; while on the
other hand, it increased the need of defining with
the utmost precision the right practice in those
matters, so that it might not be forgotten if ever the
time should come for the resumption of the Temple
services. And, if some are inclined to think lightly
of the time and thought spent upon questions which
could have no practical outcome for those who debated them, there is still a pathetic and even a heroic
aspect in the toil which preserved a sacred memory
so that it might keep alive a no less sacred hope.

The Mishnah, then, became in its turn the subject
of commentary, interpretation and expansion. The
name given to this superadded commentary is
Gĕmārā, which means 'completion.' But, whereas
there is only one Mishnah, there are two Gemaras.
The Mishnah was studied not only in the schools of
Palestine, but also in those of Babylonia. And by
the labours of these two groups of teachers there was
developed a Palestinian Gemara and a Babylonian
Gemara. In course of time the same need for
codification of the growing mass of Tradition began
to be felt in regard to the Gemaras which had
previously led to the formation of the Mishnah.
The Gemara of Palestine was ended,—not completed,—towards the close of the fourth century;
while it was not until the sixth century that the
Gemara of Babylonia was reduced to the form in
which we now have it. The name Talmud is given
to the whole *corpus* of Mishnah *plus* Gemara; and
thus it is usual to distinguish between the Palestinian

Talmud (otherwise known as the Talmud of Jerusalem) and the Babylonian Talmud.[1]

To give any account of the multifarious contents of either Talmud, even of that of Jerusalem, which is much shorter and simpler than that of Babylon, would be a work of great length and difficulty, almost amounting indeed to a translation of the huge work with the commentaries upon it.   Briefly, it consists (in both Talmuds) of a series of discussions upon the several Halachoth contained in the Mishnah.   In the course of these discussions, all manner of digressions interrupt the argument, — personal anecdotes, speculations upon points of theology or philosophy, fragments of history, scraps of science, folklore, travellers' tales—in short, anything and everything that could be supposed to have even the remotest connection with the subject under discussion are brought in, to the grievous perplexity of the reader.   To add to the difficulty, this chaotic mass is printed in an unpointed text, with no stops except at the end of a paragraph, and no sort of mark to distinguish the various elements one from the other. And, finally, the language of the two Gemaras (based

---

[1] The Hebrew names are 'Talmud Jerushalmi,' and 'T. Babli' respectively. I do not know why the former is called T. Jerushalmi; because, of the various schools in which it was developed, probably none, certainly none of any importance, had its seat in Jerusalem. It is usually understood that residence in Jerusalem was forbidden to Jews after the last war, in 135 A.D. Yet it is stated (b. Pes. 113ᵃ) that R. Joḥanan, one of the founders of the Palestinian Gemara, cited a tradition " in the name of the men of Jerusalem." On the whole, however, it seems to me most probable that the Palestinian Talmud was merely called after the name of the capital city, as indeed the T. Babli may be said to have been called after the name of the capital city of the land where the chief Rabbinical schools of the East flourished for centuries.

upon eastern and western Aramaic respectively) is far more difficult than that of the Mishnah, being, as it is, concise to a degree that Thucydides might have envied, and Tacitus striven in vain to imitate. It is full of technical terms and foreign words, which are the despair of the reader who knows only his Hebrew Bible. Yet there is order and method even in the Talmud, and it is a great mistake to suppose that its contents may be treated as a series of unconnected sentences, whose meaning is clear apart from their context, and without reference to the deep underlying principles which give vitality to the whole. The passages which will presently be cited from the Talmud may serve as illustrations of what has been said, so far as mere translations, however literal, can represent an original text so peculiar and so bizarre; and, in presenting them apart from their context, I trust I have not been unmindful of the caution just given.

The twofold Talmud is by far the most important work of the early Rabbinical literature. Yet there are others, dating from the same centuries, which can by no means be passed by unnoticed. It was stated above that the Mishnah was not the only collection of Halachoth, though it was adopted as the standard. To say nothing of the fact that the Gemaras contain many Halachoth not included in the Mishnah (hence called 'Baraitha,' i.e. external), there exists at least one independent collection of Halachoth, as a sort of rival to the Mishnah. This is known as Tosephta, a name which means 'addition' or 'supplement,' as if it had been intended merely to supply what was wanting in the standard work. Yet

it is not improbable that the existing Mishnah and
the existing Tosephta are only two out of many
contemporary collections great or small, two com-
pilations founded upon the works of many previous
teachers, and that of these two, "one was taken and
the other left." The two collections might almost
have exchanged names, so that what is now known
as the Mishnah might conceivably have come to be
looked upon as Tosephta to the other. And, although the one enjoys a sort of canonical authority
not recognised in the other, yet for historical purposes they are both of equal value, since both contain traditions dating from the earliest centuries of
the common era. The contents of Tosephta are,
as will have appeared above, mainly Halachah; but
Haggadah also is found, as in the case of the Mishnah, and in greater abundance.

The works above described, viz., Mishnah, Gemaras,
and Tosephta, have for their common purpose the
development and definition of Halachah as the rule
for the right conduct of life, the expansion into
minute detail of the principle, *Thou shalt love the
Lord thy God with all thy heart and soul and
strength.* But the Rabbinical literature includes
another very extensive class of works, in which the
same principle is dealt with in a somewhat different
manner. The generic name for works of this class is
'Midrash,' *i.e.* exposition; and the common characteristic of them all is that they are free commentaries
upon books or portions of books of the O.T.
Perhaps commentary is hardly the right word; for
the Midrash does not profess to explain every point
of difficulty in the text with which it deals, and, as

a rule, it makes no reference to grammatical and linguistic questions. The purpose of the Midrash is to expound the Scriptures with a view to edification and instruction, from the standpoint not of the scholar but of the preacher. And probably the contents of the various Midrashim are collected extracts from the sermons, as we might call them, of the Rabbis to their hearers, either in the synagogues or the schools. The general plan of a Midrash is to take a book or selected passages of a book of the O.T., and to arrange under each separate verse in order the expositions of several Rabbis. The connexion between the text and the exposition is often very slight; and, just as in the case of the Gemaras, digressions are frequent, as opportunity offers for bringing in some interesting but irrelevant topic. The method of Tradition is followed in the Midrash, though not with the same strictness as in the Talmud. Most of the expository notes are given in the name of some Rabbi, and of course the whole body of Midrash is now Tradition. But a good deal of the contents of many Midrashim is anonymous, and therefore presumably due to the compiler. In no instance in the Rabbinical literature can we say that any individual Rabbi is the author of such and such a work; at most he is the editor. But a nearer approach is made to individual authorship in the Midrash than in the Talmudic literature.

Midrash, then, is homiletic exposition of Scripture. And it will be seen from what has been said above, that the distinction between Halachah and Haggadah is applicable no less to the Midrash than to the

Talmud. That is to say, there can be Midrash whose chief purpose is to connect Halachah with Scripture, and again Midrash which chiefly aims at connecting Haggadah with Scripture. Of these two classes, the Halachic Midrashim are the more ancient, the Haggadic by far the more numerous. Of the Halachic Midrashim, the chief works are *Siphra*, on the book of Leviticus; *Siphri*, on Numbers and Deuteronomy; and *Mechilta*, upon parts of Exodus. These were compiled, according to Zunz, at a later date than the Mishnah, but contain in part older material. And while they do not exclude Haggadah, where the text suggests it, they are prevailingly Halachic, since a great part of the text dealt with is concerned with the ceremonial law. *Siphra* and *Siphri* are frequently made use of in the Talmud.[1]

The Haggadic Midrashim are very numerous, and the period of their production covers several centuries. Even the earliest of them is much later as regards date of compilation than the earliest Halachic Midrash. There is more need, on this account, of caution in using their statements as historical evidence. Yet, since those statements rest on tradition, and refer to many well-known names, there seems no reason why they should—other reasons apart—be denied all historical value. I have therefore made use of what the Midrash offered for my purpose, with, I trust, due critical caution. Of the Haggadic Midrashim, the most important in point of extent is the so-called Midrash Rabbah (or M. Rabboth), a collection of expositions upon the

---

[1] See Zunz, " Gottesd. Vortr. d. Juden," pp. 46–48.

Pentateuch and the five Megilloth (*i.e.* Ruth, Esther, Lamentations, Song of Songs, and Ecclesiastes). The ten Midrashim are of very various date, and were not gathered into one great collection till as late as the thirteenth century. Other Midrashim, of similar character, are Tanḥuma, or Jelam'denu, on the Pentateuch, Pesiqta on selected passages, and Jalqut Shim'oni on the whole of the O.T., being a vast collection of extracts from earlier Midrashim. For details concerning these and many similar works, I refer the reader to the books of Zunz, Hamburger, and others mentioned above. My object in this introduction is not to give a bibliography of Rabbinical literature, but to indicate the general scope and method of that literature, so that the reader may have some idea of the sources whence the passages, which will presently be given, have been extracted.

It will now be possible, as it is highly desirable, to attempt an answer to the question, What is the value, as historical evidence, of the Rabbinical literature? Can any reliance be placed upon statements found in works whose main purpose was not to impart exact knowledge of facts, but to give religious and moral teaching?

Nothing is easier than to pick out from the Talmud and the Midrash statements in regard to historical events, which are palpably and even monstrously false, and that, too, when the events referred to were not very far removed from the lifetime of the author of the statements. And the conclusion is ready to hand, that if, in regard to events almost within living memory, such error was possible, reliance cannot be placed upon statements concerning events more remote. Yet that hasty conclusion is refuted by the fact that the statements referring to historical events are sometimes confirmed by external testimony, such as the writings of non-Jewish historians, and sometimes, when not directly confirmed, are still in accordance with such external testimony. No one would dream of accepting as true all the historical statements of the Talmud and Midrash; but they are certainly not all false. And it ought not to be, and I believe is not, beyond the power of a careful criticism, to distinguish with some degree of probability the historically true from the historically false.

It must be borne in mind that the whole of the literature under consideration is a collection of Traditions. Now, while such a method of retaining and transmitting knowledge is exposed to the dangers of omission, addition, and alteration in a greater degree than is the case with written documents, yet on the other hand the fact that such a method was alone employed implies that the power of memory was cultivated and improved also in a greater degree than is usual with those who only or chiefly make use of writing. The Talmud and Midrash afford illustrations of both these propositions; for while we find that varying forms are handed down of one and the same tradition, the difference in the form shows that the tradition was the subject of remembrance in several minds and over considerable periods of time. It must also be borne in mind that the Talmud is not "a dateless book," as it has been called, but that the main points in its chronology

are well known, being determined by the biographical
data of the leading Rabbis. The researches of
W. Bacher[1] have shown beyond dispute that these
biographical data are, on the whole, mutually consistent; and thus we are provided with a firm
foundation on which to rest a case for the credibility
of the Rabbinical records. If the whole were a mere
tissue of extravagant inventions, there would be no
such consistency; and further, it is often possible to
mark where the historical tradition leaves off and
the legendary invention begins. Thus, R. Jehoshua
b. Levi is a perfectly well-known historical figure,
and one whose name occurs numberless times in the
Talmud and Midrash; of him various facts are
related which there is no reason to call in question,
while in addition other stories are told—such as his
conversation with the Angel of Death (b. Keth. 77[b])
—which are plainly imaginary.

In judging, then, of the reliability, as historical
evidence, of the Rabbinical records, we must take as
our guide, in the first instance, the chronology of the
lives of the Rabbis themselves, and note whether their
statements refer to matters nearly or quite contemporary. Thus, when Rabbi A. says that on a certain
occasion he walked with Rabbi B. who told him
so and so, or again, that when he was a boy he remembered seeing Rabbi C. who did so and so, he is
presumably speaking of things well within his know-

---

[1] " Agada der Tannaïten," " Ag. der Palestinensischen Amoräer," " Ag. d.
Babylonischen Amoräer." Bacher is not the only scholar who has dealt
with Rabbinical biography ; but so far as I know, his work is much more
thorough and complete than any other on the same subject ; and I would
here express my very great obligation for the help I have derived from the
invaluable works I have named above.

ledge. And though these incidental remarks may refer to things in themselves very trivial, yet they serve to extend the region of credibility. Indeed, it is perhaps in these incidental remarks that the largest harvest of historical fact is to be gathered. Because they are usually the illustration, drawn from the actual knowledge and experience of the teacher who mentions them, of the subject with which he is dealing. A Rabbi, especially one who was skilful in Haggadah, would permit himself any degree of exaggeration or invention even in regard to historical persons and events, if thereby he could produce a greater impression. Thus, an event so terribly well known as the great war, which ended with the death of Bar Cocheba and the capture of Bethar in 135 A.D., was magnified in the description of its horrors beyond all bounds of possibility. And probably no one was better aware of the exaggeration than the Rabbi who uttered it.[1] But then the purpose of that Rabbi would be, not to give his hearers an exact account of the great calamity, but to dwell on the horror of it, and to burn it in upon the minds of the people as a thing never to be forgotten. Yet there are many incidental remarks about the events of the war which are free from such exaggeration, and being in no way improbable in themselves, are such as might well have been known to the relater of them. The long passage b. Gitt. 57ª–58ª contains a variety of statements about the wars of Nero, Vespasian, and Hadrian; it is reported to a considerable extent by R. Johanan, whose informant was R. Shim'on b.

[1] Cp. what is said below, p. 252, as to Rabbinical statements concerning the former population of Palestine.

Joḥai, who himself took part in the last war. No one would dream of crediting the assertion that for seven years the vineyards in Palestine needed and received no other manure than the blood of those slain in the war. But the story that young Ishmael b. Elisha was carried captive to Rome, and discovered there and released, is in every way probable. Ishmael b. Elisha was the name of two very well-known Rabbis, one the grandson of the other, and the younger being the contemporary and rival of Aqiba. Nothing is more likely than that stories of the lives and adventures of these men should have been told amongst their friends and remembered in later times. Such stories must of course be judged on their own merits. But if they are in themselves reasonable and probable, there is nothing to discredit them in the mere fact that they are found in works like the Talmud and Midrash, embedded in a mass of Haggadic speculation. Neither Talmud nor Midrash were intended primarily to teach history; but from the manner of their origin and growth, they could hardly fail to show some traces of contemporary history. Therefore, in place of condemning as apocryphal all and sundry of the allusions to historical personages and events contained in the Talmud and Midrash, we may and ought to distinguish amongst them. And perhaps we may make some approach to a general canon of criticism on the subject, if we say that in the literature referred to, the *obiter dicta* are of most value as evidence of historical fact; or, in other words, there is more reason to suspect exaggeration or invention in statements which appear to form part of the main line of the argument, than in those

which appear to be merely illustrative notes, added
to the text and embedded in it. The purpose of
Haggadah (to which all these historical references
belong) is homiletic ; it aims at building up religious
and moral character by every means other than the
discipline of positive precept (see above, p. 12).
Reference to historical fact was only one, and by no
means the most important, form of Haggadah. Since
it is in Haggadah that the Rabbinical mind found the
outlet for its instinct of speculative inquiry, and the
play of its fancy and imagination, as already explained,
it is natural to expect that these will be most prominent and most abundant in Haggadic passages because
most in accordance with the genius of Haggadah.
When, accordingly, we find in the midst of such
fanciful and exaggerated passages occasional statements which appear to be plain, sober matter of fact,
there is the more reason to accept the latter as being
historically reliable (at least intended to be so),
because the author (or narrator) might have increased
their effect as illustrations by free invention, and has
chosen not to do so. I say that such statements may
be accepted as being at least intended to be historically reliable. They must be judged on their merits,
and where possible tested by such methods as would
be applied to any other statements professedly
historical. The narrator who gives them may have
been wrongly informed, or may have incorrectly.
remembered ; but my point is that in such statements
he intends to relate what he believes to be matter of
fact, and not to indulge his imagination.

I have made this attempt to work out a canon of
criticism for the historical value of the Rabbinical

literature, because such a canon seems to me to be greatly needed. So far as I am competent to judge, it appears to me that Jewish historians—as is only natural—make a far more legitimate and intelligent use of the Rabbinical literature for historical purposes than is generally to be observed in the writings of Christian historians who have dealt with that literature. Even in the works of Keim and Schürer, whose scholarship is above reproach, I do not remember to have found any attempt to set forth the principles on which they make use of the Rabbinical literature for historical purposes. And it is perhaps not too much to say that in most Christian writings that touch upon the Rabbinical literature there is little or no appearance of any such principles; sometimes, indeed, there is a mere reproduction of statements from previous writers, which the borrower has not verified and not always understood.

The principle which I have stated above will, of course, find its illustration in the treatment of the passages from the Rabbinical literature to be presently examined. That is to say, an attempt will be made to estimate the historical value of the statements contained in them. But it should be observed that for historical purposes they may be valuable in one or both of two ways. Whether or not they establish the fact that such and such an event took place, they at least establish the fact that such and such a belief was held in reference to the alleged event, or the person concerned in it. Thus we shall find that several instances are mentioned of miracles alleged to have been worked by Jews or Christians. The mere statement does not prove that these were actu-

ally performed, any more than the mere statement of the N.T. writers proves that the alleged
miracles of Jesus and the Apostles were actually
performed. But in the one case or in the other, the
record of alleged miracles, made in all good faith, is
clear proof of the belief that such events did take
place and had taken place.

So also we shall find many instances of discussion
upon topics chiefly scriptural, between Jewish Rabbis
and certain persons called Mīnīm.[1] Now the record
of such discussions may be, in a given case, inaccurate;
but it is proof positive of the belief that such discussions had actually occurred, and indeed may be said
to establish not merely the belief but the fact that
they had occurred. Therefore, whatever may be the
amount of actual historical fact established by the
passages from the Rabbinical writings examined in
the present work, they will at least have the value
(and it is no slight one) that belongs to records of
opinion and belief upon the subject for the illustration
of which they have been chosen.

To the consideration of those passages I will now
proceed, having given what I trust may be a sufficient,
as well as a reliable, explanation of their nature and
origin. I merely premise one word as to the classification of them, and the method by which I shall deal
with their contents. The subjects referred to in them
are so various that an exhaustive classification would
involve a great deal of repetition, since one passage
might be appropriately placed under each of several
heads. This might be avoided by arranging them

[1] The whole question of the interpretation of the word Mīnīm will be
dealt with hereafter.

in the order of their occurrence in the Talmudic treatises and the several Midrashim. But such an arrangement would not afford the slightest help to the reader who wished to find what was said upon a given subject, *e.g.* the Christian scriptures. The same objection would apply to a chronological classification, according to which the passages should be arranged under the dates of the several Rabbis responsible for them.

I have thought it best to make a classification according to the main subject dealt with in each passage. I place first of all the passages referring to Jesus; then, the much larger group of those relating to followers of Jesus. Each passage or series of passages will have its title, indicating the main subject to which it refers; and an index of all the titles will be found in the table of contents. Under each title will be given the translation of one or more passages, bearing upon the particular topic, together with sufficient commentary to explain its meaning and its connexion with the main subject. The Hebrew and Aramaic texts, numbered consecutively to correspond with the translated passages, will be collected in an appendix. Following upon the translations and commentaries, a concluding chapter will sum up the general results of the inquiry, under the two main heads of the Tradition concerning Jesus and the Tradition concerning the Minim.

PASSAGES FROM THE RABBINICAL LITERATURE,

ILLUSTRATING THE RISE AND DEVELOPMENT OF CHRISTIANITY IN THE EARLY CENTURIES

DIVISION I

A.—PASSAGES RELATING TO JESUS

BIRTH AND PARENTAGE OF JESUS

(1) b. Shabbath 104[b]. (The passage in [ ] occurs also b. Sanh. 67[a].) "He who cuts upon his flesh." It is tradition that Rabbi Eliezer said to the Wise, 'Did not Ben Stada bring spells from Egypt in a cut which was upon his flesh?' They said to him, 'He was a fool, and they do not bring a proof from a fool.' [Ben Stada is Ben Pandira. Rab Ḥisda said, 'The husband was Stada, the paramour was Pandira.' The husband was Pappos ben Jehudah, the mother was Stada. The mother was Miriam the dresser of women's hair, as we say in Pumbeditha, 'Such a one has been false to her husband.']

Commentary.[1]—The above passage occurs in a

[1] I would here express generally my indebtedness to the work of Heinrich Laible, "Jesus Christus im Talmud," Berlin, 1891. In the section

discussion upon the words in the Mishnah which forbid all kinds of writing to be done on the Sabbath. Several kinds are specified, and among them the making of marks upon the flesh. The words at the beginning of the translation are the text, so to speak, of the Mishnah which is discussed in what follows. To illustrate the practice of marking or cutting the flesh, the compilers of the Gemara introduce a tradition (Baraitha, not included in the Mishnah, see above, p. 21) according to which R. Eliezer asked the question, ' Did not Ben Stada bring magical spells from Egypt in an incision upon his flesh ? ' His argument was that as Ben Stada had done this, the practice might be allowable. The answer was that Ben Stada was a fool, and his case proved nothing. Upon the mention however of Ben Stada, a note is added to explain who that person was, and it is for the sake of this note that the passage is quoted. First I will somewhat expand the translation, which I have made as bald and literal as I could.[1]

Ben Stada, says the Gemara, is the same as Ben Pandira. Was he then the son of two fathers ? No. Stada was the name of the husband (of his mother), Pandira the name of her paramour. This is the opinion

of my work relating to Jesus I have made constant use of his book, and can hardly claim to have done more than rearrange his material and modify some of his conclusions. If it had not been my purpose to extend my own work over a wider field than that which he has so thoroughly explored, I should not have written at all.

[1] In all the translations which I shall give, I shall make no attempt to write elegant English ; I wish to keep as closely as possible to a word for word rendering, so that the reader who does not understand the original text may have some idea of what it is like, and what it really says. A flowing translation often becomes a mere paraphrase, and sometimes seriously misrepresents the original.

of Rab Ḥisda, a Babylonian teacher of the third century
(A.D. 217–309). But that cannot be true, says the
Gemara, because the husband is known to have been
called Pappus ben Jehudah. Stada must have been
not the father but the mother. But how can that be,
because the mother was called Miriam the dresser of
women's hair? Miriam was her proper name, concludes the Gemara, and Stada a nickname, as people
say in Pumbeditha *S'tāth dā*, she has gone aside, from
her husband.

The two names Ben Stada and Ben Pandira
evidently refer to the same person, and that that
person is Jesus is shown clearly by the fact that we
sometimes meet with the full name 'Jeshu ben
Pandira'—thus T. Ḥull, ii. 23, "in the name of Jeshu
ben Pandira"; and also the fact that 'Jeshu' is
sometimes found as a variant of 'Ben Stada' in parallel
passages—thus b. Sanh. 43ᵃ says, "On the eve of Pesaḥ
(Passover) they hung Jeshu," while in the same
tractate, p. 67ᵃ, it is said, "Thus did they to Ben
Stada in Lūd, they hung him on the eve of Pesaḥ.
Ben Stada is Ben Pandira, etc." Then follows the
same note of explanation as in the passage from
Shabbath which we are studying. (See below,
p. 79).

There can be no reasonable doubt that the
'Jeshu' who is variously called Ben Stada and Ben
Pandira is the historical Jesus, the founder of
Christianity. It is true that the name Jeshu'a, though
not common, was the name of others beside Jesus of
Nazareth; and even in the New Testament (Col. iv.
11) there is mention of one *Jesus who is called
Justus*. It is also true that the Jewish com-

mentators on the Talmud try to prove that another
Jesus is referred to, who is described in various
passages as having been contemporary with R.
Jehoshua ben Perahjah, about a century B.C. These
passages will be dealt with hereafter.[1] But when it
is said, as in the passage referred to above (T. Hull,
ii. 23), and elsewhere, that certain persons professed
to be able to heal the sick in the name of "Jeshu ben
Pandira," it is impossible to doubt that the reference
is to Jesus of Nazareth.

Various conjectures have been made in explanation of the epithets Ben Stada and Ben Pandira. In
regard to the first, the explanation of the Gemara
that Stada is a contraction of S'tāth dā is certainly
not the original one, for it is given as a common
phrase in use in Pumbeditha, a Babylonian town
where there was a famous Rabbinical College. But
the epithet Ben Stada in reference to Jesus was well
known in Palestine, and that too at a much earlier
date than the time of R. Hisda. This is shown by
the remark of R. Eliezer, who lived at the end of the
first century and on into the second. The derivation
from S'tāth dā would be possible in Palestine no less
than in Babylonia; but it does not seem to have been
suggested in the former country, and can indeed hardly
be considered as anything more than a mere guess at
the meaning of a word whose original significance was
no longer known.[2] It is impossible to say whether
Stada originally denoted the mother or the father of
Jesus; we can only be sure that it implied some contempt or mockery. I attach no value to the sug-

[1] See below, p. 54, No. 8.
[2] See below, p. 345, for a possible explanation of the name B. Stada.

gestion[1] that Stada is made up of two Latin words, 'Sta, da,' and denotes a Roman soldier, one of the traditions being that the real father of Jesus was a soldier.

Of the term Ben Pandira also explanations have been suggested, which are far from being satisfactory. Pandira (also written Pandera, or Pantira, or Pantiri) may, as Strauss suggested (quoted by Hitzig in Hilgenfeld's Ztschft., as above), represent πενθερός, meaning son-in-law; but surely there is nothing distinctive in such an epithet to account for its being specially applied to Jesus. The name Pandira may also represent πάνθηρ (less probably πανθήρα, the final ā being the Aramaic article, not the Greek feminine ending); but what reason there was for calling Jesus the son of the Panther is not clear to me.[2] Again, Pandira may represent παρθένος, and the obvious appropriateness of a name indicating the alleged birth of Jesus from a virgin might make us overlook the improbability that the form παρθένος should be hebraized into the form Pandira, when thᵃ Greek word could have been reproduced almost unchanged in a Hebrew form. It is not clear, moreover, why a Greek word should have been chosen as an epithet for

[1] Hitzig in Hilgenfeld's "Ztschft.," 1865, p. 344 fol.

[2] I know that the name Πάνθηρ is mentioned in this connexion by Christian writers. Origen (ap. Epiphanius, Hær. 78, cited by Wagenseil) says, Οὗτος μὲν γὰρ ὁ Ἰωσὴφ ἀδελφὸς παραγίνεται τοῦ Κλωπᾶ. ἦν δέ υἱὸς τοῦ Ἰακώβ, ἐπίκλην δὲ Πάνθηρ καλουμένου. ἀμφότεροι οὗτοι ἀπὸ τοῦ Πάνθηρος ἐπίκλην γεννῶνται. Origen doubtless knew that the Jews called Jesus 'Ben Pandira'; but, as he does not explain how Jacob, the father of Joseph, came to be called Πάνθηρ, he does not throw any light on the meaning of the term as applied to Jesus. And as there is no trace of any such name in the genealogy given in the Gospels, it is at least possible that the name Ben Pandira suggested Πάνθηρ, instead of being suggested by it.

Jesus. I cannot satisfy myself that any of the suggested explanations solve the problem; and being unable to propose any other, I leave the two names Ben Stada and Ben Pandira as relics of ancient Jewish mockery against Jesus, the clue to whose meaning is now lost.

Pappos ben Jehudah, whom the Gemara alleges to have been the husband of the mother of Jesus, is the name of a man who lived a century after Jesus, and who is said to have been so suspicious of his wife that he locked her into the house whenever he went out (b. Gitt. 90ª). He was contemporary with, and a friend of, R. Aqiba; and one of the two conflicting opinions concerning the epoch of Jesus places him also in the time of Aqiba. Probably this mistaken opinion, together with the tradition that Pappos ben Jehudah was jealous of his wife, account for the mixing up of his name with the story of the parentage of Jesus.

The name Miriam (of which Mary is the equivalent) is the only one which tradition correctly preserved. And the curious remark that she was a dresser of women's hair conceals another reminiscence of the Gospel story. For the words in the Talmud are ' Miriam m'gaddela nashaia.' The second word is plainly based upon the name ' Magdala'; and though, of course, Mary Magdalene was not the mother of Jesus, her name might easily be confused with that of the other Mary.

The passage in the Gemara which we are examining shows plainly enough that only a very dim and confused notion existed as to the parentage of Jesus in the time when the tradition was recorded. It rests, however, on some knowledge possessed at one time of the story related in the Gospels. That story undoubtedly lays itself open to the coarse interpretation put upon it by Jewish enemies of Jesus, viz., that he was born out of wedlock. The Talmud knows that his mother was called Miriam, and knows also that Miriam (Mary) of Magdala had some connexion with the story of his life. Beyond that it knows nothing, not even the meaning of the names by which it refers to Jesus. The passage in the Talmud under examination cannot be earlier than the beginning of the fourth century, and is moreover a report of what was said in Babylonia, not Palestine.

Mary the Mother of Jesus

(2) b. Hag. 4b.—When Rab Joseph came to this verse (Exod. xxiii. 17), he wept, *There is that is destroyed without justice* (Prov. xiii. 23). He said, Is there any who has departed before his time ? None but this [told] of Rab Bibi bar Abaji. The Angel of Death was with him. The Angel said to his messenger, ' Go, bring me Miriam the dresser of women's hair.' He brought him Miriam the teacher of children. He [the Angel] said, ' I told thee Miriam the dresser of women's hair.' He said, ' If so, I will take this one back.' He said, ' Since thou hast brought this one, let her be among the number [of the dead].'

(2a) Tosaphoth.—" The Angel of Death was with him : he related what had already happened, for this about Miriam the dresser of women's hair took place in [the time of] the second

temple, for she was the mother of a certain
person, as it is said in Shabbath, p. 104."

Commentary.—This passage, like the preceding
one, is centuries later than the time of Jesus. R.
Bibi bar Abaji, as also R. Joseph, belonged to the
end of the third and beginning of the fourth century,
and both lived in Babylonia. R. Joseph was head of
the college at Pumbeditha, in which office Abaji, the
father of Bibi, succeeded him. As the story is told
it involves a monstrous anachronism, which is noted
by the authors of the Tosaphoth (mediæval commentators on the Talmud). The compilers of the
Gemara can scarcely have believed that Miriam, the
dresser of women's hair, was still living in the time of
R. Joseph and R. Bibi; for, as the preceding passage
shows, she was thought to have been the mother of
Jesus. So far as I know, this is the only reference to
the Miriam in question which brings down her lifetime to so late a date; and, if we do not accept the
explanation of the Tosaphoth, that the Angel of
Death told R. Bibi what had happened long ago, we
may suppose that what is described is a dream of the
Rabbi's. Of the Miriam who, according to the story,
was cut off by death before her time, nothing whatever is known. The passage merely shows that the
name of Miriam, the dresser of women's hair, was
known in the Babylonian schools at the end of the
third and the beginning of the fourth century. The
incident of the fate of the two Miriams is merely
brought in to illustrate the text that *some are cut
off without justice.* And this again forms part of a
discussion on the duty of appearing three times in
the year before the Lord. This passage adds nothing

to our knowledge of the Rabbinical belief concerning
the mother of Jesus ; it is only given because it refers
to her, my object being, as already explained, to present as complete a series as I can of Rabbinical
passages bearing upon Jesus and Christianity.

There is, in j. Ḥag. 77ᵈ, a reference to a certain
Miriam the daughter of 'Eli, whom, on account of
the name (*cf.* Luke iii. 23), one might be tempted to
connect with the story of Jesus ; but there seems to
be no suspicion on the part of the Talmud of any
such connexion, and what is told about her does not
seem to me to point in that direction.

Jesus Alleged to be a 'Mamzer'[1]

(3) M. Jeb. iv. 13 [b. Gemara, Jeb. 49ᵇ, same
   words ; j. Gemara does not mention the
   passage]. Rabbi Shim'on ben 'Azai said, ' I
   have found a roll of pedigrees in Jerusalem,
   and therein is written A certain person *spurius
   est ex adultera* [*natus*] ; to confirm the words
   of Rabbi Jehoshua.'

Commentary.—This passage is from the Mishnah,
and therefore (see Introduction) belongs to the older
stratum of the Talmud. R. Shim'on ben 'Azai was
the contemporary and friend of Aqiba, about the end
of the first and beginning of the second century.
They were both disciples of R. Jehoshua ben
Ḥananiah (b. Taan. 26ᵃ), of whom frequent mention
will be made in these pages. R. Jehoshua, in his
early life, had been a singer in the Temple (b. Erach.
11ᵇ), and his teacher, R. Joḥanan ben Zaccai, was old

---

[1] ממזר, of spurious birth.

enough to have seen and remembered Jesus.[1]   The
Rabbis mentioned here were amongst the leading
men of their time, and on that account must have
been much concerned with the questions arising out
of the growth of Christianity.   R. Jehoshua is expressly mentioned as having been one of the chief
defenders of Israel against the Minim ; and, whatever
may be the precise significance of that term, it will
be shown subsequently that it includes Christians,
though it may possibly include others also.   R.
Aqiba also is said to have been a particularly zealous
opponent of the Christians.   Indeed, according to
one of the two conflicting opinions represented in the
Talmud, Jesus was actually a contemporary of Aqiba,
an anachronism which finds its best explanation in a
pronounced hostility on the part of Aqiba towards
the Christians.   When, therefore, Shim'on b. 'Azai
reported that he had found a book of pedigrees, in
which it was stated that 'a certain person' (pelōni)
was of spurious birth, it is certainly probable that the
reference is to Jesus.   Unless some well-known man
were intended, there would be no point in referring
to him ; and unless there had been some strong
reason for avoiding his name, the name would have
been given in order to strengthen the argument
founded upon the case.   For it is said that Shim'on
ben 'Azai made his statement 'in order to confirm
the words of R. Jehoshua.'   And R. Jehoshua had
laid it down that a bastard is one who is condemned

---

[1] It has been suggested that the John mentioned in Acts iv. 6 is the
same as Joḥanan ben Zaccai ; but there is no evidence for this identification
except the similarity of name.   Since the Rabbi was a Pharisee, it is not on
the face of it probable that he should be "of the kindred of the High
Priest."

to a judicial death,[1] *i.e.* one born of a union which was prohibited under penalty of such a death. Now Jesus undoubtedly had been condemned (though not on account of his birth) to a judicial death, as the Talmud recognises (see passages given subsequently, pp. 80, 83) and Shim'on ben 'Azai brings the evidence of the book which he had discovered, to show that in the case of a notorious person the penalty of a judicial death had followed upon unlawful birth.

The alleged discovery of a book of pedigrees in Jerusalem may be historical; for the Jews were not prohibited from entering Jerusalem until the revolt of Bar Cocheba had been suppressed by Hadrian, A.D. 135, and ben 'Azai was dead before that time. What the book was cannot now be determined. The title, Book of Pedigrees, is quite general. It is worth noticing, however, that the present gospel of Matthew begins with the words, *The book of the genealogy of Jesus Christ.* It is just possible that the book to which ben 'Azai referred was this Gospel, or rather an Aramaic forerunner of it, or again it may have been a roll containing one or other of the two pedigrees recorded in Matthew and Luke.

Covert Reference to Jesus

(4) b. Joma. 66[d].—They asked R. Eliezer, ' What of *a certain person* as regards the world to come ' ? He said to them, 'Ye have only asked me concerning *a certain person.*' 'What of the shepherd saving the sheep from the lion ' ? He said to them, ' Ye have only asked

ר יהושע אומר כל שחייבין עליו מיתת בית דין [1]

me concerning the sheep.' 'What of saving
the shepherd from the lion'? He said, 'Ye
have only asked me concerning the shepherd.'
'What of a Mamzer, as to inheriting'? 'What
of his performing the levirate duty'? 'What
of his founding his house'? 'What of his
founding his sepulchre'? [They asked these
questions] not because they differed on them,
but because he never said anything which he
had not heard from his teacher from of old.
[See a somewhat similar series of questions,
T. Jeb. iii. 8, 4.]

Commentary.—This passage is full of obscurities.
I record it here because of its reference to '*pelōni*,' 'a
certain person,' the same phrase which occurred in
the preceding extract. R. Eliezer was a very well-
known teacher at the end of the first century; and
later on will be given a passage which describes how
he was once arrested on a charge of heresy, presumably Christianity (see below, p. 187). The words
translated are a Baraitha (see above, p. 21), *i.e.* they
belong to a period contemporary with the Mishnah,
though they are not included in it. Moreover the
style of the language is that of the Mishnah, not that
of the Gemara. Further, a set of questions addressed
to the same R. Eliezer, and including some of those
translated above, is found in the Tosephta (T. Jeb. iii.
8, 4). Among the questions given in Tosephta are
those about 'pelōni,' and about the 'Mamzer.' It is
evident that the authors neither of the Gemara nor of
the Tosephta understood the full meaning of the
questions. The explanation is that the questions
were asked 'not because there was any difference of

opinion, but because R. Eliezer never said anything which he had not heard from his teacher.' The same explanation is given in reference to another set of questions addressed to Eliezer (b. Succ. 27ᵇ, 28ᵃ), and from the latter passage it appears to be Eliezer's own declaration concerning himself. But it has no bearing on the questions and answers translated above, unless it be this, that as Eliezer was known to have had some connexion with Christianity, his questioners tried to get at his own opinion concerning Jesus, and that he fenced with the questions, not caring to answer directly, and perhaps not being able to answer on the authority of his teacher. The particular point of each question I am unable to explain; but one can see an opportunity for allusion to Jesus in the questions as to the fate of ' pelōni ' in the future life, as to the ' Mamzer ' founding a house (*i.c.* a family), or a sepulchre, if it were known that Jesus was not married, and that he was buried in the grave of a stranger. I can throw no light upon the ' saving the sheep (or the shepherd) from the lion.' That this passage contains a covert reference to Jesus is the opinion of Levy, N.H.W., iv. 54ᵃ, s.v. פלוני, and also of Edersheim, L. &. T. of J. M., ii. 193, who ventures a comparison with John x. 11. Is it likely that the contents of that Gospel, supposing it to have been in existence at the time, would be known to Eliezer or his questioners ?

THE ANCESTRY OF THE MOTHER OF JESUS

(5) b. Sanh. 106ᵃ.—R. Johanan said [concerning Balaam], ' In the beginning a prophet, in the end a deceiver.' Rab Papa said, ' This is that

which they say, She was the descendant of
princes and rulers, she played the harlot with
carpenters.'

Commentary.—It will be shown subsequently that
Jesus is often referred to in the Talmud under the
figure of Balaam, and the words just translated occur
in the middle of a long passage about Balaam.   No
name is mentioned to indicate what woman is meant.
But the context suggests that the mother of Jesus is
intended; and the suggestion is borne out by the
statement that the woman mated with a carpenter.[1]
The passage, as it stands, is of a late date; for R.
Papa, who said the words, was head of the college at
Sura from 354 to 374 A.D.   Possibly it arose out of
some imperfect acquaintance with the genealogies in
the Gospels, these being regarded as giving the
ancestry of Mary instead of that of Joseph.   The
mistake might naturally arise; for if Joseph were not
the father of Jesus, and if Jesus were alleged to be
the son of David, or of royal descent, as the Talmud
itself (b. Sanh. 43ª) is by some thought to admit,[2] then
evidently his royal ancestry must have been on his
mother's side.

ALLEGED CONFESSION BY THE MOTHER OF JESUS

(6) b. Kallah. 51a.—Impudens: R. Eliezer dicit
spurium esse, R. Jehoshua menstruæ filium,
R. Aqiba et spurium et menstruæ filium.
Sedebant quondam seniores apud portam,

[1] The Munich MS. has in the margin נבר instead of נברי, *i.e.* the singular,
not the plural.
[2] This at least is one interpretation of the expression קרוב למלכות, see
below, p. 89.

præterierunt duo pueri quorum unus caput
operuit, alter revelavit.   Dixit R. Eliezer,
de illo qui caput revelaverat, 'Spurius est';
R. Jehoshua 'Menstruæ filius'; R. Aqiba
'Spurius, et menstruæ filius.' Responderunt
illi, 'Quomodo cor te inflat, ut verbis sociorum
contradixeris!'   Dixit eis 'Rem confirmabo.'
Abiit ad matrem pueri, quam vidit in foro
sedentem dum legumina vendebat.   Dixit
ei 'Filia mea, si mihi id de quo rogabo
respondeas, in seculum futurum te ducam.'
Respondit illi 'Jura mihi.' Juravit R. Aqiba
ore, sed corde irritum fecit.' Dixit ei 'Filius
hic tuus, qualis est?'   Respondit 'Quum
thalamum introivi menstrua eram, et separavit
a me conjux; paranymphus autem venit ad
me, quapropter hic puer et spurius est et
menstruæ filius.'   Responderunt (Rabbini)
'Magnus erat R. Aqiba, quum magistros
suos refutaret.' Illa hora dixerunt 'Benedictus
Deus Israel, qui R. Aqibæ secretum suum
revelavit!'

Commentary.—I give the above passage with some
hesitation, because I doubt whether it has anything
to do with the legendary history of Jesus. There is
nothing to point him out as the child in question,
and the few details which the story contains do not
agree with what we have gathered hitherto as the
Rabbinical account of the parentage of Jesus. So
far as I know, this passage stands by itself, without
being mentioned or referred to in any other Talmudic
tractate; and the tractate Kallah, in which it is found,
is of later origin than the main body of the Talmud.

4

If, as is possible, it may have been suggested by the
story in Luke ii. 41 fol., it can in no case be evidence
for opinion concerning Jesus in those centuries with
which we are concerned. And my chief reason for
inserting it is that I do not wish to leave out any
passage to which reference has been made as having
a supposed bearing on the subject. At the same
time, the fact that use has been made of the story in
the book called the *Tol'dōth Jēshū* (ed. Huldreich,
p. 22, ed. Wagenseil, p. 12), shows that it was
regarded as having reference to Jesus. In the work
"J. C. im Talmud," p. 34 fol., Laible argues that
the original author of the passage had no thought
of Jesus in his mind. It is possible that the story is
a free invention to explain the words of Shim'on
b. 'Azai (quoted above, p. 43), which refer to a
'certain person' as having been 'spurius et menstruæ filius.' If so, Laible would be justified in
saying that while the original author of the story
had no thought of Jesus in his mind, nevertheless the
real reference was to Jesus.

JESUS AND HIS TEACHER

(7) b. Sanh. 107[b].—Our Rabbis teach, Ever let
the left hand repel and the right hand invite,
not like Elisha who repulsed Gehazi with both
hands, and not like R. Jehoshua ben Perahjah,
who repulsed Jeshu (the Nazarene) with both
hands. Gehazi, as it is written . . . .[1]

---

[1] The passage referring to Gehazi will be dealt with under another head.
See below, No. 27, p. 97 fol.

What of R. Jehoshua ben Peraḥjah? When
Jannai the king killed our Rabbis, R. Jehoshua
ben Peraḥjah [and Jesus] fled to Alexandria of
Egypt. When there was peace, Shim'on ben
Shetaḥ sent to him, "From me [Jerusalem]
the city of holiness, to thee Alexandria of
Egypt [my sister]. My husband stays in thy
midst and I sit forsaken." He came, and
found himself at a certain inn; they showed
him great honour. He said, 'How beautiful
is this Acsania!'[1] (Jesus) said to him, 'Rabbi,
she has narrow eyes.' He said, 'Wretch, dost
thou employ thyself thus?' He sent out four
hundred trumpets and excommunicated him.
He [i.e. Jesus] came before him many times
and said to him, 'Receive me.' But he would
not notice him. One day he [i.e. R. Jeh.] was
reciting the Shema', he [i.e. Jesus] came before
him. He was minded to receive him, and
made a sign to him. He [i.e. Jesus] thought
that he repelled him. He went and hung up
a tile and worshipped it. He [R. Jeh.] said to
him, 'Return.' He replied, 'Thus I have received from thee, that every one who sins and
causes the multitude to sin, they give him not
the chance to repent.' And a teacher has
said, 'Jesus the Nazarene practised magic and
led astray and deceived Israel.'

Commentary.—The above passage occurs in almost
exactly the same words in b. Sotah. 47[a], and the
incident of the escape to Alexandria and the letter

---

[1] אכסניא denotes both inn and innkeeper. R. Jeh. uses it in the first
sense; the answering remark implies the second meaning, 'hostess.'

from Jerusalem is mentioned in j. Ḥag. ii. 2; j. Sanh. vi. 9.[1] The passage j. Ḥag. ii. 2 gives a very brief account of the dissension between the Rabbi and "one of his disciples," but does not give the name of the latter. This is probably the basis of what was afterwards expanded in the Babylonian Gemara.

The passage before us is the *locus classicus* for the second Talmudic theory as to the time when Jesus lived. 'Jannai the king' is Alexander Jannæus, who reigned from 104 to 78 B.C., thus a full century before Jesus lived. Shim'on b. Shetaḥ, the king's brother-in-law, and Jehoshua b. Peraḥjah (as also Jehudah b. Tabbai of the Palestinian version) were leading Pharisees of the time; and the massacre of the Rabbis, which led to the escape of one of them to Alexandria, is a historical event. The question is, how did the name of Jesus come to be introduced into a story referring to a time so long before his own?[2]   Bearing in mind that the Rabbis had

[1] Where, however, the fugitive is not Jehoshua ben Peraḥjah but Jehudah ben Tabbai.

[2] The name of Jesus is found in this passage in the codices of Munich, Florence, and Carlsruhe, used by Rabbinowicz, also in all the older editions of the Talmud. In the edition of Basel, 1578–81, and in all later ones, the censor of the press has expunged it. See Rabbinowicz Variæ Lectiones, Sanh. *ad loc.* Here is perhaps the best place to refer to the epithet ha-Nōtzri (הנוצרי) as applied to Jesus. It is well known that the name of Nazareth does not occur in the Talmud, and indeed first appears in Jewish writings so late as the hymns of Qalir (A.D. 900 *circa*), in the form Nātzrath. This is probably the correct Hebrew form; but there must have been another form, Nōtzerath, or Nōtzerah, to account for the adjective Nōtzri. Perhaps Nōtzerah was the local pronunciation in the dialect of Galilee, where the sound ō or ū frequently represents the ā or ă of new Hebrew; thus, קומי for קמי, יורדנא for ירדן (Jordan), מוגדלא for מגדלא (Magdala). With this corresponds the fact that the Syriac gives Nōtzerath and Nōtzerojo for the name of the town and of its inhabitants. That from Nōtzerath or Nōtzerah could be formed an adjective Notzri is shown by the examples

extremely vague ideas of the chronology of past
times, we may perhaps find the origin of the story in
its Babylonian form in a desire to explain the connexion of Jesus (Ben Stada, see above, No. 1), with
Egypt. The connecting link may, perhaps, be found
in the fact of a flight into Egypt to escape the anger
of a king. This was known in regard to R. Jehoshua
ben Peraḥjah, and the Gospel (Matt. ii. 13 fol.) records
a similar event in regard to Jesus. The short Palestinian story in j. Ḥag. vi. 2 shows that there was
a tradition that the Rabbi had excommunicated a
rebellious disciple, whose name is not given. As
the story now stands in the Babylonian version,
there are several details in it which appear to have
reference to Jesus, and which probably were due to
some confused remembrance of tradition about him.
In addition to the flight into Egypt, there is the fact
that Jesus was known to have set himself against
the authority of the Rabbis, and to have been the
founder of a false religion. And the rebuke, " Dost
thou thus employ thyself," *i.e.* with thinking whether
a woman is beautiful, may be based on a gross distortion of the fact that the Gospel tradition gives a
prominent place to women as followers of Jesus.
Moreover the final answer of the banished disciple in
the story, that ' one who sins and causes the multitude to sin is allowed no chance to repent,' points

Timni from Timnah, Jehudi from Jehudah. The adjective Ναζωραῖος (Acts
xxviii. 22) would seem to imply an alternative form Natzāra, the second ā
being replaced by ō in the Galilean dialect, as in Nōtzri for Nātzri. The
form Natzāra indeed is adopted by Keim as the more correct ; but I do not
see how to avoid recognising both Notzĕrah (Nāzĕrah) and Natzāra as
equally legitimate, that is as representing variations in the pronunciation,
not original difference in the formation of the name.

clearly to the historical Jesus; for the simple act of idolatry mentioned in the story cannot be called a 'causing of the multitude to sin.' What the point may be of the statement that Jesus hung up a tile, a burnt brick, and worshipped it, I cannot explain.

This passage is found in its full extent only in the Babylonian Gemara, and is probably of very late date. It is introduced as an illustration of the saying, " Let the left hand repel and the right hand invite." But there was already an illustration of that saying in the case of Elisha and Gehazi, and the whole passage is brought in, where it occurs in the tractate Sanhedrin, as belonging to the subject of Gehazi. I suggest that the mention of R. Jehoshua and Jesus was an addition founded on the Palestinian tradition and prompted by the mention of Elisha and Gehazi; and further that this addition was made in the schools of Babylonia, upon uncertain authority. It is not cited under the name of any Rabbi; and the last sentence of it, which distinctly refers it to Jesus, only does so on the authority of 'a teacher,' whose name, presumably, was not known. The glaring anachronism, of making Jesus contemporary with R. Jehoshua b. Perahjah, is more easy to understand on this theory, than if we suppose the story to have originated in Palestine at a time nearer to that when Jesus actually lived.[1]

JESUS A MAGICIAN.   (See also (1) above.)

(8) T. Shabb. xi. 15.—' He that cuts marks on his flesh '; R. Eliezer condemns, the wise permit.

---

[1] As to the other anachronism, which makes Jesus contemporary with R. Aqiba, a century after his own time, see above, p. 40.

He said to them, 'And did not Ben Stada
learn only in this way?' They said to him,
Because of one fool are we to destroy all
discerning people?'

Commentary.—The extract (1) above, and the
parallel passage j. Shabb. 13ᵈ, contain almost the same
words. I repeat them here because of their reference
to the character of Jesus as a magician. In the
earlier quotation the main reference of the passage
was to the parentage of Jesus.

It has already been shown that Ben Stada denotes
Jesus. (See above, p. 37 fol.) What is the meaning
of the statement that he brought magical charms
from Egypt concealed in an incision in his flesh? I
do not know of anything related about Jesus which
could have given rise to the detail about the cutting
of his flesh. The charge that he was a magician is
no doubt based on the belief that he did many
miracles, a belief which found ample support in the
Gospel records. We shall see later on that miracles,
whether done by Jews or Christians, were ascribed to
magic, and were not on that account despised. Now
Egypt was regarded as the especial home of magic,
an opinion expressed in the Talmud, b. Qidd. 49ᵇ:—
" Ten measures of sorcery descended into the world,
Egypt received nine, the rest of the world one." To
say that Jesus learnt magic in Egypt is to say that
he was a great magician, more powerful than others.
And as we have seen in the preceding extract (7)
there was a tradition that he had had something to
do with Egypt. As to the manner in which he is
alleged to have brought away with him Egyptian
magic, a curious explanation is given by Rashi (b.

Shabb. 104ᵇ) to the effect that the Egyptian magi-
cians did not allow anyone to carry away magical
charms from their country; and therefore, since Jesus
could not take them away in writing, he concealed
them in the manner described, or perhaps tattooed
magical signs on his flesh. Whether Rashi had any
authority for his statement, or whether he only
devised it to explain the passage before him, I do
not know. The date of the passage under consideration is to some extent determined by the fact that it
is taken from the Tosephta (see above, p. 21), a collection which represents an earlier stratum of tradition
than that embodied in the Gemara. The Eliezer who
is mentioned is of course the same as the one mentioned in (1) above, and we may take it that the
reference there, p. 36, to a ' Baraitha,' is a reference to
the present passage. The answer, that ' Ben Stada
was a fool,' does not perhaps imply any censure on
Jesus, but merely that any one would be foolish who
should act as Ben Stada was said to have done.[1]

JESUS ' BURNS HIS FOOD '

(9) b. Sanh. 103ᵃ.—For Rab Ḥisda said that Rab
    Jeremiah bar Abba said, ' What is that which
    is written: *There shall no evil befall thee,
    neither shall any plague come nigh thy dwelling*
    [Ps. xci. 10]. . . . . Another explanation:
    There shall no evil befall thee, [means], ' that
    evil dreams and evil thoughts may tempt thee
    not,' and *neither shall any plague come nigh*

---

[1] But see below, p. 345 n., for a possible alternative to the foregoing
explanation.

thy dwelling [means] 'that thou mayst not have a son or a disciple who *burns his food* in public like Jeshu the Nazarene.'

[The concluding phrase is found in another connexion, b. Ber. 17[b], see below, p. 61.]

Commentary.—This passage is Gemara, and the R. Ḥisda who cites the exposition of the Psalm is the same as the one mentioned in (1) above. He was a Babylonian, and lived A.D. 217–309. R. Jeremiah bar Abba, from whom he quoted, was his contemporary, and apparently of much about the same age.

The point of interest in the above extract is the phrase which I have translated literally, '*burns his food*, like Jesus the Nazarene.' What did Jesus do that could be so described? It is clear that as applied to him, it must have a figurative meaning. It is sometimes, however, intended quite literally. Thus, b. Betz. 29[a]: "The cook measures spices and puts them into his dish, that they may not burn [*i.e.* spoil] his food." This is evidently literal, except that in English we should not use the word 'burn' in this connexion. The phrase occurs in the Mishnah, Gitt. ix. 10, and the question has often been discussed, whether there it is intended literally or figuratively. The words are, "The School of Shammai say that a man may not divorce his wife unless he find in her a matter of shame, for it is said [Deut. xxiv. 1], *because he hath found in her a shameful matter.* The School of Hillel say [he may divorce her] even if she burn his food, for it is said, and R. Aqiba says, Even if he have found another [woman] more beautiful than she, for it is said, *If she shall not find favour in thine eyes.*" This passage

has often been cited as showing the laxity of the
Rabbinical views on the question of divorce, especially as held by the school of Hillel.   And the charge
has been met by maintaining that the phrase 'burns
his food' means, 'brings dishonour upon him,'
'brings his name into disrepute.'   Whether or not
the phrase may have some such figurative meaning,
there is good ground for taking it literally in this
famous passage of the Mishnah.   It has been well
shown in a recent work,[1] by Amram, that Hillel
and Aqiba, and the school in general who sided with
them, were declaring not what was their ethical ideal,
but what in their view the law permitted.   They
had to declare the law, not to make it; and the
reason why they did not—as they probably could
have done—lay down an interpretation of the law
more in accordance with their own ethical view,
was that the ancient custom of Israel assumed the
absolute liberty of a man to divorce his wife at his
will, and without giving reasons for his action.   The
law could not attempt more than slightly to restrict
that liberty, except at the cost of remaining a mere
dead letter.   Hillel, in this passage, declares that,
as a matter of fact, the law, in his opinion, does allow
a man to divorce his wife, even for such a trivial
offence as burning his food.   But Hillel and his
school, did not, on that account, approve of such
liberty of divorce.   On the very same page of the
Gemara, where this Mishnah is explained, b. Gitt.
90[b], a Rabbi of the school of Hillel says, "He who
divorces his first wife, the altar of God sheds tears
thereat."   To the above argument in favour of the

[1] *The Jewish Law of Divorce.*   London, 1897, p. 33 fol.

literal meaning of the phrase 'burns his food' in this disputed Mishnah, may be added that Rashi and other Jewish commentators interpret it quite literally, and give not the slightest hint of a figurative meaning. Also the fact that, whatever Hillel may have meant, Aqiba's dictum is evidently literal,[1] so that it is unlikely that Hillel's words were figurative.

But while this is quite true, it is also true that the literal meaning of the phrase will not apply in all cases where it occurs. When it is said, as in the extract from b. Sanh. 103[a], under consideration, and also in b. Ber. 17[b], "that there may not be a son or a disciple who burns his food in public," something much more serious must be intended than a literal 'burning of food.' The clue to this figurative meaning is given in the Talmud itself, b. Berach. 34[a]. The Gemara in this place is commenting on the following words of the Mishnah: "He who says 'The good shall bless thee,' lo, this is the way of heresy. He who goes before the Ark, if he makes a mistake, another shall go in his stead, and let there be no refusal at such a time." To 'go before the Ark' is to stand at the lectern to recite the prayers in the Synagogue. And the Mishnah has just remarked that some liturgical phrases are signs of heresy in the reader. Therefore the Mishnah directs what is to be done when a reader makes a mistake. Another man is to take his place and there must be no refusal on the part of the second man. That is the Mishnah. The Gemara says: "Our Rabbis have taught 'He who goes before the Ark ought [at first]

---

[1] See Edersheim, "L. and T. of J. the M.," ii. 333 n[2], where he successfully proves the literalness of the phrase in Gitt. ix. 10.

to refuse.   He who does not refuse is like food
without salt.   He who refuses too much is like food
of which the salt has burnt (or spoiled) it.' "   The
meaning of this is clear.   One who refuses too much
is *open to the suspicion of heresy*, and he is like food
that is spoiled or burnt by too much salt.   The point
of the comparison may perhaps be that as too much
salt spoils good food, so the disciple, by too much
self-will and conceit in his own wisdom, spoils the
sound teaching that is given to him, which would
have been his mental food.[1]   When, therefore, it is
said "a son or disciple who burns his food," that
means "one who is open to the suspicion of heresy."
It has already been mentioned that the phrase,
'a son or disciple who burns his food' occurs in two
passages, b. Ber. 17[b], and b. Sanh. 103[a] (translated
above).   In the former, the Gemara, in an exposition
of Ps. cxliv. 14 : ' *There is no breaking in and no
going forth, and no outcry in the streets*,' says :
' *There is no breaking in*,' that our company be not
as the company of David from which Ahitophel went
out, and ' *there is no going forth* ' that our company
be not as the company of Saul, from which Doeg,
the Edomite, went forth, and '*no outcry*,' that our
company be not as the company of Elisha from which
Gehazi went out, and '*in our streets* ' that there be
not to us a son or disciple who burns his food in
public like Jeshu the Nazarene.[2]   Now we shall see,

---

[1] With this figurative meaning of 'salt,' denoting 'independence of
mind,' may be compared Mark ix. 49, 50, "*For every one shall be salted
with fire. . . . Have salt in yourselves. . . .*"

[2] The printed text does not mention 'Jeshu ha-Nōtzri.' The reading,
however, is found in all the older editions and the MSS. See Rabbinowicz
on the passage. Note that this exposition of the Psalm is said to have been

hereafter, that Ahitophel, Doeg and Gehazi, are all, in the view of the Talmud, tainted with heresy (Minuth). These three, along with Balaam, the chief infidel, are said in the Mishnah, Sanh. x. 1, to have no part in the world to come. And the same Mishnah makes a similar declaration in regard to Jeroboam, Ahab and Manasseh. The passage in b. Ber. 17ᵇ, as quoted in the Aruch (*s.v.* קדח) reads thus, "burns his food in public, like Manasseh." And this has probably led the author of that work to explain the meaning of ' burns his food in public ' by ' sets up idols in public,' establishes false worships. But, as Rabbinowicz has shown, not "Manasseh," but " Jeshu ha-Notzri," is the original reading; and this fact is conclusive against the explanation of the author of the Aruch. It is absurd to say of Jesus that he set up idols. I conclude, therefore, that in the passage before us the reference to Jesus is intended as an example of one who inclined to heresy.[1]

It is worthy of note that the Palestinian Gemara does not make the reference to Jesus, either in Ber. or Sanh., nor does it use the phrase ' burns his food '

spoken by the disciples of R. Ḥisda (or, according to another tradition, R. Shemuel b. Naḥmani), when they left the lecture room. This tends to confirm the connexion of the phrase under discussion with R. Ḥisda.

[1] Jost, "Gesch. d. Judentums u s. Sekten," i. p. 264 n., says, speaking of the literal interpretation of ' burns his food,' "sie wird, aber, genügend widerlegt durch die in jener Zeit bekannte Bedeutung des Wortes, מקדיח תבשילו, b. Ber. 17ᵇ, b. Sanh. 103ª, wo es geradezu in dem Sinne : den *eigenen* oder *des Hauses guten Ruf preisgeben*, angewendet wird,—wie schon Zipser, Orient 1850, s. 316 nachgewiesen hat." I do not know on what authority he says that the phrase was so understood at the time, in view of the quite different interpretation given by the Talmud itself in b. Ber. 34ª.

in either passage.   The same is true of the Tosephta,
so far as I can observe.   We may, perhaps, infer that
the figurative use of the phrase originated in the
Babylonian schools, where, as we have already seen
(see above (1) (2) (7)), the Rabbis speculated a good
deal about Jesus.   Possibly R. Jeremiah bar Abba,
who used the phrase in the passage we have been
studying, was himself the author of the figurative
application of it, and also of the explanation of its
meaning, b. Ber. 34ª.   He and R. Hisda were contemporaries and friends, and the latter claimed (p. 37
above) to know something about Jesus.   To one or
other of them the origin of the phrase as denoting
a tendency to heresy may with great probability be
ascribed.

THE CLAIM OF JESUS DENIED

(10) j. Taanith 65ᵇ.—R. Abahu said : If a man say
to thee ' I am God,' he is a liar ; if [he says, ' I
am] the son of man,' in the end people will
laugh at him ; if [he says] ' I will go up to
heaven,' he saith, but shall not perform it.

Commentary.—So far as I know, this saying occurs
only here.   That it refers to Jesus there can be no
possibility of doubt.   R. Abahu, the speaker, was a
very well-known Rabbi, who lived in Cæsarea, at the
end of the third and the beginning of the fourth
century ; and we shall see hereafter that he had a
great deal of intercourse, friendly and also polemical,
with heretics, who, in some instances at all events,
were certainly Christians.   It is not necessary to
assume an acquaintance with any of the Gospels to
account for the phrases used by R. Abahu.   The

first and third do indeed suggest the Gospel of John, but it is enough to admit a general knowledge of what Christians alleged concerning Jesus from the Rabbi's own discussions with them.

The saying is based upon Num. xxiii. 19 : *God is not a man that he should lie, nor the son of man that he should repent. Hath he said and shall he not do it? or hath he spoken and shall he not make it good?* Various interpretations of these words, by Rabbis of Babylonia, are given, and then follows the sarcastic application of the text by Abahu.

Although this saying is not quoted elsewhere, nor even referred to, so far as I know, yet it belongs to a somewhat extensive group of Haggadic passages, of which the common foundation is the story of Balaam, Num. xxii.–xxiv. It will be shown presently that in the Talmud Balaam is regarded as a type of Jesus. We thus have an additional reason, beside the internal evidence furnished by the words themselves, for regarding the saying of Abahu as an anti-Christian polemic. Here may be best introduced a passage in the Jalqut Shim'oni, in which is found an amplification of Abahu's words. I give it according to the Salonica edition, as it is expunged from the later ones.

(11) Jalq. Shim. § 766.—R. El'azar ha-Qappar says, God gave strength to his [Balaam's] voice, so that it went from one end of the world to the other, because he looked forth and beheld the peoples that bow down to the sun and moon and stars and to wood and stone, and he looked forth and beheld that there was a man, son of a woman, who should rise up and seek to make himself God, and to cause the

whole world to go astray. Therefore God gave
power to his voice that all the peoples of the world
might hear, and thus he spake, ' Give heed that ye
go not astray after that man, for it is written
(Num. xxiii. 19), *God is not man that he should lie,*
and if he says that he is God he is a liar, and he will
deceive and say that he departeth and cometh again
in the end, he saith and he shall not perform. See
what is written (Num. xxiv. 23) : *And he took up
his parable and said, Alas, who shall live when God
doeth this.* Balaam said, ' Alas, who shall live, of
that nation which heareth that man who hath made
himself God.'

R. El'azar ha-Qappar, who is reported to have said
all this, was earlier than Abahu, for he died about
260 A.D. Bacher (Ag. d. Tann. ii. 506 n.[2]) shows that
only the first clause of the passage in Jalqut is to be
ascribed to El'azar ha-Qappar, *i.e.* the statement that
the voice of Balaam resounded from one end of the
world to the other. All the rest is probably of much
later date ; but it may very well have been suggested
by Abahu's words. It will be observed that Balaam
is not identified with Jesus, but is made to prophesy
his coming. That, however, Jesus is referred to is
even more evident than in the shorter saying of
Abahu. It is curious that this later Haggadah is
attached to the words not of Abahu but of El'azar
ha-Qappar.

Jesus and Balaam

(12) M. Sanh. x. 2.—Three kings and four private
    men have no part in the world to come ; the
    three kings are Jeroboam, Ahab and Manasseh

. . . . the four private men are Balaam, Doeg,
Ahitophel and Gehazi.

Commentary.—The famous chapter of the Mishnah
from which these words are taken begins by saying
that, ' All Israel have part in the world to come,' and
then enumerates the exceptions. The three kings,
Jeroboam, Ahab and Manasseh are all mentioned
in the O.T. as having introduced idolatry, perverted the true religion. And, as the four private
men are named in close connexion with the kings, it
is reasonable to infer that they were condemned for
the same offence. This conclusion is strengthened
by the fact that the preceding paragraph of the
Mishnah in this chapter excepts from the privilege
of the world to come, ' those who say the resurrection
of the dead is not proved from the Torah, and that
the Torah is not from heaven, also the Epicuros.
R. Aqiba says, He who reads in external books,
also he who whispers over a wound, and says, None
of the diseases which I sent in Egypt will I lay upon
thee, I the Lord am thy healer. Abba Shaul says,
He that pronounces the Name according to its
letters.' These are all, unless perhaps the last, aimed
at heretics who can hardly be other than Christians.
For it will be seen hereafter that the opinions and
practices here condemned were the subject of dispute between Jews and heretics (Minim). Therefore
we naturally expect that the four private men, who
are singled out for exclusion from the world to come,
are condemned on account not merely of heresy but
of actively promoting heresy. Now this is not true
in any especial sense of any one of the four. Balaam,
certainly, according to the story in Num. xxii.–xxiv.

5

did lead the people astray ; but so far as religion was concerned, he acknowledged and obeyed the God of Israel. Moreover, Balaam was not an Israelite, and therefore could not logically be included in a list of exceptions to a rule which only affected Israelites. It is evident that Balaam here does not mean the ancient prophet of Num. xxii. fol., but some one else for whom that ancient prophet could serve as a type. From the Jewish point of view there was considerable likeness between Balaam and Jesus. Both had led the people astray ; and if the former had tempted them to gross immorality, the latter, according to the Rabbis, had tempted them to gross apostasy—not unaccompanied by immorality, as will appear from some of the passages relating to Christians. This was the great charge against Jesus, that " he practised magic and deceived and led astray Israel" (see above (7) last line).

It should not be forgotten that even in the O.T., unfaithfulness in the covenant-relation between Israel and God is symbolised under the form of unfaithfulness in marriage, so that Balaam, the chief corrupter of the morality of Israel, might naturally be taken as a type of Jesus, the chief corrupter of its religion. I am well aware that this does not amount to a proof that Balaam is a type of Jesus. But it establishes a probability, which is strengthened by the consideration that the *animus* displayed against Balaam in the Talmud would be very artificial if its object had been really the ancient prophet, while it is very natural and intelligible if it was really directed against Jesus, who had dealt a blow at the national religion such as it had never received. To show the violence of the hatred against

Jesus, and also to strengthen the above contention that Balaam is a type of Jesus, I will give a passage in which they are mentioned together. By being mentioned together, it is true that Balaam is not in this case exactly a type of Jesus, *i.e.* we are not for ' Balaam ' to read ' Jesus '; but the symbol is expanded into a comparison, to suggest the conclusion, ' What Balaam was, such also was Jesus.' The passage is as follows :—

JESUS AND BALAAM IN HELL

(13) b. Gitt. 56[b], 57[a].—Onqelos bar Qaloniqos, sister's son of Titus, desired to become a proselyte. He called up Titus by necromancy. He said to him, ' Who is honoured in this world ? ' He replied, ' Israel.' ' What about joining them ? ' He replied, ' Their words are many and thou canst not fulfil them. Go, join thyself to them in this world and thou shalt become a leader, for it is written [Lam. i. 5], *Her adversaries have become the head.* Every oppressor of Israel is made a head.' He said to him, ' What is the punishment of this man ? ' [*i.e.* ' what is thy punishment '?] He replied, ' That which he determined for himself. Every day they collect his ashes and judge him, and burn him and scatter him over seven seas.'

He called up Balaam by necromancy. He said to him, ' Who is honoured in this world ? ' He replied, ' Israel.' ' What about joining them ? ' He replied [Deut. xxiii. 6], ' *Thou shalt not seek their peace or their prosperity all* [*thy*] *days.*' He said to him, ' What is the punishment of this man ? ' He replied, ' Per semen fervens.'

He called up Jesus by necromancy. He said to him, ' Who is honoured in this world ? ' He replied, ' Israel.' ' What about joining them ? ' He replied, ' Seek their good, seek not their harm. Every one who injures them, [it is] as if he injured the apple of his eye.' He said, 'What is the punishment of this man ? ' He replied, ' By boiling filth.' For a teacher has said, 'Every one who mocks at the words of the wise is punished by boiling filth.' Come and see the difference between the sinners of Israel and the prophets of the peoples of the world who serve a false religion.

Commentary.—This extract forms part of a long Midrash chiefly concerned with the war against Vespasian and Titus, and reported by R. Joḥanan (200–279 A.D.). The story of Onqelos b. Qaloniqos, nephew of Titus, is introduced immediately after the description of the death of the latter. Whether Onqelos the Proselyte, who is mentioned elsewhere in the Talmud, really was the nephew of Titus, I do not know, and the question is of no importance for the present purpose. The object of the gruesome story contained in this passage is to show the fate of the three chief enemies of Israel, *i.e.* Titus, Balaam and Jesus. Each suffers the punishment appropriate to the nature of his offence.

The modern editions of the Talmud, which have been subjected to the censor of the press, do not mention the third criminal by name. They read that Onqelos called up 'the sinners of Israel' (plural), which is obviously absurd.[1] The older editions have 'the sinner of Israel,' which is grammatically correct, but the reading 'Jeshu' is vouched for by the work that contains all the expurgated passages of the Talmud.[2] It is evident that some individual person is referred to, and that this person is not Balaam, since his case has just been disposed of. Moreover, it was some one who had 'mocked against the words of the wise,' i.e. the Rabbis. Internal evidence alone would suffice to show that Jesus was meant; and as there is authority for the reading 'Jeshu,' we may rest assured that he is the person referred to.

The passage has been introduced here, as stated above, in order to establish the fact that in the Talmud, Balaam and Jesus are classed together, and that therefore Balaam serves frequently as a type of Jesus. I do not mean that wherever Balaam is mentioned Jesus is intended, or that everything said about the former is really meant for the latter. I mean that wherever Balaam is mentioned, there is a sort of under-current of reference to Jesus, and that much more is told of Balaam than would have been told if he and not Jesus had really been the person thought of.[3] I shall henceforth assume this close

---

[1] 'The sinners of Israel' may, however, be the right reading in the last line of the passage, because there the comparison is general between 'the sinners of Israel' and 'the prophets of the heathen.'

[2] I have used the one published at Königsberg, 1860, קונטרס למלאות הסרונות הש״ס. The invaluable work of Rabbinowicz is unfortunately not available for the tractate Gittin.

[3] There is a suggestive remark in b. Sanh. 106ᵇ (immediately after

connexion in the Rabbinical mind between Jesus
and Balaam ; and if it proves a guide to the meaning of other passages where Balaam is referred to,
it will be to that extent confirmed and made more
probable. These other passages will be mentioned
presently. For the moment I return to the passage
(12), quoted above, from M. Sanh. x. 2, where it is
said that Balaam, Doeg, Ahitophel and Gehazi are
shut out from the world to come. Having seen that
Balaam here denotes Jesus, it is natural to enquire
into the meaning of the other three names. That
they merely denote the three persons mentioned
in the Books of Samuel and Kings is not probable ;
for there is nothing in the facts there recorded to
show why just these three should have been so
severely condemned. Following immediately after
Balaam-Jesus, we can hardly avoid the conclusion
that the three O.T. names denote three of the
Apostles, as having shared in the work of heresy
which Jesus began. Each of the three is elsewhere
mentioned in the Talmud as being tainted with
heresy, as will be shown hereafter (see below, pp. 99,
192). Which of the Apostles are referred to, if this
hypothesis be accepted, is a question of which the
answer must remain uncertain. One thinks, naturally,

the passage about the age of Balaam, to be given below) :—(14) Mar
bar Rabina said to his son, ' Do not multiply Midrash, in regard to all
these except in regard to Balaam, the wicked ; whatever you find in him,
expound of him.' ' In regard to all these,' i.e. the four men, Balaam, Doeg,
Ahitophel and Gehazi. Rashi, in his note on the passage, says that the
multiplying of Midrash means doing so לגנאי, with malicious intention. The
son of Mar bar Rabina, mentioned above, was the younger Rabina, contemporary with and colleague of Ashi the redactor of the Babylonian Gemara
Ashi, of course, was responsible for the inclusion in the Gemara of the
anonymous passages concerning the excommunication of Jesus (see p. 51).

of Peter, James and John. But it seems to me at least highly probable that Gehazi, at all events, means Paul. It would certainly be strange if the man who more than all else except Jesus ' troubled Israel ' (*cf.* Acts xxi. 27 fol.) should have been left out of this black list. A passage will be given presently where the story of Gehazi and Elisha is told in such a way as strongly to suggest Paul the renegade disciple of Gamaliel. (See below, No. (27), p. 97, b. Sotah. 47ª).

As for Doeg and Ahitophel, I do not know of any evidence for a particular identification. May not, however, Doeg the Edomite, who betrayed David (1 Sam. xxii. 9), possibly denote Judas Iscariot, the traitor ? And the high honour in which Ahitophel was held (2 Sam. xvi. 23) suggests him as a type of Peter. These are only guesses, and as regards the proposed identification of Doeg with Judas Iscariot, I must allow that it would be more likely that the Talmud should exalt the betrayer of Jesus into a hero than condemn him to exclusion from the world to come. At the same time, I would submit that the three names which are most prominent in the list of the Apostles, the three figures which would be most likely to dwell in the memory as connected with Jesus, are Peter, Judas Iscariot, and Paul. And therefore, in spite of difficulties, I am inclined to hold that these three are denoted by Ahitophel, Doeg, and Gehazi, in the passage we have been considering.

THE AGE OF BALAAM (JESUS)

(15) b. Sanh. 106ᵇ.—A certain heretic said to R.
Ḥanina, 'Have you ever heard how old
Balaam was ?' He replied, 'There is nothing
written about it. But from what is written
(Ps. lv. 23), *Men of blood and deceit shall not
live out half their days*, he must have been
thirty-three or thirty-four years old.' He [the
heretic] said, 'Thou hast answered me well.
I have seen the chronicle of Balaam, and
therein is written " Balaam, the lame, was
thirty-three years old when Pinḥas the Robber
killed him."'

Commentary.—R. Ḥanina lived in Sepphoris at the
end of the second and the beginning of the third
century (died 232 A.D.). The story of this conversation with a heretic was reported in Babylonia probably by Rab, who, like Ḥanina, was a disciple of
Rabbi (Jehudah ha-Qadosh. See above, p. 17). The
heretic—Min—was in all probability a Christian, as
will be shown later when the passages dealing with
the Minim come under review. And while there is
no apparent reason why a Christian should inquire as
to the age of the ancient Balaam, he might well have
inquired—especially in Galilee—about the age of
Jesus. It would seem, however, that he was not
asking for information, but had a desire to find out
whether R. Ḥanina knew anything about Jesus.
For he confirmed the Rabbi's answer by facts known
to himself. The 'Chronicle of Balaam' probably denotes a Gospel, though none of the known Gospels

states in so many words that Jesus was as much as thirty-three years old. If, however, it was believed that his ministry lasted three years, and that he was ' about thirty years old ' when he began to preach, the statement of the Christian is sufficiently borne out, though not verbally correct. R. Ḥanina must have had fairly good grounds for his opinion as to the age of Jesus, or he would not have quoted a text which would only apply to the case of a man about thirty-three or thirty-four years old.

It is curious that Balaam is here called ' the lame,' and that this epithet is mentioned, not by the Rabbi but by the Christian. It was, however, a Rabbinical opinion that Balaam was lame, and also blind of one eye. This is stated in the Gemara, b. Sanh. 105ª, in the same chapter from which is taken the extract at present under notice. This opinion about Balaam is taught by R. Joḥanan, on the strength of a fanciful interpretation of two texts—Num. xxiii. 3, xxiv. 15. It is quite possible that this is simply a fancy, without any reference to Jesus. But we may at least compare Mark. ix. 45, 46.

There remains to be noticed Pinḥas the Robber, or ' Pinḥas Listāāh,' who is said to have killed Balaam. It has been suggested by Perles (Grätz, Monatsch., 1872, p. 267, quoted by Bacher) that, assuming Balaam to represent Jesus, Pinḥas Listāāh is a corruption of Pontius Pilatus.[1] The corruption is, it

---

[1] *Cf.* the story given below (p. 87), according to which a certain person, presumably Jesus, 'took to robbery' (listāiā), and further, p. 95, where it is suggested that the allegation of robbery in reference to Jesus is due to a confusion of him with a certain robber chieftain Ben Netzer. It is worth noting that according to Matt. xxvi. 55, Jesus said, *Are ye come out as against a robber* (ὡς ἐπὶ λῃστὴν) ; λῃστής is in the Talmud לסטים, listīs.

must be admitted, a somewhat violent one, if the author who had written the one name was aware of the other. But he may have found a name to him unintelligible, and by the help of Num. xxxi. 8 have transformed it into Pinḥas Listāāh. Talmudic tradition did not, so far as I am aware, know the name of Pontius Pilate, or ascribe the death of Jesus to a non-Jewish tribunal. But it is certainly strange that a Jew should call Pinḥas [Phinehas] a robber, being, as he was, a highly honoured hero of tradition. Bacher seeks to show (*Jew. Quart. Rev.*, iii. p. 356) that the reference is to the historical Phinehas and the historical Balaam, as against the theory of Perles. And if it were not for the word Listāāh, I should agree with him. He explains its use in connexion with Pinḥas by assuming that the heretic quoted from some apocryphal work about Balaam of an anti-Israelite tendency. But was there such a work? Was Balaam of any special interest to either Jews or heretics, except as a type of Jesus? With all deference to Bacher's great authority, I cannot help thinking that under this mention of Pinḥas Listāāh there lies concealed a reference to Pontius Pilatus. The difficulty that the heretic, if a Christian, would not call Jesus by the name of Balaam, may be met by the consideration that the whole conversation comes to us in a Jewish form. As for the historical value of the incident, there is nothing to make it impossible. Such conversations were frequent, and R. Ḥanina was a well-known man. That the story only occurs in the Babylonian Gemara is not surprising, since we have already seen that there was considerable interest taken in the Babylonian schools in the traditions about Jesus.   The Palestinian Gemara contains much less than the Babylonian of such digressions from its proper subject.   But that the story is a pure invention I see no reason whatever to believe.

As it has already been suggested (see above, p. 71) that Doeg and Ahitophel represent two of the Apostles, perhaps Judas Iscariot and Peter, it is interesting to note that the text quoted above to determine the age of Balaam is also applied to these two.   On the same page of b. Sanh. 106^b it is said by R. Johanan, 'Doeg and Ahitophel did not live out half their days.   It is thus taught (Ps. lv. 23), *Men of blood and deceit do not live out half their days.*   All the years of Doeg were but thirty-four, and of Ahitophel only thirty-three.'   It is but fair, however, to admit that, as Doeg and Ahitophel had been mentioned together with Balaam in the Mishnah, the inference as to the age of the one might naturally be extended to the other, since it is only a haggadic deduction from a text of Scripture.

BALAAM (JESUS) AND THE NAME OF GOD

(16) b. Sanh. 106^a.—*And he [Balaam] took up his parable, and said, Alas, who shall live when God doeth this?*   R. Shim'on ben Laqish said: 'Woe unto him who maketh himself to live by the name of God.'

Commentary.—The text quoted is Num. xxiv. 23, and the application of it by R. Shim'on b. Laqish is a mere distortion of the original words.   What

precisely is the meaning of אל ומשי is open to
question, and is for the O.T. commentators to
decide. But by no rules of grammar or syntax
could the words be made to mean, 'Who maketh
himself live by the name of God.' This is a haggadic
variation of the text, such as the Rabbis often permitted themselves to make (see above, p. 13) for
a homiletic purpose. And it is hard to see what
purpose there could be, in the present example, other
than that of making a covert allusion to Jesus, who
had declared — according to the Gospels — that he
should rise from the dead, of course by the power
of God. The words do not apply to Balaam, at
least there is nothing recorded about him that would
give occasion for any such remark. Rashi, in his
note on the passage, does indeed refer it to Balaam,
but seems to be well aware that some one other than
Balaam is really intended. He says, "Balaam, who
restored himself to life by the name of God, made
himself God." With this passage should be compared
the saying of Abahu, (10) above, which is a somewhat
similar haggadic variation of a text of Scripture.

R. Shim'on ben Laqish, often called Resh Laqish,
was the colleague and friend of R. Johanan already
mentioned. He died somewhere about 279 A.D.

THE CHAPTER CONCERNING BALAAM

(17) b. B. Bathr. 14ᵇ.—Moses wrote his book and
the section [Parashah] about Balaam.

Commentary.—The book which Moses wrote is, of
course, the Pentateuch, with the exception of the
last eight verses, which the Talmud attributes to

Joshua. As the section about Balaam, Num. xxii.–
xxiv., forms part of the Pentateuch, the question
arises, Why was it necessary to state expressly that
Moses wrote it? Rashi answers that Moses went
out of his way to include the prophecies of Balaam,
which did not properly belong to his own subject.
Marx (Traditio Veterrima, p. 42) accepts this, and
quotes a passage from the Jerusalem Talmud to show
how much importance was attached to the Balaam
section. As this passage seems to me to suggest
more than Marx finds in it, I quote it here, adding
some preceding words which did not come within
the scope of his reference.

(18) j. Ber. i. 8 (3ᶜ).—For Rab Mathnah and Rab
Shemuel bar Naḥman says, both say, It would
be proper that the Ten Words should be read
every day. And why are they not read?
Because of the misrepresentation of the
Minim, that they might not say, 'These [i.e.
the Ten Words] only were given to Moses
on Sinai.' Rab Shemuel bar Naḥman in the
name of Rabbi Jehudah bar Zebuda says,
'It would be proper that the Parashah of
Balak and Balaam should be read every day.
And why is it not read? In order not to
weary the congregation.' Rab Huna says,
'Because there is written in it Lying down
and rising up' [Num. xxiii. 24]. Rabbi Jose
bar Rabbi Būn says, 'Because there is written
in it the going forth [out of Egypt], and
the Kingdom' [Num. xxiii. 21, 22]. Rabbi
El'azar says, 'Because it is written in the
Torah, the Prophets and the Writings.'

The first part of this passage will be mentioned in another connexion subsequently (p. 308); I quote it here because it refers to the Minim, heretics, whose false interpretation made it desirable not to introduce the Decalogue into the daily service. Coming immediately after this statement, may not the mention of the Parashah of Balak and Balaam, and its exclusion from the daily prayers, have also some reference to the misrepresentations of heretics? From the parallel passage, b. Ber. 12^b, it appears that the various reasons given by the Rabbis are reasons for the inclusion, not the exclusion, of the Parashah from the daily prayers. And the exclusion is justified on the ground that, the passage being very long, the recital of it would weary the congregation. The Babylonian Gemara distinctly says that it was proposed to include the Parashah, and that the proposal was not entertained.

There is, I admit, hardly anything in this passage to connect it directly with anti-Christian polemic; but yet I think there is enough to show that a special interest attached to the Parashah of Balaam; and we may, with a fair degree of probability, define that special interest by what we have already learnt as to the connexion between Balaam and Jesus.

THE TRIAL OF JESUS

(19) T. Sanh. x. 11.—In regard to all who are worthy of death according to the Torah, they do not use concealment against them, except in the case of the deceiver. How do they

deal with him ?   They put two disciples of
the wise in the inner chamber, and he sits in
the outer chamber, and they light the lamp
so that they shall see him and hear his voice.
And thus they did to Ben Stada in Lūd;
two disciples of the wise were chosen for
him, and they [brought him to the Beth Din]
and stoned him.

(20) j. Sanh. vii. 16 (25ᶜ, ᵈ).—The deceiver; this
denotes a private man.   Not a Sage ? [*i.e.* a
Rabbi].   No.   From the time he deceives he
is no longer a Sage.   And from the time he
is deceived he is no longer a Sage.   How do
they deal with him to work craftily against
him?   They conceal (in his case) two witnesses
in the inner chamber and make him sit in
the outer chamber, and they light a lamp
over him that they may see him and may
hear his voice.   Thus did they to Ben Stada in
Lūd, and they concealed in his case two
disciples of the wise, and they brought him
to the Beth Din and stoned him.

The Babylonian Gemara has the following
version of this incident :—

(21) b. Sanh. 67ᵃ.—[The passage of which the extract No. 1 above (the part enclosed in [ ]),
forms the conclusion.]

For it is tradition that in regard to the
rest of all who are worthy of death according
to the Torah, they do not use concealment
except in this case [*i.e.* of the deceiver].   How
do they deal with him ?   They light a lamp
for him in the inner chamber and set witnesses

in the outer chamber, so that they may see
him and hear his voice, but he does not see
them.   And one says to him, "Say to me
what thou saidst to me in private," and he
says it to him.   And another says to him,
"How shall we forsake our God who is in
heaven, and practise false worship?"   If he
repents, it is well.   If he says, "Such is our
duty and thus it becomes us to do," the
witnesses, who hear from outside, bring him
to the Beth Din and stone him.   And thus
they did to Ben Stada in Lūd, and they
hung him on the eve of Pesaḥ.

Commentary.—The legal procedure to be used in
the case of a deceiver, who has tempted others to
apostasy, is set forth in the Mishnah almost in the
same words as in the first of the above extracts.
These are from the Tosephta and the Gemaras, the
passage (20) being contained in the Palestinian
Gemara, while (21) is from the Babylonian Gemara.
The Mishnah does not contain the reference to Ben
Stada; but it is important to notice that the Tosephta
(19) does contain the name, and thus establishes the
fact that the curious and exceptional legal procedure
to be followed in the case of a deceiver was associated with the case of Ben Stada (Jesus, see above (1)),
at a time before the Tosephta was completed.   This
fact lends some support to the hypothesis of Laible,
(J. C. im Talmud, p. 76), that the legal procedure
referred to was really based upon the case of Jesus,
as traditionally reported.   In all the passages given
above, it is stated that the concealment of witnesses,
in order to trap the accused, is only practised in the

one case of a man who has tempted others to apostasy, which was of course the charge against Jesus (see above, p. 51). However that may be, and I do not feel competent to pronounce opinion on the question of the origin of this law, the point that concerns us here is this, that as early as the time when the Tosephta was compiled, there was a tradition that the condemnation of Jesus had been obtained by the fraudulent means described above. Presumably the Tosephta (19) represents the oldest form of the tradition now extant; but there is no material difference between the three passages (19), (20), (21), so far as they refer to Ben Stada. They agree in saying, first, that two witnesses were hidden in a room adjoining the one where the accused sat; second, that a lamp was lit over the accused, so that the witnesses could see as well as hear him ; third, that in the case of Ben Stada, the witnesses brought him to the Beth Din [1] and stoned him ; fourth, that this took place in Lūd (Lydda). (21) makes the important addition that " they hung him on the eve of Passover." As to the place of concealment, (19) and (20) say that the two witnesses were in the inner chamber and the accused in the outer, (21) reverses the position. It is not clear in regard to the cross-examination described in (21) whether the questioners are the two witnesses. If they are, the concealment would seem to be useless ; if not, there is nothing to show who they are. The uncertainty on this point, which the compiler of the Gemara seems to feel, may be understood if there

[1] Beth Din, literally house of judgment, an assembly of Rabbis and their disciples sitting as a court of justice. The term does not denote any special tribunal.

6

really was no law on the subject except what could be recollected in connection with the trial of Jesus. As in the passages previously examined, we have here only scanty remnants of a tradition about that trial, combined perhaps with hearsay information derived from Christians. There is no ground, as Keim rightly says (Jesus of Nazara, vi. 47 n., E.T.), for correcting the Gospel account ' by the help of the Talmud. Rather it is the Gospel account which throws light upon the Talmudic tradition. From the Gospel story are derived the two witnesses (Matt. xxvi. 60. In Mark xiv. 56, 57, several witnesses are mentioned). The Gospel speaks of ' false ' witnesses, and this is perhaps the origin of the Talmudic assertion that the witnesses were concealed in order to entrap the accused. From the Talmudic point of view the witnesses were not false, in the sense of untruthful, but were justified by their zeal for the true religion in acting deceitfully against a heretic. The mention of the outer and the inner chamber (of what building is not said) recalls Matt. xxvi. 69, where it is said that *Peter was sitting without in the court*, while the trial was going on within the house of the High Priest. The lighted lamp may have been suggested by the mention of the fire kindled in the outer court, Luke xxii. 55. And finally the statement that the witnesses carried the accused to the Beth Din may have its origin in the fact that there was, according to the Gospels, a second sitting of the council after the one at which the witnesses had been present (Mark xv. 1). The Talmudic tradition differs from the Gospel in saying that the trial took place at Lūd (Lydda), and that Jesus was stoned. These statements, as well as the remark that Jesus was hung on the Eve of Passover, belong rather to the question of the execution of Jesus, which will form the subject of the next extract.   They tend, however, to confirm what has already been pointed out, that the Talmud has preserved only a very vague and confused recollection of Jesus.   His name was doubtless held in abhorrence as that of a dangerous heretic and deceiver; but extremely little was known of him, and that little is mentioned more by way of casual remark than as being of importance on its own account.

The Execution of Jesus

(22) b. Sanh. 43ᵃ.—And it is tradition: On the eve of Pesaḥ they hung Jeshu [the Nazarene]. And the crier went forth before him forty days (saying), '[Jeshu the Nazarene] goeth forth to be stoned, because he hath practised magic and deceived and led astray Israel. Any one who knoweth aught in his favour, let him come and declare concerning him.' And they found naught in his favour. And they hung him on the eve of Pesaḥ.   Ulla says, 'Would it be supposed that [Jeshu the Nazarene] a revolutionary, had aught in his favour?'   He was a deceiver, and the Merciful hath said (Deut. xiii. 8), *Thou shalt not spare, neither shalt thou conceal him.*   But it was different with [Jeshu the Nazarene], for he was near to the kingdom.

[The whole of this passage is expunged from the later editions. It is given here on the authority of the MSS. and early editions set forth by Rabbinowicz. The words in [ ] are from MSS.]

Commentary.—To the statements contained in the foregoing passage must be added those given in Nos. (19), (20), (21), viz., that Jesus was stoned, and that his death took place in Lūd (Lydda). It is remarkable that the fact of the crucifixion in Jerusalem should have been so completely forgotten, even by the compiler of the Tosephta, to say nothing of the compilers of the Gemara. This is the more curious because there are to be found in other passages, to be given presently, allusions to a crucifixion and to a death in Jerusalem, which are probably those of Jesus. The explanation of the statement that Jesus was put to death in Lydda is probably the following : After the destruction of Jerusalem, Lydda gradually became an important centre of Rabbinical activity. In the early years of the second century, Rabbis Eliezer, Tarphon and Aqiba held their colleges there, and Lydda quite outshone Jabneh, which had been the seat first of Joḥanan ben Zaccai, and then of the Patriarch Gamliel II. after the fall of Jerusalem. Aqiba took a very active part in the insurrection under Bar Cocheba (A.D. 132–135), and Lydda was probably the headquarters of the insurgents. The name " Martyrs of Lydda " (הרוגי לוד, b. B. Bathr. 10ᵇ), was applied to some of the distinguished Rabbis who were executed at the close of the insurrection. Now we have already learnt (see above, p. 44) that the Talmud regards Jesus as having been a contemporary of Aqiba; and it is further to be observed that the Christians were persecuted by the adherents of Bar Cocheba, presumably for not acknowledging him as the Messiah.[1] Now it is quite certain that in the Talmud the insurrection of Bar Cocheba and its tragic end is remembered with much greater clearness than the fate of Jesus a century before. And the suggestion is that the more recent and important event has gathered to itself the tradition of the earlier period. Aqiba, the apostle of the insurrection, became thereby the persecutor of Christians; the place where he was most active against them was Lydda, and thus a later tradition could naturally arise that Jesus was a contemporary of Aqiba, and had been executed in Aqiba's own city of Lydda. This is in the main Laible's explanation; but I differ from him in holding that Aqiba's hostility towards the Christians was chiefly due to his own connexion with Bar Cocheba, and not so much to his hatred of Christians as such. No doubt he felt such a hatred, as did other Rabbis, e.g. Tarphon and Meir; but I do not know of any special evidence of his hostility except on the ground that I have mentioned.

The passage before us further states that Jesus was hung. With this must be combined the evidence of the passages, Nos. (19), (20), (21), that he was stoned. The connexion between the two statements is that Jesus was stoned, and his dead body then hung upon a cross. This is clear from the Mishnah, Sanh. vi.

---

[1] Justin. Mart., Apol. i. c. 31, καὶ γὰρ ἐν τῷ νῦν γεγενημένῳ Ἰουδαικῷ πολέμῳ Βαρχωχέβας, ὁ τῆς Ἰουδαίων ἀποστάσεως ἀρχηγέτης, Χριστιανοὺς μόνους εἰς τιμωρίας δεινάς, εἰ μὴ ἀρνοῖντο Ἰησοῦν τὸν Χριστὸν καὶ βλασφημοῖεν, ἐκέλευεν ἀπάγεσθαι.

4. (23) 'All who are stoned are hung, according to Rabbi Eliezer. The Sages say None is hung except the blasphemer and he who practises a false worship.' [1] The corpse was hung to a cross or else to a single beam, of which one end rested on the ground, the other against a wall (same Mishnah). It is worth noting that the technical word for a cross (צליב) is not used here. The Gospels, of course, say nothing about a stoning of Jesus, and I suggest that the Talmudic tradition is an inference from the fact that he was known to have been hung. The inference would be further strengthened by the application of the text, Deut. xxi. 23, *He that is hanged is accursed of God*, a text which Paul had to disarm in reference to Jesus (Gal. iii. 13). The Talmud knows nothing of an execution of Jesus by the Romans, but makes it solely the act of the Jews.

Here may be mentioned a passage which seems to show that there was a tradition that Jesus had been crucified.

(24) T. Sanh. ix. 7.—Rabbi Meir used to say, What is the meaning of (Deut. xxi. 23), *For a curse of God is he that is hung*? [It is like the case of] two brothers, twins, who resembled each other. One ruled over the whole world, the other took to robbery. After a time the one who took to robbery was caught, and they *crucified* him on a *cross*. And every one who passed to and fro said, 'It seems that the king

---

[1] Literally a worshipper of stars and planets. This is constantly used in the Rabbinical literature as a technical term for the adherent of a false religion, without any implication that the stars are the actual objects of worship. Idolater is not always an equivalent term ; but, with this explanation, it is the most convenient to use.

is crucified.' Therefore it is said, *A curse of God is he that is hung.*

Commentary.—R. Meir lived in the second century, and we shall see that he had some knowledge of the Gospels (see below, p. 163). It is hardly to be doubted that the above passage contains a reference to Jesus. 'One ruled over the whole world,' that is God. 'They resembled each other' suggests *He that hath seen me hath seen the Father.* The mention of the cross (צלוב) obviously accords with the Gospel story. The scornful gibe of the passers-by suggests Matt. xxvii. 37 and 39, and esp. 42, 43. The curious remark that the second 'took to robbery' (listāiā) I cannot explain, but it should be noted in connexion with what was said above (see p. 73), about Pinḥas Listāāh (Pontius Pilatus). R. Meir's interpretation of the text in Deut. is somewhat obscure ; so far as I understand it he seems to mean that the raillery of the bystanders was a cursing of God, because they said 'the King is hung,' which would be the case if Jesus were supposed to be God.

To this passage may be appended another where there is also a reference to crucifixion. It is contained in the Midrash on Esther ix. 2, and is as follows :— Zeresh, the wife of Haman, is advising him how to kill Mordecai, so that he shall not be delivered by miracle as so many had been, and she says, צלוב יתיה על צליבא דלא אשכחין חד מן עמוי דאשתזיב מניה, " Crucify him on a cross, for we do not find one out of his nation who has been delivered from it." The reference seems to be to the fact that Jesus was not saved from the cross even though it was claimed

for him that he was the Messiah; cp. Matt. xxvii.
40.

To return now to the Gemara in Sanh., at the
head of this section. It is stated there that Jesus
was put to death on the eve of Passover; the Florence
codex adds that it was also the eve of Sabbath. This
is probably dependent on the Gospel story, and it is
interesting to note that it agrees more with the
Gospel of John than with the Synoptics. From what
we have already seen, however, of the vagueness and
uncertainty of the Talmudic tradition concerning the
death of Jesus, it is unwarrantable to use this as
independent evidence.

In like manner we may ascribe to a confused
knowledge of Christian teaching the statement that
a herald went forth, during forty days before the
death of Jesus, calling upon all who could bear
witness in his favour to come and do so. The herald
is, of course, fictitious; but the forty days may have
been suggested by the forty days which are said to
have elapsed between the crucifixion and the ascension, *i.e.* before the final disappearance of Jesus.
Laible suggests the forty days of fasting ending with
Easter, and Dalman hints at the forty days' fast of
Jesus in the wilderness (Matt. iv. 2). All that can
be said with any safety is that the number forty may
have its origin in the Gospel.

The Gemara, having described the death of Jesus,
adds a remark about the statement that a herald
invited evidence in favour of Jesus, and found none.
Ulla, a Palestinian Rabbi of the end of the third
century, a disciple of R. Johanan, says, ' Would it
be thought that anything could be said in favour

of Jesus, a revolutionary? He was a deceiver, and the Merciful hath said (observe the irony of appealing to God as "the Merciful" in this case), *Thou shalt not spare nor conceal such a one.*' But, says the compiler of the Gemara, or perhaps Ulla, who raised the question, 'It was different with Jesus, because he was *near to the kingdom*.' Is this a reference to the supposed Davidic descent of Jesus? The suggestion is tempting; but I doubt whether it is warranted. The phrase "near to the kingdom" occurs elsewhere, and is applied to the family of the Patriarch Gamliel II., of whom it is said (b. B. Q. 83ª), that they were allowed to learn Greek because they were "near to the kingdom." The Patriarch was the official representative of the Jews, and since as such he must have had frequent intercourse with the government, the knowledge of Greek was necessary. Of course, Jesus stood in no such official relation to the government; but the Gospels record a remarkable hesitation on the part of Pontius Pilate to put him to death, and such hesitation might well be explained by saying that Jesus must have had friends at court, or at least that there must have been political reasons for wishing to spare him. If this suggestion, which is made by Laible (J. C. im Talmud, p. 80), be thought somewhat far-fetched, as implying a greater knowledge of the Gospel story than is probable, it may be simplified by supposing that the phrase, "near to the kingdom," was an inference from the fact that Jesus frequently spoke of "the kingdom." In this case there would be no need to bring in Pontius Pilate, and in fact the Talmudic story of the execution of Jesus does not

implicate the civil government at all.   Laible appears
to me to credit the Talmudic Rabbis with a much
clearer memory of the life and death of Jesus than
is warranted by the evidence.   That they knew of
the existence of the Gospel (or Gospels) is certain
(see below, p. 163) ; and that they had some acquaintance with the contents of the Gospel is probable;
but the frequent discussions between Jews and
Christians, of which we shall meet with many examples, lead me to think that the Rabbis gained
most of their information about Jesus from such
intercourse, and that the real tradition concerning
him amounted to hardly more than the fact that he
had been a deceiver of the people and had been put
to death.

THE DISCIPLES OF JESUS

(25) b. Sanh. 43ª.—Our Rabbis have taught, Jesus
    had five disciples—Matthai, Neqai, Netzer,
    Buni, and Thodah.   They brought Matthai
    [before the judges].   He said, ' Must Matthai
    be killed ?   For it is written [Ps. xlii. 2]:
    Mathai [= when] *shall* (*I*) *come and appear
    before God.*'   They said to him, ' Yes,
    Matthai must be killed, for it is written [Ps.
    xli. 5]: *Mathai* [= when] *shall* (*he*) *die and
    his name perish.*'   They brought Neqai.   He
    said to them, ' Must ·Neqai be killed ?   For
    it is written [Ex. xxiii. 7]: *The Naqi* [= inno-
    cent] *and the righteous thou shalt not slay.*'
    They said to him, ' Yes, Neqai must be killed,
    for it is written [Ps. x. 8]: *In secret places*

doth he slay Naqi [= the innocent].' They
brought Netzer. He said, 'Must Netzer be
killed? For it is written [Isa. xi. 1]: *Netzer*
[= a branch] *shall spring up from his roots.'*
They said to him, 'Yes, Netzer must be
killed. For it is written [Isa. xiv. 19]:
Thou art cast forth out of thy grave like an
abominable Netzer [= branch].' They brought
Buni. He said to them, 'Must Buni be
killed? For it is written [Ex. iv. 22]: *B'ni*
[= my son], *my first born, Israel.'* They said
to him, 'Yes, Buni must be killed. For it is
written [Ex. iv. 23]: *Behold, I slay Bincha*,
[= thy son] *thy first born.'* They brought
Thodah. He said to them, 'Must Thodah be
killed? For it is written [Ps. c. 1]: *A Psalm*
for Thodah [= thanksgiving].' They said to
him, 'Yes, Thodah must be killed, for it is
written [Ps. l. 23]: *Whoso sacrificeth Thodah*
[= thanksgiving] *honoureth me.'*

Commentary. — This passage is the continuation
of the preceding one, and I have only divided the
two for convenience of separate treatment. It is
probable that the passage already considered, No.
(21), which in the editions of the Talmud is found
on p. 67ª of Sanhedrin, also forms part of the
same paragraph about Jesus. Thus it would contain, first, the description of the witnesses, then the
execution, and lastly the account of the five disciples.
If this is so, then it is clear why the place of execution (Lydda) is not mentioned in the second and
third passages (22), (25), since it has already been
mentioned in (21). This is Laible's suggestion. The

reason for their being divided in the Talmud would
be that the division of subject required it, the
account of the death of Jesus being introduced in a
discussion about the stoning of certain criminals,
and the description of the manner of concealing
witnesses finding its proper place later in a discussion
upon deceivers of the people. The passage which
we have now to consider is merely a pendant to
the account of the death of Jesus, describing with
a certain ferocious humour the fate of five of his
disciples. These are said to have been condemned
to death; and when they quoted Scripture texts as
a plea for their lives, they were met with other
texts demolishing their plea. That any tribunal of
justice, or of arbitrary violence, ever conducted its
business in such a manner, it is hard to believe; and
we can only regard this fencing with texts as a
jeu d'esprit, occasioned no doubt by some actual
event. That event would naturally be an execution
of Christian disciples, if such took place. The
dialogue as given in the Talmud can certainly not
be taken as historical; but it may yet give some indication of the historical circumstances under which
it was composed. Little or nothing can be learnt
from the names of the five disciples; only the first,
Matthai, has any close resemblance to a name in the
list of the twelve (Matt. x. 2–4). The last, Thodah,
is not unlike Thaddæus; but in Hebrew that name
would be Thaddai, not Thodah. The others, Naqi,
Netzer, and Buni,[1] have no parallels in the list of the

---

[1] It is, however, worthy of note that in b. Taan. 19[b], 20[a], is related a story
of Naqdimon b. Gorion, a rich citizen of Jerusalem, and it is added in a
note that his real name was not Naqdimon, but Buni. Now Naqdimon is

Twelve; indeed, it is doubtful whether they, and Thodah, were ever names of persons at all. At most they may have been nick-names, and they certainly raise the suspicion that they have been chosen for the sake of the texts. I suggest that the case stands thus:—five disciples of Jesus, *i.e.* five Christians, were on some occasion condemned to death, that their real names, if known, were not mentioned, that one of them was designated Matthai with reference to the name attached to the first Gospel, that the play upon his name suggested a similar device in the case of the others, and that for them other names were invented, each of which had some reference to Jesus, as regarded of course by Christians. Thus Naqi, the innocent, is obviously applicable to Jesus from the Christian point of view, and is as obviously satirical from that of the Rabbis, as already shown. Nētzer, the branch, is the Hebrew word occurring in the two texts quoted from Isaiah, of which the former was interpreted Messianically, and would therefore be applied to Jesus. But perhaps more probably there is a reference to the name Nōtzri, the Nazarene, which we have ·already met with as an epithet of Jesus (for the derivation of the word Nōtzri, and its meaning, see above, p. 52 n.). Buni, as used in both the texts, is taken to mean 'my son,' a frequent designation of the Messiah, and therefore applicable by Christians to Jesus. For the name Thōdah, 'praise,' I do not know any connexion with Jesus; but it is possible that the apt retort of the second text, *whoso sacri-*

equivalent to Nicodemus. There may, therefore, be an allusion to Nicodemus, who came to Jesus by night (John iii. 1).

ficeth **Thodah** *honoureth me*, may have suggested the whole series, and thus that the name Thodah was a pure invention.

It is natural to infer from the passage that all the five disciples were condemned on the same occasion, and this at once excludes the possibility that any of the original Twelve are referred to. At least no Christian tradition exists which specifies any five out of the Twelve as having met with such a fate. But the fact that the five were called disciples of Jesus only implies that they were Christians, not that they were contemporaries of Jesus. Therefore we may look for them, if necessary, at some later period. The fact that the prisoners quoted texts of Scripture, and were met with other texts, suggests that the trial took place before a Jewish and not a Roman tribunal. Not, of course, that such a thrust and parry of texts really took place anywhere, but that it would be impossible in a Roman court and only a witty travesty of what would be possible in a Jewish one. Laible (J. C. im Talm., p. 68 fol.) makes the very probable suggestion that the story refers to the persecution of Christians under Bar Cocheba, already mentioned. It is a fantastic account of some incident of that persecution. The reasons for taking this view are, that the story occurs in the same passage as that which describes the death of Jesus, and that we have found the key to the understanding of the statements there made about Jesus in the anti-Christian hatred of Bar Cocheba, and more especially of Aqiba, his chief supporter. So far as I know, there is no other period than this (132–135 A.D.) at which Christians were persecuted and even put to death by Jews.

The Christians would, of course, be of Jewish extraction.

Other persons who are described as disciples of Jesus will be mentioned subsequently. I do not mention them here, in the division dealing with Talmudic references to Jesus, because the passages where they are alluded to are more conveniently grouped together as referring to Minûth (heresy) and Minim (heretics), and will therefore be treated separately in another main division.

I shall close this division, of which the main subject is Jesus, by a reference to the name Ben Netzer, which has been held by some to denote Jesus.

BEN NETZER

Levy (N. H. W., i. 240ª, *s.v.* בן) says that the name Ben Netzer (בי נצר) is probably an allusion to Jesus the Nazarene. Keim, (J. of N., ii. 15, Eng. Tr.) says that the Talmudists call Jesus, Ben Nētzar. This is also the view of Edersheim (L. and T. J. M., i. 222). The authority for this appears to be Abarbanel, whose work מעיני הישועה is quoted by Buxtorf (Lexicon Talmudicum, ed. Fischer, *s.v.* נצר) as follows: Speaking of the "little horn" in Dan. vii. 8, he says (26), "See, yea see, how they interpret that other 'little horn' to mean Ben Nētzer, who is Jeshua ha-Notzri, and according to the context they join in the reference to him the wicked kingdom, which is Edom, for that was his nation." What reason Abarbanel had for making this identification I do not know; but there is nothing in the passages where Ben Netzer is mentioned (b. Keth. 51ᵇ, J. Terum. 46ᵇ, Ber. r. sec. 76) to suggest Jesus. Ben Netzer is described as a sort of robber chieftain, " a robber amongst kings, a king amongst robbers," as the Talmud says. The correct explanation, as it seems beyond question, is that of Grätz (G. d. J., iv. 295, and n. 28), who shows that Ben Netzer is Odenathus, the founder of the shortlived kingdom of Palmyra, A.D. 260 *circa*. Jost (G. d. J., ii. 145 n. 4) says that this hypothesis is without evidence to support it; and if it were not for a reference in the same context to Grätz' work, it would be hard to believe that Jost had read the long note (n. 28) in which Grätz presents the evidence. It appears to me clear that Grätz is right, and if so, there can be no question of an allusion to Jesus in the name Ben Netzer. Even Jost does not allege any such allusion, though he rejects the proposed identification with Odenathus.

B.—PASSAGES REFERRING TO MINIM AND MINUTH

This division will include a much larger number of passages than the one just completed, and the greater part of them will be concerned with those Minim whose identification is one of the problems of the Talmud. It will be necessary, for the sake of clearness, to sub-divide the material in this division, with the result, as I hope, of lessening the amount of commentary upon each passage.

SECTION I.—DESCRIPTIONS AND DEFINITIONS OF MINIM AND MINUTH

I place first of all what I believe to be a reference to the most distinguished disciple of Jesus, viz., Paul.

GEHAZI (PAUL?)

(27) b. Sotah. 47ª.—Our Rabbis have taught: Always let the left hand repel and the right hand invite. Not like Elisha, who repulsed Gehazi with both his hands, and not like Jehoshua ben Peraḥjah, who repulsed Jesus the Nazarene with both his hands. What about Elisha? It is written (2 Kings v. 23), *And Naaman said, Be content, take two talents,* and

it is written (*ib.* v. 26), *and he said to him,* *'Went not my heart [with thee] when the man turned from off his chariot to meet thee*? *Is it a time to receive silver, and to receive raiment and olive gardens and vineyards and sheep and cattle and men-servants and maid-servants?'* But had he indeed received all this? Silver and raiment was what he received. R. Jitzḥaq said, ' In that hour Elisha was occupied with [the law concerning] the eight [kinds of] creeping things (Lev. xi. 29, 30]. He said to him [Gehazi], ' Wretch, the time has come to receive the punishment [for having partaken] of the eight creeping things, *and the leprosy of Naaman shall cleave to thee and to thy seed for ever.'* *And there were four leprous men* (2 Kings vii. 3), R. Johanan said these were Gehazi and his three sons. *And Elisha went to Damascus* (*ib.* viii. 7). Why did he go to Damascus? R. Johanan says that he went to turn Gehazi to repentance, and he did not repent. He said to him ' Repent,' and he answered, ' Thus have I received from thee, that everyone who has sinned and caused the multitude to sin, they give him not the chance to repent.' What did he do? Some say he set up a loadstone according to the sin of Jeroboam and made it stand between heaven and earth. And some say he wrote the Name upon its mouth, and it used to say " I " and " Thou shalt not have." And some say he drove our Rabbis from before him, as it is written (2 Kings vi. 1), *And the sons of the*

*prophets said to Elisha, Behold the place where
we sit is too strait for us,* whereas up till that
time it had not been too small.

What of R. Jehoshua ben Perahjah ? · [See
the continuation (7) above, p. 50.]

Commentary.—It must be borne in mind that this
passage is continuous with that describing the excommunication of Jesus by R. Jehoshua ben Perahjah, No.
(7) above, p. 50. The whole passage occurs in b. Sotah
47[a] and b. Sanh. 107[b]. The story of Jesus has been
given according to the latter version, for the sake of
being able to use the various readings of Rabbinowicz,
which are not available for the treatise Sotah. The
story about Gehazi is given according to the version
in Sotah, because it is somewhat fuller, and omits
nothing of importance that is found in the version in
Sanhedrin.

The connexion of a story about Jesus with a story
about Gehazi suggests that there may be, under the
figure of Gehazi, a covert reference to some person
associated with Jesus. It will not be forgotten that
Gehazi is one of the four men expressly excluded from
the world to come, and that the other three are Balaam,
Doeg and Ahitophel. We have already seen reason
to believe that Balaam is a type of Jesus (see above,
p. 64 fol.), and that Doeg and Ahitophel are elsewhere said to have been heretics (Minim), a term
which in some cases certainly denotes Christians. It
is natural, therefore, to look amongst the followers of
Jesus for the man of whom Gehazi is the type. I
suggest that the man referred to is Paul. In what
is said about Gehazi, in the passage before us and
elsewhere, there are several points of likeness to

Paul; and it would certainly be strange if the man who, more than any other except Jesus, was the foe of the traditional Judaism, and who, moreover, had been in his youth a strict Pharisee, should be passed over in silence by the defenders of that Judaism when they had occasion to refer to Christianity.

In the passage before us, the subject under discussion is the duty of attending on or accompanying a man walking forth from a town ; and a chance mention of Elisha is made the excuse for introducing a long haggadah about him, of which our passage forms part. The story translated above is, of course, a haggadic enlargement of the story in 2 Kings v. of the dismissal and punishment of Gehazi for covetousness. The curious statement that Elisha was studying the law about the eight kinds of creeping things is only a fantastic explanation of the punishment of Gehazi. Elisha said, ' Is this a time to receive silver and raiment and olive-gardens.' etc., mentioning eight things. And the objection is made that Gehazi had not received all these, but only the first two. R. Jitzhaq explains this by saying that Elisha was studying the law about the eight creeping things forbidden for food. The connexion is not, however, simply the number eight. The punishment, according to this fanciful exposition, is inflicted upon Gehazi for having broken the law about eating the creeping things. The absurdity of this explanation is somewhat diminished when we remember that it was Paul more than anyone else who repudiated the Jewish laws of clean and unclean food. In reference to the real Gehazi the explanation has no point, but in reference to Paul it has a good deal.

Significant also is the fact that Gehazi was a renegade disciple of a great master; and although this is, of course, found in the O.T. story, and is not a haggadic invention, it is none the less applicable to Paul, the disciple of Gamaliel. So, too, the fact that Gehazi went to Damascus (not stated, but implied in the statement that Elisha went thither to try and bring him to repentance) has its parallel in the fact that Paul went to Damascus, and was there as a Christian (Acts ix. 22). The answer of Gehazi to Elisha, that one who has sinned and caused the multitude to sin is allowed no chance to repent, has no meaning in reference to the real Gehazi, but harmonizes well with the case of Paul. It should be noticed that this answer is exactly the same as that which, in the companion story, Jesus makes to R. Jehoshua ben Perahjah.[1]

Further, the accounts of what happened afterwards to Gehazi deserve notice. 'Some say that he set up a loadstone according to the sin of Jeroboam.' The sin of Jeroboam consisted in setting up the calves in Bethel and Dan; and Rashi, in his comment on this passage, says that he did so by means of a loadstone which will lift metal from the earth. What may be the meaning of a loadstone in reference to Paul will be seen presently; but he so far followed the example of Jeroboam as to establish centres of worship other than Jerusalem. 'Some say that he wrote the Name upon its mouth, and it used to say " I " and " Thou

---

[1] The words of the answer are, however, a general Rabbinical maxim, not peculiar to this passage. The origin of the maxim is found in 1 Kings xiv. 16; and the Rabbinical aphorism occurs in T. Joma v. 11, b. Joma 87ᵃ, Aboth. v. 18 (in connexion with ' disciples of Balaam ').

shalt not have."' What is referred to here is again
the loadstone, and it would seem that a statue is
intended. The Name that he wrote, or carved, upon
the mouth of the figure is the name of God, the
Name which was forbidden to be pronounced. And
the words which the figure uttered are the opening
of the Ten Commandments. The meaning seems
to be that Paul set up some figure representing a
person whom he asserted to be equal with God.
That images of Christ were to be seen in Christian
churches in the time of Paul is not to be supposed ;
but that they were well known to the Rabbis of the
time to which our passage belongs, is certain. And
considering how much the doctrine of the Deity of
Christ owes to the teaching of Paul, it would not be
unnatural for a Jew to charge him with setting up
images of Christ to be worshipped as God. Possibly the clue may be found in John xii. 32 : *And
I, if I be lifted up, will draw all men unto
myself.*

'Some say that he drove our Rabbis from before
him.' This is explained by Rashi to mean that the
Rabbinical academies were crowded by the disciples
whom Gehazi drove away. Whether there is here
any reference to Paul I am not prepared to say.

As to the date of this passage, nothing can be
precisely determined. It is found only in the Babylonian Gemara, and no Rabbi is mentioned as an
authority except for some small portions. R. Johanan
belongs to the third century (d. 279 A.D.), and R.
Jitzhaq was a younger contemporary. Both lived in
Palestine. The passage about Gehazi is perhaps
older than that about Jesus, as suggested above,

p. 54, and served as the introduction to that story. But, on the other hand, the story about Jesus had a foundation in Palestinian tradition, as the story of Gehazi (Paul) had. And in both cases, what we have is a product of the Babylonian schools. Both are probably of very late date, and though one may have preceded the other, there seems no reason to place any considerable interval between them.

It is curious, by the way, that in neither story is any further reference made to that repulsion by both hands, which each story is quoted to illustrate.[1]

BEN DAMAH AND JACOB OF CHEPHAR SAMA (SECHANJA).

(28) T. Ḥull, ii. 22, 23.—The case of R. El'azar ben Damah, whom a serpent bit. There came in Jacob, a man of Chephar Sama, to cure him in the name of Jeshua' ben Pandira, but R. Ishmael did not allow it. He said, ' Thou art not permitted, Ben Damah.' He said, ' I will bring thee a proof that he may heal me.' But he had not finished bringing a proof when he died. R. Ishmael said, ' Happy art thou, Ben Damah, for thou hast departed in peace, and hast not broken through the ordinances of the wise ; for upon every one who breaks through the fence of the wise, punishment comes at last, as it is written [Eccl. x. 8]: *Whoso breaketh a fence a serpent shall bite him.*

(29) j. Shabb. 14ᵈ.—Almost word for word the same as (28), then follows:—The serpent only bit

---

[1] For the phrase, see Mechilta, Jithro, 58ᵇ.

him in order that a serpent might not bite him
in the future.   And what could he [B. Damah]
have said ? (Lev. xviii. 5) : *Which, if a man do,
he shall live in them* [*i.e.* not die in them].

(30) j. A. Zar. 40ᵈ, 41ᵃ.—Same as (29), except that
after the words " came in to cure him," is
added, " He said, We will speak to thee in the
name of Jeshu ban Pandira."

(31) b. A. Zar. 27ᵇ.—A man shall have no dealings
with the Minim, nor be cured by them, even
for the sake of an hour of life.   The case of
Ben Dama, sister's son of Rabbi Ishmael, whom
a serpent bit.   There came Jacob the Min of
Chephar Sechanja to cure him ; but R. Ishmael
would not allow him.   And he [B. Dama] said
to him, ' R. Ishmael, my brother, allow him,
that I may be cured by him, and I will bring
a text from the Torah that this is permitted.'
But he had not finished his discourse when his
soul departed, and he died.   R. Ishmael pronounced over him, ' Happy art thou, Ben
Dama, for thy body is pure and thy soul hath
departed in purity, and thou hast not transgressed the words of thy companions, who have
said [Eccl. x. 8]: *Whoso breaketh through a
fence, a serpent shall bite him.*'   It is different
in regard to Minuth, which bites a man, so
that he comes to be bitten afterwards.

Commentary.—A fifth version of this story is given
in the Midrash, Qoheleth Rabba, i. 8, along with a
good deal else referring to Minuth, of which use will
be made subsequently.   The story of Ben Damah
there given, however, does not add anything to what

is contained in one or other of the four versions already cited.

We have here to deal with an event separated by no long interval of time from the date at which it was first recorded. R. Ishmael was one of the most distinguished Rabbis whose teaching is contained in the Mishnah and Tosephta; he lived in the first half of the second century, and there is reason to believe that he did not die in the war of Bar Cocheba, or immediately afterwards (A.D. 135), but survived it some years [see below, p. 131 fol]. R. Ishmael spent the greater part of his life in Chephar Aziz, a village in the extreme south, on the borders of Idumea (M. Qid. vi. 4, Khethub. v. 8). It is not likely that he would there be brought into contact with a Galilean, and Jacob of Chephar Sama (or Sechanja) was of course a Galilean. But it is said that R. Ishmael was present at an assembly of Rabbis at Usha, in Galilee (b. B. Bathr. 28ª, ᵇ),[1] and although the date of that meeting cannot be precisely determined, it seems probable that it took place not long before the outbreak of the rebellion of Bar Cocheba, say 130. A.D. or thereabouts. Two assemblies at Usha are distinctly mentioned (b. R. ha Sh. 31ª, ᵇ), the second being immediately after the close of the rebellion. It is probable, then, that the incident of Ben Damah and Jacob of Chephar Sama (Sechanja) took place on the occasion of the first assembly at Usha. Ben Damah is elsewhere (b. Menah. 99ᵇ) said to have asked

---

[1] The assembly at Usha, here mentioned, is probably the second of the two, as that was certainly the more famous. But if R. Ishmael attended the second, there is every reason to suppose that he also attended the first. This is all that matters as far as his presence in Galilee is concerned.

permission from his uncle, R. Ishmael, to study Greek philosophy. Permission was refused by the quotation of Josh. i. 8, *Thou shalt meditate thercon* [the book of the Law] *day and night*, and the command, 'Go, seek a time when it is neither day nor night, and therein study Greek philosophy.'

Jacob of Chephar Sama or Sechanja is evidently a Christian; but, no less evidently, he cannot have been a contemporary of Jesus, still less identical with James (Jacob) the brother of Jesus, as has been suggested. The latter was put to death somewhere about the year 44 A.D.; and R. Ishmael was only a boy when Jerusalem was captured in A.D. 70. Jacob was an extremely common name, and no identification with any known Christian is possible. The place to which this Jacob belonged is called variously Chephar Sama and Ch. Sechanja. The first is thought to be the modern Khefr Sumeia, and the second the well-known Sichnin (modern Suchnin); as these two places are only nine miles apart, Jacob may quite well have been associated with both. In a passage which will be examined presently, this same Jacob is said to have talked with R. Eliezer b. Horqenos, in the High Street of Sepphoris, and to have communicated to him a saying of Jesus. [See below, p. 138 and especially p. 143]. If we suppose that Jacob was, roughly speaking, about the same age as R. Eliezer, he would belong to the third generation of Christian disciples, hardly to the second.

As to the details of the story, there is little variation among the several versions given above. In all, the Christian proposes to heal the sick man in the name of Jeshu ben Pandira, *i.e.* as the Palestinian Gemara (30) says, by pronouncing that name over the sufferer (cp. Acts iii. 6, ix. 34 ; Mark xvi. 17, 18). R. Ishmael refused to allow the cure to be performed, although his nephew pleaded that he had scripture warrant for it. He died while speaking; but the Palestinian Gemara (29) supplies what he had not time to say, by referring to Lev. xviii. 5. Ben Damah would have argued that since a man was to live by doing the things commanded in the Torah, he would be justified, for the sake of them, in saving his life.

The quotation of Eccl. x. 8 is ambiguous. It appears to have been suggested by the mere fact of B. Damah having been bitten by a serpent. But, on the other hand, according to the text, the bite of a serpent was a punishment for having " broken through a fence," *i.e.* " transgressed the ordinances of the Rabbis," according to the Rabbinical interpretation. Now Ben Damah had not done this, and therefore R. Ishmael praised him ; but he had been bitten by a serpent. Tosephta (28) does not attempt to get over the difficulty ; the Pal. Gemara (29) explains that the bite of the serpent, which killed Ben Damah, was to prevent him from meeting a worse fate hereafter ; for if he had " transgressed the ordinances of the wise," he would have been a heretic, and in the world to come would have suffered the fate of a heretic. In other words, Jacob the heretic would have infected him with the venom of heresy, if allowed to cure his wound, and thus the literal serpent saved him from the figurative serpent.

The word translated ' heresy ' is Minūth, the abstract noun from Mīn; and there can be no question but that here the heresy intended is Christianity.

This is evident from the mention of Jacob as a disciple of Jesus, and it is important as helping to decide the real significance of the terms Min and Minuth. The next extract will afford evidence of a similar kind.

The Grandson of R. Jehoshua ben Levi and a Christian Doctor

(32) j. Shabb. 14^d.—The grandson [of R. Jehoshua ben Levi] had something stuck in his throat. There came a man and whispered to him in the name of Jeshu Pandera, and he recovered. When he [the doctor] came out, he [R. Jehoshua] said to him, 'What didst thou whisper to him?' He said to him, 'A certain word.' He said, 'It had been better for him that he had died rather than thus.' And it happened thus to him, *as it were an error that proceedeth from the ruler* (Ecc. x. 5).

j. A. Zar. 40^d gives the passage in the same words as above, this page of the treatise being, indeed, to a considerable extent a repetition of that in the treatise Shabbath. The story is found also in the Midrash Qoh. rabbah, on x. 5, in a shorter form.

Commentary.—Jehoshua ben Levi is one of the best known of the Talmudic Rabbis. He lived and taught for the most part at Lūd (Lydda), where he followed his own teacher Bar Qappara, A.D. 260. But he was in close association with the two great teachers, Johanan and Rēsh Laqish, whose college was in Tiberias. It is probable that it was in Tiberias that the incident took place which is described above. For the grandson referred to was probably the son of R. Joseph (son of R. Jehoshua) who had married into the family of the Patriarch Jehudah II., and Tiberias was the latter's place of residence. A Christian doctor might be met with elsewhere, as in the case of R. Abahu, in the next extract.

The main outline of the story resembles that of Ishmael and Ben Damah, except that in the passage before us the Christian was not prevented from doing what he came to do. R. Jehoshua had not been present to interfere, but apparently only met him as he was coming away. The meaning of the quotation from Ecc. x. 5, I suppose to be, that the fact of the child having been cured by a Christian was a deplorable evil which could not be undone, as the command of a ruler given in error, and implicitly obeyed, may result in mischief which cannot be afterwards put right. This is on the lines of the explanation given by Rashi and Aben Ezra in their commentaries on Ecclesiastes. It is characteristic of the feeling of Jews towards Christians in the third century in Palestine.

That feeling is further illustrated by the following:

R. ABAHU, AND JACOB THE MIN

(33) b. A. Zar. 28ᵃ.—And yet, R. Abahu was an eminent man, and Jacob the Min applied a drug to his leg, and if it had not been for R. Ami and R. Asi, who licked his leg, he would have cut his leg off.

Commentary.—The above occurs in the midst of a

discussion on the question whether in cases of sick-
ness the help of non-Jewish physicians might be used.
R. Joḥanan laid down the rule that in cases for which
the Sabbath might be profaned, *i.e.* in very dangerous
cases, such help might not be used, but that in slighter
cases it might; the meaning of which seems to be
that all risk was to be avoided of a man dying under
non-Jewish treatment. This rule is given immediately after the story of Ben Damah, already discussed,
and is repeated just before the present passage referring to Abahu. The connexion is this, that an
exception might be made to Joḥanan's rule if the
patient were an eminent man, "and yet, R. Abahu
was an eminent man, etc."

Abahu lived in Cæsarea at the end of the third and
the beginning of the fourth century. He had very
frequent intercourse with Christians, as will be seen
hereafter, and such intercourse was not always un-
friendly. The Gemara in recording the above incident seems to suppose that Jacob the Min intended
to kill his patient by putting poison into a wound in
his leg, and says that if Abahu's two friends had not
licked the poison off (or rather perhaps sucked it out)
Abahu would have cut off his own leg rather than be
saved by a Christian. And the Gemara supports its
view by quoting Jud. xvi. 30, where Samson says,
'*Let me die with the Philistines*,' to show that the
Christian was bent on killing Abahu though he should
lose his own life in consequence. But this can hardly
be the real meaning of the incident. Abahu was 'an
eminent man,' closely associated with the court of the
Roman governor, and would therefore be attended by
a physician of his own choice. Indeed, the whole

point of the story, in reference to Johanan's rule about calling in non-Jewish physicians, implies that Abahu must himself have called in Jacob the Min, knowing him to be a Min. If so, he cannot have felt any such dislike towards his physician, as would make him cut off his own leg rather than allow the Christian remedy to be applied. His two friends, however, appear to have felt as R. Ishmael and R. Jehoshua felt, as described in the preceding passages. They licked off, or sucked out, the drug applied by the Christian; and whether they supposed it to be poison, or only disliked a Christian remedy, their antipathy to the Christian is equally apparent.

The commentary of Tosaphoth on the passage explains, rather needlessly, that the Jacob the Min who is mentioned here cannot have been the same as the Jacob of Chephar Sama (Sechanja) who attended Ben Damah. There was a period of some 170 years between them.

In b. Ḥull 84ᵃ occurs a reference to a certain Jacob the Min, who is said to have discussed a point of Halachah with Raba, a Babylonian teacher in Maḥuza, early in the fourth century.[1] As far as chronology is concerned this might be the same Jacob as the one who attended Abahu; but I do not know what he should be doing in Maḥuza. Jacob was a very common name, and there must have been many Jewish Christians who were so called.

---

[1] Cp. b. Shabb. 88ᵃ, where "a certain Min" has an altercation with Raba. The 'Jacob Minaah' who met Raba is hardly identical with the 'Jacob Minaah' who conversed with R. Jehudah (b. Meg. 23ᵃ), if this be R. Jehudah ben Jeḥesq'el, since the latter died about the time (A.D. 292) when Raba was born.

A CONTEST OF MIRACLES

(34) j. Sanh. 25ᵈ.—For example, R. Lazar and R. Jehoshua and R. Aqiba went up to bathe in a certain public bath in Tiberias. A certain Min (heretic) saw them. He said something, and the arched roof held them fast. R. Lazar said to R. Jehoshua, 'What! Jehoshua ben Hananjah, see what thou canst do.' When that Min went forth, R. Jehoshua said something, and the door held him fast, and every one who entered gave him a blow, and every one who went out gave him a thrust in the back. He said, 'Undo what ye have done.' They said, 'Undo, and we will undo.' They each did so. When they had gone forth, R. Jehoshua said, 'Well, how clever thou art!' He said, 'Let us go down to the sea.' When they had gone down to the sea, the Min said something, and the sea was divided. He said to them, 'And did not Moses your master do thus in the sea?' They said to him, 'Wilt thou not agree with us that Moses our master walked in the midst of it?' He said to them, 'Yes.' They said to him, 'Then do thou walk in the midst of it.' He walked in the midst of it. And R. Jehoshua commanded the Prince of the Sea, and he swallowed him up.

Commentary.—The foregoing tale is given as an illustration in a discussion upon magic and witch-craft, arising out of the text (Exod. xxii. 18), *Thou shalt not suffer a witch to live.* The three Rabbis mentioned are very well known characters. R. Lazar[1] is R. El'azar ben Azariah. R. Jehoshua ben Hananiah was the contemporary, and, in a sense, rival of R. Eliezer ben Horqenos whom we have already met with (see above, No. 4). Aqiba has also been frequently mentioned. All three were living at the beginning of the second century A.D. The Christian might, so far as chronology goes, have been the same Jacob of Chephar Sama who came to cure Ben Damah; but there is nothing to identify him. The story itself needs little explanation. The Rabbis go to a public bath and apparently enter a room with a vaulted roof. Levy (N. H. W., ii. 322, *s.v.* כיפה) says that what is meant is the arched recess where an idol stood; but the quotation which he gives in support of this view (b. A. Zar. 16ᵃ) does not seem to me to show this. However, it was evidently some small arch, under or in which a man could stand. The Min, whom here we may safely call a Christian (after the example of Jacob the Min, who was a disciple of Jesus), pronounced a spell, literally ' said what he said,' and the arch held them fast. Jehoshua retaliated by a spell which caused the door to hold the Christian fast, so that he blocked the way, and people as they tried to go in or out struck him. After releasing each other they all went down to ' the sea,' *i.e.* the lake of Galilee. By another spell the Christian divided the water, to show that he could do what Moses did. He incautiously admitted that Moses also walked in the midst of the divided water, and he was challenged to do the same. He fell into

---

[1] Lazar is the shorter form of Eleazar, and appears in the N.T. as Lazarus.

8

the trap ; and when he was in the midst of the water, Jehoshua commanded the 'Prince of the Sea,' the angel or spirit in charge of the lake, and the water swallowed him up.

This story is anonymous, and there is nothing to indicate its age or origin. It is certainly not contemporary with the Rabbis who figure in it, unless we admit that Jehoshua ben Hananiah enjoyed during his lifetime the reputation for magical power which was afterwards attributed to him. It should be noted that the miracles of the Christian are admitted to be as real as those of his opponent. There is complete faith in miracles all through the story. I use the term 'miracle,' though the Talmud speaks of magic, because it is well to remind the reader that what the N.T. calls a miracle (at least in English, the Greek has σημεῖα or δυνάμεις), the Talmud— reflecting current belief—regards as magic, i.e. as the result of superhuman agency employed by men who know how to call it forth. Without expressing any opinion on the reality of the alleged miracles of Jesus, I would remark that the Jews admitted them as genuine, no less than the acts performed by their own Rabbis, the difference being not in the character of the deeds, but in that of the persons who performed them. So in the story above, the rival enchanters perform exactly similar acts ; and since the story is told from the Jewish side, naturally the victory remains with the Rabbi. The fate of the Christian may perhaps contain an allusion to the story told in the Gospels, of Peter trying to walk on the water. If that story had its origin in Galilee, it might well continue to be remembered on the shores of the lake.

On the same page in which the passage above translated occurs are some further remarks on Jewish and Christian miracles, which may throw light on the probable date of the story. They would have to be included in any collection of Talmudic references to Christianity, but are hardly of sufficient importance to be treated by themselves under a separate head. They will therefore be given here.

Miracles by Jews and Minim

(35) j. Sanh. 25^d.—R. Jehoshua ben Hananiah said, 'I can take cucumbers and melons and make them into kids and goats, and they really are made into kids and goats.' R. Jannai said, ' I was walking in a certain street of Sepphoris, and I saw a certain Min take a bird, and he cast it up and it fell down and was made into a calf.' But it is not so. R. Lazar said in the name of R. José ben Zimra, ' If all who come into the world were assembled together, they would not be able to create a gnat and put breath in it.' Let us say, not that this Min took a bird and cast it up and it came down and was made into a calf, but that he called to his prince [familiar spirit] and he stole a calf from the herd and brought it to him. R. Hanina ben R. Hananiah said, ' I was going along a certain place near the gate of Sepphoris, and I saw a Min take a skull and cast it up and it came down and was made into a calf. And I went and told my father. He said, ' If thou

hast eaten of it, it is a real one ; if not, it is an illusion.'

Commentary.—R. Jannai lived in Sepphoris about the end of the second and the beginning of the third century. He was one of the teachers of R. Johanan, to whom is traditionally ascribed the codification of the Palestinian Gemara. R. Jannai's remark about the miracle which he saw is given without the support of any later teacher who vouched for it. It is simply quoted by the compilers of the Gemara as a detached saying. R. José b. Zimra was contemporary with R. Jannai, possibly an inhabitant of the same town. He is quoted by R. Lazar (*i.e.* El'azar b. Pedath), a Babylonian who migrated to Palestine about the middle of the third century. Apparently the compilers of the Gemara felt some misgiving at the assertion that animals had been produced by magic, and they quote R. José b. Zimra in support of the view that no human being can create even the smallest living creature ; but they do not on that account reject the miracle. They explain it by saying that it was done by the help of superhuman beings, who brought what was wanted, in place of the thing that was apparently changed. A similar doubt as to the reality of the miracle is expressed in the story about R. Hanina b. R. Hananiah, where his father told him that unless he had actually eaten of the calf which he said he had seen made, he could not be sure it was a real one.

All these sayings and stories about magic seem to belong to a late period, and to be merely fragments collected by the compilers of the Gemara, by way of illustration, rather than duly recorded tradition.

That the real R. Jehoshua b. Ḥananiah, a very well-known personage, should have said that he had the magical power ascribed to him above, is less likely than that such power should have been attributed to him in later times. He had indeed the reputation of being a great opponent of the Minim (heretics), and that may account for the part which he played in the contest with the Christian in the first story.

It is remarkable that nearly all the incidents mentioned above are located in Sepphoris, and that the same place was the scene of a much more important event, the meeting of R. Eliezer b. Horqenos and Jacob of Chephar Sama. It would be very interesting to know whether the Jewish Christians of Galilee possessed an original Galilean, as distinguished from the Judæan, tradition of the ministry of Jesus.

The above passages serve to show that miracles were accepted as genuine, whether done by Jews or Christians, and that they were all alike regarded as magical.

It has been impossible to avoid mentioning the word Min [1] in the above remarks, since it occurs in the texts to be translated. And I have translated it 'Christian' because the connexion with Jesus seemed to be clearly shown. But I do not wish to take it for granted that in all cases 'Min' denotes a Christian. I will therefore present here several passages in which the Talmud attempts to indicate what is a Min. And although this will still leave something to be said by way of general discussion of the question, after all the Rabbinical passages referring to 'Minim' have been given, yet a provisional definition by the Rabbis

[1] Min, plural Minim ; abstract noun Minuth, the state of being a Min.

themselves will be of much use in dealing with subsequent passages.   I proceed to give

DEFINITIONS OF MIN, MINUTH

The Fate of the Minim Hereafter

(36) T. Sanh. xiii. 4, 5.—The sinners of Israel, and the sinners of the nations of the world descend into Gehinnom in their body, and they are judged there twelve months. After twelve months their soul perishes and their body is burnt, and Gehinnom casts it out, and they are made dust and the wind disperses them and scatters them under the soles of the feet of the righteous, as it is said (Mal. iv. 3), *And ye shall tread down the wicked, for they shall be dust under the soles of the feet of the righteous, in the day that I do .make, saith the Lord of Hosts.*   But the Minim, and the apostates and the betrayers and Epiqūrōsin, and those who have lied concerning the Torah, and those who depart from the ways of the congregation, and those who have lied concerning the resurrection of the dead, and everyone who has sinned and caused the multitude to sin, after the manner of Jeroboam and Ahab, and those (Ezek. xxxii. 24) *who have set their fear in the land of the living*, and have stretched forth their hand against Zĕbūl, Gehinnom is shut in their faces and they are judged there for generations of generations, as it is said (Isa. lxvi. 24), *And they shall go forth and look upon the corpses of the men who sin against me, for their*

*worm shall not die, nor their fire be quenched,
and they shall be an abhorring unto all flesh.*
Sheol fails, they fail not, as it is said (Ps. xlix.
14), *Their beauty shall be for Sheol to con-
sume,* who hath caused them to stretch forth
their hand against Zĕbūl, as it is said (*ibid.*),
that there be no Zebul for him, and Zĕbūl
means nothing else but the Temple, as it is
said (1 Kings viii. 13), *I have surely built
thee an house of habitation* (Zĕbūl), *a place for
thee to dwell in for ever.*

Commentary.—A sharp distinction is here made
between Jewish and Gentile sinners on the one hand,
and Minim, betrayers and Epiqūrōsin on the other.
The Jewish sinners remain Jews though they sin.
The Gentile sinners have not sinned against the Torah
of Israel, because they are not bound by it. They
are punished merely *quâ* sinners ; and twelve months
in Gehinnom suffices to punish their offence. Far
greater is the guilt of those who, being Jews, have
sinned against the fundamental principles of the
Jewish religion. Apostasy in some form or another
is implied in the terms ' Minim,' ' apostates,' ' betrayers,' ' Epiqūrōsin.' These are not interchangeable.
Reserving for the moment the first, the betrayers
(Masōrōth) are explained by Rashi to mean "slanderers, who betray the wealth of Israel into the hands
of Gentiles." More particularly they are Jewish
' delators,' informers, spies, acting against Israel in
the interest of the Roman government. Epiqūrōsin
(plur. of Epiqūrōs) is plainly borrowed from the
personal name Epicurus ; but it contains also a play
on the word ' paqar ' (פקר), which means ' to be free

from restraint.' The name denotes, in general terms, a freethinker, one who disregards the restraints of traditional authority. An Epiquros was not necessarily a Jew, he might be a Gentile. Thus it is said (b. Sanh. 38ᵇ), "They teach there [in Palestine] R. El'azar said, ' Be careful to learn Torah, and know what thou shalt answer to an Epiqūrōs.' R. Johanan said, 'They taught not so except concerning an Epiqūrōs of the Gentiles.' But all the more concerning a Jewish Epiqūrōs, for he is more defiant (טפי קר פקר)." [1] In other words the Jewish Epiquros was the more dangerous opponent because he was an enemy within the camp. The term does not, so far as I know, imply the holding or rejecting of any specific doctrines, but merely the assertion of liberty of thought upon all subjects, and consequent disregard of external authority. A Gentile Epiquros would be one who, in controversy, did not from the first admit the authority of Jewish tradition as upheld by the Rabbis, a Jewish Epiquros would be one who, having formerly acknowledged the Rabbinical authority, afterwards rejected it. But a man is only an Epiquros, if I rightly understand the term, when he is considered as having relation with the Jewish religion. A Greek philosopher, teaching in Rome or Athens, would not, merely as such, be an Epiquros; but if he had a controversy with a Jew upon some question affecting Judaism, then he would be a Gentile Epiquros. A Jew became an Epiquros as soon as he showed a disposition to despise the Rabbinical authority and go his own way. Thus it is said (b. Sanh. 99ᵇ) that an Epiquros is like those who say, ' What are these

[1] See below, p. 294 fol.

Rabbis to us?' And on the same page they are
compared to "one who sits before his Rabbi, and
there has come to him a tradition from another place,
and he says, 'Thus we teach there,' instead of saying,
'Thus the teacher (Rabbi so-and-so) hath said.'"
Compare with this, Matthew v. 21, 22: *It was said
to them of old time . . . . but I say unto you.* We
may then provisionally assume that Epiqūrōs denotes
a free-thinker in the widest sense of the word.

It will be evident that the term Min denotes something similar to Epiquros, since they are both included in the passage before us, along with apostates
and betrayers. The various details of apostasy—
denial of the resurrection of the dead, of the Torah,
etc.—are not specified as being characteristic of one
class of apostates more than of another; and we may
take them as applying to Minim no less than to
Epiqurosin, while on the other hand there must be
some difference to account for the use of two terms
where one would have sufficed. The difference
between Min and Epiquros is much the same as the
difference between 'heretic' and 'free-thinker.' The
heretic usually is a free-thinker; but not every free-
thinker is a heretic. From the standpoint of Judaism
a Gentile might be a free-thinker, but not a heretic;
since, being a Gentile, he had never professed the
Jewish religion. Only a Jew could be a heretic
as regards Judaism; and he could scarcely be a
heretic without being also a free-thinker. The term
Min denotes, I believe, invariably a Jewish heretic,
i.e. one who, having been trained in the principles of
the Jewish religion, departs from them and is unfaithful towards them, violates the covenant between

God and Israel.[1] This I believe to be the root significance of the term Min, and if so it would be
practically equivalent to Jewish Epiquros. But I
think that Min, more often than Epiquros, implies not
merely freedom of thought, but the holding or rejecting of specific opinions. It does not always do so;
but it does sometimes, while I believe that this is
hardly ever the case with Epiqūrōs. We have already
met with several instances of the word Min, and have
judged from the context that the persons referred to
were Christians. So far as I know, the Talmud
seldom, if ever speaks of a Christian as Epiquros.
And I infer that the term Min carried with it the
denial of certain doctrines, as the expression of the
unfaithfulness in which his heresy consisted. A Min,
as such, was not necessarily a Christian; but, as a
matter of fact, most of the heretics who came into
strained relations with Jews were Christians, and
more particularly Jewish Christians. If they had
been Gentile Christians they would probably have
been called Epiqurosin. And thus it often happens
that 'Jewish - Christian' is a correct equivalent
of 'Min,' while yet it remains true that Min does
not properly signify 'Jewish-Christian,' but only
'heretic.'[2] This, at all events, is the meaning which

---

[1] For the probable etymology of the word Min, see below, p. 362 fol.

[2] Friedländer (*der Vorchristliche jüdische Gnosticismus*; Göttingen, 1898)
attempts to prove that the Minim were in all cases Gnostics, and more
particularly of the Ophite sect. His work will be more fully noticed in the
concluding division of this book, when having the whole of the Talmudic
evidence before us, we shall be able to judge of the value of his conclusions.
His treatment of the Rabbinical authorities is far from satisfactory, if only
because he bases his theory upon a comparatively small number of passages
not always fairly presented. For a glaring omission, hardly to be ex-
cused, see below, p. 145 n.

I provisionally adopt of the term Min. I should have preferred, if possible, to have presented all the passages referring to Min and Minuth before attempting to fix the significance to be attached to the words; but in that case it would have been difficult, if not impossible, to have given any clear idea of the bearing of each passage upon my main subject. It will be necessary to compare this provisional meaning with the context in each case, and to attempt a more precise identification of the class of persons referred to.

It remains now to remark upon the details of the passage which has led to this discussion. It should be noted that it is contained in the Tosephta, and is thus not later than the end of the second or the beginning of the third century. "Who have lied concerning the Torah." The particular point of the denial is not stated; but a comparison with M. Sanh. x. 1 makes it probable that the heretics denied that the Torah was from heaven. It is not stated that they denied the Torah, but that they lied concerning it, a charge which might cover a variety of offences. Similarly, "who have lied concerning the resurrection of the dead" does not necessarily imply that resurrection itself was denied, but that some falsehood was taught concerning it; probably, that it could not be proved from the Torah (M. Sanh. *loc. cit.*). "Everyone who has sinned and caused the multitude to sin." We have already met with this phrase in connexion with both Jesus and Paul, (see above, pp. 51, 101), and may fairly conclude that it is here directed against preachers of heresy, of whom, no doubt, Christians were the most important. "Who have set their terror in the land of the living" is a quotation from Ezek. xxxii. 24, 26, and as such, the precise point of the present application of the words remains doubtful. As used in Ezekiel, the words refer to the great nations—Asshur, Elam, Tubal, Meshech, and Edom—who had at various times oppressed Israel: and it is possible, especially in view of the following clause "Who have stretched forth their hands against Zebul (the Temple)," that the reference is to the Roman Empire, the oppressor above all others. If this is so, then it must be admitted that these two last clauses do not in any way serve to describe Minim, or heretics. But, on the other hand, it seems forced and unnatural to pass so suddenly from heretics to political enemies; and further, the Talmud nowhere else, so far as I know, threatens the Romans, or even the Roman Emperor, with the fate here described. The date of the passage forbids us to think of a time when the Roman Empire had officially become Christian, and there is no reason to suspect an interpolation in the text. The political reference seems then to be excluded, and "those who have set their fear in the land of the living," must be understood of some class of heretics. The explanation of R. Ḥisda (b. R. ha-Sh. 17ᵃ), that the reference is to "the steward, פרנס, of the synagogue, who makes himself too much feared by the congregation," does not seem adequate, in view of the severity of the punishment which is threatened. "Those who have stretched out their hands against Zebul." It is explained in the Tosephta itself that Zebul (habitation) denotes the Temple. But it does not follow that the reference is to the destruction of the Temple by the Romans. And since the whole passage seems to be directed against heresy in some form, we may perhaps interpret this clause of those who, like the Christians, repudiated the claim of the Temple to be the place where alone worship could be duly and perfectly offered. Of course the Temple ceased to exist, when Titus destroyed it; but this was only *de facto*, not *de jure*.

The sentence pronounced on all these offenders, heretics, apostates, betrayers, free thinkers, all who in their various ways sought to undermine the foundations of Rabbinical Judaism, is punishment during generations of generations in Gehinnom. When it is said that Gehinnom is shut in their faces, that can only mean that they cannot escape, though the natural meaning of shutting a door in the face of some one is that thereby his entrance is barred.

On the Rabbinical conception of Gehinnom, see Weber, *System der Altsynag. Theologie*, p. 326, 374. His translation (p. 375) of the passage which we have been studying is not sufficiently exact.

The Formula against the Minim

(37) j. Ber. 9ᶜ.—Shemuel ha-Qaton went before the Ark [to recite the prayers]. He forgot " That casteth down the proud " at the end. He paused and tried to remember them. They said to him, " The wise have not framed it thus."

Commentary.—See the commentary on the much fuller passage which follows.

(38) b. Ber. 28ᵇ, 29ᵃ.—Our Rabbis teach: Shim'on the cotton-seller arranged the Eighteen Benedictions in the presence of Rabban

Gamliel, according to their order, in Jabneh.
Rabban Gamliel said to the Wise, " Is there
anyone who knows how to compose a Benediction of the Minim?" Shemuel ha-Qaton
stood up and composed it. The following
year he forgot it, and sought [to recall it] for
two and even three hours, and they did not
call him up [from the pulpit]. Why did they
not call him up? For Rab Jehudah said, that
Rab said, " If a man makes a mistake in all
the Benedictions, they do not call him up;
but in the Benediction of the Minim they call
him up." They suspect that he is a Min. It
was different with Shemuel ha-Qaton, because
he had composed it, and it was thought
perhaps he would recover himself.

[The first sentence of this passage occurs in
b. Meg. 17^b, where follows a sort of running
commentary on the Eighteen Benedictions.
An incidental reference to the Minim occurs
(according to the reading of Rabbinowicz);
but nothing is stated beyond what is contained
in the other passage quoted in this section.]

Commentary.—This is an extremely important
passage, because it records the official condemnation
of the Minim by the Rabbis ; and it will be necessary
to determine as accurately as possible the date of the
incident here narrated.

Before entering upon that investigation, I will
notice the details of the story which call for remark.
The Eighteen Benedictions[1] are a series of short

---

[1] For a full account of them, see Hamburger, Real Encykl. f. Bibel u.
Talmud, ii., *s.v.* Schemone-Esré.

prayers still to be found in the Jewish liturgy. The
word translated Benediction serves equally for malediction, and it is rather in that sense that it is used in
regard to the Minim. In the modern liturgy the
Benediction referred to runs thus :—למלשינים אל תהי תקוה,
" May there be no hope for the slanderers," where the
word for ' slanderers ' has been put in place of the
ancient word Minim.[1]

These Eighteen Benedictions are said to have been
arranged in order by Shim'on the cotton-seller, at
Jabneh, in the presence of Rabban Gamliel. This
was Gamliel II., who held the position of Patriarch
(נשיא) after the death of Joḥanan ben Zaccai, somewhere about the year 80 A.D. Of Shemuel ha-Qaton
more will be said presently. He is said to have ' composed' the Benediction; but perhaps it would be more
correct to say ' adapted,' altered some previous formula
so as to apply to the Minim. The formula drawn up
by him was taken into use; and the following year it
fell to the lot of its author to recite it in the public
service. He forgot the words, but tried for three
hours to recall them, while the congregation waited,
and did not " call him up " from the pulpit, i.e. cause
him to leave it. The pulpit or reading-desk was
below, not above, the general level of the seats of the
congregation. According to later usage, a reader
who made a mistake in reciting this benediction would
have been made to leave the desk, because he would
be suspected of being a Min.[2] The reason given why
this was not done in the case of Shemuel ha-Qaton

---

[1] The form מלשינין suggests the transposition של מינין. Hamburger
thinks that מלשינין is the original which was altered into מינין.

[2] See j. Ber. 9ᶜ, which will be translated and explained below (p. 204).

was that as he was the author of the formula he
might be expected to remember it.

It is curious that this incident is only given in
detail in the Babylonian Gemara. It is quoted there
as a Baraitha, *i.e.* it belongs to the stratum of Tradition contemporary with that embodied in the Mishnah
and Tosephta. So far as I know, the Mishnah does
not expressly mention the " Benediction of the
Minim." In Tosephta the story is not given, but the
Benediction is referred to in a discussion of the
question how the number eighteen is to be completed
(T. Ber. iii. 25). A similar discussion is found in the
Palestinian Gemara (j. Ber. iv. 3). As these do not
throw any light on the story before us, the text of
them will be deferred till the end of the commentary
on this passage.

The incident has every appearance of being
historical; the explanation of Rab, quoted by R.
Jehudah, plainly shows that he knew of the story,
and as he was a disciple of R. Jehudah ha-Qadosh,
the grandson of the Gamliel referred to, he is a
sufficiently good witness.

To determine the date of this incident, which is
important as marking the official breach between the
synagogue and the Minim, it is necessary to examine
carefully the chronology of the life of Shemuel ha-
Qaton. The date of his death will obviously afford
a *terminus ad quem* for the date of the composition
of the formula against the Minim. The death of
Shemuel ha-Qaton is mentioned in several passages
of the Talmud and Midrash, with but slight variations
in the text. These are as follows:—

(39) T. Sotah xiii. 4.—Also, in the hour of his

death, he [Sh. ha-Q.] said, "Shim'on and
Ishmael to the sword, and their companions
to slaughter, and the rest of the people to
plunder, and many troubles will come afterwards"; and he said this in the Aramaic
tongue.

(40) j. Sotah 24^b.—The same words, with the
addition, however, of the following, after 'in
the Aramaic tongue,' "and they knew not
what he said."

(41) b. Sotah 48^b.—Same as (39).

(42) b. Sanh 11^a.—Same as (39).

The question is, to whom did the dying man refer
as "Shim'on and Ishmael"? One thinks most
naturally of Shim'on ben Gamliel and Ishmael ben
Elisha, who were executed after the capture of
Jerusalem A.D. 70. And, in spite of difficulties, I
believe that this is the right interpretation. The
detailed account in Ab. d. R. Nathan, c. 38, distinctly
implies that the two men executed were the elder
Shim'on b. Gamliel and the elder Ishmael b. Elisha.
For Ishmael there says to Shim'on, "When thou
didst sit and teach on the Mount of the House [*i.e.*
the Temple], and all the multitude of Israel sat in thy
presence, etc."

Moreover, Ishmael speaks of himself as a priest
and son of a high priest. But, if Shemuel ha-Qaton
was a member of the assembly at Jabneh over which
Rabban Gamliel presided, must not his dying words
have referred to someone whose death took place
later than the year 70? The period during which
Rn. Gamliel presided at Jabneh is usually given as
80–110 A.D. or thereabouts, so that Shemuel could

9

not have died before 80 A.D. It is therefore held, amongst others, by Jost, Grätz, Weiss and Bacher, that the Ishmael referred to was Ishmael ben Elisha the younger, grandson of the one already mentioned and contemporary with Aqiba. (See Jost, Gsch. d. Jdtums., ii. p. 74; Grätz, G. d. J., iv. 175; Weiss, G. d. j. T., ii. 102; Bacher, Ag. d. Tannaiten, i. 243). This is also the view of Rashi, at least in so far that he explains the 'companions' of Shim'on and Ishmael to be "such as R. Aqiba and R. Ḥanina ben Teradjon" (Rashi on b. Sanh. 11ᵃ). Of course, these two were companions of the younger Ishmael. Moreover, it is said (and this is the strongest evidence in favour of this view), in Mechilta (Mishpat. c. 18, p. 95ᵇ), that Aqiba uttered a solemn warning to his disciples after the execution of R. Ishmael and Shim'on. This is repeated in the late Treatise Semaḥoth c. 8, where, however, it is distinctly said that the Shim'on in question was Shim'on ben Gamliel. The passage in Mechilta is strong evidence, because that Midrash originated amongst the disciples of the younger Ishmael, who may be supposed to have known the circumstances of his death.

Yet, in spite of the above evidence, supported as it is by the great authority of Jost, Grätz, Weiss, and Bacher, there is a difficulty in the way of accepting this interpretation; because there is evidence to show that both the younger Ishmael and the younger Shim'on ben Gamliel survived the persecution of Hadrian, and died a natural death. This is unquestionably true in the case of Shim'on ben Gamliel, who died somewhere about A.D. 166. The historians above mentioned see clearly that he cannot have been the person referred to by Shemuel ha-Qaton, and accordingly state that Ishmael was executed along with " a certain Simeon," whom they do not try to identify. But there is reason for believing that R. Ishmael also died a natural death, as is shown by Hamburger (R. Encykl., ii. 526) and Frankel (Darkē ha-Mishnah, p. 106). It is said (M. Nedar., ix. 10), "When [R. Ishmael] died, the daughters of Israel raised a lament and said, ' Ye daughters of Israel, weep for Rabbi Ishmael.' " (T. Nedar., v. 6, much the same.) In the Gemara (b. Nedar. 66ᵇ) it is said, ' When R. Ishmael *lay dying*,' the word being ' shechib ' (שכיב) not ' mēth ' (מת). Now the word מת used in the other passages does not imply a violent death, while the word שכיב does imply a natural death.[1] The R. Ishmael here referred : to is undoubtedly R. Ishmael ben Elisha the younger, for he is the R. Ishmael of the Mishnah and Tosephta. And in view of the fact that a lamentation was raised for him, compare what is said (b. Sanh. 11ᵃ), אין מספידין על הרוגי מלכות, " They do not make lamentation for those slain by the kingdom " [*i.e.*, political prisoners executed as rebels, and more particularly those executed after the rebellion of Bar Cocheba]. If this can be taken as a correct statement, then R. Ishmael ben Elisha was not one of those executed at that time. Further, the view that R. Ishmael survived the persecution, or, at all events, lived some time after it had begun, is confirmed by what is recorded in b. B. Bathra 60ᵇ : " It is tradition, R. Ishmael ben Elisha said . . . . ' from the day when the wicked kingdom

---

[1] שכיב is from the root שכב, to lie, and it is used of persons who are dangerously ill. Cp. b. B. Qam. 38ᵃ, 47ᵇ, and especially 111ᵇ, where Raba says, " When I was very ill (שכיבנא), etc."

prevailed, which decrees against us wicked and hard ordinances, and prevents us from fulfilling Torah and commandments, and does not allow us to assemble to circumcise a son, etc.'" This certainly refers to the edicts which were made by Hadrian, after the suppression of the rebellion under Bar Cocheba, A.D. 135; and if so, R. Ishmael must have survived at all events the beginning of the persecution. The form of the expression, "from the day that the wicked kingdom prevailed," leads to the conclusion that some time, probably years, had elapsed since the decrees had come into force. Finally, if there be any truth in the extraordinary tale (b. A. Zar. 11ᵃ) that the skull of R. Ishmael was preserved among the Imperial treasures in Rome, that could refer quite as well to the older Ishmael, who undoubtedly was executed by the Romans, A.D. 70, as to the younger Ishmael. It is, in any case, no proof that the latter was executed.

If these considerations are well founded, then it is clear that the dying speech of Shemuel ha-Qaton did not refer to the younger Ishmael and Shim'on, unless on the assumption that the words contain a prophecy which was not fulfilled. The Talmud does not say that they were a prophecy, and does regard them as referring to persons who actually died a violent death.

There seems to me to be a quite simple explanation, which will meet all the difficulty of identifying the Ishmael and Shim'on, and which will also throw light upon the incident of Shemuel ha-Qaton's mistake in the recitation of the formula concerning the Minim. Let us suppose that Shemuel ha-Qaton was a **very** old man at the time of his death. In that case he would be contemporary with the elder Ishmael ben Elisha and Shim'on ben Gamliel, who were executed A.D. 70, and no doubt friendly with them. On his own deathbed, his thoughts may very well have gone back to the dreadful memories of the war, and have recalled the tragic fate of his two old friends— "Shim'on and Ishmael to the sword." All that he said found ample illustration in the slaughter and plunder that followed the capture of Jerusalem ; and it is not at all necessary to suppose that he prophesied the final catastrophe of the persecution under Hadrian.[1] Now if he was a very old man at the time of his death, it is easy to understand how such a failure of memory might have happened to him, as is described in the incident of the Minim-formula. Such forgetfulness is certainly much more natural to an old man than to a young one. Now the question is, Was he an old man at the time of his death ? It is generally assumed that he died young ; but, as it seems to me, the available evidence does not prove this. If it does not, on the other hand, prove that he reached an advanced age, it at least allows the possibility of his having done so. A curious story is told (j. Sanh. 18^c and elsewhere) as follows :—" It happened that Rabban Gamliel said, 'Let seven elders meet me in the upper room,' and eight entered. He said, 'Who is it that has entered without leave ?' Shemuel ha-Qaton stood up upon his feet and said, " I have come without leave; I wanted [to know] the halachah, and I have come to ask concerning it.'

---

[1] Observe the curious remark (j. Sotah. 24^b), that the hearers did not understand what the dying man said.

Rabban Gamliel said to him, ' O, Eldad and Medad !
[Num. xi. 26]; for all Israel know that if there are
two such [as they] I say that thou art one of them,'
etc." The Babylonian Gemara (Sanh. 11ª), which also
tells this story, says : " It was not Shemuel ha-Qaton
who did this [*i.e.* entered without leave], but another."
And Ḥananel, in his commentary on the passage, says
that he did it to screen the real culprit. This is
adopted by Bacher (Ag. d. Tann., i. p. 88 n. 3, where
the whole incident is admirably discussed). Now, if
Shemuel ha-Qaton was an old man, and held in high
esteem by Rabban Gamliel, he could rely on his age
and position to shield the real offender much more
confidently than if he had been only a young man.
And when Gamliel says to him, " All Israel know
that if there are two such, thou art one of them," that
seems to imply that the character and standing of
Shemuel were well known, and thus goes to confirm
the view that he was not young. Gamliel would, so
far as we can judge from his character, as elsewhere
described, have been much less tolerant of a young
man who had disobeyed his orders. There is nothing
in the epithet " ha-Qaton," " the small," to prove
that he was young. The distinguishing feature of
his character is said to have been humility, and the
epithet ' ha-Qaton " was supposed to have reference
to that. This virtue of humility caused a comparison
to be made between him and Hillel, so that he was
sometimes called a disciple of Hillel. To suppose,
however, that he actually had been a disciple of
Hillel, would be to stretch the hypothesis of his
advanced age beyond all probability ; for Hillel died
about A.D. 4, and if Shemuel had been his disciple, he

could hardly have been so at less than twenty years of age, which would make him at least ninety-six at the time when Gamliel began to preside over the assembly of Jabneh.[1]

Summing up the result of this chronological inquiry, I recognise that there is not evidence sufficient positively to decide the question whether Shemuel lived to an advanced age or not. But I submit that all the facts recorded about him, and mentioned above, not only are consistent with, but find their best explanation in, the hypothesis that he was already a very old man at the time when Gamliel began to preside at Jabneh, and I accordingly suggest that his death, and, *a fortiori*, the composition of the formula concerning the Minim, must be dated very near the year 80 A.D.

It remains only to say a word with regard to the formula itself. It was not exactly a malediction, but, as Grätz (iv. 105) well says, a kind of test-formula, for the purpose of detecting those who might be secretly inclined to heresy. The words ran, " May there be no hope for the Minim."

As already remarked, the Mishnah does not mention the formula. The passages in Tosephta

---

[1] In j. Hor. 48ᶜ it is said that when the wise were assembled in the house of Gorion, in Jericho, they heard a Bath Qol saying, ' There are two of you upon whom the Holy Spirit may worthily rest, and Hillel is one of them.' They fixed their eyes upon Shemuel ha-Qaton. In the earlier version of this story, T. Sotah. xiii. 3, Shemuel ha-Qaton is not mentioned in connexion with Hillel. But the next paragraph narrates how he, in like manner, was indicated at Jabneh. The authority for connecting Shemuel with Hillel in the same incident is R. Jehoshua ben Levi, quoted by R. Jacob bar Idi (j. Sot. 24ᶜ). So late a witness can certainly not establish the fact of their having been contemporaneous ; but his testimony may indicate a tradition that Shemuel was an old man when he died.

and the Palestinian Gemara which refer to it are the
following:—

> (43) T. Ber. iii. 25.—The Eighteen Benedictions
> which the wise have said, corresponding to
> the eighteen Invocations [mentions of the
> divine Name] in [Ps. xxix.], *Give unto the
> Lord, O ye sons of the mighty.* The bene-
> diction concerning the Minim is included in
> that concerning the seceders, and that con-
> cerning strangers in that concerning elders,
> and that concerning David in that concerning
> Jerusalem.   And if they said these on their
> own account, that would be valid.

> (44) j. Ber. 8ª.—R. Huna said, If a man saith to
> thee, They [the benedictions] are seventeen,
> say to him, ' The Wise in Jabneh have before
> now appointed that concerning the Minim.'
> R. Elazar ben R. José [1] objected in the
> presence of R. José ' But it is written [Ps.
> xxix. 3], *The God of glory thundereth* ' [*i.e.*
> that the divine name is mentioned nineteen,
> instead of eighteen, times in the Psalm].
> R. José replied, But it is taught, The bene-
> diction concerning the Minim and the sinners
> is included in ' casteth down the proud,' and
> that concerning elders and strangers in ' the
> refuge for the righteous,' and that concerning
> David in ' who buildeth Jerusalem.'

I reserve for the concluding chapter the discussion

---

[1] R. José is R. José ben Ḥalaphta, whose father was intimate with R.
Gamliel of Jabneh.   R. Jose himself may possibly have been one of the
assembly at Jabneh ; but, as he was only ordained after A.D. 135, he would
be very young when R. Gamliel died, A.D. 110 or thereabouts.

of the bearing of the "formula concerning the Minim" upon the relations between Jesus and heretics, only remarking here that Jewish Christians would probably be those who would feel most of its force as a means of detecting heresy.

R. ELIEZER ARRESTED FOR MINUTH.

(45) T. Ḥull. ii. 24.—The case of R. Eliezer, who was arrested for Minuth, and they brought him to the tribunal (במה, βῆμα) for judgment. The governor (הגמון, ἡγεμών) said to him, 'Doth an old man like thee occupy himself with such things?' He said to him, 'Faithful is the judge concerning me.' The governor supposed that he only said this of him, but he was not thinking of any but his Father who is in Heaven. He [the governor] said to him, 'Since I am trusted concerning thyself, thus also I will be. I said, perhaps these societies[1] err concerning these things. *Dimissus*, Behold thou art released.' And when he had been released from the tribunal, he was troubled because he had been arrested for Minuth. His disciples came in to console him, but he would not take comfort. R. Aqiba came in and said to him, Rabbi, shall I say to thee why thou art perhaps grieving? He said to him, 'Say on.' He said to him, 'Perhaps one of the Minim has said to thee a word of Minuth and it has pleased thee.' He said, 'By Heaven,

---

[1] Read הישיבות with b. A. Zar 16ᵇ, in place of הסיבו which makes no sense.

thou hast reminded me! Once I was walking
along the street of Sepphoris, and I met
Jacob of Chephar Sichnin, and he said to me
a word of Minuth in the name of Jeshu ben
Pantiri, and it pleased me. And I was
arrested for words of Minuth because I transgressed the words of Torah (Prov. v. 8),
*Keep thy way far from her, and come not
nigh the door of her house* (vii. 26), *for she hath
cast down many wounded.*' And R. Eliezer
used to say, ' Ever let a man flee from what is
hateful, and from that which resembles what is
hateful.'

(46)　b. A. Zar. 16ᵇ, 17ᵃ.—Our Rabbis teach,
When R. Eliezer was arrested for Minuth
they took him up to the tribunal (נרדום,
gradus) to be judged. The governor said to
him, ' Will an old man such as thou busy
himself about these vain things?' He said,
' Faithful is the judge concerning me.' The
governor supposed he said this in reference to
him; but he only said it in regard to his
Father in Heaven. He (the governor) said,
' Since I am trusted concerning thee, *Dimissus*,
thou art released.' When he came to his
house his disciples came in to comfort him,
but he would not take comfort. R. Aqiba
said to him, ' Rabbi, suffer me to say something of what thou hast taught me.' He
said to him, ' Say on.' He said to him,
' Rabbi, perhaps there has come Minuth into
thy hand and it has pleased thee, and on
account of that thou hast been arrested for

Minuth.' He said to him, 'Aqiba, thou hast reminded me. Once I was walking in the upper street of Sepphoris, and I found a man of the disciples of Jeshu the Nazarene, and Jacob of Chephar Sechanja was his name. He said to me, ' It is written in your Torah, *Thou shalt not bring the hire of a harlot*, etc. [Deut. xxiii. 18]. What may be done with it ? *Latrinae* for the high priest [may be built with it].' And I answered him nothing. He said to me, ' Thus hath Jeshu the Nazarene taught me, *For of the hire of a harlot hath she gathered them, and unto the hire of a harlot shall they return* [Micah i. 7]. From the place of filth they come, and unto the place of filth they shall go.' And the saying pleased me, and because of this I was arrested for Minuth ; and I transgressed against what is written in the Torah [Prov. v. 8], *Keep thy way far from her*, this is Minuth ; *and come not nigh the door of her house*, this is the Government.

[The remainder of the passage in A. Zar. 17ᵃ will be given below in another connexion. See p. 182.]

The same story is found in the Midrash, Qoh. Rabb. on i. 8, also in Jalq. Shim'oni on Micah i., and Prov. v. 8. These versions add nothing to what is contained in the above passages, except that (47) Qoh. Rabb. gives the dialogue between the Rabbi and Jacob more fully, as follows :—

(47) ' It is written in your Torah, *Thou shalt not*

bring, etc., What of these?' I said to him,
'They are forbidden.' He said to me, 'They
are forbidden as an offering: it is permitted
to destroy them.' I said to him, 'If so,
what shall one do with them?' He said to
me, 'He shall make with them bath-houses
and *latrinae.*' I said to him, 'Thou hast well
said.' And the halachah was concealed from
me for the moment. When he saw that I
agreed with his words, he said to me, 'Thus
hath . . . . taught me, They come from filth
and they go to filth, as is said [Mic. i. 7],
For of the hire of a harlot, etc. They shall
make seats for the public,' and it pleased me.
For this I was arrested, etc.

Commentary.—We have to distinguish two events
in this story, the arrest of R. Eliezer and his interview with Jacob the Min. First as to the arrest.
R. Eliezer lived at the end of the first and the beginning of the second century of our era; but the
dates of his birth and death are not known. His
usual residence was in Lūd, but he travelled about
the country. He was arrested, according to the
story, 'for Minuth,' *i.e.* on a charge of being a Min.
Rashi is certainly wrong when he says that Eliezer
was arrested by the Minim. From the context it
is clear that Minuth denotes the Christian heresy.
We have therefore to inquire whether there was in
Palestine, at a period within the lifetime of Eliezer, a
persecution of Christians, or if not a persecution, at
all events an official search for them. The so-called
persecution under Nero was probably confined to
Rome, and is besides too early in date (A.D. 64).

R. Eliezer must have been quite a young man at the time. But there is mentioned in Eusebius (Ecc. Hist., iii. 32), on the authority of Hegesippus, a persecution of Christians in Palestine, during which Simeon the aged bishop of Jerusalem was crucified. This took place in the year 109, during the reign, therefore, of Trajan. The charge against the bishop was that he was of the lineage of David, and also that he was a Christian. Probably it was his alleged Davidic descent rather than his Christianity which brought him under the sentence of the civil tribunal. Because already Domitian had caused inquiry to be made for descendants of the ancient royal line of David, fearing presumably lest among them might be some pretender to his own throne. It does not appear that Simeon was the only victim, though doubtless he was the most eminent. Eusebius says (*loc. cit.*) that the Christians were persecuted, or rather sought for, κατὰ πόλεις, which implies a general search throughout the country. The popular risings, which are said to have accompanied the search, would be the expression of Gentile rather than of Jewish hostility to Christianity, though no doubt the Jews might take the opportunity of assailing Christians, as they did in the case of Simeon, who is said to have been accused by certain heretics. But, on the whole, it was in the interest of the Jews to keep quiet; because, to the Gentile mind, there was too much likeness between Jews and Christians to make it safe for the former to be conspicuous while the latter were being persecuted.

It appears to me probable that the arrest and trial of R. Eliezer took place during this official search after Christians, and is therefore to be dated A.D. 109 or thereabouts.[1] How he came to be arrested is not said, because the explanation which he gives, viz., his former close association with a Christian, was a fact which he himself had forgotten until his pupil Aqiba suggested it. Yet it is possible that some popular opinion connected him with the Christians; and we have already seen that his Rabbinical companions, by their questions to him, seemed to have acted on some such suspicion (see above (4) p. 46). And it is curious to observe the embarrassment of R. Eliezer when on his trial. One would have thought that he could have saved himself by declaring that he was not a Christian, whereas he only made a skilful evasion, and owed his escape to the vanity of his judge. It is certain from all the recorded words of R. Eliezer, which are very numerous, that he was by no means a Christian; but it is none the less possible that damaging facts might be brought against him in court, connecting him with Christianity, so that his wisest course was to stave off inquiry altogether.

It is not stated where the arrest and trial took place; but it may well have happened in Cæsarea, whither Eliezer seems to have gone after his excommunication by the Rabbis of Jabneh.[2] This

---

[1] Note the fact that the judge calls him an old man. It is said (A. d. R. N., c. 6) that Eliezer was twenty-two years old when he ran away from home to learn Torah under Joḥanan ben Zaccai in Jerusalem. He appears, from this same story, to have become a distinguished pupil, if not already a Rabbi, while still in Jerusalem, therefore before the war A.D. 68–70. He must thus have been born not later than A.D. 40, probably earlier. At the time of his arrest he would be about seventy years old.

[2] He died in Cæsarea, and his body was brought thence to Lūd.—b. Sanh. 68ª.

is to some extent borne out by the fact that the judge is called by the title ' *hegmōn* ' (ἡγεμών), which usually, I believe, implies high rank, and in the present instance may denote the governor of Syria.

On being dismissed from the tribunal, Eliezer returned to his house, greatly troubled, because he had been accused of being a Christian. His disciples came in to console him, amongst them Aqiba. The latter suggested, as the reason why R. Eliezer had been arrested as a Christian, that perhaps at some time he had come in contact with that heresy and approved of it. R. Eliezer, thus reminded, recalled an interview he had once had with a certain Min called Jacob, of Chephar Sechanja, one of the disciples of Jesus the Nazarene. Jacob had expounded to him a text from Scripture, and the interpretation pleased him. Whereupon the Christian added that he had learnt it from Jesus the Nazarene.

I do not see any reason to doubt the genuineness of this incident, at all events of its main features, although Edersheim declares it to be plainly apocryphal [L. and T. of J. M., i. 537]. It may not be true that Jesus himself gave the rather unsavoury interpretation of Deut. xxiii. 18 and Mic. i. 7. And even if he did, it is certain that Jacob the Christian did not get it direct from Jesus ; because, as we have already seen, he belonged to the second or, perhaps, third generation of disciples (see above, p. 106). But I do not see on what ground we can reject the evidence of a man so well known as R. Eliezer, especially as it tells against himself. The story

is well authenticated; for, if it does not appear in
the Palestinian Gemara, where we should naturally
expect to meet with it, it is given in the Tosephta,
which is not only Palestinian, but represents an older
stratum of tradition than the Gemaras (see Introduction, p. 21).

We have already met with Jacob of Chephar
Sechanja, or Ch. Sama (see above, p. 106), and we
have to inquire when the interview between him and
Eliezer took place. The data are few and inade-
quate.[1] From the way in which R. Eliezer begins
the story, " Once on a time [פעם אחת] I was walking,
etc.," it would seem as if the incident had taken place
some years before. At least that is always the impression made on my mind by the story. Grätz
(G. d. J., iv. 47 fol.) associates the incident much
more closely with the subsequent arrest and trial.
He says that by reason of his intercourse with
Christians R. Eliezer was looked upon as a member
of the Christian community, and therefore accused
as a heretic. The only objection that I see to this
view is, that if R. Eliezer had met Jacob only a short
time previously, he would scarcely have forgotten
the incident. Also, Aqiba reminds his teacher of
what he had been told on a former occasion. Still,
these facts do not exclude the possibility of a com-

---

[1] It is probable that the interview with Jacob the Min took place after
Eliezer had been excommunicated. Before his excommunication he appears
to have lived in Jabneh or Lûd, and the interview took place in Sepphoris.
Moreover, a banished man would be more likely to venture upon intercourse
with a heretic than one who was in close fellowship with the Rabbis. From
the account of his excommunication, b. B. Mez. 59[b], it appears that this
took place shortly before R. Gamliel started on his voyage to Rome, therefore in or about the year 95 A.D.

paratively short interval only—perhaps a few months or a year or two—between the interview with Jacob and the arrest of R. Eliezer. And a short interval suits the chronology better. For we have already seen reason to believe that this same Jacob of Chephar Sechanja was living in Galilee A.D. 130, thus twenty years after the arrest of Eliezer. We cannot, therefore, safely set back the earlier date much beyond A.D. 110. It is possible, of course, but it is not likely, that there were two persons each known as Jacob of Chephar Sechanja.

As to the conversation between the Christian and the Rabbi, the interpretation of the texts quoted has nothing that is characteristic of Jesus as he is known from the Gospels.[1] It is evidently a thoroughly Jewish exposition, and therefore pleased the Rabbi; there were Jewish Christians in plenty who adhered to Rabbinical modes of thought and exposition; and seeing that Jacob was most certainly not a contemporary of Jesus, his statement, 'thus hath Jesus taught me,' means no more than that 'such is current Christian teaching.' Whether there is any parallel to this interpretation in any Jewish-Christian work I do not know.

---

[1] Friedländer (*der Vorchristliche jüdische Gnosticismus*, p. 74) rightly points out that there is nothing Christian in the exposition of Jacob, and accordingly claims the fact in support of his theory that Jacob was not a Christian but a Gnostic. But he has most strangely ignored the words— very inconvenient for his theory—'thus hath Jesus the Nazarene taught me,' whereby Jacob the Min puts the fact of his Christianity beyond dispute. Friedländer has much scorn for those shallow interpreters who hold that the Minim are Jewish Christians. Until he deals with his evidence more carefully, not to say more honestly, his scorn is hardly justified.

10

BOOKS OF THE MINIM

Under this head I collect all the passages I can find in which reference is made to heretical writings, and their treatment by Jews.

IMMA SHALOM AND A CHRISTIAN JUDGE

(48) b. Shabb. 116ᵃ, ᵇ.—Imma Shalom was the wife of R. Eliezer and sister of Rabban Gamliel. There was in her neighbourhood a ' philosoph,' who had got a name for not taking a bribe. They sought to make fun of him. She [Imma Shalom] sent to him a lamp of gold. They came before him. She said to him, ' I desire that they divide to me the property of the women's house.' He said to them, ' Divide it.' They said to him, ' For us, it is written, " Where there is a son, a daughter does not inherit." He said to them, ' From the day when ye were exiled from your land, the Law of Moses has been taken away, and the law of the Evangelion has been given, and in it is written, " A son and a daughter shall inherit alike." ' The next day he [R. Gamliel] in his turn sent to him a Lybian ass. He [the judge] said to them, ' I have looked further to the end of the book, and in it is written, " I am not come to take away from the Law of Moses and I am not come to add to the Law of Moses," and in it [the Law of Moses] is written, " Where there is a son, a daughter does not inherit." ' She said to

him, ' Let your light shine as a lamp!' R.
Gamliel said to her, ' The ass has come and
trodden out the lamp.'

Commentary. — This striking story only occurs,
so far as I know, in the Babylonian Gemara, and,
therefore, is open to suspicion from the want of contemporary evidence. On the other hand there seems
no reason to account for its being invented, if there
were no historical fact at the bottom of it. The
story may well have been told as a family anecdote
by the descendants of R. Gamliel, and have been
repeated in Babylonia by Rab, who transplanted
thither so many of the Palestinian traditions, and
whose teacher was R. Jehudah, grandson of R.
Gamliel. In the Gemara the story is tacked on to
a passage dealing with written scrolls and especially with heretical writings ; but there is not a
word of introduction to say on whose authority it
was told. The preceding passage will be given
presently ; I have placed the story here, because
the incident which it records carries us back to
an earlier date than other references to heretical
scriptures.

The R. Eliezer is the same whom we have already
several times met with. Rabban Gamliel is Gamliel
of Jabneh, under whose direction the formula concerning the Minim was arranged [see above, p. 127].
The incident took place, therefore, within the closing
years of the first or the opening of the second century.
The place was probably Jabneh.

As the purpose of Gamliel and his sister was to
expose the judge to ridicule, it is hardly likely that
they would appeal to him to decide a real difference.

In a very interesting discussion of this story,[1] Nicholson argues that the Rabbi and his sister found a pretext for their law-suit in the death of their father Shim'on, and the consequent inheritance of his property. This may be so; but if there were no real dispute (and it is evident there was not), the case might have been trumped up at any time. Nicholson gives A.D 71–3 as the probable date; and the best evidence for so early a date is the saying of the judge, " From the day that ye were exiled from your land," which can only refer to the confiscation of Jewish property in A.D. 72. I do not see much force in the contention that R. Gamliel would not have condescended to such a trick as that described in the story, after he had become president of the Sanhedrin. That dignity was probably but little known or recognised outside of Jewish circles. Still we may admit that the conduct of R. Gamliel and his sister was more appropriate to youth than to maturer years, and therefore we may accept the date A.D. 71–3 as being on the whole probable.

The judge is called a ' philosōph,' and there is no reason to read some form of ' episcopos,' as is proposed by Lowe (quoted by Nicholson, *op. cit.*, p. 146). The term ' philosōph ' or ' philosōphos ' occurs several times in the Talmud, and seems to denote a trained speaker. It is quite likely that in the present case the ' philosōph ' was a bishop ; but the term ' philosōph' has nothing ecclesiastical about it. So far as I know, there is no attempt in the Talmud to reproduce the term ' episcopos ' in a Hebrew form. The judge, whether bishop or not, was probably a Jewish not a

[1] See *The Gospel According to the Hebrews*, by E. B. Nicholson, p. 146 n.

REFERENCES TO MINIM AND MINUTH 149

Gentile Christian. That he was a Christian is beyond
question, seeing that he based his decision on a
quotation from a Gospel. R. Gamliel would not be
likely to play a trick on a Gentile judge; and a
Gentile judge would scarcely have appealed to a
Gospel in a Jewish suit. He would have decided the
case on the lines of Roman law.

Now let us examine the details of the story in
order. Imma Shālōm,[1] the sister of R. Gamliel, and
wife of R. Eliezer, applied to the court to divide for
her 'the property of the women's house,' in other
words to give to her the share in her father's property
which she ought to bring to her husband at her marriage. R. Gamliel pleaded against this, that his sister
had no title to any part of her father's property,
because he, as son, inherited it all. He supported his
plea by an appeal to the Law of Moses, though the
words which he cited do not occur in the Pentateuch.
His plea is an inference based upon Num. xxvii. 8.
The judge, mindful of the bribe he had received from
the complainant, decided against the defendant, on
the ground that the Law of Moses had been super-
seded by the law 'of the Evangelion,' according to
which a son and daughter inherit alike. I believe
that 'of the Evangelion' is the right reading in this
passage; but at the same time I doubt whether the
judge actually used the term. We shall see presently
(p. 162) that R. Meir and R. Joḥanan, in the second
and third centuries, made jests on the word Evangelion; and since the story, as we have it, was written
down long after their time, it is not safe to conclude
that the term 'Evangelion' was known and used as

---

[1] Imma Shālōm, *i.e.* Mother Salome.

early as A.D. 72. Jesus must have used some Aramaic term, at least if he used any equivalent word at all; and it would be natural to expect that a Jewish Christian, in speaking to Jews, would also have used the Aramaic term rather than the Greek equivalent. I regard the words ' of the Evangelion ' as a later gloss, though earlier than the written text of the Talmud.

There is no passage in any known Gospel which states that a son and daughter shall inherit alike. Unless some text, hereafter to be discovered, shall furnish a parallel, we can only regard the statement as a general inference from Christian principles. It is worth noting, by the way, that if there were such a rule of Christian practice, the state of things described in Acts iv. 32–37 had already ceased to exist in the year 72.

The sentence of the court having been given against him, R. Gamliel so to speak applied for a new trial by sending a bribe to the judge, a present of a Lybian ass. The next day, accordingly, the judge had reconsidered his decision. He said, ' I have read further in the end of the book, and therein it is written, " I am not come to take away from the Law of Moses, neither to add to the Law of Moses am I come," and in it [the Law of Moses] it is written, " where there is a son, a daughter does not inherit." ' There is an obvious parallel here with Matt. v. 17, though the quotation is not exact. It would be too much to infer from this that the present Gospel of Matthew was in existence at this time. But it seems probable that the judge had some written text, and was not merely quoting from memory. If there had at the time been no written text at all, it would not have occurred to the judge to say that he had 'read in *the book.*' If he had had some collection of ' Logia,' such as that of which a fragment was published by Rendell and Harris in 1897, he would have had as much as the story implies. Indeed, a collection of ' Logia,' sayings of Jesus, would better come under the description of a ' new law ' than would any work in the fuller form of one of the known Gospels. It is evident that the book, whatever it was, did not present the sayings of Jesus in anything like the same order as is found in the canonical Gospel of Matthew. For the words, *I am not come to destroy but to fulfil,* occur near the beginning of the Sermon on the Mount [Matt. v. 17], and far from the end of the Gospel. The ' Logia' fragment, already referred to, shows, where comparison is possible, an arrangement differing from that of any of the canonical Gospels. There is nothing improbable in supposing the existence of written collections of Logia in the year 72. It has been well suggested by J. E. Odgers (*Jewish Quarterly Review*, 1891, p. 16), that the first impulse to the writing down of the sayings of Jesus was given by the dispersion of the Christian community in Jerusalem, owing to the siege of the city, A.D. 69–70. The Christians did not all take refuge in Pella, as the presence of the Christian in the story plainly shows ; and written ' Logia ' may well—we may almost say must—have found their way to other places, including Jabneh, the probable scene of the story.

The reversal of the sentence naturally disappointed the original complainant, and she gave the judge a significant reminder of her present in the words, " Let your light shine as a lamp." Here, also, there

seems to be a partial reference to a text now found in
Matt. v. 16,[1] " Let your light shine before men."
How the Jewess came to know the words, unless by
report, is not easy to see ; as it is not very likely, on
the face of it, that she would read a Christian writing.
The retort is so apt, that we cannot suppose it to
have been merely invented, with no knowledge of the
words of Jesus.   By quoting them she convicted the
judge out of his own law, as well as reminded him of
the bribe he had taken.

R. Gamliel, the successful pleader, made rejoinder
in a curious saying, which may have been a popular
proverb, but which also may have been his own
original remark, " The ass has come and trodden out
the lamp."   The meaning of the retort is obvious,
and equally so its purpose in exposing the shameless
venality of the judge.   But just as the retort, " Let
your light shine," was aimed at more than the mere
fact of bribery, and had a sting for the Christian as a
Christian, so perhaps it may be in the case of the
saying about the ass and the lamp.   The phrase
occurs elsewhere, and a brief study of the subject
may throw some light on a very obscure but not
unimportant point.

The phrase is found in Pesiqta de Rab Kahana
122[b], also in j. Joma 38[c], Vajiqr. r. c. 21.   In all
these cases the phrase is used to describe the frustra-
tion of one bribe by a larger bribe from the opposite
party in a suit.   The passage in Pesiqta is more
detailed than the others, and is as follows :—" The
case of a certain woman who presented to a judge a
lamp of silver ; but her opponent went and presented

[1] In fact Matt. v. 15, 16, and 17 seem to underlie the story.

to him an ass of gold. On the morrow the woman
came and found the judgment reversed. She said,
' My lord, let justice shine before thee like a silver
lamp.' He said to her, ' What shall I do for thee ?
The ass has trodden out the lamp.' "

Bacher (Ag. d. Pal. Amor., ii. 424 n.) holds that
this story is founded upon the story of Imma
Shalom and R. Gamliel. And I think he is right
in this opinion, even though the Pesiqta should be,
as it possibly is, earlier in date than the completion
of the Babylonian Gemara. At all events the
evidence of the Pesiqta places the story on
Palestinian ground. If we may conclude that the
phrase originated with Gamliel, then we are free to
inquire whether there is anything significant in the
mention of a lamp and an ass as the bribes to the
judge. It is, of course, easy to discover symbolism
where none is intended ; and quite possibly the ass
and the lamp were costly gifts and nothing more.
But there is evidence elsewhere to show that there
was some obscure connexion in thought between
Jesus and an ass, so that the latter served as a kind
of symbol of the former. In the Midrash Qoh. r.
on i. 8, a passage which will be given below (see p.
211 ff.), R. Jehoshua b. Ḥananiah says to his nephew,
who had been led astray by the Minim of Capernaum and rescued from them, " Since *the ass* of
that wicked one is roused against thee, thou canst
no longer dwell in the land of Israel," etc. The
plain meaning is that the young man had been
damaged in character and repute by contact with
Christianity ; and this would hardly have been
described by a metaphor so peculiar unless there was

an implied reference to Jesus in the mention of
the ass.[1] What may have suggested this reference
I cannot positively say. But possibly it is an
allusion to the alleged Messianic dignity of Jesus.
In Ber. r. c. 75 § 6, it is explained that the ass is
a symbol of the Messiah. And the passage just
quoted from Qoh. r. i. 8 tends to confirm this
suggestion, because the young apostate had been
made by the Christians to ride on an ass on the
Sabbath. These are nothing more than slight and
obscure hints, and there may be nothing in them ;
but they are worth collecting and recording, on the
chance that their meaning may be more clearly
understood in the light of future researches.

If there really was, in contemporary thought, some
association of an ass with Jesus, then the story of
R. Gamliel and his bribe to the judge gains additional
point. The object of the whole plot was to expose
the venality of this Jewish Christian, by bribing him
to alter his own decision. The rectitude of the Jew
had been corrupted by the spirit of Christianity, the

---

[1] In this connexion may be mentioned the caricature found on a wall in
Rome, where there is shown a crucified figure having an ass's head ; a
soldier kneels before the cross, and underneath is written, "Alexamenos
worshipping his God." This brutal parody of Christian belief evidently
shows that in the mind of the 'artist' there was an association of Jesus with
an ass. The charge of worshipping an ass was brought against the Jews, as
is shown by the well-known passages in Josephus (c. Apion, ii. 7) and
Tacitus (Hist., v. 3, 4). The Jews in their turn tried to pass it on to the
Christians. See an article by Rösch, on the *Caput asininum*, in the Stud. u.
Kritik., 1882, p. 523, where the origin and development of this fable are
described. Rösch makes no mention of the Rabbinical allusions, though he
refers to the Talmud for another purpose. I think the passages mentioned
in the text may fairly be connected with the fable of the ass-worship.

For another possible reference to the association of Jesus with an ass, see
below, p. 224 n.

light of the true religion had been extinguished by a mischievous heresy, and the witty Rabbi expressed both these facts by saying, " The ass has come and trodden out the lamp."

How the Books of the Minim are to be Treated

(49) T. Shabb. xiii. 5.—The margins[1] and books of the Minim they do not save, but these are burnt in their place, they and their ' memorials ' [*i.e.* the sacred names in the text]. R. José the Galilean says, ' On a week-day one cuts out the memorials and hides them and burns the rest.' R. Tarphon said, ' May I lose my son! if they come into my hand I would burn them and their memorials too. If the pursuer were pursuing after me, I would enter into a house of idolatry, and I enter not into their houses. For the idolaters do not acknowledge Him [*i.e.* God] and speak

---

[1] The word גליון means the unwritten portion of a book, the margin. But, as in modern books, the margins of ancient MSS. were used for annotations ; and it is reasonable to suppose that these annotations would include texts of Scripture, quoted as illustrations. Hence the question would arise whether, although the *corpus* of the book was heretical, the marginal citations of Scripture were to be regarded as sacred. Jost (Gsch. d. Jdtums. ii. 40 n.) says that גליון (giljon) plainly denotes ' evangelion ' in the passage before us. No doubt the Gospels are included amongst the ' Books of the Minim ' ; but I do not think it can be shown that ' giljon ' by itself ever means a Gospel. If that were the case, there would be the less occasion for the plays on the word ' Aven-giljon ' and ' Avon-giljon ' which will be mentioned below (s. p. 162). Friedländer (d. Vorchr. jüd. Gnosticismus, p. 83 fol.) identifies the ' giljōnīm ' of the Minim with the Diagramma of the Ophite sect of the Gnostics. This may be correct ; but as the Talmud never gives any indication of what the ' giljonim ' contained beyond ' memorials,' the guess is hazardous.

falsely concerning Him ; but these [*i.e.* the Minim] do acknowledge Him and speak falsely concerning Him. And concerning them the Scripture says [Isa. lvii. 8], *And behind the door and the door-post thou hast set thy memorial.'* R. Ishmael said, ' Whereas, in order to make peace between a man and his wife, God says [cp. Num. v. 23], *Let my name which is written in holiness be blotted out in water,* how much more the books of the Minim, which put enmity and jealousy and strife between Israel and their Father who is in Heaven, should be blotted out, and their memorials too. And concerning them the Scripture says [Ps. cxxxix. 21], *Do I not hate them, O Lord, which hate thee, and I loathe them that rise up against thee. I hate them with a perfect hatred, and they have become to me as enemies.'* And even as men do not save them [the books] from burning, so they do not save them from falling, nor from water, nor from anything which destroys them.

(50) (51) No important variation. See Appendix.

Commentary. The Rabbis whose words are cited here lived in the early part of the second century. Tarphon[1] is well known as a bitter opponent of Christianity. Ishmael is the same whom we have

---

[1] Tarphon is often identified with Tryphon, the interlocutor in Justin Martyr's Dialogue. Beyond some resemblance of name, there is little, if anything, on which to found such identification. It is possible that Justin may have heard of, or perhaps even met, Tarphon, though certainly not in Ephesus. But no one who knows Tarphon in the Talmud would recognise him in the feeble Jew who serves Justin as a man of straw. Tarphon, not Tryphon, is the proper form of the name.

previously seen, protesting against the cure of his nephew by a Christian doctor. It is evident then, from their strong denunciations, that the Books of the Minim included Christian writings. But the phrase is indefinite, and cannot be fairly restricted to writings explanatory of the Christian religion. We shall see, in another passage (p. 158), that copies of the Hebrew Scriptures were sometimes written by Minim, in the ordinary way of business, and the question arose whether such copies might be used by Jews. In the present passage that question is not directly raised; but one of the difficulties which it suggested is mentioned, viz., the fact that in. heretical writings the name of God often occurred, whereby the reader was placed in the dilemma of having either to destroy the divine Name along with the book, or to preserve the heretical book for the sake of the divine Name. R. José the Galilean enjoins the quaint device of cutting out [1] and keeping the divine Name wherever it occurred, and burning the rest. What was to be done with the collected scraps is not said. R. Tarphon and R. Ishmael were at least consistent, in deciding that heretical books were to be destroyed, no matter what they contained.

BOOKS OF THE LAW WRITTEN BY MINIM

(52) b. Gitt. 45ᵇ.—Rab Bodia said to Rab Ashi, ' " At more than their price," this is why " they do not receive them." At their price they do

---

[1] I follow here the reading of the Vienna Codex, and the early printed text, also Siphre, p. 6ᵃ, as against the Erfurt Codex, which has instead of קורא קודר, i.e. 'reads' the name instead of 'cuts out' the name.

receive them.' Learn from this, that one may read in a Book of the Law which is found in the hand of an idolater. Ought it, perhaps, to be concealed? Rab Naḥman said, 'We have received [tradition] that a Book of the Law, if written by a Min, is to be burnt; if written by an idolater, it is to be concealed.' If found in the hand of a Min, it is to be concealed; if found in the hand of an idolater, some say it is to be concealed, some say it may be read. [In regard to] a Book of the Law written by an idolater, one [teacher] teaches that it is to be burnt, another [tradition] is that it is to be concealed, and another that it may be read. There is no contradiction.

Commentary.—Apart from the difficulties in connexion with books written by Minim for their own use, there was the difficulty of deciding whether a book of the law might be used if written by, or found in the possession of, some one other than a Jew. Such a book might have been written in order to be sold to Jews for their own use. Or, if found in the possession of a non-Jewish person, it might still have been written by a Jew, and therefore might be lawful for a Jew to use. The text in the Mishnah, of which the passage before us is the commentary, says, " We do not receive books, tephillin,[1] and mezūzōth[2] from idolaters at more than their price." R. Bodia explains, what is surely obvious, that books, etc., might be received from

---

[1] Tephillin, phylacteries, small parchment boxes, containing certain texts, and worn on the arm and the head.

[2] Mezūzōth, similar small boxes, containing texts, but fastened to the doorpost of the house. Mezuzoth may be called the 'tephillin' of the house.

idolaters, only that more than their proper price must not be given for them. As a contemporary of R. Ashi (the editor of the Babylonian Gemara), R. Bodia lived at the end of the fourth century or the beginning of the fifth. R. Naḥman, whose explanation is more to the purpose, is Naḥman bar Jacob, a Babylonian teacher who died A.D. 300.[1] A clear distinction is made between an idolater and a Min, in deciding how to deal with books of the law whose origin was doubtful. It should be noticed that the Mishnah text does not say anything about Minim in this connexion. The distinction is made against the Min and in favour of the idolater. The Min is not in this case necessarily a Christian, but is certainly a Jewish heretic. Therefore a book written by a Min was condemned outright, and must be burnt. If found in his possession, even though it might have been written by a Jew, it was considered as tainted with heresy, and must be 'concealed,' *i.e.* withdrawn from use, treated as an Apocryphon. On the other hand, a book if written by an idolater must be 'concealed'; but, if found in his possession, according to some authorities it must be 'concealed,' according to others it might be used.

A few lines further down on the same page of the Talmud (b. Gitt. 45ᵇ) are two more references to Minim. I do not translate the whole passage, because it is chiefly taken up with technical questions having no bearing on the subject of heresy; and, further, it is exceedingly difficult to render into intelligible English. The first reference occurs in a *dictum* of R. Hamnuna,

---

[1] He received several Palestinian traditions from R. Jitzḥaq, a disciple of R. Joḥanan, who visited him in Nehardea.

son of Raba of Parshunia. He says, 'Rolls of the Law, tephillin and mezuzoth, written by a Min, a betrayer, an idolater, a slave, a woman, a child, a Samaritan or an apostate Israelite, are ceremonially unfit for use' (פסולין). This also occurs b. Men. 42ᵇ. The second reference is merely the following:—" Concerning a proselyte who reverts to his wickedness: [he will revert] to his wickedness much more if he be a Min."

These references are added merely to make the list of references to Minim as complete as possible. They are of very late date, and add nothing new to what is contained in other more important passages.

THE BOOKS OF THE MINIM DO NOT DEFILE THE HANDS

(53) T. Jad. ii. 13.—The rolls and books of the Minim do not defile the hands.

The books of Ben Sira and all books which have been written from that time onward do not defile the hands.

Commentary.—There is hardly anything to be said on this passage, which is a mere statement that the books of the Minim are not to be regarded as sacred. It may seem strange that such a statement should be necessary, especially in view of such denunciations of them as those uttered by R. Tarphon and R. Ishmael (see above, pp. 154–5). The reason probably is, that the books of the Minim, though heretical, made mention of sacred names and things, and might therefore be supposed to be themselves holy.

It is remarkable that the Mishnah does not mention

the books of the Minim either in the parallel passage
M. Jad. iii. 5, or, so far as I know, in any other
place. The 'external books' referred to in M.
Sanh. x. i. are understood by the commentators to be,
or to include, the books of the Minim; but they are
not so called in the Mishnah.

On the same page of T. Jadaim, a few lines below
the passage just cited, there is an apparent reference
to Minim which ought to be noticed, if only to guard
the reader from a mistake, and myself from a charge
of omitting an important passage. Mention is there
made (ii. 16) of הלכות מינין, 'halachoth concerning the
Minim'; and for some time I was under the delusion
that the reference was to ordinances concerning
heretics, made at Jabneh. A comparison, however,
with j. Bicc. iii. 6 (p. 65ᵈ) shows conclusively that
the word מינין denotes here not 'heretics,' but simply
'kinds' or 'sorts,' and the reference is to the seven
'kinds' of fruit for which Palestine was famous. The
word מין is a common noun as well as a proper noun;
and to a non-Jewish reader it is not always easy
to distinguish between the two usages. (See below,
p. 364).

The Books of the Bē Abidan (and Bē Nitzraphi

(54) b. Shabb. 116ᵃ.—R. Joseph bar Ḥanin asked
R. Abahu: 'Those books of the Bē Abīdan,
does one save them from burning or not?'
Yes and no; he was undecided. Rab did not
go to the Bē Abīdan, much less to the Bē
Nitzraphi. Shemuel did not go to the Bē
Nitzraphi; but he did go to the Bē Abīdan.
11

They said to Rab, 'What is the reason thou
didst not come to the Bē Abīdān?' He said
to them, 'There is a certain palm tree by the
road, and it is an offence to me; if it were
uprooted, the place of it would be an offence
to me.' Mar bar Joseph said, 'I have been
amongst them, and I was not respected by
them.' On one occasion he went and they
sought to endanger him. R. Meir called it
Aven giljon, R. Johanan called it Avon
giljon.

Commentary. This passage forms part of a longer
one, of which we have already examined two portions.
It follows immediately after No. (51) and immediately
precedes (48); I have broken it up for convenience of
treatment. It obviously comes under the general
head of 'Books of the Minim,' but the portion at
present under examination is interesting on its own
account, because it mentions the Bē Abīdān and the
Be Nitzraphi. These are of sufficient importance to
be treated separately. And having in the previous
sections dealt with all the passages that I know of
which refer to the Books of the Minim, I shall present
here those which mention the Bē Abidan and the Bē
Nitzraphi. What these names mean is not certain,
and I shall endeavour to explain them presently.
Meanwhile I will consider the rest of the passage.

R. Abahu we have already met with (see above,
No. 10). He lived in Cæsarea at the end of the third
and beginning of the fourth century. This is evidence
that the question put to him referred to things in
Palestine. The printed text in the modern editions
give the name of his questioner as Joseph bar Ḥanin,

and this is correct, although the Munich MS. gives
'Joseph bar Ḥama.' The latter, the father of Raba,
was a Babylonian, who, so far as I know, never came
in contact with Abahu. Joseph bar Ḥanin, or
Ḥanina, was the teacher of Abahu ; his name in this
passage is vouched for by the Oxford MS. See
Rabbinowicz, *ad loc.* Mar bar Joseph, if the reading
be correct, would be the son of Joseph b. Ḥanin.
Whatever the books of the Bē Abīdān may have
been, it is clear that they included books which were
heretical, and distinctly Christian. That they were
heretical is shown by the context, because the books
of the Minim have just been mentioned (see No 51).
And that they were Christian is shown unmistakably
by the concluding words, which contain plays upon the
name Evangelion. This concluding sentence is not
found in the modern editions, but is contained in the
MSS. and early editions, and is here given on the
authority of Rabbinowicz. Probably both witticisms
are reported by R. Abahu, who was a disciple of R.
Joḥanan, the author of one of them. And R. Joḥanan
must have been aware of the saying of R. Meir, since
his own jest is only a variation of the older one.
'Aven giljōn' means 'a worthless thing of a book
[roll],' or, since 'Aven' in the O.T. generally has some
reference to idolatry, 'a book of idolatry.' In
like manner Avon giljon may be rendered 'a book
of iniquity.' R. Meir, to whom belongs the credit of
the original *jeu d'esprit*, lived in Palestine in the latter
half of the second century. His teachers were R.
Aqiba, whom we have already met with as a fierce
opponent of Christianity, and Elisha ben Abuja, himself inclined to heresy, and well acquainted with the

books of the Minim. The gibe of R. Meir is clear
proof that in his time the term Evangelion was in
common use, and we may perhaps conclude from the
passage before us that it was a generic term for the
' Books of the Minim,' or, at all events, that it included more than one book. After referring to
' books ' in the plural, the passage reads, ' R. Meir
called *it* Aven giljon.' I have already (p. 149) pointed
out that the use of the word Evangelion in the story
of R. Gamliel and the Christian judge (a passage which
forms the continuation of the one at present under
examination) is probably a later gloss. It would at
all events be unsafe to rely upon its authenticity in
that story.

Now what are the ' Bē Abīdān ' and ' Bē Nitzraphi '? ' Bē ' is a shortened form of Bēth, house.
Neither ' Abīdān ' nor ' Nitzraphi ' are regular
Aramaic, still less Hebrew, words. They are hybrids,
and contain some polemic allusion. ' Abīdān ' is
apparently connected with the root ' abad ' (אבד), to
destroy, and both form and derivation may be compared with Ἀβαδδών (Rev. ix. 11). Nitzraphi [the
vocalization is uncertain] is almost certainly connected with the word Notzri, Nazarene, while the
form suggests a niph'al from the root tzaraph (צרף), to
unite. It is tempting to infer for Bē Nitzraphi the
meaning ' house where Nazarenes assemble.' And
whether or not this be the intention of the inventor
of the word, it suits the sense in the few passages
where the word occurs. These passages I will introduce here, so that we may have all the available
evidence for an answer to one of the minor problems of the Talmud. In addition to the passage

already translated, we have the following, which
I will translate successively and comment on together :—

(55) b. Shabb. 152ᵃ.—Cæsar said to R. Jehoshua
ben Ḥananjah, 'What is the reason that thou
comest not to the Bē Abīdān?' He said to
him, 'The mountain is covered with snow
[my head is white, I am too old], its slopes
are frozen [my beard is white], its dogs do
not bark [my voice is feeble], its grinders do
not grind [my teeth are gone].'

(56) b. A. Zar. 17ᵇ.—They said to him [El'azar
ben Perata], 'What is the reason that thou
comest not to the Bē Abīdān?' He said to
them, 'I have become an old man, and I am
afraid lest ye should trample me with your
feet.'

(57) b. Erub. 79ᵇ, 80ᵃ.—What is an Ashērah in
general? Rab said, 'Every [tree] which
priests guard and do not taste of its fruits.'
And Shemuel said, 'Like those who say,
These dates are for the wine of the Bē
Nitzraphi, which they drink on the day of
their feast.'

[b. A. Zar. 48ᵃ has substantially the same.]

These are, so far as I know, all the passages
which mention either the ' Bē Abīdān ' or the ' Bē
Nitzraphi.' Whatever these places were, it is plain
that they were to be found in Palestine. This is shown
by the fact that all the Rabbis mentioned in the foregoing passages lived in Palestine during the whole or
part of their lives. The extraordinary explanation
of Hamburger (R. Encykl., ii. 95, 96) may therefore

be dismissed, viz. that 'Be Abīdān' is Bezabde, a
town on the west side of the Tigris, and 'Be
Nitzraphi' is Nicephorium on the Euphrates! Why
should R. Jehoshua ben Ḥananiah, who never was
in Babylonia in his life, be taken to task because he
had not gone to Bezabde on the Tigris? And was it
only in these two remote and little known cities that,
as Hamburger says, "theological disputations were
held between Ormuzd priests, Christians and Jews?"

Jost (Gsch. d. Jdtums., ii. 40 n.) says that the term
'Bē Abīdān' belongs to the Persian time, and means
place of assemblage. But why should a Persian word
be used to describe an institution which R. Jehoshua
ben Ḥananiah and R. El'azar ben Perata, both
Palestinians of the second century, were in a position
to attend? Jost seems to feel some doubt of his own
assertion, for he adds the suggestion that perhaps
'Bē Abīdān' is a corruption of 'Bē Ebiōnim' (house
of the poor). This is better, but scarcely convincing.
His suggestion that Be Nitzraphi is a corruption of
'Bē Nitzranin' (נצרנין ? נוצרין) is unintelligible to
me; perhaps it involves a printer's error.

I have not been able to discover that Grätz in his
history makes any allusion to either of the two names,
still less gives any explanation of them. Nor, so far
as I know, does Bacher explain them in his three
works on the Agada.[1] I have not found anything
bearing on the subject in Weiss' G. d. j. T. Levy
(N. H. W., i. p. 8) suggests that אבידן may be con-

---

[1] The only reference, so far as I know, made by Bacher, is in A. d. Pal.
Am., ii. 97, n. 4, where he says, that the meaning of Be Abīdān has never
yet been explained, but that in any case the 'Books of the B. Abidan' are
equivalent to the 'Books of the Minim,' so far as Abahu is concerned.

nected with בידין, which is the rendering in the
Targums of the Gk. πύθων (ventriloquist, fortune-
teller). Such persons, he says, were seldom, in the
later Grecian period, absent from popular merry-
makings, and might have been conspicuous in a place
of public debate. Yet something more serious is
surely implied than this; an Emperor would hardly
ask an eminent Rabbi why he had not come to listen
to a ventriloquist; nor would it be carefully noted
that some Rabbis did, and some did not, go to the
place where such persons were to be met with. It
should be noted also (as Levy admits) that the word
πύθων is rendered in the Mishnah by פיתום (Sanh.
vii. 7).

I venture to suggest that (Bē) Abīdān represents
the word ῷδεῖον, odeum, a species of theatre for
musical performances, frequently used as a law-court
or *as a place for philosophical disputations*.[1] Such
buildings were erected in several of the cities of
Palestine,[2] as is shown by the existing ruins (see
Schürer, G. d. J. Volkes, ii. 24, and elsewhere).
Hadrian built one in Rome, and of course the original
᾽Ωιδεῖον was in Athens. Now there are various
accounts in the Talmud and Midrash of disputations
between R. Jehoshua ben Ḥananiah, the Emperor
Hadrian, and 'the men of the Bē Athina,' *i.e.* literally
the 'House of Athens' (see b. Bechor. 8b, Qoh.

---

[1] εἰ δὲ φήσει τις ὅτι δόξαν οὗτοι καὶ τιμὰς ἐθήρευον, ἐπὶ τοὺς σοφοὺς ἐλθὲ καὶ τὰς
σοφὰς ᾽Αθήνησι σχολὰς καὶ διατριβάς· ἀναπέμπασαι τὰς ἐν Λυκείῳ τὰς ἐν ᾽Ακαδημίᾳ,
τὴν Στοάν, τὸ Παλλάδιον, τὸ ᾽Ωδεῖον.   (Plut. De Exil., p. 602 B.)

[2] Grätz (G. d. J., iv. 313 n.) quotes from Malala (Histor., x. p. 261) the
following words, showing that Vespasian built an Odeum in Cæsarea :—
ἔκτισε γὰρ καὶ ἐν Καισαρείᾳ . . . ἐκ τῆς ᾽Ιουδαικῆς πραίδας ὁ αὐτὸς
Οὐεσπασιανός ᾠδεῖον μέγα πανυ θεάτρου ἔχον διάστημα μέγα οντος καὶ αὐτοῦ τοῦ
τόπου πρῴην συναγώγης τῶν ᾽Ιουδαιῶν.

r. i. 7, and elsewhere). It is not recorded that R.
Jehoshua was ever in Athens; but he visited Rome
(see below, p. 228), where there was an 'Aθήναιον
founded by Hadrian. The Athenæum was not the
same as the Odeum; but in both institutions philosophical disputations were held, and a Jew would not
be likely to make any careful distinction between the
two. May not the debates between R. Jehoshua and
the men of the ' Be Athina' represent what really
took place in an Odeum, either in Palestine or
Alexandria ? The Rabbis living in Palestine must
certainly have heard and known the name ὠδεῖον in
the common speech of the Greek inhabitants of the
towns, where such buildings existed. Further, the
study of Greek philosophy was looked upon with
disapproval amongst the Rabbis, who regarded it as
a danger to their religion (see above, p. 106). Therefore it was natural that they should not willingly
encounter Greek philosophers, though sometimes
obliged to do so. The term ' Bē Abīdān,' though
only a hybrid word, may be translated ' House of
Destruction'; and I suggest that it is a play on the
word ὠδεῖον or odeum, nearly alike in sound,[1] though
not intended as a transliteration. I venture to think
that this explanation of ' Bē Abīdān ' meets the re-
quirements of the references to it in the passages
quoted above. An ὠδεῖον was a place to which a Jew
might on occasion go, because it was not a heathen
temple. It was a place where philosophical disputa-

---

[1] אבידן and ὠδεῖον seem at first sight somewhat far removed from each
other in sound. But, for the first syllable, compare אוקינוס and ὠκεανός,
bearing in mind that ב and ו are frequently interchanged. And, for the
termination, compare סימן and σημεῖον, an exact parallel.

tions were held, such as we know that R. Jehoshua did engage in ; and it was a place where books (including Christian books) would most naturally be found. Finally, it was a place well known in several Palestinian cities, and not, so far as I am aware, familiar to the Babylonian Rabbis.

There remains to be considered the term Bē Nitzraphi. What this means, we can only infer from the two passages quoted above (54), (57). It is evident that the ' Be Nitzraphi ' was considered to be a worse place to go to than the Bē Abīdān ; for while Rab wc.ld not go to the latter, much less to the former, Shemuel went to the latter, but would not go to the former. Moreover, while the ' Bē Abīdān ' is first mentioned in connexion with R. Jehoshua and R. El'azar (first half of the second century), the ' Bē Nitzraphi ' is only mentioned in connexion with Rab and Shemuel, whose sojourn in Palestine occurred in the beginning of the third century. It appears from (57) that the ' Bē Nitzraphi ' was a place where wine was used for religious purposes, while at the same time it could not have been a heathen temple, because no Rabbi would have entered such a place or have had any inducement to do so ; and thus the fact that he did not go there would call for no remark. Moreover, the 'Bē Nitzraphi' was a Palestinian institution, although the fact of its being mentioned only in connexion with Rab and Shemuel, both chiefly known as Babylonian teachers, might suggest that it was a Babylonian institution. This cannot indeed be said to be impossible, owing to the scantiness of the evidence upon which any conclusion can be based. But it is not likely, because a comparison is made

between the Bē Abīdān, which we have seen to be
purely Palestinian, and the Be Nitzraphi; and it is
stated that Shemuel went to one but not to the other.
Evidently he could have gone to both.   It appears to
me most probable that the ' Bē Nitzraphi ' is a
synagogue or meeting-place of Christians, more
particularly Jewish Christians or Nazarenes, Nōtzrim.
In this case the wine which "they drank on the
day of their feast" would be the wine of the Lord's
Supper.   While a Jew would certainly not enter a
place where Gentile Christians assembled, we know,
and shall see in passages to be quoted hereafter, that
Rabbis of undoubted orthodoxy, such as Abahu, had
close intercourse with Jewish Christians; and not only
so, but that a Rabbi (Saphra) was actually appointed
by the Jewish Christians of Cæsarea to be their teacher
on the recommendation of this same Abahu.   If anything, this proves too much, because the ' Bē
Nitzraphi,' or Jewish Christian place of meeting,
might seem to be not such a terrible place after all.
Yet Abahu, with all his readiness to hold intercourse
with Jewish Christians, was a stout opponent of their
teaching, and had many a debate with them.   I rest,
therefore, in the conclusion that ' Be Nitzraphi ' denotes a meeting-place of Jewish Christians; and I
would explain the name as a hybrid, combining a
reference to Nōtzrim, Nazarenes, with the notion
of assembly (root, tzaraph).   I do not know that
Nitzraphi is the correct form; as the word is only
found in an unpointed text, it is difficult to say what
the proper vowels are.

In conclusion it should be pointed out that there
is no mention of books in connexion with the ' Bē

Nitzraphi.' That institution is only referred to because the mention of the ' Bē Abīdān ' suggested it. Also, if my explanation of ' Bē Abīdān ' be correct, the books referred to would not be exclusively Christian books. But undoubtedly Christian books would be included, perhaps even as early as the time of R. Jehoshua, certainly in the time of Rab and Shemuel, and afterwards. Because, by the middle of the second century, Christian writers had composed Apologies for their religion in answer to the arguments of Gentile opponents ; and the Dialogue of Justin Martyr with Tryphon the Jew, though probably fictitious in substance, may nevertheless represent a fact ; for the dialogue form would scarcely have been chosen, unless such disputations were already familiar by common usage to those who would read the book. That a Jew, to say nothing of Tarphon, would have spoken as Justin makes his Jew speak, is not likely ; but in other respects the Dialogue may be taken as a representation, from the Christian side, of what went on in a ' Bē Abīdān.' There was no great difference, from this point of view, between an ᾠδεῖον and the ξυστός, where Justin says that he conversed with the Jew.

THE NAZARENE DAY

(58) b. A. Zar. 6ᵃ (*ib.* 7ᵇ).—For R. Taḥlipha bar Abdimi said that Shemuel said: ' The Nazarene day, according to the words of R. Ishmael, is forbidden for ever.'

(59) b. Taan. 27ᵇ.—On the eve of Sabbath they did not fast, out of respect to the Sabbath ;

still less [did they fast] on the Sabbath itself.
Why did they not fast on the day after
Sabbath ?   R. Joḥanan says, 'Because of the
Nazarenes.'

Commentary.—There is little to be said upon these
two meagre references to the Christian Sunday.   It
is curious that both occur in the Babylonian Gemara,
and that the Palestinian tradition does not appear to
contain any allusion to the 'Nazarene day.'   It is
true that R. Joḥanan was a Palestinian teacher ; but
his dictum (in 59) is quoted only by a Babylonian, *i.e.*
by the compiler of the Gemara, presumably R. Ashi,
in the fourth century.   In (58) the 'words of R.
Ishmael' have no reference to the Sunday, but are
a general declaration concerning heathen festivals.
Shemuel, a Babylonian (A.D. 180–250), merely asserts
that, according to the rule of R. Ishmael, the 'Nazarene day' is forbidden for ever.   The context shows
that what is forbidden on that day is intercourse with
those who observe it as a festival.   In (59) the subject
under discussion is the reason for certain fasts, kept
by the אנשי מעמד, men appointed to be present and
to repeat prayers while sacrifices were offered, of
course in the time when the Temple was still in existence.   In Sopherim, c. 17, § 5, the passage (59) is
referred to, and R. Joḥanan's explanation is given,
though without his name.   Then follows his remark,
" but the sages have said that in the days of the
מעמדות [the assistants at the sacrifices] men did not
pay any attention to the idolaters."   R. Joḥanan
transferred to the time of the Temple a feature of
the religious life of his own totally different time.
It should be observed that the word נוצרי, 'Nazarene,'

and not the word Minim, is used to designate the obnoxious day.

Having examined the passages which, so far as they go, describe Minim, I proceed to give those which attempt to define Minim and Minuth. I am aware that in so doing I am not following the logical order; but I trust that the reason given above (p. 123) may be a sufficient justification.

GENTILE AND MIN (i.)

(60) T. B. Mez., ii. 33.—Gentiles, and those that keep small cattle and those that breed the same, are neither helped out [of a pit] nor cast into it. The Minim and the apostates and the betrayers are cast in and not helped out.

This passage is included and discussed in the following.

(61) b. A. Zar. 26ᵃ, ᵇ.—R. Abahu taught, in presence of R. Johanan, Idolaters and shepherds of small cattle are neither helped out nor cast in; but the Minim, and the betrayers and the apostates (mūmarim) are cast in and not helped out. He [R. Johanan] said to him, ' I teach *every lost thing of thy brother* [Deut. xxii. 3] to include the apostate, and thou hast said, they are cast in.' He [R. Joh.] excludes the apostate. Then did he mean to teach this both of the apostate who eats *nebhēlōth* from desire, and of the apostate who eats *nebhēlōth* to offend ? [Because] some suppose

that he who eats *nebhēlōth* to offend is a Min,
some say an apostate.   Rab Aḥa and Rabina
are divided.   One says, ' he who eats *nebhēlōth*
from desire is an apostate, he who eats *nebhēlōth*
to offend is a Min.'   The other says, ' even he
who eats *nebhēlōth* to offend is an apostate.'
Then what is a Min?   He who serves false
gods [lit. gods of the stars].   It is rejoined,
' If he eat a single flea or fly, he is an apostate.'
Now here [*i.e.* in R. Abahu's dictum] it is a
case of eating to offend, and therefore he
includes the apostate ; there [*i.c.* in R.
Johanan's dictum] he [the apostate] wished
to taste what is forbidden [and is therefore
excluded].

Commentary. — The foregoing passage is a fair
specimen, both in matter and style, of a halachic
discussion.   To make the meaning clear, considerable
explanation of detail is necessary.   " Idolaters,"
literally, worshippers of stars, are the ordinary
heathen, Gentiles, and I have used the term Idolaters
for convenience.   " Are neither helped out nor cast
in," *i.e.* out of or into a pit.   Gentiles are not to be
endangered or delivered from danger.   On the other
hand, Minim, betrayers and apostates, are to be
endangered and not to be delivered from danger.   As
regards Minim and betrayers, *i.e.* political informers,
delatores, this is not disputed.   The question is raised,
however, in regard to the apostate (*mūmar*), whether
he ought to be included in the severer treatment
dealt out to Minim.   R. Abahu taught that he should
be included, R. Johanan on the other hand maintained
that he should not.   And the point to be settled

accordingly is whether there is a distinction between a Min and an Apostate. An Apostate (*mūmar*) is one who deliberately transgresses the ceremonial law, especially in regard to food, by eating forbidden things. *Nebhēlōth* means the flesh of an animal that has died of itself, which flesh is forbidden as food [Lev. vii. 24]. A man who eats *nebhēlōth* is undeniably a *mūmar*. But, says the Gemara (in reference to the dictum of R. Johanan, who excluded the *mūmar* from the severer treatment), a *mūmar* may eat *nebhēlōth* either from desire, because he is hungry, or in order to offend, *i.e.* from wilful defiance of God. Does R. Johanan apply his words to both of these? Because some say that the latter is a Min, while some say that he is still only a *mūmar*. The discussion between R. Johanan and R. Abahu must have taken place not later than A.D. 279, the year of R. Johanan's death. The point raised was discussed by R. Aha and Rabina, Babylonian teachers during the early years of the fourth century. The former (R. Aha bar Jacob) held that a *mūmar* who ate *nebhēlōth* from desire was only a *mūmar*, while one who did so to offend was a Min. The latter (Rabina the elder) held that a *mūmar* in either case was only a *mūmar*, and that a Min was a heathen idolater. The Gemara decides, as between R. Johanan and R. Abahu, that even if a man eat a single flea or fly (both of which are forbidden food), he is a *mūmar*; but that. R. Abahu had in view the *mūmar* who ate in order to offend, and therefore declared that such *mūmar* was to be severely dealt with, like a Min or an informer; on the other hand, R. Johanan had in view the *mūmar* who only ate because he wished to taste forbidden

food, and therefore declared that such *mūmar* should
be excluded from the severer treatment.

It should be observed that this whole discussion
arises upon two Baraithas, *i.e.* decisions contemporary
with, but not included in, the Mishnah.   One is that
already quoted at the head of this passage, from T. B.
Mez. ii. 33.   The other is found in T. Horai. i. 5,
and is to the effect that everyone who eats reptiles
(שקצים) is a *mūmar*.[1]   These two passages are considerably earlier than the period of R. Johanan and
R. Abahu, and yet more so than that of Aḥa and
Rabina.   The discussion upon them may therefore
be considered as academic rather than practical, so far,
at all events, as regards the difference between a
mūmar and a Min.   And a comparison of the two
discussions seems to show that whereas R. Johanan
and R. Abahu knew well what a Min was, R. Aḥa
and Rabina did not know, except as a matter of
speculation.   Rabina would not have said that a
Min was an ordinary Gentile if he had had actual
knowledge of the Minim.

So far as regards the subject of Minim, the passage
we have just studied is of very little value, being
concerned only with the subject of the *mūmar*.   It
was necessary, however, to deal with it because of
its mention of Minim, and it could not be made
intelligible without the dry and tedious explanation
just given.

It may be sufficient to refer, without translation, to
a short passage b. Hor. 11ᵃ, where the same question
concerning the *mūmar* and the Min is discussed and
decided in the same way as in the passage just ex-

---

[1] Cod. Erfurt reads 'Meshummad,' משומד.

amined. Nothing fresh is added, and the explanation of the one passage suffices for the other.

The following extract is hardly less dry and difficult than the foregoing; but it must be included, since it brings out a somewhat different aspect of the subject.

GENTILE AND MIN (ii.)

NO DEALINGS WITH THE MINIM

(62) T. Ḥull. ii. 20, 21.—Flesh which is found in the hand of a Gentile (נכרי) is allowed for use, in the hand of a Min it is forbidden for use. That which comes from a house of idolatry, lo! this is the flesh of sacrifices of the dead, because they say, 'slaughtering by a Min is idolatry, their bread is Samaritan bread, their wine is wine offered [to idols], their fruits are not tithed, their books are books of witchcraft, and their sons are bastards. One does not sell to them, or receive from them, or take from them, or give to them; one does not teach their sons trades, and one does not obtain healing from them, either healing of property or healing of life.'

Commentary.—The ordinary Gentile is here distinguished from the Min, and the latter is judged more severely, presumably on the ground that the ceremonial law in regard to food is unknown to the former, and wilfully violated by the latter. The argument is, 'flesh found in the hand of a Min is forbidden for use, because that which is slaughtered

12

by a Min is [for] idolatry, and that which comes from
a house of idolatry is the flesh of sacrifices of the
dead' [cp. Ps. cvi. 28]. The various statements
about the Minim rest upon anonymous authority—
'they say'—and perhaps only represent current
opinion in the time when the Tosephta was compiled.
The context of the passage shows that the Minim
here described are, or at all events include, Jewish
Christians. The passage does not occur, so far as I
know, either in the Mishnah or the Gemaras; but in
b. Ḥull. 41ᵃ, ᵇ there is a parallel to some sentences of
Tosephta preceding the portion just translated. The
Mishnah on the page just mentioned (M. Ḥull. ii. 9.,
b. Ḥull 41ᵃ) says that a hole to catch the blood of
slaughtered animals is not to be made in the street,
שלא יחקה המינין, 'that one may not imitate the Minim.'
(See also j. Kil. 32ᵃ, where the same statement
occurs.)   T. Ḥull. ii. 19 has לא יעשה כן מפני שעושה את חוקי
מינין, "he shall not do so because he would be doing
the statutes of the Minim." Rashi and the other
commentators explain the Minim to be idolaters,
ordinary Gentiles. If this were the meaning, it is
not evident why the usual term for a Gentile was not
used. The reference must be to heretics, possibly,
though not necessarily, Jewish Christians; but I do
not know of any heretical practice such as that
described.

Here may be added a passage which seems to show
that the distinction between Min and Gentile was
scarcely understood in the Babylonian schools.

(63) b. Ḥull. 13ᵇ.—A teacher said, 'a thing
slaughtered by an idolater is *nebhelah* (see
above. p. 175) and he is suspected of being a

Min. Rab Naḥman said that Rabah bar Abuha said there are no Minim among the idolatrous nations. But we show that there are. Say that the majority of idolaters are not Minim. He [R. Naḥman] thought of this that R. Ḥija bar Abba said that R. Joḥanan said, Foreigners outside the land are not idolaters, but follow the custom of their fathers. R. Joseph bar Minjomi said that Rab Naḥman said 'there are no Minim among the idolaters.' In reference to what? Do you say, In reference to slaughtering? Here we have 'a thing slaughtered by a Min': if he be an Israelite, it is forbidden. What if he be an idolater? But [if you mean] in reference to 'casting-down' [into a pit], we have, 'They cast down a Min who is an Israelite'; what if he be an idolater?

Commentary.—In addition to what has been said on the preceding passages in the present group, it is only necessary to say that the foregoing seems to be a purely academical discussion amongst teachers who had no practical experience of Minim. R. Naḥman bar Jacob (died 300 A.D.) taught in Nehardea till A.D. 258, then at Shechanzib till his death. He was the son-in-law of Rabah bar Abuha, the Resh Galutha after 250 A.D. R. Ḥija bar Abba was a pupil of the Palestinian R. Joḥanan, he lived in the latter half of the third century and the beginning of the fourth. R. Joseph bar Minjomi was an otherwise unknown pupil of R. Naḥman. The purpose of the discussion seems to be to reconcile the dictum that there are no Minim among idolaters with the statements of the teacher who said that an idolater who slaughtered an animal for sacrifice was suspected of being a Min. From this latter it would follow that a Min was only a particularly zealous idolater, and this is the view generally taken by Rashi (see his comment on the present passage, and elsewhere). The Gemara accounts for the opinion that there are no Minim amongst idolaters, by a reference to the saying of R. Joḥanan that there is no idolatry outside the Holy Land. This means that the worship of gods other than the God of Israel is only idolatry, false worship, when practised in the Holy Land, by those who might be supposed to know the true religion. There might therefore be, in foreign countries, persons who in Palestine would be called Minim; but they are not so called, because the name implies a distinction which only holds good in Palestine.[1] The Gemara, however, does not accept the dictum that there are no Minim amongst idolatrous nations, and proves their existence by showing that it is implied in certain ordinances referring to Minim who were of Jewish origin. But it is quite plain that the discussion does not rest upon any real knowledge of, or personal contact with, Minim. This will be of importance when we come to gather up the evidence so as to present a general account of the use of the term Minim.

[1] But the same Rabbi Joḥanan says (b. A. Zar. 65ᵃ), 'A proselyte who lets twelve months go by without being circumcised is like a Min among the idolaters.' From which may be inferred that Joḥanan did not hold the opinion that there were no Minim among the idolaters; and, further, that he would define a Min as one who professed to hold the Jewish religion without observing the ceremonial law.

THE JEWISH ORIGIN OF THE MINIM

(64) j. Sanh. 29ᶜ.—R. Joḥanan said, 'Israel did not go into exile until they had been made twenty-four sects of Minim.' What is the reason? *Son of man, I send thee to the children of Israel, to the rebellious peoples that have rebelled against me* [Ezek. ii. 3]. It is not written here, *to the rebellious people*, but *to the rebellious peoples which have rebelled against me, they and their fathers have sinned against me, unto this day.*

Commentary.—This is a little bit of haggadah, not at all a strict exegesis of the text of Ezekiel. So far as I know it does not occur elsewhere in the Gemaras or the Midrashim. It forms part of a long chapter upon that section of the Mishnah which enumerates those persons who shall have no part in the world to come. Amongst these, according to R. Joḥanan, in a passage immediately preceding the one before us, are to be included the followers of Joḥanan ben Kareah [Jer. xliii.]. This opinion is based upon an exposition of Hos. v. 7, not because that text distinctly refers to the son of Kareah, but merely because it might be applied to him. This dictum of R. Joḥanan appears to serve as an excuse for introducing the one before us, which in like manner is only a fanciful deduction from a text in Ezekiel. The prophet speaks of the children of Israel as '*rebellious peoples*' instead of '*people.*' And, whether or not the Hebrew text is correct in giving the plural form, and whatever the prophet may have meant if he did use the plural, it is out of the question that he should have meant what R. Joḥanan deduced from his words. Probably the Rabbi was quite aware of this. His object was not to expound Ezekiel, but to find a Scripture basis, however slight, for an opinion of his own concerning heretics. He knew the Minim, of his own day and earlier, as heretics who disregarded the true religion of Israel as summed up in the Torah. They were rebellious against the God of Israel; and thus, as the word used by Ezekiel was applicable to them, haggadic logic inferred that the rebellion denounced by Ezekiel was that of the Minim. The twenty-four sects of Minim are arrived at by the simple calculation that each of twelve tribes was divided into at least two sections. Hence twenty-four. (This, at all events, is the explanation of the anonymous commentator on the passage in the Palestinian Gemara.) The only point worth noticing is that R. Joḥanan's dictum implies the Jewish origin of Minim. They were not Gentiles, but unfaithful Jews. The passage therefore, while entirely worthless as a comment on Ezekiel, is valuable as evidence for the historical definition of the term Minim, coming from a contemporary authority.

HAGGADAH AGAINST MINUTH

(65) b. A. Zar. 17ª.—*Keep thy way far from her* [Prov. v. 8], this is Minuth; *and come nob near the door of her house*, this is the Government. Some say, *Keep thy way far from her*, this is Minuth and the Government; *and come not near the door of her house*, this is harlotry.

How near [may one come]? R. Ḥisda said,
Four cubits. How do our Rabbis expound
this: 'The price of a harlot'? According to
R. Ḥisda. For R. Ḥisda said, Every harlot
who begins by being hired ends by hiring, as it
is said [Ezek. xvi. 34], *Whereas thou givest hire
and no hire is given to thee and thou art
contrary.* He differs from R. Pedath, for R.
Pedath said, The Torah only forbids approach
for uncovering nakedness, as it is said [Lev.
xviii. 6], *None of you shall approach to any
that is near of kin to him to uncover their
nakedness.* Ulla, when he came from the
college, used to kiss the hands of his sisters.
Some say he kissed their breasts. He [Ulla]
contradicts himself; for Ulla said, Approach in
general is forbidden on the ground of [the
maxim], 'Away, away, Nazirite, they say,
approach not the fence round the vineyard.'

The horseleach hath two daughters [crying],
Give, give [Prov. xxx. 15]. What is '*Give,
give?*' Mar Uqba said, ' It is the voice of two
daughters who cry from Gehinnom, saying in
this world, Give, give.' And who are they?
Minuth and Government. Some say that R.
Ḥisda said that Mar Uqba said, The voice of
Gehinnom crying out and saying, ' Bring me
my two daughters who cry and say in this
world, Give, give.' *None who come to her
return, neither do they attain the paths of life*
[Prov. ii. 19]. But if they do not '*return,*'
how should they '*attain?*' Here is a difficulty. If they do '*return,*' they do not

'*attain' the paths of life.*'   It is to be inferred
that everyone who departs from Minuth dies.
But [there is the case of] a certain woman
who came before R. Ḥisda and said, that the
lightest of the lightest sins she had done was
that her youngest was begotten by her eldest
son.   And he [R. Ḥisda] said, 'Make ready
her shroud!'   But she did not die.   From her
saying, 'the lightest of the lightest sins she had
done,' presumably Minuth was still in her;
and because she had not thoroughly turned
from it she did not die.   Some say [one who
turns] from Minuth dies, [one who turns] from
sin [does] not.   But [there is the case of] the
woman who came before R. Ḥisda, and he
said, 'Make a shroud for her!' and she died.
From her saying, 'the lightest of the lightest
sins she had done,' presumably Minuth was
still in her, and she died [in parting] from
it and not from her sin.   But it is tradition,
they said, concerning El'azar ben Dordaia
. . . .[1] he bowed his head between his knees
and groaned with weeping until his soul
departed.   And there went forth a Bath Qol
[voice from heaven], saying, 'Rabbi El'azar
ben Dordaia is summoned to the life of the
world to come.'   Here he was in sin, and
died [in parting from it].   There [referring to
the incident omitted], so long as he clave to
the woman, it was like Minuth.   Rabbi wept
and said, 'One man earns heaven in how many

[1] Here follows an obscene story to show how a great sinner may repent
and yet die.

years! and another in a single hour. It is not enough for repentant sinners that they should be received, but they must also be called Rabbi!'

Commentary.—This passage forms the continuation of No. (46), where is related the arrest of R. Eliezer for Minuth. But whereas that famous incident is mentioned no less than five times in the Talmud and Midrash, the present passage (with the exception of the first few sentences) occurs, so far as I know, only here.

The haggadic interpretation of Prov. v. 8 would seem to be due to R. Eliezer himself.[1] For he says (see above, p. 139), 'I transgressed that which is written in the Torah, *Keep thy way far from her*, this is Minuth ; *and go not near the door of her house*, this is the Government.' R. Eliezer's misfortune was due to both these evils ; he had been contaminated with heresy, and was a prisoner in the power of the state. The variation, according to which the first half of the verse refers to both Minuth and the Government, while the second denotes harlotry, is probably much later, and seems to belong to a time when Minuth and the Empire were blended by the adoption of Christianity as the state religion. That this great change did not pass unnoticed in the Rabbinical literature we shall have evidence later on.

R. Ḥisda, whose opinions are cited more than

---

[1] According to Bacher, A. d. Tann., ii. 310 n., the application of Prov. v. 8 to Minuth is ascribed to R. Jehoshua ben Qorḥa, in "the second version of the Aboth de R. Nathan 7ᵇ." This reference I have not been able to verify. R. Eliezer was considerably earlier in date than R. Jeh. b. Qorḥa.

once, was a Babylonian whom we have already several times met with. In conjunction with R. Huna, he presided over the college at Sura. He was born A.D. 217, and died A.D. 309. He was a pupil of Rab, and also of Mar Uqba, whose name occurs in the present passage. R. Pedath, probably the elder of two who bear the same name, was a Babylonian contemporary with Rabbi in Palestine. He is scarcely known except as the father of the more distinguished R. El'azar ben Pedath. Ulla is Ulla ben Ishmael, of Palestinian origin (see Bacher, Ag. d. Bab. Amor., p. 93, n. 3), who afterwards migrated to Babylonia. He was not liked in the country of his adoption, a fact which perhaps may account for the rather uncivil reference to him.

The maxim, 'Away, away, Nazirite, they say; approach not the fence round the vineyard,' is quoted b. Shabb. 13ª, b. Pes. 40ᵇ, b. Jeb. 46ª, b. B. Mez. 92ª, b. A. Zar. 58ᵇ, Bamm. r. x. 8 p. 38ᶜ. It means, 'Keep away from temptation,' the Nazirite, of course, being forbidden to taste wine. The earliest authority for it is R. Johanan (b. A. Zar. 58ᵇ, 59ª), who, however, refers to it as a familiar saying. It is indeed called a proverb (מתלא, משל) in the last of the above-mentioned passages, and probably occurs elsewhere; but I have not been able to find it.

The explanation of the text Prov. xxx. 15 is not very clear, except to this extent, that it is interpreted of Minuth and the Empire, as in the case of the former text [Prov. v. 8]. This interpretation appears to be due to Mar Uqba (see above), and to have been handed down in more than one form, for one of which the authority is R. Ḥisda, a disciple of Mar Uqba. It should be noted that R. Ḥisda was also the authority in the Babylonian schools for the story about the mother of Jesus (see above, No. (1), p. 36), and for the remark about Jesus in reference to 'burning his food' (see above, No. (9), p. 56). Further, in b. Ber. 12ᵃ (a passage which will be examined hereafter, p. 308), the same R. Ḥisda mentions the Minim. These facts serve to show in what direction R. Ḥisda was looking when he endorsed Mar Uqba's interpretation of the text in Prov. xxx. 15. It is possible, and perhaps probable, that this interpretation was of Palestinian origin; at all events, hostility against both Minuth and the Empire would naturally be more bitter in the west than in the east. At the same time it must be admitted that there does not seem to be any trace of this particular haggadah in the Palestinian Midrash. R. Ḥisda improved on Mar Uqba's interpretation of the text. The earlier teacher said that the 'two daughters' who cried 'give, give' were Minuth and the Empire. This left it uncertain what was meant by the 'horseleach' whose daughters they were. R. Ḥisda said that the horseleach meant Gehinnom [Gehenna, which in this case may be fairly rendered Hell], 'who cries and says, Bring me my two daughters who cry and say in this world Give, give'; in other words, Heresy and the Empire are the rapacious offspring of Hell, and Hell cries out for them.

Following on this text is an interpretation of Prov. ii. 19, on similar lines, *None who come to her return, neither do they attain the paths of life.* Like

the preceding haggadah, it is introduced without any
mention of a Rabbi as its author.   But in this case
the source can be traced in the Palestinian tradition.
In the Midrash Qoh. r. [on i. 8, a long passage of
which use will be made hereafter], occurs the following, which will be seen at once to be a close parallel
to the incident at present under consideration.

(66) Qoh. r. i. 8.—The case of a woman who came
to R. Eliezer to become a proselyte.   She said
to him, ' Rabbi, receive me.'   He said to her,
' Relate to me thy deeds.'   She said, ' My
youngest son is by my eldest son.'   He
stormed at her.   She went to R. Jehoshua
and he received her.   His disciples said to
him, ' R. Eliezer drove her away and thou
receivest'!   He said to them, ' When her
mind was set on becoming a proselyte she
no longer lived to the world [?], as it is
written [Prov. ii. 19], *None that go unto her
return again, and if they return, they do not
attain the paths of life.*'

Commentary.—This passage occurs in the midst of
a long series of references to Minuth, all of which,
moreover, are concerned with Palestinian personages.
It is, on the face of it, much more likely that a
woman desiring to abjure Minuth—in this instance
Christian heresy—should go to a Palestinian Rabbi
rather than to a Babylonian like Ḥisda.   At the same
time it is true that the Midrash on Qoheleth is later
than the Babylonian Gemara, and occasionally quotes
from it (see Zunz, G. Vortr., p. 265).   But, in the
present instance, the Midrash gives the shorter form
of the story; and the version in the Babylonian

Gemara, at present under consideration, is not only longer, but appears to be introduced as merely a case for discussion. Bacher (Ag. d. Tann., i. 188 n. 4,) regards the version in Qoh. r. as the original. If so, then this haggadic interpretation of Prov. ii. 19 is traced back to the second century. And seeing that the haggadah on Prov. v. 8 is due to R. Eliezer, the contemporary of R. Jehoshua, it is at least probable that the interpretation of Prov. xxx. 15 also dates from the same period, and from one or other of the two famous Rabbis already named. In that case R. Ḥisda merely added his own comment upon each text to a tradition brought from Palestine.

We resume now the discussion of the passage in the Babylonian Gemara. The object of the argument is to decide whether they who recant from Minuth die or not. The Gemara says, " It is to be inferred that they die." Then by way of proof to the contrary is introduced the case of the woman who came before R. Ḥisda, accusing herself of gross crimes. It is to be observed that the Gemara does not know whether this woman really died or not, and it attempts to prove its point on either supposition. It seems likely that what came before R. Ḥisda was not the woman herself, but the story of the woman who had gone to R. Eliezer and R. Jehoshua, mentioned merely as a case in point, and submitted to him for his opinion. He gave his opinion (viz. that she would die) in the words, ' Make ready her shroud ! ' If, as a matter of fact, she did not die, then, says the Gemara, she was still unrepentant ; if she did die, then she died in parting from her heresy and not from her sin. This uncertainty as to whether she died or not can be traced to the original story in

Qoh. r. There R. Jehoshua, when asked why he received her, said, ' When her mind was set on becoming a proselyte, she no longer lived *to the world*' (לעולם). I have translated these words literally, but I do not feel certain what exactly is meant by ' to the world.' The Rabbinical literature does not recognise, so far as I know, the sharp distinction between ' the world' and the spiritual life which is common in the N.T., especially in the Fourth Gospel. So that possibly here, as elsewhere, לעולם should be translated ' for ever.' But still I believe that the sense which R. Jehoshua intended is given by the translation ' to the world,' *i.e.* he meant that the woman by her repentance died to her past life and would never live in it again. This is the opinion of Hamburger (Encykl., ii. 514). Apparently this was not understood in the Babylonian schools, hence the uncertainty as to whether or not the woman really died.

The story about R. El'azar ben Dordaia (which I have not transcribed or translated because it is gross and has no bearing on the main subject) is introduced by way of an objection to the argument that the woman did not die because of her sin. El'azar ben Dordaia, it is urged, sinned no less grievously, and was forgiven, but yet he died. The objection is met by saying that while he was in his sin it was, as it were, Minuth to him, and he died in parting from it, not merely in repenting of his sin. This is mere hairsplitting, and shows that in the Babylonian school where this discussion was carried on there was only a vague notion of what Minuth was, and an inclination to identify it with sexual immorality.

Note that El'azar ben Dordaia was not, strictly speaking, a Rabbi, but was only greeted with that title when summoned by the divine forgiveness to heaven. And note finally the jealousy of Rabbi, *i.e.* R. Jehudah ha-Qadosh, whose epithet of 'The Holy' would lead one to expect something different.

MINIM AND CIRCUMCISION

(67) Shem. r. xix. 4, p. 36ᵈ.—Because Israelites who are circumcised do not go down to Gehinnom. R. Berachjah said, 'That the Minim and the wicked of Israel may not say, "We are circumcised, we shall not go down to Gehinnom," what does the Holy One, Blessed be He, do? He sends an angel and effaces their circumcision, and they go down to Gehinnom, as it is said [Ps. lv. 20], *He hath put forth his hand against such as be at peace with him, he hath profaned his covenant*; and when Gehinnom sees that their circumcision is a matter of doubt, it opens its mouth and swallows them alive and *opens its mouth without measure*' [Isa. v. 14].

Commentary.—R. Berachjah was a younger contemporary of Abahu in the early years of the fourth century, and, like him, lived in Palestine. There were indeed two Rabbis of this name, of whom the elder lived perhaps half a century earlier. The one who is the more frequently mentioned (especially in the Midrash) is probably the younger.

The passage before us is of no great importance

in itself, except that it implies the Jewish origin
of the Minim. Circumcision would not concern any
Gentile. The Minim are evidently Jewish heretics,
and, though not necessarily in every case Christians,
must certainly have included some. If so, then it is
important to notice that as late as the fourth century
there were Jewish Christians who were circumcised.
The conclusion is either that the practice was kept
up amongst Jewish Christian families, or else that the
Jewish Christian community received very numerous
proselytes. The former is the more likely, because
the term Minim, whatever it may denote, must at
least refer to the main body of heretics, so called,
whoever they were, and not to those who joined them
from time to time.

THE PRINCIPLE OF MINUTH : THE HOUSE OF STRAW

(68) Bamm. r. xviii. 17, p. 75ᵈ.—R. El'azar said,
There was in them [*i.e.* Doeg and Ahithophel]
the principle of Minuth. What were they
like? Like a house filled with straw, and
there were openings in the house, and the
straw entered them. After a time that straw
which was inside those openings began to
come forth. But all knew that that had
been a house [full] of straw. So Doeg and
Ahithophel. From the beginning no Mitzvoth
[precepts of the Law] were in them ; although
they had been made Sons of the Law, they
were as in their beginning, for *wickedness was
in the midst of* them, within them [cp. Ps.
lv. 11].

Commentary. — The Midrash on Exodus dates, according to Zunz (G. Vortr., p. 261), from the twelfth century, but contains material that is much earlier. The passage before us is part of such earlier material. It is not indeed to be found in exactly the same words in the older literature ; but the substance of it is contained in the Palestinian Gemara, and there are traces of it in that of Babylon. In j. Sanh. 27ᵈ is the following :—

> (69) The Epiquros : R. Joḥanan and R. Lazar, one said, '[He is] like one who says These Scribes'!; the other said, '[He is] like one who says These Rabbis'! R. El'azar and R. Shemuel bar Naḥman, one said, '[He is] like an arch of stones ; as soon as one stone is loosened all are loosened.' The other said, '[He is] like a house full of straw. Although you clear away the straw from it, the chaff inside [clings to and] loosens the walls.'

This latter passage carries us back to the third century. R. Lazar is the same as R. El'azar, and both names denote R. El'azar ben Pedath. He was a Babylonian who came to Palestine and taught in Tiberias, where he died in A.D. 279, about the same time as R. Joḥanan. R. Shemuel bar Naḥman was a Palestinian (see Bacher, A. d. Pal. Amor., i. 477), contemporary with R. Joḥanan and R. El'azar, though perhaps somewhat younger, as he appears to have been living in A.D. 286 (Bacher).

In both passages the subject of discussion is the heretic or the freethinker (on the relation of Epiquros to Min, see above, p. 121 fol.). A Jewish Epiquros was practically the same as a Min. The point of

13

comparison between the heretic and the house full
of straw is this, that the original character of each
remains unchanged in spite of changes in outward
appearance or condition.   Though the straw be
removed, the chaff remains; though the heretic put
on an appearance of piety, the taint of heresy is in
him still.   Thus Doeg and Ahithophel are said to
have in them the principle of Minuth, the taint of
heresy, in spite of the fact that they were made 'sons
of the Torah,' *i.e.* brought up in the Jewish religion.
In b. Ḥag. 16ᵇ it is said of these two that there was
'a gnawing passion in their heart' (טינא בלבם), *i.c.* a
secret desire to rebel, in spite of outward conformity.
We have already seen (above, p. 70) that Doeg and
Ahithophel are treated in the Rabbinical literature as
types of heresy, and that there is probably some
covert reference to Christianity in the condemnation
of them.   The present passage does not contradict,
though it does not confirm, the latter supposition.
The Gemara does not explain in what the ' principle
of Minuth' consisted, but leaves it to be inferred, or
rather takes it for granted as being generally known,
on the strength of other references to it elsewhere.
The simile of the arch of stones is used by R. Joḥanan,
j. M. Qat. 83ᶜ, though for a different purpose.   The
simile of the house of straw is ascribed, in the second
passage above (j. Sanh. 27ᵈ), to R. Shemuel bar
Naḥman, and that of the arch of stones to R. El'azar.
It is probable that these two should be interchanged,
in which case the version in Bamm. r. would be in
harmony with that in the Palestinian Gemara.

SCRIPTURAL INDICATIONS OF MINUTH

(70) Siphri, § 115, p. 35ª.—*And ye shall not walk after your heart* [Num. xv. 39], this is Minuth, according as it is said [Ecc. vii. 26], *And I find a thing more bitter than death, even the woman whose heart is snares and nets, and whose hands are bands,* and *the king shall rejoice in God* [Ps. lxiii. 11.]

Commentary.—The book Siphri is almost contemporaneous with the Mishnah (see Zunz, G. Vortr., p. 46). It was compiled, or rather edited, somewhat later; but parts of its contents are older. It may be dated about the middle of the third century. The above passage is the earliest authority for the interpretation of the phrase *after your heart* in the sense of heresy. This really amounts to a definition that Minuth consists in following the dictates of one's own selfish nature, as against those of the lawful authority. The result of so doing is, indirectly, the rejection of beliefs and practices enjoined on those who hold the true religion. A Min, accordingly, disregards the authority of the Rabbis as teachers of religion and expounders of the Torah, both written and unwritten, and also maintains doctrines and practices which are not those of the true religion. This dictum, that ' after your heart ' denotes Minuth, became a sort of canon of exegesis in the later literature. In support of it Siphri quotes two texts, Ecc. vii. 26 and Ps. lxiii. 11. The first of these does not appear to have any reference to heresy; but the citation of it may be explained either on the ground

of the symbolism common in the O.T., which represents religious unfaithfulness under the figure of
fornication, or on the ground of the immorality
with which heretics, and particularly Christians, were
frequently charged. The second text needs to be
given in full in order that its bearing on Minuth may
be understood. It runs: *But the king shall rejoice in
God ; everyone that sweareth by him shall glory, for
the mouth of them that speak lies shall be stopped.*
A verse of which the learned editor of Siphri rather
naïvely says that it clearly refers to Minuth.

The above passage is referred to in b. Ber. 12^b,
where, however, the text cited in support of the interpretation is Ps. xiv. 1, *The fool hath said in his heart
there is no God.*[1] This gives at least one of the
implications of Minuth, for, if the Minim did not
theoretically deny the existence of God, it was quite
sufficient (as later Christian history abundantly shows)
that they should be heretics in order to be at once
branded as atheists. Rashi, on the passage in Ber.
12^b, says :—Minuth : those who turn the sense of the
Torah into an exposition of falsehood and error.

There is a further reference to this interpretation
of the phrase 'after your heart' in the Midrash
Vajiq. r. as follows :—

(72) Vajiqr. r., § 28, p. 40^c, ^d.—R. Benjamin ben
      Levi said they sought to withdraw the Book
      Qoheleth because they found in it things that

---

[1] Cp. also (71) Siphri, § 320, p. 137^b top: [Deut. xxxii. 21], *I will
provoke them with a foolish nation.* These are the Minim. And he said
thus [Ps. xiv. 1], *The fool hath said in his heart, There is no God.*

In b. Jebam., 63^b the same occurs : the application of Ps. xiv. 1 is
ascribed to R. Eliezer, *i.e.*, probably, R. Eliezer ben Horqenos in the first
century. He had already applied Prov. v. 8 to Minuth. See above, p. 139.

lead to Minuth. They said, Ought Solomon
to have said thus? [Ecc. xi. 9], *Rejoice, O
young man, in thy youth; and let thy heart
cheer thee in the days of thy youth.* Moses
said [Num. xv. 39], *And ye shall not walk
after your heart*; and Solomon said [Ecc., *ut
supra*], *Walk in the ways of thy heart, and in
the sight of thine eyes.* But the band is loosed,
and there is no judgment and no judge. As
soon as he [Solomon, in the same verse] said,
*But know, that for all these things God will
bring thee into judgment*, they said, Solomon
hath spoken well.

R. Shemuel bar Naḥmani said they sought
to withdraw the Book Qoheleth, because they
found in it things that lead to Minuth. They
said, Ought Solomon to have said thus? *What
profit is there to a man of his labour* [Ecc. i.
3]. Perhaps he means even of his labour in
hearing Torah? They said again, If he had
said *Of all his labour*, and had then been
silent, we should have said he does not say this
except in reference to his labour which does
not benefit; but the labour of hearing Torah
does benefit.

Commentary.—Little needs to be added to what
has already been said. R. Benjamin ben Levi was a
Palestinian of the fourth century (see Bacher., Ag. d.
Pal.|Amor., iii. 661 fol.). R. Shemuel bar Naḥmani
is written by mistake for R. Shemuel bar Jitzḥaq (see
Bacher, as above, p. 662, n. 2), who was contemporary
with R. Abahu, and thus lived at the beginning of
the fourth century. The proposal to withdraw the

book of Ecclesiastes, *i.e.* to declare it uncanonical, is referred to in b. Shabb. 30^b. ' They ' who desired to do this are ' the Wise,' *i.e.* the Rabbis.   In the passage in b. Shabbath the reason given is merely the alleged contradiction of certain texts in the book, not any tendency to Minuth.   In the Mishnah, Jad. iii. 8, the discussion which ended in the retention of the book is said to have taken place " on the day when R. E'lazar ben Azariah was made Nasi," *i.e.* at Jabneh, about 100 A.D. (see below, p. 386 n.).   It is worth noting that R. Gamliel II., who was temporarily deposed in favour of R. El'azar ben Azariah, was the same who ordered the composition of the formula against the Minim (see above, No. 38, p. 126 fol.).   It is thus at least conceivable that an alleged heretical tendency in the book of Ecclesiastes may have been one reason in favour of declaring it uncanonical. The fact at all events remains, that though the book was admitted, the suspicion of its orthodoxy was not wholly quenched, as is seen in these references and explanations in the later literature.

The passage just translated appears in a slightly different form in the Midrash Qoh. r., on i. 3 (p. 1^c), and also in Pesiqta 68^b and Pesiqta r., § 18, p. 90^b. These add nothing of importance to what has already been given.

(73) b. Sanh. 38^b.—R. Jehudah said that Rab said the first man was a Min, as it is said [Gen. iii. 9], *And God spake unto the man and said, Where [art thou]*?   Whither hath thy heart inclined ?

Commentary.—The meaning of this haggadah is that the sin of Adam, in disobeying the command of

God, was the same in kind as that of the heretic, who rejects the divinely-appointed authority.

This saying does not occur, so far as I know, anywhere else, not even in Ber. r., which mentions and comments on the text. R. Jehudah is R. Jehudah ben Jehesq'el, a disciple of Rab, already frequently mentioned.

Immediately following on the passage are two other sayings, one that Adam effaced his circumcision, the other that he denied God. Both of these may be taken as expansions of the statement that he was a heretic.

In Ber. r. xix. 1, p. 42^b, it is said that the serpent [Gen iii.] was also a Min. The idea is the same.

In Shem. r., p. 73^c, ^{d}, Moses is accused of being a Min, because he expressed a doubt as to the resurrection of the dead. This passage will be dealt with later (see p. 315).

SIGNS OF MINUTH; LITURGICAL VARIATIONS

(74) M. Meg., iv. 8, 9.—He that saith I will not go before the Ark in coloured garments, shall not do so in white ones. [He that refuseth to do so] in sandals, shall not do so even barefoot. And he that maketh his tephillin round, it is danger, and there is no [fulfilling of] commandment in it. If he place it [the tephillin] upon his forehead or upon the palm of his hand, lo, this is the way of Minuth. If he cover it with gold, and place it on his robe, lo, this is the way of the Ḥitzonim.

If one say, 'The good shall bless thee,' lo,

this is the way of Minuth. [If one say],
'Thy mercies reach to the nest of the bird,'
'Let thy name be remembered for good,'
'We praise, we praise,' they silence him.

Commentary.—This is one of the few passages in
which the Mishnah refers directly to Minuth. It is
also one of the most obscure. To 'go before the ark'
is to stand up to read the prayers in the synagogue.
The Mishnah enumerates several signs by which a
reader, who is inclined to heresy, can be detected.
The difficulty is to identify the form of heresy referred
to. Those who desire to wear white garments when
reading the prayers may be the Essenes, who are
said to have always worn a white robe. This explanation, however, will not apply to those who desire to
be barefoot when they read. It is again quite uncertain what heretics are censured in the reference to
those 'who make their tephillin round.' Of those
who wear the tephillin on the forehead or on the palm
of the hand, it is said 'this is the way of Minuth.'
It is remarkable that the Gemara, the earliest commentary on the Mishnah, can give no explanation of
these allusions. It only says (b. Meg. 24[b]) that the
reason for the prohibition is 'lest Minuth should be
propagated,' a reason which is obvious in itself, and
does not throw light on the difficulty. The Gemara
is altogether silent on the last clause, 'he who
covereth his tephillin with gold, lo, this is the way of
the Ḥitzonim.'[1] The name Ḥitzonim means simply
'outsiders,' and whether or not it refers to the Essenes,

---

[1] In b. Gitt. 45[b], and b. Menaḥ 42[b], the phrase, 'cover the tephillin with
gold,' occurs and is understood quite literally. Nothing is there said about
the Ḥitzonim. Such tephillin are simply said to be not according to the
halachah.

it is surely not, as Edersheim suggests, the origin of
that name (see L. and T. J. M., i. 333). He explains
'cover the tephillin with gold' as equivalent to
'praying at sunrise,' which is a somewhat strained interpretation. I do not think it is possible to identify
the various forms of heresy, or even to say with
certainty that separate forms of heresy are referred
to. It is conceivable that the Mishnah only meant to
point out that certain practices were not in accordance
with the accepted usage, and therefore that those who
adopted those usages laid themselves open to suspicion of heresy. Yet, on the other hand, considering
how many points of ritual were, if not open questions,
at least subjects of discussion between the Rabbis,
it is noteworthy that the practices referred to in
this passage are condemned without qualification ; so
that the conclusion can hardly be avoided, that the
Mishnah had some particular, and not merely general,
intention in its reference.

It is not, however, only in aberrations from prescribed ritual that signs of Minuth were, according
to the Mishnah, to be detected. Certain liturgical
formulæ were also branded as heretical. The first
of these is, 'The good shall bless thee.' The Babylonian Gemara in Megillah does not notice this
formula. The Palestinian Gemara gives only the
brief comment, 'two powers' (שתי רשויות). This
is a phrase of which several instances will be presented later. It denotes the heretical doctrine that
there are two divine powers in heaven ; in other words,
the denial of the unity of God. If this is the intention of the words in the Mishnah, 'the good,' which
is plural, refers to God, and, of course, implies more

than one. 'Thee' in this case refers to the worshipper. But since, in all the other formula quoted, it is God who is addressed, it seems likely that it is so in this phrase as well, and that 'the good' are the human beings who bless God. The heresy would seem to consist in the implication that God is blessed only by the good, and not by all his creatures, including the bad. This is the explanation of Rashi (*ad loc.*), who, however, does not say in what way the wicked bless God. Tosaphoth accepts this, but gives the alternative view of the Palestinian Gemara. It is worthy of note that only in connexion with this formula is it said, 'lo, this is the way of Minuth.' In connexion with the others it is said merely, 'they silence him' [who uses them]. The next formula is, 'Thy mercies extend over the nest of the bird' [or extend 'to' the nest, etc.]. The Palestinian Gemara explains this to imply either an expression of jealousy, God has mercy on the birds but not on me'; or secondly, a limitation of the mercy of God, as if it extended only to the nest of the bird; or thirdly, a misrepresentation of the purpose of God, by saying that what are really the decrees of God are only acts of mercy. The Babylonian Gemara gives the same alternatives. (See also Mishnah Ber. v. 3, and the two Gemaras thereupon, where these heretical formulas are mentioned in a passage almost identical with the one under consideration.) Of the three alternatives, the last is probably the right explanation, and the heresy consists in saying that God acts towards his creatures not as one who commands, but as one who loves. When we remember the Pauline antithesis of Law and Grace, or, indeed, the general N.T. doctrine that God is love, it is easy to understand why such an innocent and beautiful phrase should be deemed heretical.

The third formula is, ' Let thy name be remembered for good,' or ' on account of what is good.' This is explained by saying that a man ought to thank God for the ill as well as for the good that befalls him. Whether heresy or only want of piety is condemned here, I do not know. The Gemaras agree in the explanation.

The fourth formula is, ' We praise, we praise.' Here the ground of objection is the repetition of the word, as implying that there are two who are to be praised. The Gemaras agree that the reference is to the doctrine of ' two powers.' And the Palestinian Gemara adds, in the name of R. Shemuel bar Jitzhaq, the reason why those who use the formula are to be silenced, ' *That the mouth of those who speak lies may be stopped*,' Ps. lxiii. 11. (For the application of this text to Minuth, see above, p. 196.)

The formulæ above mentioned are heretical variations introduced into the liturgy ; and they must date back to a time when Jews and Jewish Christians worshipped together in the Synagogue, or, at all events, to a time when the presence of such heretics might reasonably be feared. I say Jewish Christians, because they were the class of heretics most likely to be affected by regulations concerning the liturgy to be used in worship. No doubt other heretics would be detected if any such were present ; but the Jewish Christians were the most important. We may reasonably connect the censure of these liturgical formulæ with the enactment of the 'formula concerning the Minim' (see above, p. 125 fol.), and refer them, or rather the Mishnah enumerating them, to the end of the first century. This may account for the fact that the Gemara cannot explain the reasons of the various censures upon ritual, and can only partially explain those upon the liturgical formulæ. When the Gemaras were compiled, Jewish Christians had probably ceased to worship with Jews in the synagogues. Their aberrations in ritual were wholly forgotten and unknown, and only some knowledge of their aberrations in doctrine remained.

Signs of Minuth; Liturgical Omissions

(75) j. Ber. 9ᶜ.—R. Aḥa and R. Judah ben Pazi were sitting in a certain synagogue. There came one and went before the Ark, and left out one benediction. They came and asked R. Simon. He said to him [sic], in the name of R. Jehoshua ben Levi, " When a servant of the congregation omits two or three benedictions, they do not make him turn back. There exists difference of opinion.[1]   In general, they do not make any one turn back, except him who has omitted 'that makest the dead to live,' 'that bringest down the proud,' 'that buildest Jerusalem.' I say that [such a one] is a Min."

Commentary.—The incident here related belongs to the beginning of the fourth century, or possibly

---

[1] אשכח תני ופליג.   'One is found teaching and differing.' I have not found this technical phrase explained anywhere, and only give what seems to me to be the meaning.

the end of the third. R. Simon is R. Simon bar
Pazi, who was a disciple of R. Jehoshua ben Levi,
and younger contemporary of R. Johanan. He
owned land in the south of Palestine (j. Demai 25ᵃ, ᵇ),
and lived and taught there. R. Judah ben Pazi was
his son—Pazi being the general family name, and
not that of the father alone (see Bacher, A. d. P. A.,
ii. 438, n. 2]. R. Judah b. P. and R. Aḥa both
dwelt in Lūd (Lydda) (j. Sanh. 18ᶜ, ᵈ), and there,
no doubt, was the synagogue referred to in the
story. In reciting the liturgy, the reader omitted
a single one of the [eighteen] benedictions. The
question arose whether he ought to be made to turn
back and recite what he had left out. R. Simon was
consulted, presumably after the service was ended,
and he gave in answer a dictum of his teacher R.
Jehoshua b. Levi, that when a servant of the congregation omits two or three benedictions, he is not
to be turned back. It is not clear to me whether
what follows is part of R. Simon's answer, or part
of R. Jehoshua's opinion, or the opinion of the compilers of the Gemara. But, whichever it be, the
opinion is clearly expressed that if a man leaves
out the benedictions referring to ' the raising of the
dead,' ' the casting down of the proud,' and ' the
building of Jerusalem,' that man is a Min. It will
be shown hereafter that the doctrine of the resurrection was one of the main points in dispute between
Jews and Minim. The words ' that bringest down
the proud ' are the conclusion of the formula against
the Minim (j. Ber. 8ᶜ, see p. 136 above). The
formula concerning the ' building of Jerusalem ' included the prayer for the restoration of the throne

of David ; but it is not clear to me why the omission of that prayer should be characteristic of a Min. So far as I know, the point is never raised in the polemical discussions of Jews with Minim.

It does not appear that the reader in this story was suspected of being a Min on account of his omissions, at least, if he were so suspected, nothing came of the suspicion. The incident is made the occasion for remarking that certain omissions do point to heresy. On the whole, I am inclined to believe that the opinion to this effect is the opinion of R. Simon, and that his reply might be paraphrased thus :—' R. Jehoshua's decision does not wholly meet the present case. As to that, there is a difference of opinion. In general, I should say that a reader ought not to be stopped except he leave out the three benedictions specified, because in that case I say he is a Min.' It should be observed that this does not imply that Jews and Minim were still in the habit of worshipping together, and therefore does not contradict what was said above (p. 204). The Minim had their own places of assembly, and did not mix with the Jews. But, of course, it might happen, and probably did happen from time to time, that a Jew inclined gradually towards heresy and joined the Minim. His heresy might show itself in the recital of the liturgy before he finally broke with the Synagogue. There was, accordingly, reason for keeping up the use of the detective formula (see above, p. 135) ; and it would seem that two other prayers, of the eighteen, were made use of for the same purpose.

THE KINGDOM TURNED TO MINUTH

(76) M. Sotah, ix. 15.—R. Eliezer the Great
says . . . . When the Messiah is at hand,
insolence will abound . . . . and the Kingdom will be turned to Minuth, etc.
[The latter phrase occurs also b. Sanh. 97ᵇ,
Shir. r. on ii. 13, p. 17ᶜ, and Der. eretz zuta,
c. x. In these cases it is ascribed to R.
Nehemjah. In b. Sanh. 97 ᵇ it is repeated
by R. Jitzḥaq.]

Commentary.—This passage forms part of a piece
of haggadah appended to the tractate Soṭah in the
Mishnah. Bacher (A. d. Tann., ii. 222, n. 4) seems
to regard it as not properly belonging to the Mishnah,
an opinion which I do not venture to call in question.
The first part of the haggadic appendix contains re-
flections on the deaths of several Rabbis, ending
with that of Jehudah ha-Qadosh, the editor of the
Mishnah. Then follows a retrospect of the religious
decline which set in after the destruction of the
Temple. By a natural transition, there follows a
forecast of the troubles that will immediately precede the coming of the Messiah.[1] And one of the
signs of his coming will be that the Kingdom. *i.c.*
the Roman Empire, will be turned to Minuth. As
the text stands, the author of the saying about the
Kingdom is R. Eliezer the Great, *i.c.* R. Eliezer
ben Horqenos, who has been already frequently

[1] On the doctrine that the advent of the Messiah will be heralded by woes
and calamities, see Weber, System d. Altsyn. Theologie, 336 ; Drummond,
Jewish Messiah, p. 209 fol. Matt. xxiv. is almost entirely on the lines of
current Jewish belief.

mentioned as one of the leading teachers at the end of the first century. No other Rabbi is named until the passage containing the forecast of future trouble is completed. But it is extremely doubtful if the whole passage is from R. Eliezer. The sudden changes of language, from Hebrew to Aramaic and back again, seem to show that different traditions are combined. Probably only the words in Aramaic are his, and perhaps not even those. The reference to the Kingdom occurs in the Hebrew part. It is to be observed that although the remark about the Kingdom occurs elsewhere (see references above), it is nowhere ascribed to R. Eliezer, except in the present instance. In all the other instances it is given as the dictum of R. Nehemjah, who was a disciple of R. Aqiba, in the middle or latter half of the second century. Even as the text stands in the Mishnah, it is allowable to argue that the words are not expressly ascribed to R. Eliezer, though at first sight they seem to be. The most probable explanation is that of Bacher (loc. cit.), viz., that the saying is due to R. Nehemjah, that it, along with other similar sayings of his, was incorporated with the references to the destruction of the Temple (which may have been said by R. Eliezer), and the whole passage added to the haggadic conclusion of tractate Sotah. That the addition is a very late one is shown by the fact that allusion is made to the death of Rabbi, i.e. R. Jehudah ha-Qadosh who edited the Mishnah. Thus the passage, although included in the received text of the Mishnah, is really, as Bacher says, a Baraitha (see above, p. 21). It is curious that the Palestinian Gemara does not comment on either the reference to the destruction of the Temple or the forecast of the advent of the Messiah; certainly not in connexion with the end of tractate Sotah, and I believe not elsewhere. The same is true of the Babylonian Gemara.

As to the statement itself that the kingdom shall be turned to Minuth, there is here no reference to the proclamation by Constantine the Great in favour of Christianity, A.D. 313. R. Nehemjah lived considerably more than a century before that event. There is not the slightest reason to suspect so late an addition to the text of the Mishnah as this would imply, nor to father it on R. Nehemjah if it had been made. The conversion of the Empire to Minuth is merely a way of saying that the spread of heresy and the consequent decay of religion will be universal. R. Jitzhaq, who also mentions the conversion of the Empire to Minuth as a sign of the advent of the Messiah, probably lived till the time when Constantine the Great, by his successive edicts, virtually adopted Christianity as the religion of the state. But R. Jitzhaq, if he knew of the event, makes no special reference to it. He merely repeats the words as R. Nehemjah had said them. All, therefore, that can be learned from the passage is, that Minuth was in the second century sufficiently known and dreaded, that it could serve as an illustration of the calamities which were to herald the coming of the Messiah.[1]

[1] Bacher (A. d. P. Am., ii. 481, n. 5) gives a saying of R. Abba b. Kahana: "When thou seest in the land of Israel the seats in the schools filled with Minim, then look for the feet of the Messiah," Shir. r. on viii. 9; Ech. r. on i. 13. The present texts in these places have, not 'Minim' but 'Babliim,' *i.e.* Babylonians. Bacher, on the authority of Perles, says that this is an ancient gloss, and that 'Minim' is the original reading. Yet he shows some hesita-

14

Here may be added a reference to Christian Rome.

ROME PRETENDING TO BE THE TRUE ISRAEL

(77) j. Nedar. 38ª.—R. Aḥa in the name of R.
Huna: Esau the wicked will put on his
'tallith' and sit with the righteous in Paradise
in the time to come; and the Holy One,
blessed be He, will drag him and cast him
forth from thence. What is the meaning?
*Though thou mount on high as the eagle, and
though thy nest be set among the stars, I will
bring thee down from thence, saith the Lord*
[Obad. 4]. The stars mean the righteous, as
thou sayest [Dan. xii. 3], *They that turn
many to righteousness [shall shine] as the stars
for ever and ever.*

Commentary. — The R. Huna here mentioned
was R. Huna of Sepphoris, a disciple of R. Joḥanan,
and must not be confounded with the earlier Babylonian R. Huna, head of the college at Sura about
the middle of the third century. R. Aḥa lived at
Lydda in the first half of the fourth century. He
was therefore contemporary with the adoption of
Christianity as the official religion of the Roman
Empire. The above passage contains an unmistakable allusion to that event. 'Esau the wicked' is a
stock phrase in the Talmud to denote the Roman
Empire. That Esau should wrap himself in his
tallith (the scarf worn by a Jew when praying) means

tion; and, indeed, it is easier in this connexion to understand a reference
to Babylonians than to Minim. I have therefore not included this passage
in my collection.

that the Roman Empire, now become Christian, pretended to be the true Israel, in accordance with the doctrine laid down in Gal. iii. 7. The claim of the Christian Church to be the true Israel must have been very exasperating to Jews, perhaps all the more that the first to teach it had once been a Jew himself.

I proceed now to give a series of passages which may be grouped together under the head of

SECTION II. POLEMICAL DISCUSSIONS WITH MINIM

I will take, in the first place, some passages which mention or describe encounters between Jews and Minim. Afterwards, passages containing discussions of special doctrinal points.

THE MINIM OF CAPERNAUM AND R. ḤANANJAH, NEPHEW OF R. JEHOSHUA

(78) Qoh. r., i. 8, p. 4ᵇ.—Ḥanina, son of the brother of R. Jehoshua, came to Chephar Naḥum, and the Minim worked a spell on him, and set him riding on an ass on the Sabbath. He came to Jehoshua his friend, and he put ointment on him and he was healed. He [R. Jehoshua] said to him, 'Since the ass of that wicked one has roused itself against thee, thou canst no longer remain in the land of Israel.' He departed thence to Babel, and died there in peace.

Commentary.—This story occurs in the middle of a long passage containing abundant references to

212 CHRISTIANITY IN TALMUD

Minim. The story of the arrest of R. Eliezer for
Minuth (see above, p. 139 fol.), the attempted cure
of Ben Damah by a Min (p. 104 fol.), and the story of
the woman who desired to become a proselyte (p. 188
fol.), precede the present story. Those that follow
it will be given afterwards (p. 218 fol.).

The Midrash known as Qoheleth Rabbah, on the
book of Ecclesiastes, is of very late date, but nevertheless contains abundance of ancient material. The
present story I believe to be ancient, in spite of traces
of late date in the style, for two reasons. First, the
motive that suggested it was one that would lose its
force if the man of whom the story was told had been
dead for a long time. Second, the references to the
Minim of Capernaum only occur in connexion with
persons of the first or second century. At a later
time they seem to be quite unknown. If, therefore,
the story had been made up at some considerably
later date than the time of R. Jehoshua and his
nephew, it is probable that his alleged intercourse
with Minim would have had a different historical
setting. The R. Jehoshua of the story is R. Jehoshua
ben Ḥananjah, who has already been frequently
mentioned, and who lived at the end of the first and
the beginning of the second century. Ḥananjah
(not Ḥanina as in the text) his nephew, was a well-
known teacher, though by no means so distinguished
as his uncle. He did remove from Palestine to
Babylonia, probably before the outbreak of the war
of Bar Cocheba. And there he finally established
himself, although he once at least returned to
Palestine (b. Succ. 20ᵇ). Even in the time of R.
Gamliel II., before he left Palestine, Ḥananjah

appears to have been a Rabbi, and to have enjoyed a considerable reputation as such (b. Nidd. 24[b]). By his residence in Babylonia[1] he escaped the persecution which followed upon the defeat of Bar Cocheba; and it would seem that he took advantage of the confusion and weakness of the Palestinian schools to assert the independence of his own and other Babylonian seats of learning. After order had been restored in Palestine, and the scattered Rabbis had gathered under the leadership of R. Shim'on ben Gamliel, a sharp controversy took place between the latter and R. Ḥananjah. Messengers were sent to Babylonia to demand the submission of R. Ḥananjah to the authority of the Palestinian Patriarch. The story of the dispute is given in j. Nedar. 40[a], j. Sanh. 19[a], b. Berach. 63[a], [b], and is admirably discussed by Bacher, Ag. d. Tann., i. 390 n. 4. The date of this dispute may be roughly given as 150 A.D., possibly somewhat earlier.

Now it was evidently the interest of the Palestinian Rabbis to depreciate the authority of R. Ḥananjah if they could; and the suggestion of his intercourse with the Minim would answer their purpose. Here we find the motive for the story contained in the passage translated above. Whether true or not, it is evident that there was a reason for telling the story. Also it would seem natural that the story should become current at a time not long after the dispute just mentioned, possibly even while it was going on. It does not appear that R.

---

[1] The name of the place where he lived was Nahar Paqod (or Nahar Paqor); see Neubauer, Geogr. d. Talm., 363 ff. Also, for the name Paqod, cp. Schrader, Keilinschrift. d. A. T. 423 (E.T. ii. 117).

Ḥananjah ever made any formal submission; but there is no doubt that the authority of the Nasi in Palestine was successfully asserted as against the schools of Babylonia. R. Ḥananjah was left in peace, having failed to realise his ambition. The story before us ingeniously presents him as a man for whom allowances had to be made. No one disputed his learning or his eminence as a teacher, but he had unfortunately permitted himself to be tainted with heresy, and therefore was obliged to leave the country. Such seems to be the intention of the story.

In its details the story is very interesting. That the Minim here denote Christians there can be no possible doubt. The phrase 'the ass of that wicked one' contains an unmistakable reference to Jesus. And the mention of Chephar Nahum, i.e. Capernaum, confirms the reference, that city having been the headquarters, so to speak, of Jesus during the earlier part of his public career. If Christians were to be found anywhere in Galilee in the second century, Capernaum was the most likely place to contain them.[1]

The story represents Ḥananjah as having been the victim of magic. With this may be compared the stories given above (p. 112 ff.) of Christian miracles. He was made to ride on an ass on the Sabbath,

---

[1] I do not go into the question whether Capernaum is now represented by Tell Ḥum or Khan Minyeh. The fact that Minim are associated, in the story under consideration, with the city of Capernaum, goes to confirm the theory that Khan Minyeh marks the true site. This theory seems to me to be, on other grounds, preferable to the one which identifies Capernaum with Tell Ḥum. Is it not possible that ancient Capernaum included both sites ?

presumably as a sort of imitation of Jesus. With
the mention of the ass in this connexion, compare
what is said above (p. 154 n). Whether the story
is based on a real incident in the life of R. Ḥananjah
there is not sufficient evidence to show. But the
case of R. Eliezer, discussed above (see p. 144) is a
well-authenticated instance of intercourse between
a Rabbi and a Min, and thus makes it quite possible
that R. Ḥananjah also had some dealings with the
Minim. If he had, then they must have taken place
before the year 130 A.D.

It should be observed that this story is not contained in either the Palestinian or the Babylonian
Gemara, nor in any of the older Midrashim, although
R. Ḥananjah is several times referred to as a well-
known teacher. In the Midrash Qoheleth rabbah,
which is the sole authority for the story, there is
nevertheless a passage which to some extent confirms
its antiquity. It is said (on vii. 26) that R. Isi of
Cæsarea (fourth century) expounded this verse in
reference to Minuth, and gave several examples of
the good who escaped, and the bad who were ensnared.
Amongst his instances are El'azar ben Damah and
Jacob of Chephar Sechanja, and also Ḥananjah and
the Minim of Chephar Naḥum. This shows that the
story is not necessarily of late date, although it now
occurs only in an almost mediæval midrash (see below,
p. 219).

THE MINIM AND R. JONATHAN

(79) Qoh. r., i. 8.—R. Jonathan—one of his
disciples ran away to them [*i.e.* the Minim].
He came and found him in subjection to

them. The Minim sent after him, saying thus
unto him, ' And is it not thus written [Prov. i.
14], *Thou shalt cast in thy lot with us ; one
purse shall there be for us all.*' He fled, and
they fled after him. They said to him, ' Rabbi,
come and show kindness to a girl.' He went
and found them . . . . with a girl. He said,
' Is it thus that Jews act ? ' They said to him,
' And is it not written in the Torah, *Thou shalt
cast in thy lot with us ; one purse,*' etc. He
fled and they fled after him, till he came to
the door [of his house] and shut it in their
faces. They said, ' Rabbi Jonathan, go, prate
to thy mother that thou hast not turned and
hast not looked upon us. For, if thou hadst
turned and looked upon us, instead of our
pursuing thee, thou wouldst have pursued us.'

Commentary.—R. Jonathan, here mentioned, is R.
Jonathan ben El'azar, a Palestinian Rabbi of the
third century, contemporary with and associate of
Johanan and Resh Laqish. He lived in Sepphoris.
The Minim with whom he had the unpleasant adventure described in this passage may have been those
of Capernaum, as the present passage follows, without
a break, after the story about R. Hananjah. The
connexion is so close that the present story begins
by saying that the disciple of R. Jonathan ran away
' to them,' suggesting that the Minim of Capernaum
are still referred to. I do not feel certain that this
connexion is anything more than literary. But it is
at least probable that Christians of Galilee are referred
to, and certainly possible that Capernaum is the city
where they dwelt. If not Capernaum, then Sepphoris

is probably intended, because Jonathan, when he escapes from the Minim, appears to take refuge in his own house, since he shuts the door in their faces.[1]

As regards the details of the story little needs to be said. It is plain that the words ' And is it not written . . . . fled after him ' should be omitted, on their first occurrence, to avoid a break in the story. The reference to alleged immorality practised by Christians in their secret assemblies does not need to be enlarged upon. It should be noted that the Rabbi, in rebuking the Minim, implies that they are Jews, or at least of Jewish birth. The pursuit of the Rabbi by the Minim is curious, and perhaps indicates the dread as well as dislike felt by Jews towards the heretics.

This story, like the preceding one, is found only in the Midrash Qoheleth rabbah, a compilation of very late date. Thus much, however, can be said in support of the authenticity of the story, that R. Jonathan is known to have had polemical discussions with Minim, as will be shown subsequently (see below, p. 254). Moreover, the fact that he took the trouble to lay down a canon of interpretation of Scripture referring to Minuth (Ber. r. 48, 6, see below, p. 319), shows that he had had occasion to study the subject. With the incident of the flight of a disciple and the attempt of his teacher to bring him back, may be compared a story quoted by Eusebius from Clemens Alexandrinus (Euseb., Hist., iii. 23). The conclusion of the story, however, is quite different from that of the Jewish one.

---

[1] See above, p. 115, on Sepphoris as the scene of several incidents in which Minim were concerned.

I proceed to give the conclusion of the passage in
Qoheleth rabbah, from which the three preceding
anecdotes have been taken.

THE MINIM AND R. JEHUDAH BEN NAQŌSA

(80) Qoh. r., i. 8.—R. Jehudah ben Naqōsa—the
Minim used to have dealings with him.   They
questioned him and he answered; they questioned and he answered.   He said to them,
'In vain! ye bring trifles.   Come, let us agree
that whoever overcomes his opponent shall
split the brains of his opponent with a club.'
And he overcame them, and split their brains,
till they were filled with wounds.   When he
returned, his disciples said to him, 'Rabbi,
they helped thee from heaven and thou didst
overcome.'   He said to them, 'And in vain!
Pray for this man and this *sack*; for it was
full of precious stones and pearls, but now it is
full of black ashes.'

Commentary.—R. Jehudah ben Naqōsa was a
younger contemporary of Rabbi (Jehudah ha-Qadosh),
and disciple of R. Jacob, and of R. Ḥija.   Very little
is known of him, and the story just translated occurs,
so far as I am aware, nowhere else.   That the duel
between R. Jehudah and the Minim really was of the
savage character described cannot be accepted, though
it is not clear why a polemical debate should be
described by such a violent metaphor.   The remark
of the disciples to the Rabbi, and his reply, are interesting.   They ascribed his victory to heavenly assist-
ance.   According to the commentators on the passage,
R. Jehudah had transgressed the commandment,

'*Come not near her*' (*i.e.* have nothing to do with
Minuth ; see above, p. 182 ff.), and thus, if he escaped,
it was owing to divine protection. The Rabbi replied
that his deliverance was in vain. 'Pray for this man,'
i.e. 'for me,' and for 'this sack,' *i.e.* 'my head,' which
was formerly like a sack full of jewels and now is like
a sack full of ashes. Apparently his mind had been
contaminated with heresy, and was filled with evil
thoughts in place of its former learning and piety.

The three stories which have now been given
from Qoheleth rabbah form one continuous passage,
together with the story of the arrest of R. Eliezer
for Minuth, the story of El'azar ben Dama, and that
of the woman who came to R. Eliezer and R.
Jehoshua to be received as a convert. All the six
are given as illustrations of Minuth, and form a
haggadic exposition of the words, Eccl. i. 8, *All
things are full of weariness.* Now, in this same
Midrash, on vii. 26 (p. 21ᵈ) it is said

(81) "R. Isi of Cæsarea expounded this verse
('*whoso pleaseth God shall escape from her, but
the sinner shall be taken by her*') in reference to
Minuth. 'The good is R. El'azar, the sinner
is Jacob of Chephar Neburaia. Or, the good
is El'azar ben Dama, the sinner is Jacob of
Chephar Sama. Or, the good is Ḥananjah,
nephew of R. Jehoshua, the sinner is the Minim
of Chephar Naḥum. Or, the good is Jehudah
ben Naqōsa, the sinner is the Minim. Or, the
good is R. Jonathan, the sinner is his disciple.
Or, the good is R. Eliezer and R. Jehoshua,
the sinner is Elisha.'"

It is evident at a glance that there is a strong

likeness between this list of examples of Minuth and
the series of stories contained in the earlier part of
the Midrash.   Placed side by side, the likeness
becomes still more apparent.

(*A.*) R. Isi's Series (Qoh. r. on vii. 26).	(*B.*) Series of Stories (Qoh. r. on i. 8).
1. El'azar and Jacob of Ch. Neburaia.	1. Eliezer's arrest.
2. El'azar ben Dama, and Jacob of Chephar Sama.	2. El'azar ben Dama and Jacob of Chephar Sama.
3. Ḥananjah and the Minim of Capernaum.	3. Eliezer and Jehoshua and the would-be convert.
4. Jehudah ben Naqōsa and the Minim.	4. Ḥananjah and the Minim of Capernaum.
5. Jonathan and his disciple.	5. Jonathan and his disciple.
6. Eliezer and Jehoshua and Elisha.	6. Jehudah ben Naqōsa and the Minim.

It will be seen that four stories are common to
both lists (A 2, 3, 4, 5, and B 2, 4, 6, 5).   In A 6
Eliezer and Jehoshua are both concerned with a
heretic.   So they are in B 3, though the heretic is
not the same.   The only marked discrepancy is
between A 1 and B 1.   It should also be observed
that neither series extends beyond the six examples,
and that the series B is given anonymously where it
occurs in the Midrash on Eccl. i. 8.   Now, since the
series B is substantially the same as the series A, I
suggest that R. Isi of Cæsarea is really the author of
B, and that B gives the substance of what he said
in his exposition on Minuth, while A only gives the
heads of his discourse.   R. Isi lived in the fourth
century, probably about the middle of it.   And
although not himself an eminent teacher, he moved
in the same circle in which Abahu had moved, and

was thus in a position to hear much concerning the Minim and their intercourse with Jews. The slight discrepancies between A and B may be explained in this way. The compiler of the Midrash preferred to take the famous case of R. Eliezer's arrest rather than the obscure one of Jacob of Ch. Neburaia[1] (a contemporary of R. Isi, of whom more will be said below). His object was not to illustrate the teaching of R. Isi, but to expound the verse Eccl. i. 8 in reference to Minuth; and for this purpose, R. Isi's series was ready to his hand. The difference between A 6 and B 3 may rest only on a scribal error. The opponent of Eliezer and Jehoshua is said in A 6 to be Elisha, in B 3 the woman who desired to be received as a convert. The latter version is probably correct. Elisha is supposed to be Elisha ben Abujah, who certainly did become a heretic ; but he had little if anything to do with Eliezer and Jehoshua, being much younger. He was contemporary with Aqiba and Meir. Moreover, it is very unusual to speak of him simply as Elisha. I suggest that אלישע may be a corruption due to similarity of sound, of האשה, ' the woman.

R. JEHOSHUA, CÆSAR AND A MIN

GOD HAS NOT CAST OFF ISRAEL

(82) b. Ḥag. 5ᵇ. *And I will hide my face in that day* [Deut. xxxi. 18]. Raba said, The Holy

---

[1] Friedländer (Vorchr. jüd. Gnosticismus, p. 108), says that this is " offenbar Jacob von Kephar Sechanja," an assumption for which there is no warrant. Jacob of Ch. Neburaia was a very well known character, contemporary, or nearly so, with R. Isi, who here mentions him (see below, p. 334 fol.). Friedländer does not give the text of the passage, and he leaves the reader to suppose that the last clause contains the full name ' Elisha ben Abujah.' This is not the case, and the fact ought to have been stated.

One, Blessed be He, saith, Though I have
hidden my face from them, yet *in a dream I
will speak with him* [Num. xii. 6]. R. Joseph
said His hand is stretched out over us, as it is
said [Isa. li. 16], *In the shadow of my hand have
I covered thee.* R. Jehoshua ben Ḥananjah
was standing in the house of Cæsar. A certain
Min[1] showed him [by signs] a nation whose
Lord hath turned away his face from them.
He [R. Jehoshua] showed him [by signs] His
hand stretched out over us. Cæsar said to
R. Jehoshua, 'What did he shew thee?' 'A
people whose Lord hath turned away his face
from them, and I showed him His hand stretched
out over us.' They said to the Min, 'What
didst thou show to him?' 'A people whose
Lord hath turned away his face from them.'
'And what did he show to thee?' 'I do not
know.' They said, 'A man who does not know
what is shown him by a sign, one shows it to
him before the King.' They took him out and
slew him.

When the soul of R. Jehoshua was passing
away, our Rabbis said, 'What will become of
us at the hands of the Minim?' He said to
them [cp. Jer. xlix. 7] 'Counsel hath perished
from the children, their wisdom is corrupted,'
when counsel hath perished from the children
[of Israel] the wisdom of the peoples of the
world is corrupted.

Commentary.—This is one out of several examples
to be found in the Talmud and the Midrash of con-

---

[1] The modern texts read אפיקורום ; Rabbinowicz gives מין throughout.

versations between R. Jehoshua ben Hananjah and a
Roman emperor, the particular emperor being
Hadrian. These stories are doubtless in some cases
overlaid with legendary matter; but there is, beyond
reasonable question, some historical fact at the bottom
of them. Not only is it known that Hadrian was in
the habit of conversing with learned men wherever
he met them, but he actually mentions in a letter that
he conversed in Alexandria with a patriarch of
the Jews. (See the passage quoted by Grätz, Gsch.
d. J., iv. p. 450, from Vopiscus.) This patriarch of
the Jews can be no other than R. Jehoshua, who is
known to have gone to Alexandria. Grätz and
Bacher both accept the general fact of intercourse
between Hadrian and R. Jehoshua, and admit the
genuineness of this particular story. (Grätz as above;
Bacher, Ag. d. Tann., i. 176).

As related in the Talmud, in the present passage
the story is introduced to illustrate the doctrine that
although God might have hidden his face from his
children, nevertheless he had not withdrawn his
favour; he still held communion with them and still
protected them. The latter is the statement of R.
Joseph, who is presumably the authority for the story
which then immediately follows. R. Joseph was a
Babylonian, head of the school of Pumbeditha (b. 259,
d. 322 or 333). Where he got the story from is
suggested by a remark in b. Bechor. 8ᵃ, in introducing a marvellous tale (also about Hadrian and R.
Jehoshua) with the words 'R. Jehudah said that Rab
said,' etc. R. Jehudah (ben Jehezq'el) was the teacher
of R. Joseph (Bacher, Ag. d. Bab. Amor., p. 101).
Rab, of course, as the disciple of R. Jehudah ha-

Qadosh (Rabbi), came in the direct line of the Palestinian tradition. The story in Bechoroth lies too far off the main line of my subject to justify me in translating it.[1]

The story before us needs little explanation. R. Jehoshua and the Min stood in the palace, in the presence of the emperor. The Min made a pantomimic sign to the Rabbi, intended to signify that God had turned away his face from the Jews. The Rabbi replied with another gesture implying that God's hand was still stretched out over his people. The Min must evidently have been acquainted with the O.T. scriptures, since both the sign and the countersign are dramatized texts (Deut. xxxi. 18, and Isa. li. 16). Probably therefore he was a Christian, though not necessarily a Jewish Christian, as the incident took place in Alexandria. A Jewish Christian would scarcely have taunted a Jew with the great disaster which had befallen the Jewish people. The exchange of pantomimic signs between the Jew and the Min attracted the attention of the emperor and the other bystanders, who asked for an explanation. The Rabbi explained both the gestures. The Min professed ignorance of the answer which the Rabbi

---

[1] Two allusions to Christianity have been suspected in this passage (see Bacher, *loc. cit.*). One is the saying, "If the salt have lost its savour, wherewith do men salt it?" *cp.* Matt. v. 13. The other is a reference to a she-mule which bore a foal, the allusion being, presumably, to the birth of Jesus from a virgin. As regards the first, the saying about the salt may have been a proverb quoted by Jesus no less than by R. Jehoshua. And as regards the second, there would be more point in it if R. Jehoshua was speaking to Christians. His opponents in the story appear to be heathen philosophers in Rome. Still, in view of the curious association of Jesus with an ass (see above, p. 154), there may be something in the reference to the foal of a mule.

REFERENCES TO MINIM AND MINUTH 225

had made to his sign. They said to him that if he
had not understood it, he should be shown the
meaning in the presence of the emperor ; whereupon
they took him out and put him to death. This
appears to mean, that as he had not understood that
the Jews were protected by their God, this should be
proved to him by the imperial sentence, condemning
him to death for having insulted a Jew. Whether
Hadrian would ever have acted so is open to question.
Certainly, the incident took place before the revolt
of Bar Cocheba had broken out, at a time when
Hadrian was well disposed towards the Jews. Moreover, R. Jehoshua himself appears to have enjoyed
in a high degree the favour of the emperor, who
might on that account resent an insult offered to him,
while perhaps taking no notice of one offered to any
other Jew. Of course the story is told from the
Jewish side. It is given as an instance of the success
of R. Jehoshua in repelling the attacks of the Minim.
Accordingly, there follows a sort of obituary notice
of R. Jehoshua, regarded as a defender of the faith.
When he was dying, the Rabbis said, ' What will
become of us by reason of the Minim ? ' The dying
man replied by an ingenious perversion of the text
Jer. xlix. 7, *Is counsel perished from the prudent ?
Is their wisdom vanished ?* He rendered it thus,
' (When) counsel is perished from the *children*, (then)
the wisdom of them [*i.e.* the Gentiles] is corrupt.'
The children (בנים = also the prudent, the understanding) are of course the children of Israel. That
' *their* wisdom ' means ' the wisdom of the Gentiles '
is the Rabbi's own interpretation. His meaning
appears to be, that the power of the Gentiles to
15

molest ceases with the power of the Jews to defend. A somewhat roundabout way of saying that the Jewish religion would never want a defender so long as it was attacked.

The date of the death of R. Jehoshua is not known with certainty ; but it must have taken place before the outbreak of the war in 132 A.D., as he is never mentioned in connexion with any of the incidents of the war. He must therefore have been an old man at the time of the above incident. And it is probable that it was during this visit to Alexandria that the conversation took place in which the emperor (Hadrian) asked him why he did not visit the Bē Abīdān (see above, p. 165).

R. JEHOSHUA AND A MIN

(83) b. Erub. 101ª.—A certain Min said to R. Jehoshua ben Hananjah, ' Thou brier ! for it is written of you [Mic. vii. 4] *The best of them is a brier.*' He said to him, ' Fool, look at the end of the verse, for it is written [ibid.], *The upright is* (from) *a thorn hedge*, and a fence.' What is [meant by] *The best of them is a brier ?* Just as these briers are a protection to the gap in the wall, so the good amongst us are a protection to us. Another explanation, *The best of them is a brier*, because they thrust the wicked down to Gehinnom, as it is said [Mic. iv. 13], *Arise and thresh, O daughter of Zion. For I will make thy horn iron, and I will make thy hoofs brass. And thou shalt beat in pieces many peoples*, etc.

Commentary.—I give the above passage here because it is associated with R. Jehoshua ben Ḥananjah. The classification of the numerous passages dealing with the controversies between Jews and Minim is not easy. On the whole it seems best to give first those in which a discussion takes place between a Jew and a Min, and then those in which some text is interpreted polemically against the Minim. The passages which describe actual discussion between opponents will be arranged, as far as possible, in the chronological order of the Rabbis who took part in them.

Of the present passage little need be said by way of explanation. It is found, so far as I am aware, nowhere else, and is anonymous. As the preceding words are those of R. Jehudah (ben Jehezq'el), it is possible that he is the authority for the story. We have seen that other stories concerning R. Jehoshua are due to him (see above, p. 223). There is nothing to show when or where the incident took place. Neither is there anything especially heretical in the taunt of the Min. The repartee only serves to show how the Rabbi turned aside the scornful gibe of his opponent. The thorn hedge serves as a protection where there is a gap in the wall, so as to prevent intrusion. So the righteous amongst Israel serve to defend the people against their enemies, especially heretics. The second interpretation, which brings in the idea of the thorns thrusting the wicked down to Gehinnom, may be later than R. Jehoshua, as it is more ferocious in its sentiment than his sayings generally are.

R. Jehoshua, R. Gamliel, R. El'azar ben
Azariah, R. Aqiba and a Min

God keeps the Sabbath

(84) Shem. r., xxx. 9, p, 53[c, d].—The case of R[n.] Gamliel, R. Jehoshua, R. El'azar ben Azariah, and R. Aqiba, who went to Rome and preached there that the ways of the Holy One, Blessed be He, are not as [the ways of] flesh and blood. For [a man] decrees a decree, and tells others to do, and himself does nothing. But the Holy One, Blessed be He, is not so. A Min was there. After they had gone forth, he said to them, 'Your words are nothing but falsehood. Did ye not say, God saith and doeth? Why does He not observe the Sabbath?' They said to him, 'O most wicked! is not a man allowed to move about in his dwelling on the Sabbath?' He said to them, 'Yes.' They said to him, 'The upper regions and the lower are the dwelling of God, as it is said [Isa. vi. 3], *The whole earth is full of his glory.* And even a man that sins, does he not move about to the extent of his own stature on the Sabbath?' He said to them, 'Yes.' They said to him, 'It is written [Jer. xxiii. 24], *Do I not fill heaven and earth? saith the Lord.*'

Commentary.—The journey to Rome of the four Rabbis here named is an incident often mentioned in the Rabbinical literature. It took place in the year A.D. 95.[1] R[n.] Gamliel is Gamliel II., grandson of the Gamliel of Acts v. 34, and president (Nasi) of the assembly called the Sanhedrin of Jabneh (see above, p. 127). R. Jehoshua has been mentioned several times. R. El'azar ben Azariah was one of the members of the assembly of Jabneh, and during the temporary deposition of Gamliel was elected president in his place. R. Aqiba has often been mentioned previously (see above, p. 84).

The scene of the 'preaching' of the Rabbis would be one of the synagogues in Rome, where of course the Min had been amongst their hearers. It is not easy to define the form of heresy of this Min. From the fact of his being a listener to the preaching of the Rabbis, it would seem that he was of Jewish extraction—like all the Minim whom we have hitherto met. This is borne out by the quotation of texts from scripture, which would have no authority for a Gentile. On the other hand, the point of this argument is that God does not keep the Sabbath; and a Jewish Christian would not be likely to hold an anti-Jewish doctrine of the Sabbath. It should, however, be borne in mind that, while the term 'Jewish Christian' is usually applied to those Christians of Jewish origin who continued to observe the Jewish law, nevertheless the possibility always remained that Jews, on being converted to Christianity, entirely ceased to observe the Jewish law. Paul himself is an example of a Jew who became a Christian but by no means—in the technical sense—a Jewish Christian. It is not, indeed, certain that the Min, in the passage

---

[1] Bacher, Ag. d. Tann., i. 84, n. 2, where will be found a useful collection of references to the event in the Rabbinical literature.

before us, was a Christian at all. But it is probable that
he was, since a Christian would be more likely than
a heathen to be familiar with the O.T. scriptures,
and to take an interest in the preaching of Jewish
Rabbis, especially if he himself was of Jewish origin.

The argument of the Min, that God does not himself observe the Sabbath though he has commanded
men to observe it, may perhaps be compared with
the thought expressed in John v. 17, *My Father
worketh even until now, and I work*; though it
by no means follows that the Fourth Gospel was in
existence at this time. The idea that God never
ceases from working is found in Philo.[1]

The reply of the Rabbis is ingenious, but it only
amounts to saying that God's ceaseless energy is no
proof that he does not keep the Sabbath. The answer
serves to refute the Min, but not to establish the
contention of the Rabbis.

It is curious that, in this story, the four Rabbis are
grouped together, and it is not said who was the
spokesman. All four preached, and apparently all
four replied to the heretic. It is impossible to
determine which of the four is especially referred to,
since Gamliel, Jehoshua and Aqiba all had controversies with heretics at various times, and thus any
one of the three might have done so in the present
instance.

The abusive term, 'O most wicked,' is, literally,
'wicked of the world,' *i.e.* 'most wicked man in the
world.'

---

[1] Philo., de Allegor., i. 3. παύεται γὰρ οὐδέποτε ποιῶν ὁ θεός, ἀλλ' ὥσπερ ἴδιον τὸ καίειν πυρὸς καὶ χιόνος τὸ ψύχειν, οὕτω καὶ θεοῦ τὸ ποιεῖν · καὶ πολύ γε μᾶλλον, ὅσῳ καὶ τοῖς ἄλλοις ἅπασιν ἀρχὴ τοῦ δρᾶν ἐστιν.

R. Gamliel and the Minim

The Resurrection of the Dead

(85) b. Sanh. 90[b].—The Minim asked Rabban
Gamliel, ' Whence [do ye prove] that the
Holy One, Blessed be He, revives the dead ? '
He said to them, ' From the Torah, from the
Prophets, and from the Writings.' And they
did not accept his answer. ' From the Torah,'
as it is written [Deut. xxxi. 16], *Behold, thou
shalt sleep with thy fathers and arise.*' They
said to them [the Minim to R[n.] Gamliel], ' But
is it not said, *and this people shall arise* ? ' etc.
' From the Prophets,' as it is written [Isa.
xxvi. 19], *Thy dead shall live; my dead
bodies shall arise. Awake and sing, ye that
dwell in the dust; for thy dew is as the dew
of herbs, and the earth shall cast forth the
shades.* ' But are there not the dead whom
Ezekiel raised ? ' ' From the Writings,' as it
is written [Cant. vii. 9], *and thy mouth like the
best wine, that goeth down smoothly for my
beloved, causing the lips of them that are asleep
to speak.* ' But, do not their lips move in this
world ? '

Commentary.—Rabban Gamliel appears as the
representative of Judaism in several dialogues with
non-Jews. In another part of the treatise from which
the present passage is taken (b. Sanh. 39[a]), five such
dialogues are given, in which R. Gamliel replies to
the questions of an opponent. In the common text
this opponent is called a liar, כופר ; but Rabbinowicz

(D. Soph. on the passage), shows that the true
reading is קיסר, Cæsar, an emperor; and he connects
these dialogues with that visit of Gamliel and the
other Rabbis to Rome, mentioned in the preceding
section (see above, p. 228). The reading 'Min' is
found, according to Hamburger, in the versions of
the stories in the Midrash and the Yalqut; but the
authority of Rabbinowicz is decisive on the point. I
therefore exclude the dialogues referred to, as having
no bearing on my subject.

In the passage under consideration there is nothing
to show when or where the dialogue took place.
But, judging from the context, where there follows
immediately a dialogue between 'the Romans' and
R. Jehoshua, it is not unlikely that the Minim put
their question to R. Gamliel in Rome, at the time of
the journey already mentioned, A.D. 95. This is
Bacher's suggestion (A. Tann., i. 87, n. 4). The
doctrine of the resurrection of the dead was one of
the most frequent subjects of controversy between
Jews and Minim, as will be seen from several passages
to be presented below. Neither side disputed the
fact of resurrection. The question was whether
there was proof of the doctrine in the O.T.
scriptures. The Jews of course maintained that there
was, while the Minim maintained the contrary. The
controversy could have no interest unless both parties
were concerned with the Hebrew scriptures; so that
it is clearly Christians who are referred to as Minim,
when the doctrine of resurrection is the subject of
discussion. The Christian position was that the
resurrection of the dead was consequent on the
resurrection of Christ (cp. John xiv. 19, and 1 Cor.

xv. 20 fol.)   And that position would be weakened
if a valid proof of the doctrine could be produced
from the O.T. ; because, in that case, the resurrection
of Christ would be shown to be unnecessary, at all
events as an argument for the resurrection of men
in general.

In the passage before us the Minim challenged R.
Gamliel to give a proof from the O.T. scriptures
of the doctrine of resurrection.   He replied by
quoting three texts, one from each of the three
divisions of the O.T.   His opponents did not accept
his proof.

The proof from the Torah was founded on Deut.
xxxi. 16, where the Rabbi reads the text *thou shalt
sleep with thy fathers and arise* contrary to the plain
sense and the grammatical construction.   His opponents immediately detected the fallacy and pointed it
out.   The words " *and arise* " belong to the second half
of the text, and refer, not to Moses but, to *this people.*

The proof from the prophets was based on Isa.
xxvi. 19, where God calls on the dead to arise.   The
rejoinder of the opponents was to the effect that the
prophet Ezekiel had called the dead to life by special
command from God, and that therefore the special
command did not establish the general principle.

The proof from the writings was a far-fetched
application of Cant. vii. 9, where the point is that the
lips of the dead move, thus showing that they live
after death.   The Minim reply that this movement
of the lips takes place in the grave, and belongs to
this world, not to the next.   The Gemara adds, in
support of the view of the Minim, the saying of R.
Johanan that the lips of the dead move in their graves

when anyone quotes a halachah which they have taught.

The Minim, it is said, did not accept these answers as amounting to a proof. R. Gamliel therefore strengthened his case by quoting Deut. xi. 9, *the land which the Lord sware unto your fathers to give them.* The land was to be given to "*your fathers,*" not "*to you.*" Hence the 'fathers' must live after death. Another tradition says that R. Gamliel's final answer was (Deut. iv. 4), *Ye that did cleave unto the Lord your God are alive, every one of you, this day.* This is explained to mean that 'as ye stand up, everyone of you, this day, so ye will stand up in the world to come.'

It would appear that the Minim accepted the final answer of the Rabbi; at least the Gemara says that they did not accept his answer until he had quoted his final text. On the whole, however, it cannot be said that a strong case was made out on the Jewish side. If the Minim did admit the force of the appeal to Deut. xi. 9, with its reference to the patriarchs, it is just possible that they did so with the recollection that Jesus himself had founded an argument for the doctrine of resurrection upon a somewhat similar reference to the patriarchs (Matt. xxii. 31, 32). I do not press this point, because the Talmud would not, in any case, allow the Minim to be the victors in the discussion; therefore we cannot assume that they really confessed themselves overcome. At most the debate came to an end. It would not have been difficult to have refuted even the last argument of the Rabbi, by showing that the land promised to the fathers was not, as a matter of fact, given to them but to their descendants.

R. Gamliel and a Min

God has Departed from Israel

(86) b. Jeb. 102ᵇ.—A certain Min said to R. Gamliel, 'A people whose Lord has drawn off [departed] in regard to them, as it is written [Hosea v. 6], *They shall go with their flocks and with their herds, to seek the Lord, and they shall not find Him; He hath drawn off from them.*' He said to him, 'Fool, is it then written *drawn off in regard to them?* It is written *drawn off from them.* If [in the case of] a childless widow [the phrase were] 'the brothers draw off in regard to her,' there would be some ground for your argument.'

Commentary.—In the foregoing translation I have used the phrase 'draw off' to represent the double meaning of the word *ḥalatz* (חלץ). This word, in addition to its ordinary meaning of 'depart,' has also a technical meaning in connexion with the law of the deceased brother's widow (Deut. xxv. 5–10). If a man die leaving no children, one of his brothers shall do the duty of a husband towards her. And if such brother refuse, then the widow shall perform a ceremony expressing contempt of him. She shall publicly 'draw off' (ḥalatz) his shoe from his foot, spit in his face, and say, *Thus shall it be done unto the man that doth not build up his brother's house.* In this case the widow 'draws off in regard to the brother,' performs the ceremony in regard to him (חלץ ליה); but she does not 'depart from' him; he rejects her by refusing to do the duty required of him. This is the technical use of ḥalatz, and it requires the preposition 'le,' ל, 'in regard to.' The non-technical use of ḥalatz, in which the meaning is 'depart,' requires the preposition 'min,' מן, 'from.'

Now the argument of the Min, and the answer of Gamliel, will be more intelligible. The Min says, 'A people whose Lord has rejected them,' ḥalatz 'in regard to them' (technical use), for it is said, Hosea v. 6, *he hath departed from them.* R. Gamliel at once replies that the text does not bear out the construction put upon it. The text reads 'ḥalatz min,' 'depart from,' which is neutral, and only implies estrangement, not that God had rejected his people. Even if, as the Min assumed, 'ḥalatz min' were equivalent to 'ḥalatz le,' that would only imply, in the text, that the people had rejected God. For the purpose of the Min's argument, the text ought to read that the people 'ḥaletzu lo' (technical term), implying that God had rejected his people. It might be true that there was estrangement between God and Israel; but it was not true that He had rejected his people, they had rather rejected him. If, added R. Gamliel, the technical term 'ḥalatz le' was used of the brothers and not of the widow, then the argument of the Min would be valid; because, in that case, it would prove that God had rejected his people.

The above explanation is, I believe, correct in substance; at all events it brings out the point of R. Gamliel's reply, viz., that God had not cast off his people. As to the date and place of this dialogue, no hint is given in the text. The alleged rejection of Israel refers of course to the destruction of Jerusalem and the Temple by Titus in A.D. 70. After that great disaster, it might well seem that God had rejected his people ; and we shall find that in several controversial dialogues the non-Jewish opponent taunts the Jew with the loss of the divine protection (cp. the story given above, p. 222). In the present instance there seems to be no reason for locating the incident elsewhere than in Palestine. A knowledge not merely of the O.T. scriptures but of the Jewish Law is implied on the part of the Min, to whom, otherwise, the answer of R. Gamliel would have been unintelligible. Probably the Min was some Christian of Jabneh, where R. Gamliel dwelt ; though whether he was a Jewish Christian is open to question, on the ground that one who was himself a Jew would scarcely have taunted a Jew with the calamity that had befallen the nation.

BERURIA AND A MIN

(87) b. Ber. 10ᵃ.—A certain Min said to Beruria, 'It is written [Isa. liv. 1], *Sing, O barren that didst not bear.* Sing, because thou didst not bear.' She said to him, 'Fool, look at the end of the verse, for it is written [ibid.], *For more are the children of the desolate, than the children of the married wife, saith the Lord.* But what is meant by *O, barren that didst not bear, sing?* The congregation of Israel, which is like a woman who hath not borne children for Gehenna, like you.'

Commentary.—Beruria was one of the famous women of the Talmud. She was the wife of R. Meir, and daughter of R. Ḥanina ben Teradjon.

Her father was one of those who were executed during the persecution of Hadrian after the suppression of the revolt of Bar Cocheba. Her husband, Meir, had been a disciple of Aqiba; and after his death, during the same persecution, Meir was virtually, though not officially, the leader of the Rabbis who carried on the Tradition. The date of the dialogue is therefore the middle, or the latter half, of the second century. The place cannot be determined, except that it was somewhere in Palestine. Meir lived at one time near Lūd (Lydda), at another near Tiberias, perhaps also in Sepphoris. (See b. Erub. 53ᵇ, j. Sota 16ᵇ, j. Ber. 5ᵇ). Beruria, whose name is said to represent Valeria, was almost unique amongst Jewish women in being learned in halachah. She might, in fact, have been a Rabbi, if she had been a man. An opinion which she gave, on a point of halachah, is mentioned with approval, T. Kelim ii. 1. The dialogue before us shows at least that she knew her scriptures well.

The Min quoted to her part of the verse Isa. liv. 1., not applying it indeed to her, because she had children, but apparently referring—as the prophet had referred—to Zion, as representing the Jewish people. Why, he asked, should one that was barren sing for joy? Apparently he meant, why should the Jewish people, crushed and decimated by persecution, nevertheless rejoice? Beruria answered by bidding him first look at the conclusion of the verse, where it is said that the children of the barren are more than the children of the married wife. Then she retorted by accepting his interpretation of the text and turning it against him, 'You say that Israel is like

a barren woman, and ask why then should she rejoice? Because she does not bear children for Hell,
such as you.' Her answer shows clearly enough
the hostility felt by Jews towards the Christians, in
the second century, at a time when the latter were
steadily increasing in numbers. R. Meir, the husband
of Beruria, was the inventor of the nickname Aven-
giljon to denote the Gospels, which is of course a
play upon the word εὐαγγέλιον, (see above, p. 163).
Beruria, probably, had no thought in her mind except
abhorrence of the Minim, when she gave her rather
severe answer. The expression " children for Hell "
(Gehenna) suggests a comparison with the phrase
Matt. xxiii. 15. And while it is exceedingly doubtful
whether the contents of the Gospel were known to
the Rabbis, except very imperfectly through hearing
them referred to or quoted by Christians, nevertheless
it is not unlikely that Christians should occasionally
address Jews in the terms of that terrible denuncia-
tion in Matt. xxiii. And in any case Christians
could not complain if the terms of the Gospel were
cast back at them, being as much, or as little, deserved
on the one side as on the other. Beruria probably
had never seen the passage in Matthew's Gospel, but
she may well have heard language not unlike it from
Christians.

RABBI (JEHUDAH HA-QADOSH) AND A MIN

(88) b. Ḥull. 87ᵃ.—A certain Min said to Rabbi,
' He who formed the mountains did not create
the wind. And he who created the wind did
not form the mountains, as it is written [Amos

iv. 13], *For, lo, he that formeth the mountains
and [he] that createth the wind.*' He [Rabbi]
said to him, 'Fool, look at the end of the
verse, *The Lord of Hosts is his name.*' He
[the Min] said to him, 'Give me time, three
days, and I will refute you.' Rabbi sat three
days fasting. When he was about to eat,
they said to him, 'The Min is standing at the
gate.' He said [Ps. lxix. 21], *They gave me
also gall for my meat.* He [the Min] said to
him, 'Rabbi, I bring thee good tidings.
Thine enemy hath not found an answer, and
hath fallen from the roof and he is dead.' He
[Rabbi] said to him, 'Wilt thou dine with
me?' He said 'Yes.' After they had eaten
and drunk, he [Rabbi] said to him, 'Wilt
thou drink the cup of blessing or receive forty
gold pieces?' He said, 'I will drink the cup
of blessing.' There went forth a Bath Qol
and said, 'The cup of blessing is worth forty
gold pieces.' R. Jitzhaq said, 'Even yet that
family exists among the great ones of Rome,
and they call it the family of Bar Livianos.'

Commentary.—This curious anecdote is introduced
by way of illustration into a halachic discussion, and
is not intended as a haggadic invention. The question
debated was suggested by the mention of an act recorded of R[n.] Gamliel II. On one occasion a man
had slain an animal, and before he could fulfil the
commandment to cover the blood which had been
shed [Lev. xvii. 13], another man forestalled him,
thus depriving him of the merit of fulfilling the
commandment. R[n.] Gamliel ordered that the second

man should pay to the first ten pieces of gold, as being the equivalent of a commandment. The Gemara asks the question whether this sum is the equivalent of a commandment or of a blessing (benediction), and says that in the case of the "cup of blessing" after a meal, if this be regarded as the fulfilling of a commandment then the equivalent is ten gold pieces; but if it be regarded as a blessing, then the equivalent is forty gold pieces, since there are four separate benedictions. The story is introduced in order to prove that the equivalent of the 'cup of blessing' is forty gold pieces; and the proof is given by the fact that Rabbi (Jehudah ha-Qadosh) named that sum to his guest, and also by the assertion that a Bath Qol (voice from heaven) declared that sum to be the equivalent of the 'cup of blessing.'

That is the purpose of the story from the point of view of the Gemara. There was no occasion for the introduction of a Min, as the guest of the Rabbi, if the story had been invented to solve the halachic problem. And although the question of the Min to Rabbi which opens the story, is the same as a question asked of R^n. Gamliel by Cæsar (b Sanh. 39^a, see above, p. 231), yet the conclusion of the story is quite different. The Min quoted the text Amos iv. 13, *He that formeth the mountains and [he that] createth the wind*, and argued, from the use of two distinct verbs, that two distinct creative beings were referred to. The Rabbi answered by telling him to look at the end of the verse, *The Lord of Hosts is his name*, implying that the Creator was one and not two. The Min was not satisfied, and asked for time in which to
16

think of a rejoinder. The Rabbi gave him three days, and himself spent the time in fasting, being apparently in fear of his antagonist. At the end of the time, however, another Min comes to his house, bringing the ' good tidings' that the Rabbi's opponent had destroyed himself, having been unable to think of the rejoinder he desired. In return for his welcome news, he was pressed to stay to dinner; and at the end of the meal his host offered him his choice between drinking the cup of blessing and receiving forty gold pieces. The Rabbi supposed that being a Min, he would not care to act as a Jew by making the responses after the benedictions, and might prefer to receive a reward in money. The Min, however, chose the former, whereupon, so the story goes, a voice from heaven proclaimed that the equivalent of the ' cup of blessing' was forty gold pieces.

A curious note concludes the story, to the effect that ' that family,' presumably that of the Min who brought the ' good tidings,' was well known amongst the great ones of Rome, and that it was called the family of Bar Livianos.

The Jew in this story is R. Jehudah ha-Qadosh, the compiler of the Mishnah, who died A.D. 220, so that the incident belongs to the end of the second, or the beginning of the third, century. Where it took place, there is no evidence to show. Rabbi (as Jehudah ha-Q. is usually called) spent the greater part of his life in Galilee; at various times he lived in Usha, Shefaram, Beth Shearim and Sepphoris. The last-named city may be regarded as especially his place of residence, since he dwelt there seventeen years and died there. We may suppose that the incident of the story before us took place in Sepphoris ; and with this agrees the fact that, as we have already seen, many of the stories about Minim are located in Sepphoris.

In the story itself, nothing turns upon the particular question of the Min to Rabbi. And since this is identical with a question addressed to R^n Gamliel by Cæsar, it is possible that it has been borrowed from the earlier incidents, the actual question of Rabbi's opponent not being known. The interest of the story before us is contained in its dramatic development. It is certainly surprising that a man should commit suicide because he could not refute the argument of an opponent. The second Min, however, is more interesting than the first ; and the remark of R. Jitzḥaq, at the end of the story, seems to indicate that he was not an unknown man. The words in which he delivered his message, ' I bring you good tidings ' (מבשר טובות), might seem to suggest εὐαγγέλιον ; but the phrase is common in New Hebrew, as the N.T. term is in Greek. We cannot therefore infer a reference to the Gospel in the language of the Min, though the phrase is certainly appropriate, if he was a Christian. He must have been a Jewish Christian, since he was evidently familiar with the Jewish ceremonial of the benediction after the meal, and was willing to take part in it as if he had been a Jew. The friendliness shown towards a Min by a Jew in this instance is in sharp contrast to the feeling indicated in most of the stories concerning the Minim.

The historical note about the family of this Min is a riddle which I have not been able to solve. R.

Jitzḥaq, the authority for it, is, indirectly, the authority for the story itself, although it is given anonymously. He evidently knew about it, since he knew the Min who is mentioned in it. R. Jitzḥaq was a Babylonian by birth, but spent the greater part of his life in Palestine, chiefly in Tiberias (where he studied under R. Johanan), and in Cæsarea. He belonged therefore to the end of the third and the beginning of the fourth century. The name 'Bar Livianos' is written in most of the MSS. and early texts, 'Bar Lulianos' (see Rabbinowicz on the passage), and in one MS. 'Ben Ulianos.' The name Lulianos usually represents Julianus. R. Jitzḥaq said that the family called by this name existed in his own time, amongst the great ones of Rome,[1] and that the Min was a member of it. It is not clear how a Jewish Christian should be a member of a great Roman house. Some light is thrown on the question by the fact that R. Jitzḥaq had a disciple whose name was Luliani bar Tabrinai, *i.e.* Julianus bar Tiberianus (see Bacher, Ag. d. Pal. Am., ii. 210, n. 7). This man was a Jew, since he was a Rabbi; and his Roman name does not imply Gentile birth. Many Rabbis had Greek or Roman names. The remark of R. Jitzḥaq may accordingly be explained thus: the name of the Min was Julianus (or Lulianos), a name simply borrowed from a great Roman family. R. Jitzḥaq's disciple, Luliani, may have been a relative of the Min in a younger genera-

---

[1] This term, however, is sometimes applied to distinguished Romans living in Palestine, as in b. A. Zar. 18ᵃ, where "the great ones of Rome" attended the funeral of R. José b. Qisma, probably in Cæsarea, certainly in Palestine. The Min in the story is more likely to have been associated with a Roman family in Palestine than in Rome.

tion, and perhaps had the vanity to assert a connexion with the Roman family.

R. Ishmael ben Jose and a Min

two powers in heaven

(89) b. Sanh. 38^b.—A certain Min said to R. Ishmael ben R. José, 'It is written [Gen. xix. 24], *And the Lord rained upon Sodom and Gomorrah brimstone and fire from the Lord.* It ought to have been *from himself.*' A certain fuller said [to R. Ishmael], 'Let him alone; I will answer him. For it is written [Gen. iv. 23], *And Lamech said to his wives, Adah and Zillah, hear my voice, ye wives of Lamech.* It ought to have been *my wives.* But the text reads so, and here also the text reads so.' He said, 'Whence did you get that?' 'From the saying of R. Meir.'

Commentary.—This anecdote forms part of a long passage containing many polemical discussions between Jews and non-Jews. These will be dealt with, so far as they relate to Minim, in reference to the various Rabbis who took part in the dialogue. It would have been interesting to present the whole passage at once; but for convenience of explanation it is better to break up the material into its component parts. R. Ishmael ben José was the son of R. José ben Ḥalaphta, and belonged to the circle of Rabbi (Jehudah ha-Qadosh) mentioned in the preceding section. He lived, probably in Sepphoris, at the end of the second century and the beginning of the third. This serves to fix the date of the incident within rather wide limits indeed, but otherwise is of no importance; because, although the Min addressed his question to R. Ishmael, he was answered, not by that Rabbi, but by a bystander who heard the question.

The Min quoted Gen. xix. 24, and drew attention to the fact that in that text the name of the Lord was mentioned twice, *The Lord rained . . . . from the Lord.* He suggested that this implied the existence of more than one divine being.[1] A fuller, who heard the remark, asked to be allowed to answer the Min. He quoted Gen. iv. 23, where a similar grammatical peculiarity occurs in reference to Lamech. The inference was that as Lamech was only one being, so God was only one. As for the form of the phrase, the scripture (or rather the author of the scripture) chose to say so, in the one text as in the other. On being asked, as it would seem by R. Ishmael, where he learned his answer, the fuller replied that it was from the teaching of R. Meir. Probably R. Meir had used the argument in a public address in the synagogue.

R. Jitzhaq (see above, p. 244), a century later, strengthened the argument (Ber. r., § li., p. 105ª, ᵇ) by quoting 1 Kings i. 33 and Esther viii. 8 in addition to Gen. iv. 23. He did not refer to the use of Gen. xix. 24 by the Minim; but unless this text were made use of by heretics, there would have been no object in strengthening the counter argument.

[1] On the doctrine of Two divine Powers, see below, p. 261 fol.

R. Ḥanina, R. Hoshaia, and a Min

ISRAEL AND THE GENTILES

(90) b. Pes. 87ᵇ.—R. Hoshaia said, 'What is that which is written [Judg. v. 11], *The righteousness of his rule in Israel.* The Holy One, Blessed be He, did righteousness in Israel in that he "scattered" them amongst the nations.' And this is what a certain Min said to R. Ḥanina, 'We esteem ourselves better than you. It is written .concerning you [1 Kings xi. 16], *He dwelt there six months*, etc. This refers to us. You have been in our midst these many years and we do nothing to you.' He said to him, 'Wilt thou allow a disciple to join in [the discussion] with thee?' R. Hoshaia joined in with him. He said to him, 'Because ye did not know how ye might destroy us. Not all of them [the Jews] are amongst you. As for those that are amongst you [if ye destroyed them] ye would be called a broken kingdom.' He said to him, 'By the Temple of Rome! we are always thinking so.'

Commentary. — R. Hoshaia belonged to the younger generation of the disciples of Rabbi (Jehudah ha-Qadosh), and there is some reason to believe that the latter, and not R. Ḥanina, was the one to whom the remark of the Min was addressed. Rabbinowicz (D. Soph. on the passage) gives a reading, 'Jehudah Nesiah' in place of R. Ḥanina. This would naturally denote the grandson of Rabbi; but Rabbi himself is sometimes so called. R. Hoshaia is described as a disciple. This would suggest Rabbi, rather than R. Ḥanina, as his teacher, and would exclude Jehudah Nesiah. Since, however, the question is answered by R. Hoshaia, it is of no great importance to whom it was addressed. The date of the incident may be placed in the first half of the third century. The scene was probably Cæsarea, where R. Hoshaia seems to have spent most of his life.

The story occurs in the middle of a haggadah upon the dispersion of Israel among the nations. R. Hoshaia explained the text, Judg. v. 11, *The righteousness of his rule in Israel*, by slightly altering the word ' his rule,' *pirzōnō*, so as to make it read as if it were derived from the root *pazar*, to scatter. Whence he drew the moral that God had shown his righteousness, had done good to Israel by scattering them amongst the nations. In illustration of this striking interpretation, the dialogue with the Min is added, in which R. Hoshaia virtually explains his meaning. The Min quotes the text 1 Kings xi. 16,[1] *He dwelt there six months until he had cut off every male in Edom.* *Edom*, said the Min, refers to us (*i.e.* the Romans, according to a very common identifiication in the Talmud and the Midrash). The argument of the Min is this :—Israel showed cruelty to Edom in the days of old; but Edom, *i.e.* Rome, has done nothing to Israel, though for many years Jews have been living in the midst of the Gentile nations in the Roman empire. Therefore the Romans are

---

[1] I give this in full. The Talmud often gives only a few words of a quotation, although the whole verse is necessary to establish the point with a view to which the quotation was made.

more generous than the Jews. The answer to this challenge is given, not by the person addressed, whether R. Ḥanina or Rabbi, but by R. Hoshaia. Instead of denying, as he might well have done, the alleged forbearance of the Romans towards the Jews, he boldly declared that the Romans would have killed all the Jews if they had known how. But Israel was scattered abroad, and in that fact lay their safety. This was the blessing of God in scattering Israel, according to the exposition of Judg. v. 11 already given. If, continued R. Hoshaia, the Romans had killed the Jews who were in their midst, their empire would be called a broken kingdom ; the reason apparently being that the Jews were good citizens and also numerous, so that the destruction of them would have been a loss to the empire. The Min admitted the justice of the retort.

There is nothing in this dialogue to distinguish the Min from any heathen citizen of the empire, except the fact that he was aquainted with the O.T. scriptures. He could hardly have been a Jew ; for, as remarked in connexion with another anecdote (see above, p. 224), a Jew, even though he were a Jewish Christian, would hardly have taunted another Jew with the misfortunes or the faults of Israel. The Min was probably a Christian ; but as opposed to the Jew, it is remarkable that he speaks as a Roman citizen, not as a Christian. I need hardly remind the reader that the date of this incident must be nearly a century earlier than the time when Christianity became the official religion of the Roman empire. It is impossible to identify this Christian. There is some reason to believe that Hoshaia met and conversed with Origen, who was, like himself, resident in Cæsarea. But there is nothing in the present instance to suggest that the Min was a Christian bishop. Whatever a layman might do, a bishop would hardly swear by the great temple of Rome. As Cæsarea was the seat of the government, the Min may have been some official in the city who happened to be a Christian.

R. Ḥanina and a Min

THE REJECTION OF ISRAEL

(91) b. Joma 56ᵇ. — A certain Min said to R. Ḥanina, ' Now are ye unclean children, for it is written [Lam. i. 9], *Her uncleanness is in her skirts.*' He said to him, ' Come, see what is written concerning them [Lev. xvi. 16], *That dwelleth with them in the midst of their uncleanness*; at the very time when they are unclean, the Shechinah dwelleth in the midst of them.'

Commentary. — There is very little that needs explanation in this fragment of dialogue. We have, as in other cases, quotation of scripture by a Min, with an anti-Jewish purpose. The Min accordingly was probably a Christian not of Jewish extraction. The point of the taunt to the Jew was the apparent abandonment of Israel on the part of God. The previous extract (90), shows one way in which the Jews met and refuted the insinuation. R. Ḥanina in the present instance gives another. The challenge of the Min and the answer of the Rabbi are little

better than mere word-fencing. The incident only
serves to show how both Jews and their opponents
were conscious of the change in the national status
of Israel since the destruction of the temple by
Titus, and the final overthrow under Hadrian. The
Jews were by no means disposed to gratify either
Christian or heathen by the admission of defeat; and
though the sorrow was heavy in his heart, the Jew
would turn a proud face to the Gentile and meet
scorn with scorn.

R. Ḥanina has already been mentioned, not merely
in the preceding section, but earlier (see above, pp.
72, 73). He was of Babylonian origin, and only
came to Palestine comparatively late in life. He
lived in Sepphoris, and is thought to have died about
the year 232. He was more than eighty years old at
the time of his death. No doubt the interview with
the Min took place in Sepphoris, a place which has
already been very frequently mentioned in connexion
with Minim.

R. Ḥanina and a Min

THE LAND OF ISRAEL

(92) b. Gitt. 57ª. — A certain Min said to R.
Ḥanina, 'Ye speak falsely' [in reference to
the alleged enormous population of Palestine
in former times]. He said to him, '*A dear
land* it is written of her [Dan. xi. 41].
Whereas in the case of this deer, its skin
does not contain it, so the land of Israel while
the people lived in it was wide, and now that
they are now longer living in it, is contracted.'

Commentary. — This can only be regarded as a *jeu d'esprit* of R. Ḥanina. It occurs in a famous haggadah concerning the land of Israel, where several Rabbis utter the wildest exaggerations as to its former fertility and the population of its cities. No Rabbi seriously believed that there were " 600,000 cities on the King's mountain, each of which contained as many people as came out from Egypt, while three cities contained each twice as many." A too literal Min, prototype of other Minim in later days, was shocked at the monstrous exaggeration, and exclaimed to R. Ḥanina, " Ye lie ! " The Rabbi gave him an answer worthy of the occasion, being only a witty play upon words. It is written, he said, in Daniel xi. 41, *a dear land.*[1] Now the skin of this *deer*, when it is stripped off, is no longer large enough to hold the carcase of the animal ; it shrivels up. In like manner, the land of Israel was large enough to hold all those people while they lived in it. Since they have gone, it has shrivelled up, and is no longer large enough. You behold it in its shrunken state.

I have expanded R. Ḥanina's answer in order to bring out the point of it; and I leave it, without further comment, as a piece of Rabbinical wit, genuine haggadah in its sportive mood. It would be ridiculous to treat it seriously, and found upon it a charge of falsehood against the Rabbis.

In b. Kethub. 112[a] is a reference to this same repartee of R. Ḥanina, but the play upon the word

---

[1] More correctly, 'a glorious land.' I have used the word 'dear' in order to reproduce the pun. Tzebi means 'glory,' and also 'a gazelle' or deer. Thus the words quoted may be rendered either 'a dear (glorious) land,' or 'the land is a deer' (gazelle).

'tzebi' is expanded into a series of similes; and although R. Ḥanina is mentioned, the Min only addresses to him a remark upon the actual fertility of Palestine. On the same page of b. Kethub. is a remark make by a Min to R. Zera, which is found in a somewhat different form in b. Shabb. 88ᵃ.

R. JANNAI, R. JONATHAN, AND A MIN

THE GRAVE OF RACHEL

(93) Ber. r., § 82, p. 155ᵇ.—*And Rachel died and was buried* [Gen. xxxv. 19]. Burial followed close on death, in the *way to Ephrath (the same is Bethlehem).*
R. Jannai and R. Jonathan were sitting. There came a certain Min and asked them, 'What is that which is written [1 Sam. x. 2], *When thou art departed from me this day [thou shalt find two men by Rachel's tomb, in the border of Benjamin at Zelzah]?* Is not Zelzah in the border of Benjamin, and the tomb of Rachel in the border of Judah? As it is written [Gen. xxxv. 19], *and she was buried on the way to Ephrath,* and it is written [Mic. v. 2], *Bethlehem Ephrathah.'* R. Jannai said to him [Isa. iv. 1], '*Take away my reproach*'! [R. Jonathan] said to him '[the text means], *When thou departest from me this day by Rachel's tomb, thou shalt find two men in the border of Benjamin at Zelzah.'* Others say [that the answer of R. Jannai was] '*When thou departest from me this day in the border*

of *Benjamin in Zelzah, thou shalt find two men by the tomb of Rachel,'* and this is the correct answer.

Commentary.—The difficulty which prompted the question of the Min was as to the locality of Bethlehem. According to Mic. v. 2 [v. 1 Hebr.] Bethlehem Ephrathah is in the land of Judah. According to Gen. xxxv. 19, Rachel was buried *in the way to Ephrathah, which is Bethlehem.* But it is said in 1 Sam. x. 2, *Rachel's tomb in the border of Benjamin at Zelzah.* Whence it would seem that Bethlehem Ephrathah was also 'in the border of Benjamin,' This contradiction is several times referred to in the Rabbinical literature, and various solutions of it given. Bacher [A. d. T., ii. 50, n. 5] mentions one by R. Meir, but does not give the reference. There is also one in T. Sot., xi. 11, where no author's name is mentioned.

In the story before us a Min came to where R. Jannai and R. Jonathan were sitting, and asked them to explain the difficulty. R. Jannai apparently was unable to do so, and turning to R. Jonathan said, in the words of Isaiah [iv. 1], ' *Take away my reproach,*' *i.e.* ' Help me out ; do not let me lie under the reproach of being unable to answer.' (This is the interpretation of the commentary ' Japheh Toar ' upon the passage.) R. Jonathan accordingly explained the verse, in one or other of two ways, both of which are given. The point of his answer is that ' *in the border of Benjamin at Zelzah* ' denotes a different place from that where Rachel's tomb was. Therefore, there was nothing to prove that Bethlehem Ephrathah, the site of the tomb, was not in the land of Judah.

The interest of the dialogue, for the purpose of this

work, lies in the fact that a Min should come and consult a Rabbi upon a question of interpretation of scripture. This shows that the relations between the Jews and the Minim were not always hostile.

R. Jannai and R. Jonathan both lived in Sepphoris, and were contemporary with R. Ḥanina mentioned in the preceding sections. R. Jonathan is the same whom we have already met with as having an unpleasant adventure with the Minim (see above, p. 215). The Min in the present instance is evidently a Jewish Christian, since no one else (except a Jew) would be interested in the interpretation of the texts about Bethlehem. The importance of these texts was the same both for Jews and for Jewish Christians, since upon them depended the question of the birthplace of the Messiah. The prophecy Mic. v. 1 was interpreted of the Messiah, as is shown by the Targum on the passage,[1] and also by the quotation in Matt. ii. 4–6. It was therefore a difficulty for Jewish Christians as well as for Jews, that the text in 1 Sam. appeared to contradict the prophecy in Micah. That the interpretation of R. Jonathan was contrary to the plain meaning of the text is of small importance.

R. SIMLAI AND THE MINIM

THE DOCTRINE OF TWO POWERS IN HEAVEN

(94) j. Ber., 12ᵈ, 13ᵃ.—The Minim asked R. Simlai how many gods created the world? He said to them, Do ye ask me? Go and ask the first man, as it is written [Deut. iv. 32], *Ask*

---

[1] Targum on Mic. v. 1 :—מנך קדמי יפוק משיחא.

*now of the former days which were before thee,
since God created man upon the earth.* It is
not written here *(they) created*, but *(he)
created.* They said to him, It is written
[Gen. i. 1], *In the beginning God created.*
He said to them, Is it written *(they) created?*
It is only written *(he) created.*

R. Simlai said, ' In every passage where the
Minim go wrong, the answer to them is close
by.'

They (the Minim) returned and asked him,
'What of that which is written [Gen. i. 26],
*Let us make man in our image, after our
likeness.*' He said to them, ' It is not written
here [*ib.* 27], *And they created man in their
image*, but *And God created man in his image.*'
His disciples said to him, ' Rabbi, thou hast
driven away these men with a stick. But
what dost thou answer to us?' He said to
them, ' At the first, Adam was created out of
the dust, and Eve was created out of the man.
From Adam downwards [it is said] *in our
image according to our likeness.* It is impossible for man to exist without woman, and
it is impossible for woman to exist without
man, and it is impossible for both to exist
without the Shechinah.'

And they returned and asked him, 'What is
that which is written [Josh. xxii. 22], *God,
God the Lord, God, God the Lord, he
knoweth.* He said to them, ' It is not written
here ' *(they) know*, but it is written *(he)
knoweth.*' His disciples said to him, ' Rabbi,

thou hast driven these men away with a stick. But what dost thou answer to us ?' He said to them, 'The three [names] are the name of one, just as a man says, Basileus, Cæsar, Augustus.'

They returned and asked him, 'What is that which is written [Ps. l. 1], *God, God the Lord hath spoken and he called the earth.*' He said to them, 'Is it written here (*they*) *have spoken* and *have called*? It is only written, (*he*) *hath spoken* and *hath called the earth.*' His disciples said to him, 'Rabbi, thou hast driven these men away with a stick. But what dost thou answer to us ?' He said to them, 'The three [names] are the name of one, just as a man says, labourers, masons, architects.'

They returned and asked him, 'What is that which is written [Josh. xxiv. 19], *For he is a holy God*' [where the word '*holy*' is plural]. He said to them, 'It is written there not *they are holy*, but *he* [*is holy*]. (He is a jealous God.)' His disciples said to him, 'Rabbi, thou hast driven these men away with a stick. What dost thou answer to us ?' R. Jitzḥaq said, 'Holy in every form of holiness.' For R. Judan said, in the name of R. Aḥa, 'The way of the holy One, Blessed be He, is in holiness. His word is in holiness, his sitting is in holiness, the baring of his arm is in holiness. He is fearful and mighty in holiness. His ways are in holiness [as it is written, Ps. lxxvii. 13], *Thy way, O God, is*

17

in the sanctuary. His footsteps are in holiness
[Ps. lxviii. 24], *The goings of my King, my
God, in the sanctuary.* His sitting is in
holiness [Ps. xlvii. 8], *God sitteth upon the
throne of his holiness.* His word is in holiness
[Ps. cviii. 7], *God hath spoken in his holiness.*
The baring of his arm is in holiness [Isa. lii.
10], *The Lord hath made bare his holy arm.*
He is fearful and mighty in holiness [Exod.
xv. 11], *Who is like thee, glorious in holiness
[fearful in praise]*?

They returned and asked him, ' What is
that which is written [Deut. iv. 7], *For what
great nation is there that hath a God, so nigh
unto them, as the Lord our God, whensoever
we call upon him?'* He said to them, ' It is not
written here *call upon them,* but *call upon him.'*
His disciples said to him, ' Rabbi, thou hast
driven away these men with a stick. What
dost thou answer to us ? ' He said to them,
' He is near in every manner of nearness.'

The above passage is contained, with but
slight variations, in Ber. r., viii. 9. Parts of it
are found in Shem. r., xxix., Debar. r., ii.

Commentary.—R. Simlai, of Babylonian origin,
lived in Palestine, and for the most part in Lydda.
He spent some time, however, in Galilee, where he
became the friend and attendant of R. Jannai. He
thus belonged to the same circle as the Rabbis mentioned in the sections immediately preceding the
present one. The date of the story may be given as
about the middle of the third century. I am inclined
to think that R. Simlai lived in Lydda after his so-

journ with R. Jannai in Galilee. He is referred to in the Babylonian Gemara, A. Zar. 36ᵃ, as R. Simlai of Lydda. It seems natural to suppose that he was head of an academy after, and not before, being the disciple and attendant of R. Jannai. But the data for fixing the chronology of his life are scanty and somewhat contradictory (see Bacher., A. d. Pal. Am., i. 552 fol. ; also Grätz, G. d. J., iv. 265).

The long passage translated here contains the fullest account of the discussions between R. Simlai and the Minim. Moreover, as it is given in the Palestinian Gemara, it is the nearest in time to the date when the incidents related took place ; and not only so, but R. Simlai was the associate of the Rabbis who represent the main line of tradition embodied in the Palestinian Gemara. We may therefore infer that the series of dialogues here recorded contains the substance of actual discussions between R. Simlai and the Minim. That is to say, we may be certain that the doctrinal question which forms the basis of all the dialogues was really debated, that the texts quoted were really those used by the Minim, and that the replies of R. Simlai contain the actual arguments used in refutation of the heretical exegesis. It need not be supposed that all the six dialogues took place in immediate succession. This is unlikely, from the fact that some of the answers are mere repetitions. R. Simlai probably had several encounters with the Minim at various times ; and the passage before us may be considered as a list of these, arranged according to the texts made use of. The phrase, 'the Minim returned and asked,' hardly means more than that 'on another occasion they asked.'

It will be observed that in every dialogue but the first the disciples of R. Simlai asked him to give them a reply other than that which he had given to the Minim. In each case the curious phrase occurs, ' Rabbi, thou hast driven these men away with a stick.' This appears to mean, 'thou hast put them off with a mere quibble,' instead of dealing seriously with their question. So, at all events, the disciples seem to have intended the phrase. Yet the answers which the Rabbi gave to the Minim were surely more to the point than those which he gave to his disciples. Those who argue from plural nouns are adequately refuted with singular verbs. And it must be remembered that the written text of Scripture was, for both parties in the controversy, the final authority. The time is, even now, not so far distant when similar questions were decided by appeal to texts. The intention of the disciples in asking for other explanations was perhaps that they wished for an interpretation of the text without reference to its polemical use, an indication of what it did mean rather than of what it did not mean. R. Simlai did not always succeed so well in positive exposition as he did in controversial negation. His explanation of the words, *let us make man*, etc., is no explanation. The words were used before the creation of Adam and Eve, and could not gain their meaning from what was only possible after that event. If this be dismissed as absurd, then the alternative seems to be that R. Simlai regarded the account of the creation in Gen. ii. as a record of events prior to those related in Gen. i., so that Adam and Eve were already in existence when God said, *Let us make man*, etc. I suspect that R. Simlai was quite unable to explain the use of the plural in *let us make man,* etc., and escaped from the difficulty by a piece of haggadah, striking but irrelevant.

His answers to the argument from the triple designation of God are reasonable enough. It is curious that the interpretation of the phrase concerning the holiness of God is ascribed, not to R. Simlai, but to R. Jitzḥaq, a younger contemporary, and not impossibly one of R. Simlai's own disciples. It is nowhere said indeed, so far as I know, that there was this relationship between the older and the younger man ; but it is noteworthy that, in the last of his explanations, R. Simlai uses the same idea as that which R. Jitzḥaq had used in reference to 'holiness,' a fact which would seem to suggest that R. Simlai took up the idea, on hearing his disciple expound it, having himself been unable to explain the text to which Jitzḥaq applied it. If this be thought to be too far-fetched, then the conclusion is that R. Simlai's own explanation had been forgotten, or that he never gave one, and that the compilers of the Gemara inserted the later explanation of R. Jitzḥaq in this appropriate place.

The question, so often asked in preceding sections, Who are the Minim referred to in the passage ? is of special importance here, because the controversy recorded turns upon a great theological subject. It is known, and frequently referred to in the rabbinical literature, as the doctrine of 'Two Powers in Heaven.' And as the present passage is the longest which treats of that subject, here will be the best place to discuss it. Other passages having reference to this doctrine will be given later, and

mention has already been made of it.   But it will be
convenient to inquire here, once for all, what is the
doctrinal implication of the phrase, 'Two Powers in
Heaven.'   We shall then have a means of deciding
in other passages, as well as in the present one, Who
were the Minim who held the doctrine?

The phrase itself, 'Two Powers in Heaven,' occurs
in Siphri, § 329, p. 139ᵇ.   More often it occurs in the
shorter form 'two powers,' as in Mechilta 66ᵇ, and
elsewhere.   But in every case it is implied that the
two powers are supposed to be in heaven.   It is
evident, therefore, that the doctrine referred to is
not that of a dualism consisting of a good and an
evil power, hostile to one another.   The doctrine of
the Two Powers cannot be that of the Persian, or
the Manichæan dualism; because, according to those
systems, the evil power certainly did not work in
conjunction with the good power in the creation of
the world or in anything else.   The Persian dualism,
comprising Ahuramazda and Ahriman, is referred to
in the Talmud, in a polemical discussion, b. Sanh.
38ᵇ, and it is worth notice that the opponent of the
Jew is there called a Magus and not a Min.   There
are, it is true, instances where the term Min is used,
and where a Persian is almost certainly intended
(see b. Ber. 58ᵃ), but this does not occur in reference
to the doctrine of the Two Powers.

The various Gnostic systems maintained a dualism,
or rather a plurality, of superhuman Powers; and
the Jews of Palestine were more likely to come into
contact and collision with Gnostics than with the
adherents of the forms of religion just mentioned.
Is the doctrine of the Two Powers, then, a Gnostic

doctrine? It was one of the main tenets of most
Gnostic systems that the world was created by the
Demiurgus, an inferior God, regarded as an emana-
tion from the supreme Deity, and far removed from
him. The Demiurgus was, by some Gnostics,
identified with the God of the Jews; and the
superiority of Christianity over Judaism was explained by saying that the latter was the religion
whose object of worship was the Demiurgus, while
the former was the revelation, through Christ, of the
supreme God. Neither Christ, nor the supreme God,
according to Gnostic teaching, had any share in
creating the world. Christ certainly not; and the
supreme God only so far as he willed it, and dele-
gated the task to the inferior being, the Demiurgus.
The whole point of the Gnostic doctrine was that
the supreme God should be thought to have no
immediate contact with the world of matter.

Now the doctrine of the Two Powers in Heaven,
which is ascribed in the Talmud and the Midrash
to the Minim, is almost always mentioned in connexion with the creation of the world. And the
texts which are urged against it are such as to show
that not only did the supreme God himself create
the world, but that he did so alone, without any
associate. And the refutation is always directed
especially to the second point. The Gnostics certainly did not teach that creation was the work of
the supreme God; but equally they did not teach
that it was the work of two deities acting together.
Hence it would seem that the doctrine of the Two
Powers is not a Gnostic doctrine; and the only
exception is perhaps this, that where the two powers

are referred to in connexion with some other subject than the creation of the world, there may be—I do not say there is—a reference to Gnosticism.

There remains the question whether the doctrine of the 'Two Powers in Heaven,' associated in creation, was a Christian doctrine? And in answering that question it must be borne in mind that we are not at liberty to range through all the various forms of Christianity taught in the first three centuries, but must confine our attention to those which may reasonably be supposed to have been familiar to the Christians of Palestine. Now a doctrine of two powers in heaven, associated in creation, is clearly taught in the Epistle to the Hebrews. The opening words of that epistle are (Heb. i. 1): *God . . . . hath, at the end of these days, spoken unto us in his Son, whom he appointed heir of all things, through whom also he made the worlds.* Whatever may be the precise meaning of 'worlds' (αἰῶνας), it certainly includes that of the world of which God, according to the O.T., was the creator. The relation of Christ to God in the theology of the Epistle to the Hebrews was quite different from that of the Demiurgus to God, in the Gnostic systems. And the difference consists in the fact that the Demiurgus was placed as far off from God as was consistent with his retaining a spiritual nature, while Christ was regarded, in the epistle, as in closest possible union with God, short of actual identity of person or complete equality of rank. The theology of the Epistle to the Hebrews might, from the Jewish point of view, be naturally described as a doctrine of Two Powers in Heaven, or even as a doctrine of two Gods. The same might be said of the purely Pauline and the Johannine theologies, from the Jewish point of view. It is therefore evident that the doctrine of Two Powers, which is ascribed to the Minim in the Talmud, is a Christian doctrine.[1]

Of the three types of Christian theology just mentioned, the one most likely to be found amongst the Christians with whom the Jews of Palestine came into contact, is, beyond question, that of the Epistle to the Hebrews. Whatever may be the place of origin, or the destination of that Epistle, it was addressed to Jewish Christians; and it is not unreasonable to suppose that it would become generally known amongst Jewish Christians where-ever they might be, whether in Rome or in Palestine. That the Epistle to the Hebrews was known, not merely to the Jewish Christians of Palestine, but to the Rabbis, is indicated by a polemical reference (b. Nedar. 32[b]) to the priesthood of Melchizedek, upon which is founded one of the characteristic doctrines of the Epistle to the Hebrews. [The passage will be translated (139) and explained below, see p. 338.] This polemical reference was made by R. Ishmael, whom we have already met with several times as an opponent of Minim [see above, pp. 105, 130, 156], and dates from the early years of the second century.

We may, therefore, conclude that the theology of

---

[1] This is shown clearly by a passage (95) in Pesiqta. r., xxi. pp. 100[b], 101[a], "If the son of the harlot [*i.e.* Jesus] say to thee, 'There are two gods,' say to him, 'I am He of the Red Sea, I am He of Sinai'" [*i.e.* there are not two gods but one]. A few lines further down, the same argument is met by the text, 'God spoke' [sing. not plur.]. See below, p. 304.

the Epistle to the Hebrews was known to, and accepted by, the Jewish Christians of Palestine early in the second century, and that the doctrine of the Two Powers in Heaven is the Jewish description of the doctrine of that Epistle, concerning the relation of Christ to God. Whether all Jewish Christians, in Palestine or elsewhere, adopted the Christology of the Epistle to the Hebrews, must remain an open question. It is quite likely that some of them adhered to the primitive doctrine as to the person of Jesus, which did not in any way trench upon the Jewish conception of the Unity of God. There were certainly different sects or parties amongst the Jewish Christians, as is shown by the names Ebionite and Nazarene. And it is possible that the former term denoted those who did not accept the Christology of the Epistle to the Hebrews. The solution of this question I leave to New Testament scholars.

As regards the main subject of this book, it may now be taken that the term Minim includes Jewish Christians holding a theology similar to that of the Epistle to the Hebrews. In the concluding division of this work I shall endeavour to place this fact in its proper relation to the general history of the Jewish Christians.

R. Abahu, R. Saphra, and the Minim.

(96) b. A. Zar. 4ᵃ.—R. Abahu commended R. Saphra to the Minim as being a great man. They remitted to him thirteen years' tolls. One day they found him. They said to him, ' It is written [Amos iii. 2], *You only have I*

known, of all the families of the earth, therefore I will visit upon you all your iniquities. One that hath anger, would he vent it against his friend?' He was silent, and said to them nothing at all. They put a towel over his head and railed at him. R. Abahu came and found them. He said to them, 'Why do ye rail at him?' They said to him, 'And didst not thou tell us that he was a great man? Yet he does not know how to tell us the explanation of this text.' He said to them, 'I said this to you of him as a Talmudist. Did I ever say so of him as a Scripture-teacher?' They said to him, 'Why are ye different, and know [how to explain scriptures]?' He said to them, 'We, who live in your midst, give our minds to it and examine [the scriptures]. They [*i.c.* the Babylonians] do not examine them.' They said to him, 'Do thou tell us.' He said to them, 'I will make a parable of what the thing is like. [It is like] a man who lends to two men, one his friend and the other his enemy. He recovers [payment] from his friend little by little, but from his enemy all at once.'

Commentary.—The date of this very curious incident is the beginning of the fourth century. R. Abahu, already mentioned, was the disciple of R. Johanan, and lived in Cæsarea. R. Saphra was a Babylonian, on a visit to Palestine, and is well known, though not prominent, in the history of the Talmudic tradition. No doubt was ever expressed of his entire loyalty to the Jewish religion. Yet here we find him, and that, too, on the recommendation of R. Abahu, accepted by the Minim as a teacher. From the fact that they remitted to him thirteen years' tolls, it would seem that they engaged him as their teacher, offering him at least an honorarium if not a salary. This fact is important for the history of the Minim, as bearing on their relation to Judaism. There is, so far as I know, nothing in the scanty notices of R. Saphra, to be found elsewhere in the Talmud, that throws any light upon the incident here related. He was held in high esteem in Babylonia, where it was triumphantly reported (b. Gitt. 29^{b}) that he had, in a judicial decision, proved three ordained Rabbis of Palestine to be in error. He was intimate with Abahu, and it is perhaps worthy of note that it was he who reported in Babylonia, on the authority of Abahu, the account of the abortive schism of Ḥananjah, nephew of R. Jehoshua, concerning whom the allegation of Minuth had been made (see above, p. 211). It does not appear, however, that R. Saphra knew anything of the story about Ḥananjah's adventure with the Minim of Capernaum. There is something so strange in the assertion that a Rabbi so well known as Saphra should become a teacher amongst the Minin, that one is inclined to suspect a confusion between the well-known Saphra and some obscure man of the same name. But there is no evidence for this. Abahu speaks of Saphra as a great man, and a Babylonian. And there is no hint of any other being intended than the R. Saphra elsewhere mentioned, who, moreover, is known to have been an associate of Abahu. There is no ground whatever for dismissing the story as a fiction. The time in which Abahu lived was not so remote but that the traditions of his school were well known when the Babylonian Gemara was compiled. The incident under discussion would not be less strange even if the Rabbi concerned were not the well-known Saphra. What is remarkable is that any Rabbi should have become a teacher amongst the Minim. And if such an occurrence had never been known, it is not likely to have been invented. If it had been invented, and related by way of a jest against R. Saphra, the story would have done more justice to the jest and not have mentioned the alleged fact as a mere matter of course.

Bacher (A. d. Pal. Am., ii. 96 f.) suggests that R. Saphra was engaged by the Minim not as a teacher but as an assistant in collecting the Imperial revenue, which they farmed. This is on the strength of the phrase, "remitted to him thirteen years' tolls." But this suggestion, even if it be deemed a fair inference from the phrase just quoted, does not solve the difficulty. For the Minim were annoyed with him on account of his ignorance of Scripture, not of his blundering in finance. If they had engaged him as an accountant, they could not have charged Abahu with having given a misleading recommendation, when R. Saphra failed as an interpreter of Scripture. It is possible that the collection of the tolls in Cæsarea was in the hands of a Christian; but it is not clear what is meant by the remission of 'thirteen years' tolls.' All that can be said is that the Minim made some sort of a present to R. Saphra, in return for the benefit which they hoped to derive from his services.

I see no alternative but to accept the story as showing that the relations between the Minim and the Jews, at all events in the beginning of the fourth century, were not always hostile. That the Minim here mentioned were Jewish Christians, and of a strongly Jewish type, is evident from the fact that a Jewish Rabbi of unquestioned orthodoxy could be acceptable to them. That they were heretics is plain from Abahu's answer to them. The story itself needs little further explanation. The Minim were dissatisfied with their new teacher, and asked R. Abahu why it was that the stranger could not explain the Scriptures, while Abahu and the Jews of Cæsarea were able to do so. The answer was that the necessity of refuting the Minim in controversy made them study the Scriptures very closely. The Babylonian Jews, who did not encounter Minim, had no inducement to such close study. This is of some importance as showing that the Minim were confined to Palestine, or, at least, were not numerous elsewhere.

R. Abahu, at the request of the Minim, gave his own interpretation of the text (Amos iii. 2) in the form of a parable. The Jews, being favoured by God, received the punishment of their sins by instalments, so that they might not be too severely dealt with. The other nations will receive their punishment once for all and will suffer in proportion.

R. Abahu and the Epiqurosin. Enoch

(97) Ber. r., xxv. 1, p. 55ᶜ.—The Epiqurosin asked R. Abahu, they said to him, ' We do not find death in the case of Enoch.' He said to them,

'Why?' They said to him, 'There is mention here [Gen. v. 24] of "taking," and there is mention elsewhere [2 Kings ii. 5], *to-day the Lord taketh away thy master from thy head.*' He said to them, 'If ye are arguing from the idea of "taking," there is mention here of "taking," and there is mention elsewhere [Ezek. xxiv. 16], *Behold, I take away from thee the desire of thine eyes.*' R. Tanḥuma said, 'R. Abahu has answered them well.'

Commentary.—The Epiqurosin, here mentioned, are no doubt the same as the Minim. Bacher (A. d. Pal. Am., ii. 115 n. 4) gives 'Minim,' but does not mention the edition of the Ber. r. from which he quotes.

The point of the dialogue is obvious. The Minim seem to have wished to show that Enoch was a type of Jesus, as regards his ascension into heaven. In support of their contention, that the words (Gen. v. 24), *and God took him,* did not imply death, they quoted 2 Kings ii. 5, where the same word is used of Elijah on his ascent into heaven. R. Abahu refuted the argument by giving an instance (Ezek xxiv. 16) where the use of the word clearly implied death. It is true that there is here no direct allusion to Jesus, but unless such an allusion was intended there would seem to be no reason why the Minim should contend that Enoch did not die, nor why R. Abahu should have refuted their contention. At the same time, it is not easy to see why Elijah should not have served as the type of Jesus, since even Abahu admitted the fact that he did not die and that he did ascend to heaven. I leave it to those who are familiar with

the early Christian writings to say whether Enoch is
ever regarded as a type of Jesus in reference to his
ascension. In Ep. Hebr. xi. 5, a writing which was,
as we have seen, known to the Minim (above, p. 265),
Enoch is mentioned, but only as an instance of faith.
It is there stated, however, that Enoch did not die.
It is possible that in the dialogue before us there is
no reference to Jesus, but merely a defence of a
Christian text against a Hebrew one.[1]

R. Tanḥuma, who is reported to have approved the
answer of Abahu, lived in Palestine in the fourth
century, and had, himself, an adventure with the
Minim (see below, p. 282).

R. ABAHU AND A MIN. ANACHRONISM
IN SCRIPTURE

(98) b. Ber. 10ª.—A certain Min said to R. Abahu,
'It is written [Ps. iii. 1], *Psalm of David,
when he fled before Absalom his son.* And it is
written [Ps. lvii. 1], *Of David ; Michtam,
when he fled before Saul, in the cave.* Was the
incident [of Absalom] first? Yet since the
incident of Saul was first, it ought to have
been written first.' He said to him, 'To you,
who do not interpret "contexts," there is a
difficulty ; to us, who do interpret "contexts,"
there is no difficulty.'

---

[1] It is worth notice that the LXX., in Gen. v. 24, render נקח (took) by
μετέθηκε, 'translated,' and that the latter word is used in Heb. xi. 5.
Both R. Abahu and the Minim understood Greek ; and thus the discussion
may have turned on the question whether the Hebrew word was correctly
rendered in the text in the Eυ. to the Hebrews.

Commentary.—Rabbinowicz (D. Soph, *ad loc.*) gives a variant according to which the question of the Min is הי מנייהו קדים מעשה דאבשלום קדים או מעשה דשאול קדים: This is the reading of the Munich MS. I do not adopt it, however, because it appears to be intended as a gloss, in explanation of the question of the Min. The reading of the Agadath ha-Talmud, also quoted by Rabbinowicz, is הי מעשה הוה ברישא לאו מעשה דשאול ברישא: which 'seems to confirm the reading of the printed text. The difficulty raised by the Min is obvious; the Psalm which refers to the earlier event comes after that which refers to the later one. R. Abahu replied that the difficulty was only felt by those who did not interpret 'contexts.' He meant that there were reasons, apart from succession or priority in time, why the Scripture mentions one event in connexion with another. The Scriptures were regarded as containing the whole of revealed truth, and therefore as being much more than a mere historical record. Religious and moral lessons were taught in it, for the sake of which historical consistency was disregarded. The principle of deduction from 'contexts,' סמוכין to which R. Abahu referred, was followed in the Rabbinical schools long before his time. R. Eliezer, in the first century, made use of it, as did also R. El'azar ben Azariah, his younger contemporary. R. Aqiba appears to have been the first to formulate the principle into a canon of interpretation, in the form כל פרשה שהיא סמוכה לחברתה למדה הימנה, *i.e.* 'every section is explained by the one that stands next to it.' (Siphri, on Num. xxv. 1, § 131, p. 47ª). In the third century, R. El'azar ben Pedath gave a Scripture proof of the principle, or at least warrant for it, from

18

Ps. cxi. 8, *They are established* (סמוכים) *for ever and ever*, *i.e*, 'The סמוכים are for ever and ever'; they are eternally true. This dictum of R. El'azar ben Pedath is mentioned in the Gemara, immediately after the answer of R. Abahu to the Min. The printed text wrongly ascribes it to R. Johanan. Rabbinowicz shows, on the authority of the Munich MS., that the true reading is 'El'azar.' R. Abahu did not explain to the Min how he would apply the principle in the case of the two texts quoted. The illustration given in the Gemara, in connexion with the saying of R. El'azar, refers to a different pair of texts. That the Minim did not follow this principle in their interpretation of Scripture is evident, not merely from R. Abahu's statement, but from the fact that, as he pointed out, the difficulty would not have been felt by them if they had followed the principle.

R. Abahu and a Min. The Souls of the Departed

(99) b. Shabb. 152[b].—A certain Min said to R. Abahu, 'Ye say that the souls of the righteous are stored up under the Throne of Glory. How did the necromancer call up Samuel by witchcraft?' [1 Sam. xxviii. 12]. He said to him, 'That happened within twelve months [from death]. For it is tradition, that during twelve months a man's body remains, and his soul goes up and comes down; after twelve months the body perishes, and his soul goes up and does not come down again.'

Commentary.—It will be noticed that in the preceding passage, as well as in the present one, there
is no polemical intention in the question of the
Minim to R. Abahu, but only a desire for instruction.
This helps to make clearer such a friendly attitude
of both parties to each other as is implied in the story
of R. Saphra already discussed (see above, p. 266).
On the other hand, the passage does not throw any
light upon the theology of the Min; the question is
not in itself heretical, but merely an inquiry by one
who was a heretic.

R. Abahu and a Min. God a Jester; God a Priest

(100) b. Sanh. 39ᵈ.—A certain Min said to R.
Abahu, ' Your God is a jester, for he said to
Ezekiel [Ezek. iv. 4], *Lie upon thy left side,*
and it is written [*ib.*, 6], *and thou shalt lie on
thy right side.*' There came a certain disciple
and said to him [Abahu], ' What is the meaning of the Sabbath-year?' He said, ' I will
say to you a word which will answer both of
you. The Holy One, Blessed be He, said to
Israel [Exod. xxiii. 10, 11], *Sow six years, and
refrain the seventh,* that ye may know that
the land is mine.' But they did not do so,
but sinned, and were carried away captive.
It is the custom of the world that a king of
flesh and blood, against whom a city is rebellious, if he is cruel will slay all the people,
if he is merciful he will slay half, and if he is
full of mercy he chastises the great ones among

them with chastisement. Thus did the Holy
One, Blessed be He, chastise Ezekiel, that he
might wipe away the sins of Israel.'

   A certain Min said to R. Abahu, 'Your
God is a priest, for it is written [Exod. xxv.
2], *That they take for me a heave-offering.*
When he buried Moses, wherewith did he
purify [bathe] himself?   If you say, 'with
water,' then see what is written [Isa. xl. 12],
*Who hath measured the waters in the hollow
of his hand.'* He said to him, 'With fire did
he purify himself, as it is written [Isa. lxvi,
15], *For behold the Lord will come with fire.'*
[He said], 'Does then purification by fire
avail?' He said, 'The very essence of purification is in fire, as it is written [Num. xxxi.
23], *All that abideth not the fire, thou shalt make
to pass through the water.'*

Commentary.—There is little to be said upon these
two anecdotes. The questions contain nothing
characteristic of Minuth, and only serve to illustrate
the relations between R. Abahu and the Minim.
They occur in the middle of a long passage, containing many references to Minuth, and several instances
of dialogues between Jewish Rabbis and Minim.
These have been, or will be, dealt with in connexion
with the several Rabbis mentioned.

R. ABAHU AND A MIN. THE COMING
OF THE MESSIAH

(101) b. Sanh. 99ᵃ.—And this is what a certain
   Min said to R. Abahu, 'When will the Messiah

come ?' He said to him, 'When darkness
hath covered these men [*i.e.* covered you].'
He said, 'Thou art cursing me!' He said,
'The text is written [Isa. lx. 2], *For behold
darkness shall cover the earth and gross darkness the people ; but the Lord shall arise upon
thee and his glory shall be seen upon thee.*'

Commentary.—The reference in the opening words
is to an anonymous parable of a cock and a bat
who were waiting for the dawn. The cock said to
the bat, I am waiting for the light, for the light is
mine ; but what have you to do with light ? In other
words, none but Jews have any concern with the
coming of the Messiah. This, says the Gemara, is
the point of the answer, made by R. Abahu to a
certain Min, etc., and then follows the above passage.
The only interest in it is that it is, so far as I know,
the only passage where a Min refers to the Messiah.
If the Minim are, or include Jewish Christians, one
would naturally expect that the alleged Messiahship
of Jesus would be a subject of controversy. This,
however, is not the case ; and the fact might be used
as an argument in support of the theory that the
Minim are not Christians. In the present instance
the Min can hardly have been a Jewish Christian,
because Abahu by his answer implies that he is a
Gentile. But the incident is too slight to serve as
the foundation for any argument.

R. ABAHU AND A MIN (SĀSŌN)

(102) b. Succ. 48ᵇ.—A certain Min, whose name
was Sāsōn, said to R. Abahu, Ye will draw

water for me, in the world to come, for it is
written [Isa. xii. 3], *With joy [sāsōn] shall ye
draw water*, etc. He said to him, ' If it were
written *for joy*, it would be as you say. But
it is written, *with joy* [with sāsōn]; we shall
make a waterskin of the skin of this man [*i.e.*
of your skin], and draw water from it.'

Commentary.—This is only a piece of witty repartee
and needs no comment. The name Sāsōn occurs
elsewhere ; there was a Rabbi 'Anani bar Sāsōn,
as Bacher points out, who appears to have been a
contemporary of R. Abahu. There is nothing to
imply that Sāsōn was a Min, beyond the mere statement of the text.

This concludes the series of dialogues in which R.
Abahu was concerned. Several are of but small importance, and are only given here for the sake of
completeness. It is my endeavour to present to the
reader every passage in the Talmud in which Minim
and Minuth are referred to.

R. AMI AND A MIN. THE RESURRECTION
OF THE DEAD

(103) b. Sanh. 91ª.—A certain Min said to R.
Ami, ' Ye say that the dead live. But, lo,
they are dust ; and how shall dust live ? ' He
said to him, ' I will tell thee a parable. Unto
what is the thing like ? Unto a king of flesh
and blood who said to his servants, Go, build
for me a great palace in a place where there
is neither water nor dust. They went and
built it. After a time it fell. He said, Build

it again, in a place where there is dust and
water. They said to him, We cannot. He
was angry with them, and said to them, Ye
have built it in a place where there was neither
water nor dust; how much more in a place
where there is water and dust.

' But, if thou dost not believe [that dust can
live], go into the valley and see the mouse,
which to-day is half flesh and half earth, and
to-morrow has crept out and is become altogether flesh. And, lest thou say, This is
through length of time, go to the hill and see
that to-day there is but one snail; to-morrow
the rains have fallen, and the place is filled
with snails.'

Commentary. — R. Ami was a disciple of R.
Johanan, and thus a contemporary of R. Abahu. The
Min would seem to have been an unbeliever in resurrection altogether. If so, of course, he cannot have
been a Jewish Christian. The argument of the
Minim against the resurrection was usually a denial
that the doctrine could be proved from the Torah.
This appears from the passage already quoted (see
above, p. 232), where Rn. Gamliel tries to refute their
argument. The Mishnah at the head of this section
of Sanhedrin is the famous one [M. Sanh. x. 1], already
several times mentioned, which enumerates those who
have no portion in the world to come. Amongst
others, it specifies those who say that there is no
resurrection from the dead. The common text adds
the words, מן התורה, ' according to the Torah'; but
Rabbinowicz, on the passage, shows that these words
are an interpolation. This is confirmed by the

Tosephta (T. Sanh. xiii. 5), which condemns "those who lie concerning the resurrection of the dead," but does not allude to a denial of scripture proof for the doctrine. The words interpolated are probably from the Gemara, a few lines further down (p. 90ᵇ), where the question is raised 'what is the proof of the resurrection *according to the Torah*?' The scripture proof of the doctrine is merely a special branch of the general subject. Accordingly, the Gemara, here and elsewhere, deals with the subject, sometimes in reference to the general, sometimes to the special question. The Minim ask Rn. Gamliel for a proof of the resurrection of the dead, and he gives them texts from Scripture (see above, p. 231, No. 85). A few lines further down, on the same page of Sanhedrin, the 'Romans' ask R. Jehoshua b. Ḥananjah the same question, and he also answers them by quoting texts. Then follows a passage in which, according to the received text, it is alleged that the 'Books of the Minim' contain denials of the scripture proof of the doctrine of resurrection. But the correct reading is not Minim, but Cuthim (Samaritans), as is shown by the parallel passages, Siphri, p. 33ᵇ, *cp.* 87ᵃ, also by the MS. authority cited by Rabbinowicz. On the last line of p. 90ᵇ of Sanhedrin is a passage in which an Emperor (קיסר), puts to Rn. Gamliel the very same question which the Min puts to R. Ami in the passage at present under consideration. The answer is different in the two cases, but in both it is addressed to an opponent who denies the doctrine of resurrection in general, not merely the scripture proof of it. The denial is natural enough coming from a heathen emperor (presumably Hadrian). But I do not know what class of heretic—Min—denied that doctrine. In the time when R. Ami lived, the end of the third and beginning of the fourth century, there were no Sadducees. The denial of the resurrection of the dead was not a Gnostic tenet.[1] I am inclined to think that the opponent of R. Ami was really a heathen, incorrectly or inadvertently called a Min in the Gemara.

The passage is evidently introduced merely for the sake of R. Ami's answer. His parable of the building of the palace is easily explained. If God could form man out of nothing, much more could he form again a living being out of dust. The Rabbi's curious illustrations from the natural history of the mouse and the snail rest upon what in his time were accepted facts.

GEBIHA B. PESISA AND A MIN. THE RESURRECTION OF THE DEAD

(104) b. Sanh. 91ᵃ.—A certain Min said to Gebiha ben Pesisa, 'Woe to you guilty who say that the dead live. If the living die, how shall the dead live?' He said, 'Woe to you guilty who say that the dead do not live. If those who were not, live, those who have been, live all the more.' He said to him, 'Thou callest me guilty. Suppose I prove it by kicking thee and tearing thy scalp from thee.' He said, 'If thou doest thus, thou shalt be called a faithful physician, and shalt receive a great reward.'

---

[1] The resurrection of the body, however, was denied by the Gnostics.

Commentary.—This passage follows immediately after the one about R. Ami, just translated. I have included it here, because it deals with the same subject, not because it belongs chronologically to this place. Gebiha ben Pesisa is a legendary character, traditionally contemporary with Alexander the Great. Two anecdotes are given on the same page of Sanhedrin, describing how Geb. b. Pesisa acted as advocate for the Jews before Alexander the Great. I can throw no light upon him. The repartee about the resurrection of the dead was connected with his name, and for that reason presumably he is mentioned by the compiler of the Gemara immediately after R. Ami.

The meaning of his further answer to the threat of violence is, that if the Min killed him, he would confer immortality and thus prove himself a great physician by giving life by means of death. A rather dangerous doctrine for physicians.

R. TANḤUMA, CÆSAR AND A MIN. ALL ONE PEOPLE

(105) b. Sanh. 39ª.—Cæsar said to R. Tanḥuma, 'Come, let us all be one people.' He said, 'So be it. But we, who circumcise ourselves, cannot become like you. Do ye circumcise yourselves and become like us.' He said to him, 'Thou hast spoken well. Nevertheless, everyone who prevails over a king, they cast him into the *vivarium*.' They cast him into the *vivarium*, but [the beast] did not eat him. A certain Min said to him (Cæsar), 'The

reason why [the beast] did not eat him is that it was not hungry.' They cast him [the Min] [into the vivarium] and [the beast] ate him.

Commentary.— R. Tanḥuma lived in Palestine, in the generation after R. Abahu, thus about the middle of the fourth century. Bacher (A. d. Pal. Am., iii. 467) admits that this anecdote rests upon a historical event, and supposes that the emperor referred to must have been a Christian. The emperors contemporary with R. Tanḥuma were, with one notable exception, Christians. That exception was Julian the Apostate (A.D. 361–363), and I suggest that the Emperor in the story is intended for Julian, rather than for one of the Christian emperors. It is true that Julian is nowhere mentioned by name in the Talmud (unless the reading לוליגוס מלכא, j. Ned. 37ᵈ, be preferred to the reading מ׳ דוקליטינוס in the parallel passage, j. Shebhu. 34ᵈ). There is, however, no *a priori* reason why he should be entirely ignored, at all events in the Babylonian Gemara. It is known that Julian was disposed to be friendly towards the Jews, even to the extent of offering to rebuild the Temple in Jerusalem. His friendship was, no doubt, influenced in part by his dislike of the Christians, in part, perhaps, also by his desire to have the Jews on his side in his contemplated war with Persia. No Christian emperor would be described as suggesting to a Jew, in a friendly conference, that he and his countrymen should forsake their religion and become one people with their sovereign. There is extant a letter to the Jews in which Julian speaks of his desire to see their holy city rebuilt, and *to join with them* in offering praise there to the All-Good (καὶ ἐν αὐτῇ δόξαν δώσω

μεθ᾽ ὑμῶν τῷ κρείττονι, cited by Grätz, iv. n. 34).
This hope was never realised, and the projected rebuilding of the Temple was abandoned. The Jews
do not appear to have been greatly in favour of the
project, perhaps because it was due to a pagan
emperor in the interests of pagan rather than of
Jewish religion.

The story before us seems to reflect such a relation
between the emperor and the Jews. Julian actually
was in Antioch in the year 362 ; and R. Tanḥuma,
though not the Nasi, was one of the few eminent
representatives of his people in Palestine. He was
therefore a likely personage for the emperor to con-
verse with if he held any intercourse with Jews, as he
certainly did. I do not mean to suggest that the
story refers to anything so definite as the project
of rebuilding the Temple, only that it describes an
incident made possible by such an intention on the
part of Julian. If this be so, then the reply of the
Rabbi would reflect the view which the Jews took of
the overtures of a heathen emperor, viz., that they
would not purchase his friendship at the cost of their
religion, even for the sake of seeing their Temple
rebuilt. The emperor would naturally be mortified
at such a rebuff; but it is in keeping with the
character of Julian, the philosopher, that he should
have admitted the force of the Rabbi's argument,
while punishing him for his rashness in opposing the
imperial will. The story goes on to say that the
Rabbi was cast into the vivarium,[1] to be devoured by a

---

[1] Vivarium ; this is evidently the equivalent of ביבר, although vivarium
in classical Latin does not mean a den of wild beasts, such as is clearly
implied in the story.

wild beast, and that for some reason the beast would not touch him. Amongst the bystanders was a Min, who explained the reason of the Rabbi's safety by the suggestion that the beast was not hungry. Whereupon he was sent to prove the worth of his own suggestion by being himself cast into the den, where he was immediately devoured. If the Min were a Christian, it is conceivable that Julian should have so dealt with him; or, if not that, it is not unnatural that the author of the story should have so expressed his own dislike of the Christians under cover of the known antipathy towards them of Julian.

This anecdote does not, of course, throw much light, if any, upon the general subject of the Minim; but, if the suggestion made above be warranted, it is at least interesting as affording a glimpse into a period of Jewish history concerning which the Rabbinical literature is almost silent.

R. Idi and a Min: Metatrōn

(106) b. Sanh. 38ᵇ.—R. Naḥman said, 'He who knows how to answer the Minim like R. Idi, let him answer; if not, let him not answer.' A certain Min said to R. Idi, 'It is written [Exod. xxiv. 1], *And he said unto Moses, Come up unto the Lord.* He ought to have said, *Come up unto me.*' He [R. Idi] said, ' This is Metatrōn, whose name is as the name of his Master. For it is written [Exod. xxiii. 21], *For my name is in him.*' ' If so, worship him.' ' It is written [*ibid.*], *Provoke him not* [*i.e.* Do not mistake him for me].' ' If so,

what have I to do with [*ibid.*] *he will not pardon thy transgressions ?* ' He [R. Idi] said to him, ' Be sure of this, that even as a guide we would not receive him ; for it is written [Exod. xxxiii. 15], *If thy presence go not [with us, carry us not up hence]*.'

Commentary.—Rab Idi[1] is classed by Bacher (A. d. P. A., iii. 704) amongst the Palestinian Amoras of the fourth century, though without any indication of the place where he lived. R. Naḥman, who refers to him, is R. Naḥman bar Jitzḥaq, a Babylonian, president of the College at Pumbeditha, who died A.D. 356. R. Idi appears to have travelled in Babylonia, and may there have met with R. Naḥman. His dispute with the Min probably took place in Palestine, as it is said, b. Ḥull. 13ᵃ, that there are no Minim amongst the Gentiles, and b. Pesaḥ., 56ᵇ, that there are no Minim in Nehardea.

The dialogue between R. Idi and the Min belongs, in any case, to the fourth century. Friedländer, in his work *der Vorchristliche jüdische Gnosticismus*, p. 103 fol., makes some use of the passage before us, and begins by transferring it to the Tannaite period, thus antedating it by nearly two hundred years ! In accordance with his theory, he regards the Min as a Gnostic, on the strength of the identification which he proposes between ' Metatrōn ' and the Gnostic ' Horos ' ("Ορος, Metator). But he overlooks the fact that it is the Jew, and not the Min, who mentions Metatrōn. And the Rabbi's argument surely is that the Min is

[1] ' Idi ' is the correct reading. The form ' Idith,' as in the text, occurs only here, and the evidence of the authorities quoted by Rabbinowicz shows that even here the name should be read ' Idi.'

wrong in hinting at a second God, because the reference is to Metatrōn, and not to a second God. If the Min was a Gnostic, and if Metatrōn were identical with Horos, then the Rabbi would merely have been playing into the hands of the Min.

The point in dispute is the doctrine of the Two Powers in Heaven, which we have already met with in other polemical discussions (see above, p. 262 fol.). The Min quoted a text, which appeared to imply the existence of more than one divine being, *And he said unto Moses, come up unto the Lord.* If it were God himself speaking, then He ought to have said, *Come up unto me.* Who was it to whom Moses was told to go up? The Jew was ready with his answer. The reference was to Metatrōn, a recognised personage in the Rabbinical theology, where he always appears as the chief of the angels, nearest to God but subject to God, acting as his messenger and representative, but never regarded as being in any sense himself God. Metatrōn is so far from being identical with the Logos of the Jewish Alexandrine philosophy, or with the Horos of Gnosticism, that he may be regarded as the expression of the Rabbinical rejection of those conceptions. In other words, the doctrine of Metatrōn is the reply of the Rabbinical theology to the doctrine of the Logos and to the Gnostic systems. No doubt there is common to all three conceptions the idea of a delegation of divine power; but, in the case of Metatrōn, the line is sharply drawn between servant and Master, creature and Creator. This is shown, in a curious way, in a passage (107) [b. Ḥag. 15ª], which describes how Elisha ben Abujah entered

Paradise, and there " saw Metatrōn, to whom was given power to sit and write down the merits of Israel. He [Elisha b. A.] said, ' It is taught that on high there is no sitting, no strife, no parting and no joining. Can there be, heaven forbid, two powers ? ' They brought out Metatrōn *and gave him sixty lashes of fire.*" This was done, as Tosaphoth rightly explains, to show that Metatrōn was not superior in kind to the other angels, however much he might be in degree. Friedländer, in the work already referred to (*Vorchr. jüd. Gnosticismus*, 102), quotes, or rather paraphrases, this passage ; " Bei seinem Eindringen in das Paradies sah Acher [El. b. Abujah], wie berichtet wird, zu seinem schrecken eine *zweite Gottheit* im Himmel, den *Metatron.*" Friedländer, however, does not mention the concluding words, translated above, which expressly contradict the assertion that Metatrōn was a second God. Elisha ben Abujah may have believed that Metatrōn was such ; but the Talmud stamps that belief as a heresy. And it is quite clear that the Rabbinical theology recognised Metatrōn, while it certainly did not admit the Gnostic conception with which Friedländer would identify Metatrōn.

I now return to the dialogue between R. Idi and the Min. The former has explained that the reference in the text quoted by the latter, *Come up unto the Lord*, is to Metatrōn, for his name is as the name of his Master, as it is written [Exod. xxiii. 21], *For my name is in Him.* The Min rejoins, ' Then why do you not worship him ? ' If, that is, the name and by implication the power of God is committed to Metatrōn, why should he not be worshipped ?

A question very much to the point, if the Min, as suggested above (p. 265 fol.), be a Jewish Christian whose theology was that of the Epistle to the Hebrews. The Jew meets the argument by a rather strained interpretation of the text: *Provoke him not.* The word translated ' provoke ' he derives from another root, meaning ' to change '; and he translates, ' Do not mistake him for me.' His object is to emphasise, as much as possible, the intrinsic difference between God and the inferior being (Metatrōn), which was already clearly marked in the original text. The Min replies that if there be such a marked difference between the two, why is it said *he will not pardon your sins?* Does not this imply that he, of whom this is said, has power to pardon or withhold pardon ? And if so, can he be only a subordinate, to whom worship must not be offered ? The answer of the Rabbi is rather obscure, ' Be assured of this, that even as a guide we would not receive him, for it is written, *If thy presence go not with us, carry us not up hence.*' The connexion of this with the argument of the Min is suggested by the remark of Rashi, in his commentary on the verse in Exodus, that it was not the function of the angel to pardon sins ; he was to be a guide, and nothing more. *He will not pardon your sins,* because that is out of his department. The Rabbi seems to have interpreted the words in a similar way. Metatrōn was sent as a guide, with no power to pardon sins. ' But even as a guide,' he goes on, ' we would not receive him.' The promised guide, to whom the words in, Exod. xxiii. refer, was never sent. For it appears from Exod. xxxiii. 12–17 that Moses prayed that God

19

himself would lead his people, and that his prayer was granted. Thus, from the Jewish point of view, the argument of the Min was completely met. So far from there being, as suggested, a second God, there was only an angel, supreme amongst angels perhaps, but by more than a little ' lower than God.'

Friedländer makes the needless remark (*op. cit.*, p. 104) that the Rabbi, driven into a corner, only extricated himself by a violent exegesis that made nonsense of the text. The real matter in dispute was not a point of exegesis, but a fundamental theological doctrine. And even if exegesis had been in question, the Rabbi was only following the usage of the schools in applying exegetical methods which were haggadic and not scientific. This will already have appeared, from the numerous examples we have seen of Rabbinical interpretation of Scripture.

R. ABINA AND A MIN

(108) b. Sanh. 39ᵃ.—A certain Min said to R. Abina, ' It is written [2 Sam. vii. 23], *Who is like thy people, like Israel, one nation in the earth?* What is their excellence? Ye also are mingled with them, for it is written [Isa. xl. 17], *All the nations are as nothing before him.*' He said to him, ' Your own [prophets] bear witness concerning us, for it is written [Num. xxiii. 9], *It shall not be reckoned among the nations.*'

Commentary.—Abina is the name of two Rabbis, both Palestinian, and both living in the fourth century, though not in the same generation. Bacher holds that the Abina of this passage is the elder of the two.[1] The passage is of little importance. The Min sought to show that Israel had no claim to pre-eminence over the other nations, on the ground that all the nations were as nothing before God. The Rabbi retorted by quoting the words of a heathen prophet, viz., Balaam, to the effect that Israel was not to be reckoned amongst the nations. The Min evidently was a Gentile, and therefore probably a Christian, since no other Gentile would be able to quote from the O.T. scriptures. It is possible that the reference to Balaam has something of the anti-Christian animus noted above (p. 66 fol.). But if this were the intention, we should expect the reference to be made more prominent.

This concludes the series of passages in which Jewish Rabbis meet Minim in controversy. I shall next present a further series of passages containing polemical allusions to the Minim. To some extent I have classified them, according to their subject matter; but I shall have to include several in a miscellaneous group, having little or nothing in common except the allusion to Minim. I give, first, a group of texts referring to the doctrine of the Unity of God and the opposed doctrines of Two Powers in Heaven.

SECTION III. POLEMICAL ALLUSIONS TO THE MINIM

MAN CREATED SOLITARY

(109) M. Sanh. iv. 5.—For this reason man was created solitary [for various reasons], and in

[1] A. d. P. Amor., iii. 539.

order that Minim might not say there are
several Powers in Heaven.

(110) T. Sanh. viii. 7.—Man was created last.
And why was he created last? That the
Minim might not say there was a companion
with Him in the work.

Commentary.—I have omitted from (109) a few lines,
in which are suggested several rather fantastic reasons
why man was created solitary. My object, of course,
is not to expound Haggadah, but to examine references
to Minim. It should be noticed that in (109) the
Minim are charged with believing in several Powers
in Heaven; in (110) they are charged with asserting
the existence of a being who aided God in the work
of creation. The commentators on (109) explain the
passage thus, that, if several men had been created at
once, the Minim might say one deity had created one
man, another another, and so on. It is not evident
what doctrine is aimed at in (109). At first sight it
would seem to be that of mere Gentile polytheism,
but the ordinary Gentiles are never, so far as I know,
called Minim. The Gnostics did, it is true, believe
in 'several Powers' in Heaven, but not several
creators, and the argument of the Mishnah has no
point, unless the doctrine combatted be that of
several *creators*. It is possible that the word
translated 'several' may only imply 'more than one,'
in which case the passage would be in harmony with
most of the others where the doctrine of the Minim
touching the creation is alluded to.

In the second passage (110) it is clear that only
two Powers are alleged. Man is said to have been
created last in order that the Minim might not say

that He, *i.e.* God, had a companion in the work of creation. That ' He ' refers to God and not to man is evident from the sense of the passage, and is moreover explicitly stated in the Gemara [b. Sanh. p. 38ᵃ]. If it were in the power of the Minim to show that a being, other than the Supreme God, had shared in the work of creation, then that would have been a strong argument in their favour, supposing them to have been, as suggested above (p. 265 fol.), Jewish Christians of the type represented by the theology of the Epistle to the Hebrews.

The two passages (109) and (110) are reproduced in the Babylonian Gemara (b. Sanh. 38ᵃ), but not in that of Palestine. There is no discussion of either passage in the Gemara. There is, however, in the same context a further reference to the denial of the Unity of God by the Minim. Indeed, this part of b. Sanhedrin is full of allusions to heresy, several of which have already been examined.

THE UNITY OF GOD. TEXTS APPEALED TO BY THE MINIM

(111) b. Sanh. 38ᵇ.—We teach there R. Eliezer says, ' Be careful to learn Torah, and know what thou shalt answer to an Epiquros.' R. Johanan said, ''They only taught this concerning a Gentile Epiquros, but [it applies] all the more to a Jewish Epiquros, for he is more defiant.'

R. Johanan said, ' In every place [*i.e.* text of Scripture] which the Minim misinterpret, the context refutes them. [Gen i. 26], *Let us make man in our image;* [*ib.* 27], *And God*

created [sing.] *man in his image.* [Gen. xi. 7],
*Go to, now, let us go down and there confound
their language* [*ib.* 5]; *And the Lord went
down* [sing.] *to see the city and the tower.*
[Gen. xxxv. 7], *For there God was* [plur.]
revealed to him ; [*ib.* 3], *unto God who answered*
[sing.] *me in the day of my trouble.* [Deut. iv.
7], *For what great nation is there that hath a
God so nigh* [plur.] *unto them as the Lord our
God is whensoever we call upon him* [sing.].
[2 Sam. vii. 23], *And what one nation in the
earth is like thy people, even like Israel, whom
God went* [plur.] *to redeem unto himself* [sing.]
for a people. [Dan. vii. 9], *Until thrones
were set, and one that was ancient of days did
sit.* What do these words mean, according to
[the theory] of R. Joḥanan? For R. Joḥanan
said, 'The Holy One, Blessed be He, doeth
nothing except he have taken counsel with the
family above, as it is said [Dan. iv. 17], *The
sentence is by decree of the watchers and the
demand by the word of the holy ones.* All
this may be admitted ; but what is to be said
of *until thrones were set* ? One for Him and
one for David ; for it is tradition, 'One for
Him and one for David ; the words of R.
Aqiba.' R. José said to him, 'Aqiba, how
long wilt thou make the Shechinah profane ?
It is One for justice and one for righteousness.'
He [Aqiba] received it [*i.e.* the correction] from
him, or he did not receive it. Come and see.
For it is tradition, 'One for justice and one
for righteousness ; the words of R. Aqiba.'

R. El'azar ben Azariah said to him, ' Aqiba,
what hast thou to do with Haggadah ? Be
off to 'wounds' and 'tents.' It is 'One for
his throne and one for his footstool. A throne
to sit on and a footstool for the support of
his feet.'

Commentary.—The first part of this passage, referring to the Epiquros, has been dealt with already
(see above, p. 120 fol., where the meaning of the term
Epiquros is examined). The advice of R. Johanan
concerning the Jewish Epiquros is usually understood
to mean that such an opponent was to be shunned
as dangerous. This is not what R. Johanan said.
He adopted the words of R. El'azar b. Arach, ' Know
what to answer to an Epiquros,' and said, ' This was
spoken in reference to the Gentile Epiquros ; but
it applies *all the more* to the Jewish one.' In other
words, the Jew was to be especially careful how he
replied to a Jewish Epiquros, because he was more
dangerous. But that is not the same as saying that
the Jew was not to meet the Jewish Epiquros in
argument. And, since a Jewish Epiquros was
practically a Min, we have already met with many
examples of such polemical encounters.

The connexion between Epiquros (freethinker) and
Min (heretic) is indicated in the present passage by
the word '*p'qar*' (פקר), which means in general ' to
be free from restraint, thence to act as a freethinker,'
and (in relation to Scripture) ' to interpret heretically.'
The name Epiquros, borrowed, of course, from the
Greek, was adopted for the sake of the play upon
the word '*p'qar.*' R. Johanan said that the Jewish
Epiquros '*p'qar*' more than the Gentile one ; also

that the Minim '*p'qaru*' in their interpretation of Scripture.

The examples given of texts relied on by the Minim and refuted by the context have, with the exception of the last, been already dealt with. The last is Dan. vii. 9, *Until thrones were set, and one that was ancient of days did sit.* The Gemara asks what is the explanation of this, according to the theory of R. Joḥanan (*i.e.* that the context refutes the heretical misuse of the text). The refutation is found, hardly in the context, but so far away as Dan. iv. 17. R. Joḥanan, accordingly, understood that the 'thrones,' which the heretics said were intended for, and implied the existence of, more than one God, were for the use of the 'family above,' the angels with whom God was said to take counsel. It is not surprising that this text caused some perplexity to the Rabbinical interpreters of Scripture. In addition to the explanation of R. Joḥanan, the Gemara gives three earlier interpretations. R. Aqiba said that the thrones were for God and David; whereupon R. José [ha-Galili] rebuked him for 'making the Shechinah profane,' in other words, associating a man with God in equality of dignity. Possibly David stands for 'the Son of David,' *i.e.* the Messiah; and Aqiba may have been thinking of Ps. cx. i., *The Lord said unto my lord, sit thou at my right hand.* R. José felt the danger of such an explanation, in admitting the possibility of other divine beings associated with God. His own explanation, a very forced one, was that both thrones (assuming them to have been only two) were for the use of God. He sat on one to dispense justice, on the other to do righteousness, or rather to show mercy.

R. Aqiba, according to one tradition, adopted this explanation. Another contemporary, R. El'azar ben Azariah, rebuked him as R. José had done (probably on the same occasion), and in his turn suggested the explanation that one throne was for God to sit on, the other to serve as a footstool. This, again, was a forced interpretation, evidently intended to guard against the danger involved in that of R. Aqiba. It is remarkable that R. Aqiba, who was sufficiently alive to all danger of heresy, should not have detected the fault in his own interpretation of the text. The rebuke that he knew nothing of Haggadah, but only of Halachah, was unduly severe; though it is no doubt true that he was greater in the latter department than in the former. The reference to 'wounds' and 'tents' denotes the halachahs concerning injuries and ceremonial uncleanness. R. Aqiba, as a master of Halachah, was virtually one of the founders of the Mishnah. His work, in beginning the codification of the halachahs, was made use of by R. Jehudah ha-Qadosh, to whom the completion of the Mishnah is due.

77. The Unity of God. An Offering to JHVH

(112) Siphri, § 143 p. 54ᵃ.—Shim'on ben Azai says, Come and see: In all the offerings [mentioned] in the Torah, it is not said, in connexion with them, either 'God' or 'thy God' or 'Almighty' or 'of Hosts,' but 'JH,' a singular [not plural] name. So as not to give to the Minim an occasion to humble us.

(113) b. Menaḥ. 110ᵃ.—Tradition: R. Shim'on

ben Azai said, Come and see what is written
in the chapter on offerings, viz., that it is not
said, in connexion with them, either God [El] or
'God' [Elohim], but JHVH, so as not to give
to the adversary an occasion to distinguish.

(114) Siphra. 4ᶜ.—The same, in substance, as (112),
but ascribed to R. José [ben Ḥalaphta], instead
of to Shim'on ben Azai.

The saying is also found in Jalqut Shim'oni,
§ 604.

Commentary.—Shim'on ben Azai was a younger
contemporary of R. Aqiba, in the early years of the
second century. The point of his remark, in the
above passages, is that all offerings prescribed in the
Torah are mentioned in connexion with the individual
name of God, *i.e.* JHVH, and not with the generic
names for God, which are mostly plural in form.
The older texts, Siphri and Siphra, have ' Minim,' as
the opponent against whom Ben Azai directed his
remark. The Gemara in b. Menaḥoth reads merely
' the adversary,' and it is remarkable that Rabbinowicz
gives no variant in support of the reading ' Minim.'
There can, however, be no doubt that ' Minim ' is
the original reading, whatever may be the explanation of the alteration in the Gemara. Bacher (A. d.
Tann., i. 422) says that the Minim here are the
Gnostics. This may be so, but I venture to submit that Bacher does not quite accurately represent
the argument of Ben Azai. Bacher regards the
names ' God,' ' Almighty,' ' Hosts,' as being intended
to refer to the divine power, whereas the name
JHVH refers to the divine goodness. The Gnostics
held that the laws concerning offerings were given

by the Demiurgos, who was powerful but not good. But if this had been the argument of Ben Azai, the Gnostics would have met it by denying that the name JHVH implied the divine goodness. The point is, that the name JHVH is an individual name, which could not possibly be applied to more than one divine being; whereas the other names might be, and were, so interpreted. Siphri expressly says, that the name JHVH is an individual name. And that the Gemara evidently took the same view, is shown in the concluding words of (113), "so as not to give the adversary an occasion to *distinguish*," *i.e.* to distinguish between a plurality of divine persons. The argument is directed merely against the doctrine of Two Powers, already familiar from previous discussions. The term Minim, as used here, might certainly include the Gnostics; but there is nothing to prove that the Minim, in this passage, are in any way different from the Minim who have been already considered.

In Echa. r. on i. 1, p. 10ª, is a Haggadic interpretation by Ben Azai, founded on the word Echa (איכה) (115): "Israel did not go into exile until they had denied the one only [God], the practice of circumcision, the ten commandments and the five books of Torah." The Minim are not mentioned here, but are probably intended. With the form of the expression, cp. the saying of R. Joḥanan quoted above, p. 181 fol.

THE UNITY OF GOD. TWO POWERS

(116) Siphri, § 329, p. 139ᵇ.—[Deut. xxxii. 39],
See now, that I, even I, am He. This is the

answer to them that say there is no power in heaven. He that says there are two powers in heaven, they answer him, and say unto him [*Deut., ibid.*], *And there is no God with me.* And, lest [one should say], He cannot make alive or kill, or do evil or do good, learn to say [Deut., *ibid.*], *I kill and I make alive.* And Scripture says [Isaiah xliv. 6], *Thus saith the Lord, the King of Israel and his redeemer, the Lord of Hosts, ' I am the first and I am the last, and beside me there is no God.'*

(117) Mechilta, p. 66ᵇ.—Scripture says [Dan. vii. 9], *I beheld, until thrones were set,* and it says [*ib.* 10], *A fiery stream issued and came forth from before him.* So as not to give to the peoples of the world an opportunity to say, ' These are two powers.' But *I am the Lord your God.* I am [God] on the sea and on the dry land, in the past and in the future, in this world and in the world to come. As it is said [Deut. xxxii. 39], *See, now, that I, even I, am He*; [Isa. xlvi. 4], *Even to old age I am He*; [*ib.* xliv. 6], *Thus saith the Lord, the King of Israel and his redeemer, the Lord of Hosts, ' I am the first and I am the last.'* And it says [*ib.* xli. 4], *Who hath wrought and done it, calling the generations from the beginning? I, the Lord, the first, etc.* R. Nathan says, Hence is an answer to the Minim who say, ' There are two powers.' For when the Holy One, Blessed be He, stood up and said, ' I am the Lord thy God,' who stood up and protested ?

Commentary.—For the general question of the doctrine of Two Powers in Heaven, see above, p. 262. These two passages belong to the stratum of tradition contemporary with the Mishnah. The Minim are not mentioned in (116), but are clearly intended, as is shown by (117). In (117) 'the peoples of the world' may be an error for 'the Minim,' caused by the fact that in the same context there are several polemical allusions to 'the peoples of the world,' where the ordinary Gentiles are intended.

R. Nathan was a Babylonian, settled in Palestine, contemporary with R. Jehudah ha-Qadosh.

In Mechilta, Beshallach, § 4 p. 37ᵇ, there is another allusion to the doctrine of two powers, based on the text [Dan. vii. 9] about the thrones. The doctrine is ascribed to the 'peoples of the world,' not to 'the Minim.'

THE UNITY OF GOD. "HE WHO WILL ERR, LET HIM ERR"

(118) Ber. r. viii. p. 22ᵈ.—R. Shemuel bar Naḥman, in the name of R. Jonathan, said, When Moses was writing the Torah, he wrote the deeds of each day [of creation]. When he came to this verse, as it is written [Gen. i. 26], *And God said, let us make man in our image, according to our likeness,* he said, 'Lord of the world, how thou art giving a chance to the Minim! I am astonished!' He said to him, 'Write; and he who will err, let him err!'

Commentary. — R. Jonathan has already been mentioned several times in connexion with Minim;

(see above, p. 216) R. Shemuel bar Naḥman was one of his disciples.

The grim humour of the reply to Moses is somewhat spoiled by a feeble explanation added on to it. The explanation is the same as that given by R. Joḥanan (see above, p. 296), that God took counsel with 'the family above,' i.e. the angels. In the present passage, the explanation is contained in a second speech, beginning, "And the Holy One, Blessed be He, said to Moses," etc. I have ventured to regard this merely as a gloss, and to leave R. Jonathan's daring invention untouched. It is by far the best retort which the Rabbis made to the Minim on this text.

THE UNITY OF GOD. GOD HAS NO SON

(119) j. Shabb. 8ᵈ.—[Dan. iii. 25], *Like a son of God.* Reuben said, In that hour, an angel descended and struck that wicked one [*i.e.* Nebuchadnezzar] upon his mouth, and said to him, Amend thy words: Hath He [*i.e.* God] a son? He turned and said [v. 28], *Blessed be the God of Shadrach, Meshach and Abednego, who*—it is not written, *hath sent his son,* but—*hath sent his angel, and hath delivered his servants who trusted in him.*

Commentary.—This is part of a haggadic interpretation of the story, in Dan. iii., of the three men cast into the furnace. The fact that, in v. 25, Nebuchadnezzar uses the phrase 'son of God,' while in v. 28 he speaks of a '*messenger,*' not of a '*son,*' of God, is ingeniously turned to account as an argument

against the Christian doctrine. There can be no
question that the polemic here is anti-Christian. Of
Reuben, the author of this haggadah, nothing is certainly known. Probably he is the same as Reuben
ben Aristobulos, who belonged to the generation after
the war of Bar Cocheba, and of whom one or two
sayings are recorded.

The Minim are not alluded to in this passage.

With this reference to Christian doctrine may be
connected another, equally unmistakable, upon the
same subject.

The Unity of God. God has no Son

(120) Shem. r. xxix. 5, p. 51ᵇ.—Another explanation
[Exod. xx. 2], *I am the Lord thy God.* R.
Abahu said, A parable of a king of flesh and
blood; he reigns, and he has a father or a
brother. The holy one, blessed be He, saith,
I am not so [Isa. xliv. 6], *I am the first,* I
have no father; *and I am the last,* I have no
son, *and beside me there is no God,* I have no
brother.

Commentary.—For other anti-Christian sayings of
R. Abahu, see above, p. 266 fol. The Minim are not
mentioned. There can be no question that the
Christian doctrine is here attacked; and it is worth
noticing that the text made use of by R. Abahu [Isa.
xliv. 6] is one which we have met with already as
an argument against the Minim (see above, p. 300).
This goes to strengthen the contention that the
Minim are—or include—Jewish Christians. But
hitherto, as will have been observed, in the passages

where the doctrine of the two powers is ascribed to the Minim, there has been no decisive proof that Christians were referred to. The following passage appears to supply that proof.

The Unity of God. The Son of the Harlot

(121) Pesiq. r. xxi. p. 100[b].—R. Ḥija bar Abba said, If the son of the harlot shall say to thee, 'These are two Gods,' say unto him, ' I am He of the Sea ; I am He of Sinai,' . . . . [another explanation], R. Ḥija bar Abba said, If the son of the harlot shall say to thee, 'These are two Gods,' say unto him [Deut. v. 4], *Face to face the Lord spake* [sing. not plural] *with you.*

Commentary.—This is part of a haggadah on the Ten Commandments, and more particularly on the words, ' I am the Lord thy God.' In the course of the discussion many texts are introduced which we have already met with in connexion with the doctrine of Two Powers. R. Ḥija's remark was occasioned by the quotation of [Dan. vii. 9], *Until thrones were set,* a text which gave a good deal of trouble to the Rabbinical interpreters (see above, p. 296 fol.). Those who deduced from this text the doctrine of Two Powers were the Minim. In the present passage the doctrine of two Gods[1] is ascribed to the ' son of the Harlot.' This phrase can refer to none

---

[1] The terms 'Two Powers' and 'Two Gods' are interchangeable, though the former is the more usual. The Minim, who are credited with holding the doctrine of 'Two Powers,' asked R. Simlai, ' How many Gods created the world ?' (see above, p. 255).

other than Jesus, the story of whose birth was thus coarsely represented in the Rabbinical tradition (see above, p. 41 fol.). Hence the inference that the Minim included Christians, though it does not follow that all Minim were Christians. Friedmann, in the edition of Pesiqta, from which I quote the above passage, has a suggestive note (p. 101ᵃ), "Son of the harlot: this is to be interpreted 'son of Minuth.' 'Min' is rendered in the targum 'zan,' see Aruch. *s.v.* זן. And perhaps the reference here is to what is suggested in Midrash Tillim on Psalm xxii. 1, '*My God, my God, why hast thou forsaken me*'; *i.e.* the God of the Red Sea, and the God of Sinai. The Midrash, perhaps, had in view him who prayed, 'My God, my God, why hast thou forsaken me.'" 'Minuth,' according to this view, is closely akin to 'zanuth' (fornication), even etymologically. If this is correct, it throws light on the real significance of the term 'Min,' and shows that the fundamental idea of heresy in the Rabbinical theology is the same as in that of the prophets, viz., spiritual unfaithfulness symbolised as conjugal unfaithfulness. This subject will be more fully dealt with in the concluding section of this work.

The Midrash in Ps. xxii. 1 appears to explain the double use of 'my God' by the twofold revelation of God to his people, first at the Red Sea, second on Sinai. The Psalmist accordingly is not appealing to two Gods, but to one and the same. Friedmann adds, that the Midrash probably had in mind the utterance of Jesus on the Cross [Matt. xxvii. 46], which is a quotation of Ps. xxii. 1 in the Aramaic, not in the Hebrew.

There can be no doubt that in the passage before us, the reference is to Jesus; and this, in connexion

20

with passages previously considered, establishes the
close association of Minuth with Christianity.

R. Ḥija bar Abba was a Babylonian settled in
Palestine; he belonged to the group of disciples of
R. Joḥanan, and may thus be placed in the latter half
of the third century and the beginning of the fourth.

THE UNITY OF GOD. TWO POWERS:
A SECOND GOD.

(122) Debar. r. ii. 33, p. 104ᶜ.—[Prov. xxiv. 21],
Meddle not with them that are given to change.
Meddle not with those who say there is a
second God. R. Jehudah bar Simon said
[Zech. xiii. 8], *And it shall come to pass that
in all the land, saith the Lord, two parts therein
shall be cut off and die.* The mouths that
say, There are two powers, shall be cut off
and die. And who will remain in existence?
[Zech., *ibid.*], *And the third part therein shall
be left,* these are Israel, who are called *thirds*,
for they are threefold, Priests, Levites, Israelites, from three fathers, Abraham, Isaac, and
Jacob. Another explanation, because they
praise the Holy One, Blessed be He, with
three 'holies'—holy, holy, holy. R. Aḥa said,
The Holy One, Blessed be He, was angry with
Solomon, because he had said this verse [Prov.
xxiv. 21]. He said to him, 'In the matter of
hallowing my name, thou hast spoken in terms
of " Notariqon," [1] *Meddle not with them that are*

---

[1] 'Notariqon,' a species of cipher, or cryptogram, usually formed by
reading the initials of several words as one word. In the present instance
nothing more seems intended than a play upon the words שְׁנַיִם, two, and
שׁוֹנִים, 'given to change.'

given to change.' Immediately he [Solomon]
turned and made the matter plain [by saying,
Ecc. iv. 8], *There is one and there is no
second ; he hath neither son nor brother.* He
hath neither brother nor son, but [Deut. vi. 4],
*Hear, O Israel, the Lord our God, the Lord
is one.*

The above passage occurs, almost in the
same words, in Bamm. r. xvi. 14, p. 66ᶜ.

Commentary.—It is only needful to point out that
here the doctrine of Two Powers is usefully paraphrased as the doctrine of a second God. This confirms what has been said in explanation of the doctrine
under previous heads. The Minim are not mentioned,
but are clearly intended.

R. Jehudah bar Simun was a Palestinian, of the
fourth century. If the interpretation of the text in
Zechariah may be taken literally, it would show that
the Minim as compared with the Jews were in a
majority. But it is more probable that the 'two
parts' (lit. the 'two mouths') are only used to serve
as the basis for the interpretation "the *mouths* which
say there are *two* Gods." In like manner the word
translated 'given to change' (שונים) is connected with
the word meaning 'second' (שני).

In Pesiqta r., p. 98ᵃ, there is a passing reference
to the doctrine of Two Powers. Moses charges
the angels with holding that doctrine, and refutes
them with the text, *I am the Lord thy God*
[Exod. xx. 2].

THE TORAH. THE 'CARPING' OF THE MINIM

(123) j. Ber. 3ᶜ.—And they recited the 'Ten
Words,' '*Hear* [*O Israel*],' '*And it shall be
if thou hearest*,' '*And he said.*' R. Ami in the
name of Resh Laqish [said], 'This shows that
the benedictions do not hinder.' R. Ba said,
'That proves nothing; we do not learn anything thence. For the "Ten Words," these
are the very essence of the Shema'.' R.
Mathnah and R. Shemuel bar Naḥman both
said, 'It was sought that they should recite
the "Ten Words" every day. And why do
they not recite them? Because of the misrepresentation of the Minim, that they might
not say, "These alone were given to Moses
on Sinai."'

(124) b. Ber. 12ᵃ.—And they recite the 'Ten
Words,' '*Hear* [*O Israel*],' '*And it shall be if
thou hearest*,' '*And he said*,' 'True and stead-
fast,' 'Service,' and the 'Blessing of the Priests.'
R. Jehudah said that Shemuel said, 'Even in
the surrounding districts [of Jerusalem] they
sought to recite thus; but they had already
discontinued it because of the carping of the
Minim.' For it is tradition also, R. Nathan
said, 'In the surrounding districts they sought
to recite thus, but they had already discontinued it because of the carping of the Minim.'
Rabah bar Rab Huna thought to establish it
in Sura; but R. Ḥisda said to him, 'They
have already discontinued it, because of the
carping of the Minim.' Amemar thought to

establish it in Nehardea; but R. Ashi said
to him, 'They have already discontinued it,
because of the carping of the Minim.'

(125) b. Pesaḥ. 56ª.—Our Rabbis have taught,
How did they connect [the words of] the
Shema'? They said, '*Hear, O Israel, the
Lord our God the Lord is one,*' and they did
not divide [the words]: the words of R. Meir.
R. Jehudah said, They did divide (them), but
not so as to say, ' Blessed be the name of the
glory of his kingdom for ever and ever.' And
we, on what ground do we say it? [*i.e.* Blessed
be the name, etc.]. According to the exposition of R. Shim'on ben Laqish. For R.
Shim'on ben Laqish said [Gen. xlix. 1], *And
Jacob called together his sons, and said, Gather
yourselves together and I will declare*; Jacob
sought to reveal to his sons the end of the
days, but the Shechinah departed from him.
He said, 'Perhaps, Heaven forbid, there has
been a defect in my marriage-bed, as there was
to Abraham, from whom proceeded Ishmael,
and to Isaac my father, from whom proceeded
Esau.' His sons said to him [Deut. vi. 4],
*Hear, O Israel, the Lord our God the Lord
is one.* They said, ' Even as in thy heart there
is but One, so in our heart there is but One.'
In that hour Jacob our father began to say,
'Blessed be the name of the glory of his
kingdom for ever and ever.' Our Rabbis said,
'How shall we act? If we say it [*i.e.* Blessed,
etc.], Moses our master did not say it. If we
do not say it, Jacob did say it.' They ordered

that men should say it in a whisper. R.
Jitzḥaq said (some say that one of the school
of R. Ami said), A parable of a king's daughter
who smelt spices [and desired them]. If she
said so, she would be disgraced ; if she did
not say so, she would suffer. Her servants
began to bring them to her silently. R. Abahu
said, They ordered that men should say it in a
loud voice because of the carping of the Minim ;
but in Nehardea, where there are no Minim,
they even now say it in a whisper.'

Commentary.—The three passages translated above
are connected together by their subject-matter, the
main point in them all being some peculiarity in the
recital of the daily prayers, which was said to be due
to the 'carping' of the Minim. In (123) and (124)
it is explained that this was the reason why the
Decalogue was not recited every day. In (125) an
explanation is attempted of the origin and varying
method of recital of the liturgical response, " Blessed
be the name of the glory of his kingdom for ever and
ever." The Shema', which is mentioned in all three
passages, is the central point of the liturgy, and
consists of three groups of verses from Scripture, viz.,
Deut. vi. 4–9, *ib.* xi. 13–21, and Num. xv. 37–41.
The term Shema' is used in a stricter sense, to denote
the opening words of the first of these groups, *i.e.* the
words, *Hear* [Shema', שמע], *O Israel, the Lord thy
God, the Lord is one.* The second group is referred
to, from its opening words, as, '*And it shall be,*' and
the third, in like manner, as, '*And he said.*' In the
liturgy, the response, ' Blessed be the name,' etc.,
comes immediately after '*Hear, O Israel,*' etc., and

is thus seen to be an interpolation into the Scripture text. The Decalogue was intended to be recited immediately before the Shema'.[1]

It is clear, from the contents of the above passages, that nothing was certainly known concerning the omission of the Decalogue, or the addition of the response, except the fact that both were due to the 'carping of the Minim.' In other words, both gave to the Minim the opportunity to misrepresent the Jewish religion and to advance their own heretical opinions. If the Decalogue were repeated every day, it was thought that the Minim would say that only the Ten Commandments [Hebr., the Ten Words] were given to Moses, and that all the rest was un-inspired. Of more importance is the addition of the response, " Blessed be the name," etc. This follows immediately after " *Hear, O Israel, the Lord our God, the Lord is one.*" This text is the watchword of the Divine Unity ; and it was in connexion with this that the misrepresentation of the Minim was most to be expected. In (125) it is said by one Rabbi that in the recital of this text the words were divided by a pause, so that presumably the meaning would be, " The Lord is our God ; the Lord is one." By another Rabbi it is said that the words were not divided by a pause, and that the response was not added. In this case the text would read, " The Lord our God the Lord, is one " ; and perhaps this form

---

[1] In the *Jewish Quarterly Review*, April 1903, p. 392 ff., there is a very interesting account of a papyrus fragment in Hebrew, containing the Decalogue *immediately followed by the Shema'*. The fragment appears to date from the first century of our era, and the text shows slight divergencies from the Massoretic text. The papyrus is now in the Cambridge University Library.

would lend itself to heretical misrepresentation, by those who denied the Divine Unity, more than the first form.   However this may be, the addition of the response after the word ' one ' would be much more likely to lead to misrepresentation, especially if, as is stated in (125), it was originally said in a whisper. The effect would be that, in the recital of the liturgy, after the declaration of the Divine Unity followed a pause during which something was whispered.   The reason why it was whispered at first is no doubt truly indicated in the fantastic haggadah of (125), viz., that it was an extra-biblical interpolation into a Scripture text.   But it appears that this practice of whispering the response was misrepresented by the Minim ; and consequently it was ordered that the response should be said aloud, so that there might be no uncertainty as to the words really used.   Apart from that reason, the older method of whispering the response was preferred ; and accordingly, in places where there were no Minim, the practice was kept up.   This is expressly stated by R. Abahu, who explains why it was ordered that the response should —where there were Minim—be said in a loud voice.

The attempts described in (124) of several Rabbis to introduce in Babylonia some practice already discontinued owing to the Minim, refer, I think, to the recital of the Decalogue before the Shema', and not to the response after it.

It remains to inquire into the date at which the order was made in regard to the recital of the response in a loud voice.   With this object in view, 1 include here another passage, in which mention is made of ordinances directed against the Minim.

(126) M. Ber. ix. 5.—All who concluded benedictions in the sanctuary used to say 'from the
world' [*i.e.* from of old]. After the Minim
corrupted [religion] and said that there was
only one world, they ordered that they should
say 'from world to world' [*i.e.* 'from age to
age,' 'for ever and ever']. And they ordered
that a man should greet his companion with
the Name, as it is said [Ruth ii. 4], *And,
behold, Boaz went,* etc.

This passage is from the Mishnah, and thus older
than the three previous ones. Although the Minim
are here mentioned, it is doubtful whether they are
really intended. The mention of the change in the
liturgy, by the substitution of the fuller doxology
'from world to world,' may be nothing more than an
inference from Neh. ix. 5, and the reason for it a
recollection of the Sadducees. It is true that the
Minim are said to have denied the doctrine of
Immortality ; but, as has been already shown (see
above, p. 232 fol.), what they really denied was
the Scripture proof of the doctrine. Moreover, the
liturgical alteration referred to in (126) seems a rather
feeble counterblast against a denial of Immortality.

Grätz (G. d. J., iv. 458) suggests the revolt of
Bar Cocheba, 135 A.D., as the date when the two
ordinances referred to in (126) were made. This is
possible, and perhaps not improbable ; but I cannot
find any sufficient evidence for the suggestion. It is
remarkable that the Mishnah passes over in silence
the famous change in the liturgy made by Gamliel II.
at Jabneh, when the 'formula concerning the Minim'
was drawn up (see above, p. 125 fol.), and incorpor-

ated in the Eighteen Benedictions.   If the ordinance
about greeting with the Name, *i.e.* the sacred name
JHVH, had any reference to the Minim, it is at
least possible that it was made at the same time as
the formula against the Minim.   Liturgical precautions against Minuth seem to imply a time when
Minim might be expected to be present in the synagogues where the liturgy was recited.   Thus the
regulations referred to in (123), (124), and (125), the
origin of which was clearly unknown to those who
recorded them, may, with some probability, be referred
to the same period.   But certainty on the point is
unattainable; and it should be noted that in regard
to (125), R. Hananel, in his 'commentary on the
passage, appears to have read in his text of Pesaḥim
that the ordinance was made in Usha.   If this rests
on anything historical, then the date would be that
of the famous assembly at Usha, held after the
suppression of the revolt of Bar Cocheba, say about
140 A.D.   But in the references to the decrees of that
assembly, no mention is made of liturgical changes,
or of the Minim.   The attention of the assembly
seems to have been mainly given to questions affecting property and family life, in view of the disorders
resulting from the war and the subsequent persecution
by the Romans.   No manuscript authority is quoted
by Rabbinowicz in favour of the reading which mentions Usha.   On the whole, while disclaiming any
certainty, I think it is probable that the liturgical
changes referred to in the passages under consideration were made by the assembly at Jabneh, in the
time of Gamliel II., say about the end of the first
century.

For some other liturgical peculiarities deemed heretical, see above, p. 199 fol.

IMMORTALITY

(127) Shem. r. xliv. 6, p. 73ᶜ, ᵈ.—Another explanation [Exod. xxxii. 13]: *Remember Abraham [Isaac and Israel]*. Why does he mention the three Fathers? R. Levi said, 'Moses said, Lord of the world, are the dead living? He said to him, Moses, thou art become a Min,' etc.

Commentary.—This passage is of interest only as showing that to deny the Scripture warrant for immortality is a sign of Minuth. For the attitude of the Minim to the doctrine of Immortality, see above, pp. 232, 280. The rest of the passage quoted has nothing to do with Minuth. R. Levi was a younger contemporary of R. Joḥanan.

SECTION IV. MISCELLANEOUS PASSAGES REFERRING TO MINIM, MINUTH

THE GROUND OF DEPARTURE OF THE MINIM

(128) T. Meg. iv. 37.—Hence R. Shim'on ben El'azar used to say, One man alone is not competent to reply to a corrupting speech; for the Minim take their ground of departure from the answer that Aaron gave to Moses.

Commentary. — The reference is to Exod. xxxii. 22–24, in which Aaron excuses himself to Moses for having made the golden calf. The Erfurt MS. of Tosephta reads, 'The answer which Moses gave to

Aaron,' which is obviously an error. The 'ground of departure' of the Minim would seem to be the rejection of the authority of Moses implied in the act of making the calf. R. Shim'on ben El'azar was a disciple of R. Meir, in the second half of the second century. There is nothing to identify the Minim with Christians in this passage; what is said would apply to all Jewish heretics.

In (129) b. Meg. 25^b there is a somewhat different version of the above passage. R. Shim'on ben El'azar says, 'Let a man always be careful in his answers; for from the answer which Aaron gave to Moses, the Minim [so acc. to the MSS.] have gone astray; for it is said [Exod. xxxii. 24], *I cast it in the fire, and there came out this calf.*' The commentators explain this to mean that the Minim inferred from the answer of Aaron that there was some truth in so-called false religion.

Do not give Place to the Minim

(130) T. Par. iii. 3.—They said, in the presence of R. Aqiba, in the name of R. Ishma'el, Cups of stone were hung on the horns of the oxen; when the oxen stooped to drink, the cups were filled. He said to them, 'Do not give occasion to the Minim to humble you.'

Commentary.—The phrase, 'Do not give occasion to the Minim to humble you,' occurs also in the following passages: (i) M. Par. iii. 3, where the speaker is R. José, and the printed text has צדוקים in place of מינין; (ii) T. Joma iii. 2, where the speaker is R. Aqiba. The subject-matter in every case is different. The Mishnah in Joma does not contain the phrase; but in the Babylonian Gemara, Joma 40^{b}, it is quoted in a Baraitha apparently from the Tosephta. Here the printed text has צדוקים in place of מינין ; but the latter is the reading of the MSS. and of the early editions, as shown by Rabbinowicz.

The literal meaning of the phrase is clear; but the application of it is very difficult to understand. In every instance where it occurs, the matter under discussion is a minute detail of ritual, connected with either the killing of the red heifer [Num. xix. 1–13] or the casting of lots for the scape-goat [Lev. xvi. 8 fol.]. In the time of R. Aqiba (or R. José, *i.e.* probably R. José ben Ḥalaphta) the ritual in question was no longer practised, having ceased to be possible when the Temple was destroyed. The discussion upon them was therefore purely academic. Accordingly the difficulty arises, What reason was there to fear the Minim? From all that we have learnt hitherto, it does not appear that the Minim took part or interest in the discussions upon halachah in the Rabbinical assemblies. The frequent controversies between Minim and Jewish Rabbis turned chiefly upon the interpretation of texts of Scripture, and were concerned with doctrine rather than with ritual. If the ceremonies referred to had been actually performed in the time of R. Aqiba, it would be more easy to understand that the Minim might have found occasion to criticise, and in some way to 'humble,' the Jews. But the ceremonies had long been disused, together with all else that depended upon the existence of the Temple.

Since, then, the discussion related to the manner

in which these ceremonies had once been performed, or ought to have been performed, we may interpret the phrase about the Minim as a suggestion that the opinions of those to whom R. Aqiba (or R. José) addressed the remark were heretical, or at least would support the contentions of the Minim. I can offer no better explanation than this, and am aware that it is not complete. I cannot show in what way the opinions put forward tended to favour heresy. The commentators on the passage in b. Joma 40^b, where the discussion refers to the scape-goat, explain that the Minim will say that Azazel, for whom the scape-goat was intended, was a second God, and thus will taunt the Jews with admitting the doctrine of Two Powers. But that criticism on the part of the Minim, if it were made at all, would be applicable to the original text in Lev. xvi., not merely to one small detail of the ritual connected with the scape-goat. And as for the reference to the 'cups of stone' hung on the horns of the oxen, it is hard to see what this has to do with Minuth, or why the Minim should object to it more than to the whole series of ceremonies of which it was a small part. If it were alleged that the Minim did object to, or rather deny the validity of, the whole procedure in reference to the red heifer and to the scape-goat, then it might be pointed out that these two are mentioned in the Epistle to the Hebrews, a writing with which we have seen reason to believe the Minim were familiar. It is, of course, possible that such a reference underlies the phrase we are considering, but in itself it is quite too slight and vague to serve as the foundation for any such conclusion.

An alternative explanation is that the reference is not to the Minim but to the Sadducees. This is supported by the printed text of the Mishnah, and by the fact that in two other passages of b. Joma, 19[b] and 53[b], the Sadducees are undoubtedly referred to in a discussion upon certain matters of ritual. It is true that the Sadducees passed out of history along with the Temple, at least it is probable they did so. But there might, and indeed did, remain the tradition of Sadducean practice and theory; and the phrase under consideration would, in this case, mean that the opinions against which Aqiba protested were, in his judgment, Sadducean. But there is nothing to establish any connexion between the opinions put forward and the teaching or practice of the Sadducees. And if there were, it is a question whether it would have been worth while for R. Aqiba to have referred to a virtually extinct opponent. The Minim, whoever they were, were by no means extinct in the time of R. Aqiba; and although it be now impossible to explain the precise force of his remark, there can be little doubt that he intended it to guard against a danger which he felt to be real.

A CANON OF MINUTH.

(131) Ber. r. xlviii. 6, p. 97[b], [c].—R. Jonathan said, Everywhere that 'hypocrisy' (הנופה) occurs in a verse, the Scripture speaks of Minuth; and the common element in them all is [indicated by Isa. xxxiii. 14], *The sinners in Zion are afraid; trembling hath seized the hypocrites.*

Commentary.—This is really only an *obiter dictum*

founded on the text in Isaiah.   It never was applied
as a regular canon of interpretation.   It amounts to
little more than the assertion that the essence of
Minuth is ' hypocrisy.'   The word so translated has
the root-meaning of ' change,' ' substitution,' and
thence ' pretence.'   It is most frequently used in
reference to religion, and implies either the pretence of being religious, or the fact of being irre-
ligious ; thus, either ' hypocrisy ' or ' godlessness.'   R.
Jonathan accordingly declared that Minuth consisted
in hypocrisy, an outward profession of religion, *i.e.*
the Jewish religion, together with the denial of the
substance of it.   The text in Isaiah was intended
as a convenient reminder of the alleged connexion
between hypocrisy and Minuth, but probably R.
Jonathan's remark about Minuth was suggested to
him by the occurrence of the word ' hypocrites,'
when he was expounding the text in Isaiah.

For R. Jonathan, see above, pp. 216, 254.

A CHANCE FOR THE MINIM.   " I HAVE HARDENED
PHARAOH'S HEART "

(132) Shem. r. xiii. 3, p. 24^b.—Another explanation : *For I have hardened his heart* [Exod. x.
1].   R. Johanan said, ' Here is an " opening
of the mouth " for the Minim to say, It was
not in his [Pharaoh's] power that he should
repent, as it is said, *For I have hardened his
heart.*'   R. Shim'on ben Laqish said to him,
' Let the mouth of the Minim be shut !   But
[Prov. iii. 34], *Surely he scorneth the scorners !*
For the Holy One, Blessed be He, warns a

man once, twice, thrice; and [if] he does not turn, then He closes his [the man's] heart against repentance, so as to punish him for the sin which he committed. Even so [of] Pharaoh the wicked. When the Holy One, Blessed be He, had sent to him five times, and he had not taken heed to His words, then the Holy One, Blessed be He, said to him, Thou hast stiffened thy neck, and thou hast hardened thine heart. Lo, I add to thee uncleanness to thy uncleanness.'

Commentary.—R. Johanan and his colleague R. Shim'on ben Laqish have been frequently mentioned. They lived in Tiberias in the latter half of the third century. Who are referred to as the Minim in this passage is not clear. Bacher (A. d. P. A., i. 258 n. 1) says that "the Minim here are Gnostics, who held that the God of the O.T. did not desire the good," and therefore did not allow Pharaoh to repent. I do not presume to say that this interpretation is incorrect. Yet the argument of R. Shim'on ben Laqish seems to show that the point in dispute was, not the goodness or otherwise of God, but the possibility of repentance on the part of Pharaoh. The Minim are charged by R. Johanan with saying, ' It was not in the power of Pharaoh to repent, because God hardened his heart.' The rejoinder to that is that Pharaoh could have repented, and was given five opportunities to repent, and that only when he had neglected all these did God close his heart against repentance, so that Pharaoh might be justly punished for his sins. That many Gnostics thought that the God of the O.T. did not desire the

21

good, is perhaps true. But if the Minim are to be
identified with such Gnostics, then we should expect
that the question of the goodness of God would be
frequently debated between Minim and Jews; and
this we have not found to be the case.

An alternative interpretation is not impossible.
We have already found reason to connect with the
doctrines of the Minim the teaching of the Epistle to
the Hebrews (see above, pp. 265 fol.). Now, in that
Epistle, vi. 6, there is a remarkable saying about
repentance, *It is impossible to renew them to repentance.* The writer of the epistle applies this to
those who were once enlightened . . . . and fell away.
And, of course, such a case as that of Pharaoh does
not come within the range of the principle laid down.
But that would not prevent an opponent from saying
that the Epistle to the Hebrews taught the impossibility of repentance. And if, further, such
impossibility was held to be not merely on the part
of man but on the part of God, then R. Johanan
might with justice say that the text which he quoted,
I have hardened his heart, bore out the doctrine
which he supposed the Minim to hold. R. Shim'on
ben Laqish agreed with him in supposing that the
Minim held such a doctrine; but he sought to show
that the text quoted did not support it, and that if
a man did not repent, it was his own fault. God
did not prevent him from repenting, but only, after
repeated warning, accepted the fact and inflicted
punishment.

It is worth notice that this very case of Pharaoh
is mentioned in the Epistle to the Romans, ix. 17, 18,
For the Scripture saith unto Pharaoh [cp. Exod. ix.

16], '*For this very purpose did I raise thee up, that I might show in thee my power, and that my name might be published abroad in all the earth.*' *So then he hath mercy on whom he will, and whom he will he hardeneth.* That the Epistle to the Romans was known to the Rabbis is extremely doubtful. But it may have been known to the readers of the Epistle to the Hebrews ; and if not that, there is at least so much of connexion of thought between the two epistles as to make it probable that the idea of the unconditional sovereignty of God would be acceptable to the readers of the Epistle to the Hebrews.

On the whole, therefore, while admitting that the Minim in the present passage may represent Gnostics, I think it more probable that, as elsewhere, so here they denote Jewish Christians holding the doctrines of the Epistle to the Hebrews.

Four Classes of Minim

(133) Jalq. Shim., Ps. lx. 9 (7). — Another explanation [Ps. lx. 9], *Gilead is mine.* R. Shim'on ben Laqish said, ' If the Minim say to thee that the Holy One, Blessed be He, doth not revive the dead, say to them, Behold Elijah, who was of Tishbi in Gilead, testifying that I have revived the dead by his hand. *And Manasseh is mine.* If they say to thee that the Holy One, Blessed be He, doth not receive repentance, say to them, Behold Manasseh, testifying that I received him in repentance, as it is said [2 Chron. xxxiii. 13], *And he prayed to the Lord ; and he was*

intreated of him and heard his prayer. Ephraim is the defence of my head. And if they say unto thee that the Holy One, Blessed be He, doth not visit the barren, Behold Elkanah of whom it is written [1 Sam. i. 1], *A son of Tohu, a son of Zoph, an Ephraimite,* testifying that I visited Hannah. *Judah is my sceptre.* And if they say unto thee that the Holy One, Blessed be He, doth not deliver from the fire, Behold Hananiah and his companions testifying that He delivered them from the fire; as it is said [Dan. i. 6], *Now among them were of the children of Judah, Daniel, Hananiah.*

Commentary.—The above passage occurs, with no important variations, in Bamm. r. xiv. 1 ; and in Tanhuma, Nissa, § 30. The author is undoubtedly R. Shim'on ben Laqish, as Bacher points out.

The text of Ps. lx. 9 is not interpreted, but is forced by sheer violence to suggest a refutation of four heretical doctrines, which are ascribed to the Minim. It is only indeed in connexion with the first heresy, viz., the denial of the resurrection of the dead, that the Minim are mentioned ; but they are clearly intended in all four instances of alleged heresy. Moreover, the heresy that God does not receive a penitent is expressly ascribed to the Minim in the passage translated above (p. 320), where the refutation is given by R. Shim'on ben Laqish. I do not know of any ground for ascribing, either to Gnostics or to Jewish Christians, the doctrines that God does not give children to the barren women, and that he does not save men from the fire. Who, therefore, are meant by the Minim in these two instances, I am unable to suggest.

Words of the Minim

(134) Siphri, § 48, p. 84ª.—R. Shim'on ben Menasja says [Prov. v. 15], *Drink waters out of thine own well*, drink the waters of thy creator; and do not drink foul waters, lest thou be drawn with the words of the Minim.

Commentary. — R. Shim'on ben Menasja was a contemporary of R. Jehudah ha-Qadosh, in the beginning of the third century.

The application of the text in Prov. v. 15 to the Minim is chiefly of interest because it is found in an early Midrash. In itself it contains nothing new. We have already seen that this chapter of Proverbs was by other Rabbis interpreted in reference to Minuth (see above, p. 185).

92. "They that hate Me." The Minim

(135) Siphri, § 331, p. 140ª.—[Deut. xxxii. 41], *I will render vengeance to mine adversaries*, these are the Cuthiim [Samaritans]; as it is said [Ezra iv. 1], *And the adversaries of Judah and Benjamin heard that the children of the captivity were building the Temple. And I will recompense them that hate me*, these are the Minim; and thus He [*i.e* God, in Scripture] saith [Ps. cxxxix. 21, 22], *Do I not hate them which hate thee, O Lord? and am I not grieved with those that rise up against thee? I hate*

them with a perfect hatred; they have become as enemies to me.

Commentary.—Observe that the Minim are here distinguished from the Samaritans. In a few passages the reading varies between Minim and Cuthiim.

For the application of Ps. cxxxix. 21, 22 to the Minim, see above, p. 156, where R. Ishmael cites the same text in reference to the books of the Minim.

A REPLY TO THE MINIM. GENEALOGIES

(136) b. B. Bath. r. 91ª. — And R. Ḥanan bar
Rabba said that Rab said, The mother of
Abraham was Amathlai bath Carnebo ; the
mother of Haman was Amathlai bath Orbathi ;
and thy signs are, ' Unclean, unclean,' ' Clean,
clean.'   The mother of David was Nizzebath
bath Adael, the mother of Samson was Zelalponith, and his sister Nesiin. To what does
this tend ? To an answer to the Minim.

Commentary.—R. Ḥanan b. Rabba was a son-in-law of Rab, the disciple of R. Jehudah ha-Qadosh, who carried to Babylonia the tradition embodied in the Mishnah. Rab is the sole authority for the names of personages in the above list. He may have invented them. Only one, Zelalponith, is found in the O.T., and that, in a slightly different form, 1 Chr. iv. 3. Whether Rab intended them to serve as an 'answer to the Minim,' there is nothing to show. The Gemara does not explain how they could serve such a purpose. Rashi says, "The Minim asks us concerning these more than concern-

ing other women, and we reply that [the names] have
been handed down to us, orally, by the prophets."
Why the Minim, whether Gnostics or Jewish
Christians, should have been curious on the subject,
I do not know. Possibly the reference to 'endless
genealogies,' 1 Tim. i. 3, may have some bearing on
the point.

THE MINIM AND THE NEW MOON

(137) M. R. ha-Sh., ii. 1.—If they do not know
him, they send another with him to vouch for
him. Formerly they used to receive evidence
as to the new moon from anyone. Since the
Minim acted perversely, they ordained that
they should not receive evidence except from
such as were known.

Commentary.—This passage is from the Mishnah,
and its extreme terseness of style requires some expansion. The subject under discussion is the question
of determining the time of new moon, the time upon
which depended the date of the festivals in the suc-
ceeding month. The beginning of the month was
the day on which the new moon was first seen after
conjunction with the sun. Evidence was therefore
taken from those who had seen the new moon. Such
witnesses must of course be trustworthy; therefore
(and here our passage begins), if a witness was unknown to those appointed to receive evidence, another
man accompanied him, in order to vouch for his
credibility. Formerly anyone might give evidence.
But from the time that the Minim introduced some
mischievous practice, it was ordered that only the

evidence of such witnesses as were personally known should be received.

This is an interesting as well as an obscure passage; ·and though both the Gemaras make some reference to it, they do not give a complete explanation.

In the first place, there is no doubt that the reading 'Minim' [מינין] is the correct one. It is the reading of the Mishnah, as printed separately, and of the text of the Mishnah incorporated in the Gemaras. (See Rabbinowicz on b. R. ha-Sh. 22^b.) The verse of the Mishnah immediately following (R. ha-Sh., ii. 2) mentions the Samaritans [כותים], as having introduced some corrupt practice. Thus the Mishnah is aware that the Samaritans are not the same as the Minim, and therefore the mention of the Minim is intentional. When we turn to the Tosephta and the Gemaras, we find a source of confusion in a story about certain people called Baithusin [בייתוסין] who also introduced corrupt practices. The Tosephta gives this story [R. ha-Sh., i. 15], and does not say anything about the Minim. It says, " Formerly they used to receive evidence from any man. On one occasion the Baithusin hired two witnesses to come and deceive the Wise; because the Baithusin do not admit that Atzereth [Pentecost] should be on [any day] except the day after a Sabbath." [Therefore they sought to influence the calculation upon which the day of the feast ultimately depended.]

The Palestinian Gemara R. ha-Sh. 57^d, in its comments upon the alleged corrupt practices, appears to depend upon the notice in Tosephta just mentioned. The Minim are not referred to by name. It is stated that the ' corrupt practice ' consisted in keeping Pente-

cost on the day after a Sabbath, and assuming that
that day had been consecrated as the feast day;
whereas the right day, according to the view of the
Talmudic Rabbis, the fiftieth day from the first
Paschal day, might fall later in the week.   After this
explanation has been given there follows the story
about the Baithusin and their false witnesses.   It is
possible, therefore, that the explanation about the
fiftieth day being kept on a Sunday does not refer
to the Baithusin, but to the Minim.

In the Babylonian Gemara, R. ha-Sh. 22^b, the
printed text has the following:—(138) " Formerly
they used to receive evidence concerning the new
moon from any man.   [This is the quotation of the
Mishnah.]   Our Rabbis have taught: What corrupt
practice did the ' Baithusin ' commit?   On one occasion," etc., and then follows the story about the false
witnesses.   Now the correct reading in this passage is
not ' Baithusin,' but ' Minim ' (see Rabbinowicz on
R. ha-Sh. 22^b).   The alteration has no doubt been
made on account of the mention of the Baithusin in
the story which follows.   That story, a graphically-
told anecdote, seems to me to have obscured the reference to the Minim, and led to the belief that the
Mishnah, in its charge against the Minim, was really
referring to the Baithusin; accordingly the story is
quoted in explanation.   Who the Baithusin were is
not certain, probably the name indicates more than
one religious party at different epochs.   The story of
their false witnesses implies Jerusalem for the scene
of it, and, if historical, is thus earlier than A.D. 70.
But the ' corrupt practices ' which had to be guarded
against continued long after that date.   In the

Palestinian Gemara, R. ha-Sh. 57[d], it is stated that R. Nehorai once went to Usha[1] to corroborate a witness for the new moon.   Thereupon follows immediately the explanation already given about the day of Pentecost being kept on a Sunday.

Now, whether the Minim are identical with the Baithusin or not, it is quite possible that the Minim may have had their own reasons for holding a similar view with regard to the proper days of Passover and Pentecost.   If the Minim were Jewish Christians, it is easy to understand that they would have an interest in the date of Pentecost, and the corresponding fiftieth day previous to Pentecost.   The Jewish Christians kept the Jewish feasts, but read into them a Christian meaning, and connected with Passover and Pentecost the death of Jesus and the gift of the Holy Ghost.   Jesus was crucified on a Friday, and, according to the Gospels, rose again on the Sunday following.   The first Christian Pentecost was likewise on a Sunday.   Now, according to the Jewish usage, the fourteenth day of Nisan, the day of Passover, might fall upon any day of the week.   The Jewish Christians would naturally prefer that it should fall on a Friday, so that the fast and feast days should correspond with those of the original Passion-week and the subsequent Pentecost.   Since it was the custom, according to the Mishnah, to fix the appearance of the new moon by the evidence of eye-witnesses, and to determine the days of the month accordingly, Jewish Christians could give evidence as

---

[1] The Sanhedrin, or at least the Nasi and his colleagues, met at Usha A.D. 130 *circa*, and again in A.D. 140 *circa*.   Probably the visit of R. Nehorai took place at the earlier date.

well as others. And, whether or not they ever attempted to influence the determination of the days of the month, their evidence would be open to suspicion, because they were known to be biassed in favour of a particular day of the week for the fourteenth of Nisan.

If, then, according to the reading of the Mishnah, the Minim are really referred to in connexion with the subject of the new moon witnesses, there is some amount of ground for identifying them with Jewish Christians. That the Minim in this instance can be Gnostics is out of the question. The Gnostics did not pay any regard to the 'set feasts' of the Jewish religion, and would not care what might be the day of the week on which they fell.

THE MINIM AND ALEXANDER THE GREAT

In Vajiqr. r. xiii. 5, p. 19ᶜ, it is related that Alexander the Great showed honour to the High Priest, Shim'on ha-Tzaddiq, and that the 'Minim' remonstrated with him for doing so. The story occurs in Josephus, Antiq., xi. 8, 5, and is repeated in b. Joma 69ᵈ, and Pesiqta d. R. Kahana, Parah, p. 41ᵃ. Neither of the two Hebrew texts mentions the word ' Minim.' The text in Joma has simply '*they* said to him'; the text in Pesiqta has '*his courtiers* said to him.' The reading 'Minim,' or rather 'Minai,' in Vajiqr. r. may be explained as being, at the late date of the compilation of this Midrash, merely a general term for enemies of the Jews. It is sufficient to mention this passage without going to the trouble of translating it.

CHRISTIANITY IN TALMUD

In like manner it will be sufficient to mention, without comment, some few passages which merely allude to Minim, but contain nothing of importance for the study of them. These passages are as follows :—

MINIM, CASUAL REFERENCES

(i) b. Ber. 7ᵃ, Sanh. 105ᵇ, A. Zar. 4ᵇ.—R. Jehoshua ben Levi is annoyed by a Min, who lived near him. The fact is mentioned on account of the device which the Rabbi made use of, unsuccessfully, to draw down a curse upon his enemy.

(ii) b. Ber. 54ᵃ—The Minim say there is only one world. See above, p. 313 fol. The reading ' Minim ' is correct, yet it is possible that the original reference was to the Sadducees.

(iii) *Ib.*, 56ᵇ.—A Min asks R. Ishmael to interpret certain dreams. There is no reference to Minuth.

(iv) *Ib.* 58ᵃ.—A Min converses with R. Shesheth. There is no reference to Minuth. Probably the Min in this instance was a Persian, and a fire-worshipper. If so, ' Min ' may represent ' Mani.'

(v) b. Meg. 23ᵃ.—Jacob the Min asks a question of R. Jehudah. There is no reference to Minuth. Tosaphoth doubts whether Jacob was a Min at all.

(vi) b. B. Bathra 25ᵃ.—R. Shesheth would not turn to the east because the Minim teach concerning it. Here, as in No. (iv), Minim

probably denotes fire-worshippers. It should
be added, however, that Rashi believes the
reference to be to ' the disciples of Jesus.'

(vii) b. Sanh. 37ᵃ.—R. Kahana answers the question
of a Min concerning a woman who is נדה.
No reference to Minuth.

(viii) M. Jad. iv. 8.—' A Min of Galilee' said
to the Pharisees, etc., see Geiger, Urschrift,
p. 146 ; Schürer, G. d. J. V., ii. 318. The
Min here is a political rather than a religious
partisan. Probably a follower of Judah of
Galilee is meant. The date of the passage
is uncertain, probably not earlier than the
codification of the Mishnah by Rabbi.
Therefore it cannot be quoted as the earliest
instance of the use of the term Min. The
printed text of the Misnah reads Tzadduqi
in place of Min ; but the latter reading is
shown by Schürer to be the right one.

As the printed texts of the Talmud are subject to
the censorship of the press, it is frequently the case
that the word Min (Minim) is struck out and replaced by Tzadduqi, Cuthi, Romi, or some other
innocent word. This defect is found in most of the
printed texts since the edition of Basle, 1578. The
comparison of manuscripts, and early editions, as
performed by Rabbinowicz,[1] has made it possible to
correct these mischievous errors. A few passages

---

[1] The invaluable work of Rabbinowicz, entitled Diqduqe Sopherim, is
unfortunately incomplete. It extends over perhaps three-fourths of the
Talmud, including the most important of the treatises.

remain, in which the reading Tzadduqi, or Cuthi, is the right one. I subjoin a list of references to such passages as I have met with where this is the case. There are probably others. My purpose, however, is not to collect references to the Sadducees, or to the Samaritans, but to give a list of the references to the Minim as complete as I can, and also as free as possible from the intrusion of what does not belong to it.

In the following passages, the reading Tzadduqi is correct, and the reference is to the Sadducees.

(A.) Mishnah (collected by Schürer, *op. cit.*, ii. 317 fol.); Erubh. vi. 2 (uncertain); Macc. i. 6; Parah. iii. 7; Nidd. iv. 2; Jad. iv. 6, 7, 8. (B.) Talmud. Joma 19^b, 53^a; B. Bathr. 115^b; Macc. 5^b; Nidd. 33^b. (C.) Tosephta; Ḥagg. iii. 35.

97. JACOB OF CHEPHAR NEBURAIA

A passage has already been quoted (see above, p. 219) from the Midrash Qoh. r. (on vii. 26, p. 21^d), in which it is stated that " R. Isi of Cæsarea expounded this verse in reference to Minuth : The good is R. El'azar, the sinner is Jacob of Chephar Neburaia," etc., after which follows a list of five other examples of contrasted saints and sinners. There can be no possible doubt that the intention of R. Isi was to pronounce Jacob of Ch. N. a Min. It is therefore desirable to ascertain what may be known about this Jacob. I have not included him in the list of those Minim who had polemical discussions with Jews, because no such controversies are ascribed to him. Controversies he certainly had, but in the records of them he is not called a Min. Moreover, certain sayings of his are mentioned with approval, and the Babylonian Gemara does not seem to have any suspicion of his ' Minuth.' I have therefore thought it best to deal with him in a separate section, and to put that as an appendix to the main body of evidence collected on the subject of Minuth.

Jacob of Chephar Neburaia lived in the fourth century, and is most frequently mentioned in connexion with Tyre and Cæsarea. The site of the village from which he took his name has not been identified. He 'targumed' Hagg. ii. 19, in the synagogue Maradta in Cæsarea, and his exposition was approved by the Rabbis (j. Bicc. iii. 3. 65ᵈ, b. Sanh. 7ᵃ, and Midr. Samuel c. 7 (6)[1]). He expounded Ps. lxv. 2 at Tyre ; and his exposition is quoted in j. Ber. 12ᵈ. In b. Meg. 18ᵃ it is quoted, but is ascribed to *R. Jehudah* of Chephar Neburaia. This is the result of a confusion between Jacob of Ch. N. and R. Jehudah bar Naḥmani, who had been interpreter (מתרגמן) of R. Shim'on ben Laqish.

Further, Jacob of Ch. N. was involved in controversy with R. Ḥaggai of Tyre upon questions of halachah. Two instances of this are given, and appear together in several passages in the Rabbinical literature. The two halachic decisions which he gave were, first, that the son of a Gentile woman might be circumcised on the Sabbath ; and second, that the rules relating to the killing of cattle for food applied also to fishes. For both these decisions he was called to account by R. Ḥaggai, who ordered him on each

---

[1] This reference is given by Bacher, A. d. P. A., iii. 710, 3. I have not the means of verifying it.

occasion to come and be scourged for having given a
wrong decision. Jacob asked R. Ḥaggai by what
authority he scourged him? The Rabbi quoted
texts to show that Jacob's teaching was wrong, after
which Jacob lay down and submitted to be scourged.
The first of these two incidents is described in j.
Kidd. 64ᵈ, j. Jebam. 4ᵃ. The two together are found
in Ber. r. vii. 2, Bamm. r. xix. 3, Pesiqta d. R. Kahana,
§ Parah., 35ᵇ, 36ᵃ, Tanhuma, Huqqath, 56ᵇ, 57ᵃ.

In b. Kethub. 65ᵃ a halachic decision by Jacob of
Ch. N. is mentioned and debated, with no hint that
any suspicion attached to him. In j. Shabb. 17ᵇ
there is the following:—Jacob of Chephar Neburaia
asked R. Ḥaggai, 'Is then a child that is born in
the twilight circumcised in the twilight?' He said
to him, 'If thou and I were entering in at one door,
perhaps we might be able to decide the point.' The
meaning of this plainly is, that Jacob was no longer
considered by the Rabbi to be in fellowship and thus
open to conviction on Jewish principles. It is nowhere said that Jacob was excommunicated, but it
seems reasonable to infer that in some way he was
excluded from the community of Israel and regarded
as a heretic. His question to R. Ḥaggai may indicate that he still regarded himself as being a
member of the community.

In the passage already mentioned, Qoh. r. vii. 28,
21ᵈ, he is charged with Minuth, in contrast with a
certain El'azar otherwise unknown.

The above passages contain, I believe, all that is
known of Jacob of Chephar Neburaia. They are
too scanty to be of much use, and for that reason I
have not translated them. Scanty as they are, how-

ever, they prove that Jacob of Ch. N. was a real
person, and that he became a heretic. It is therefore needless, and unwarranted, to say, as Friedländer
says (Vorch. jüd. Gnosticismus, p. 108), that in the
list of contrasted saints and sinners, Qoh. r. vii. 26,
Jacob of Ch. N. is plainly Jacob of Ch. Sechanja
(see above, p. 221 n.) We may also perhaps infer
that the distinction between Jew and Min was not
regarded, from the side of the Minim, as being a
very sharp one. Here may be compared the very
curious story of R. Saphra and the Minim of Cæsarea
(see above, p. 266 fol.). There the Minim, strange as
it seems, actually engaged a Jewish Rabbi to be their
teacher. It is true he did not suit them; but that
was owing to his defective knowledge of Scripture,
not to the fact of his being a Jew. Is it possible
that Jacob of Ch. N. stood in some similiar relation
towards the Minim, and that less staunch than R.
Saphra, he was perverted by those to whom he
ministered? That he did become a Min is shown
not merely by the passage in Qoh. r., but also by
that in j. Shabb. 17ᵇ, where R. Ḥaggai speaks of
himself and Jacob as not entering at the same door.
But it is worthy of note that his apostasy does not
appear to have been known outside of his own
country. He is mentioned in the Babylonian
Gemara, Kethub. 65ᵃ, and an opinion given by him
is debated without any reference to his being a Min.
Further, if I am right in supposing that the passage
j. Shabb. 17ᵇ refers to a time after he had become a
Min, then it would seem that he still kept up his
interest in halachah. If so, he might be a Jewish
Christian, but scarcely a Gnostic. There is, however,

nothing to show what was the change which turned him from a Jew into a Min. He remains a shadowy figure, tantalising by its vagueness, the ghost of an ancient heretic.

THE PRIESTHOOD OF MELCHIZEDEK

(139) b. Nedar. 32ᵇ.—R. Zechariah said, in the name of R. Ishmael, The Holy one, Blessed be He, sought to cause the priesthood to go forth from Shem. For it is said [Gen. xiv. 18], *And he was priest of God Most High.* As soon as he put the blessing of Abraham before the blessing of God, he caused it to go forth from Abraham, as it is said [*ib.* 19], *And he blessed him and said, 'Blessed be Abraham of God Most High, possessor of heaven and earth, and blessed be God Most High.'* Abraham said to him, 'Do they put the blessing of the servant before the blessing of his owner?' Immediately it was given to Abraham, as it is said [Ps. cx. 1], *The Lord said unto my Lord, Sit thou at my right hand until I make thy enemies the footstool for thy feet.* And further down it is written [*ib.* 4], *The Lord hath sworn, and will not repent, Thou art a priest for ever after the order of Melchizedek,* according to the saying of Melchizedek. And this is what is written [Gen. xiv. 18], *And he was priest of God Most High.* He was priest; his seed were not priests.

Commentary.—The point of the above haggadah is that the priesthood was taken away from

Melchizedek and given to Abraham. God, it is said, had at first intended that the priesthood should 'go forth from Shem,' *i.e.* should be handed down along the line of his posterity. Melchizedek is here identified with Shem, as elsewhere in the Midrash. The divine purpose, however, was changed, and the priesthood was caused to descend in the line of Abraham. Tosaphoth points out that Abraham himself was one of the descendants of Shem, and gives the explanation that the priesthood was taken away from all the other descendants of Shem, and given to Abraham and his posterity. In any case it was taken away from Melchizedek. Now Melchizedek was the subject of a great deal of speculation in the early centuries of the common era. There was a Gnostic sect who called themselves after his name, regarding him as an incarnation of the divine power. Also, in the Epistle to the Hebrews, Melchizedek is represented as a type of Christ, and the comparison is worked out in detail [Heb. vii.]. Evidently the intention of R. Ishmael, in his haggadah, was to destroy the foundation for this exalted conception of Melchizedek, by showing that the priesthood was taken away from him. This R. Ishmael is the same whom we have already met with several times as an opponent of Minim. It was he who forbade the attempted cure of his nephew, Ben Damah, by a Min who was beyond question a Christian (see above, p. 103 fol.). It was he, also, who severely condemned the Scriptures of the Minim (see above, p. 156 fol.). He lived in Palestine at the end of the first, and well on into the second century.

The depreciation of Melchizedek would serve as

an argument against both the Gnostic sect and the Christian readers of the Epistle to the Hebrews; but I see no reason to restrict the reference to the first. The Melchizedekites do not appear to have been a very important or very aggressive sect, certainly not more prominent than the Jewish Christians. It has been suggested above (p. 265) that the doctrine of Two Powers in Heaven, ascribed to the Minim, is the Jewish version of the Christology of the Epistle to the Hebrews. I take the present passage to be additional evidence in support of the view that the teaching of that Epistle was known to the Rabbis, and that the Minim were, or at least included, Jewish Christians whose theology was represented in that Epistle. It should be noticed that R. Ishmael, as well as the author of the Epistle to the Hebrews, made use of Ps. cx. 4 in support of his argument. The Rabbi interpreted the words דברתי על (Eng. version, *After the order of*), to mean *according to the saying of* Melchizedek. That is, Melchizedek himself, by what he had said, forfeited the priesthood so that it passed to Abraham. The citation of Ps. cx. may, however, be due not to the Rabbi's acquaintance with the Epistle to the Hebrews, but merely to the fact that Melchizedek is mentioned in the Psalm. That his argument does impugn the doctrine of the Epistle to the Hebrews there can be no question.

This completes the series of passages in which I have found a reference to Christianity, in the person of its Founder or of his followers. That the whole material is exhausted I do not venture to affirm.

The Rabbinical literature is enormous, and, moreover, has never been indexed, so that I dare not claim to have overlooked nothing. Nevertheless, I believe I have gathered all the important passages, and nearly all the less important ones. A few I have intentionally left out, which have been thought to have some polemical reference, but in which I could find no allusion, however remote, to Christianity. Also, I have omitted passages where a mere verbal likeness might be traced to some phrase in the New Testament. The subject of parallel passages did not come within the limits which I had marked out for my work.

It remains now to collect the general results of the mass of evidence presented in the foregoing pages ; and to this task I shall devote the concluding section of this book.

DIVISION II

GENERAL RESULTS

I HAVE called this book by the title of " Christianity
in Talmud and Midrash," and have offered to the
reader a number of passages from the Rabbinical
literature of the first four centuries containing what
I believe to be references to Christianity, either in the
person of its Founder, or of his followers. In doing
so I have been unable to avoid giving provisional
answers to questions which cannot be fully answered
until all the evidence has been presented, and have
thus, to some extent, taken for granted what ought
to be proved. In this concluding section I shall try
to complete my case by a general review of the evidence, and shall show first that Jesus is referred to in
the Rabbinical literature ; and second, that the Minim,
who are so often mentioned, are, or at all events
include, Jewish Christians. Under the first head I
shall, after proving as I hope that the historical Jesus
of Nazareth is referred to, sum up the main heads of
the traditions concerning him, and inquire into their
origin and value. Under the second head I shall in
like manner, after presenting the case for the Christianity of the Minim, collect the evidence for their

theology, their relation to Judaism, and whatever else may serve to give clearness and distinctness to the picture. The problem of the Minim has often been discussed, for it is one of the riddles of the Talmud. The solution of that problem attempted here may claim at least the merit of being based upon a larger body of evidence than has, so far as I know, ever been collected before. If the reader is dissatisfied with that solution, he has now before him the materials for a better.

CHAPTER I

Jesus in the Talmud and Midrash

Is the historical Jesus of Nazareth mentioned in the Rabbinical literature? Or, to state the question somewhat differently, are the persons variously named Ben Stada, Ben Pandira, Jeshu, Jeshu ha-Nōtzri, one and the same individual, and he, Jesus of Nazareth? The answer to this question is clearly given by a comparison of parallel passages. Thus :—

(a) T. Sanh. x. 11 (see above, p. 79, No. (19)), " And thus they did to Ben Stada in Lūd, ... and they brought him to the Beth Din and stoned him."

(b) b. Sanh. 67ᵃ (see above, p. 79, No. (21)), " And they bring him to the Beth Din and stone him; and thus they did to Ben Stada in Lūd, and they hung him on the eve of Pesaḥ."

(c) b. Sanh. 43ᵃ (see above, p. 83, No. (22)), " On the eve of Pesaḥ they hung Jeshu ha-Nōtzri." . . . " Jeshu ha-Nōtzri goeth forth to be stoned because he hath practised magic, כישף, and deceived and led astray Israel."

(d) b. Shabb. 104ᵇ (see above, p. 35, No. (1)), " And did not Ben Stada bring magic spells, כשפים, from Egypt? "

There can be no reasonable doubt that Ben Stada
is here equivalent to Jeshu ha-Nōtzri.[1] Next, let us
compare Ben Pandira with Jeshu ha-Nōtzri. We
have

(e) T. Ḥull ii. 24 (see above, p. 138, No. (45)). R.
Eliezer said, " Once I was walking in the street of
Sepphoris ; I found Jacob of Chephar Sichnin, and he
said a word of Minuth in the name of Jeshu ben
Pantiri."

(f) b. A. Zar. 16ᵇ, 17ᵃ (see above, p. 138, No. (46)).
R. Eliezer said, " Once I was walking in the upper street
of Sepphoris, and I found a man, one of the disciples
of Jeshu ha-Nōtzri, and Jacob of Chephar Sechanja
was his name," . . . . "and he said to me, Thus hath
Jeshu ha-Nōtzri taught me."

The name Jeshu ben Pantiri in (e) is, on the same

---

[1] Note that the form Jeshu ben Stada does not occur. Ben Stada is
clearly identified with Jeshu ha-Nōtzri ; but the possibility remains that
originally they were not identical. R. Eliezer, who mentions Jeshu ben
Pandira, mentions also Ben Stada, with no indication that the two names
denote one person. I venture to suggest, as worth consideration, the hypothesis that Ben Stada originally denoted "that Egyptian" [Acts xxi. 38 ;
Josephus Antiqq., xx. 8, 6 ; B. J., ii. 13, 5], who gave himself out as a
prophet, led a crowd of followers to the Mount of Olives, and was routed
there by the Procurator Felix. This man is called a sorcerer ; at least he
promised that the walls of Jerusalem should fall at his approach. Now R.
Eliezer said of Ben Stada that he brought magical spells from Egypt ; and
the Rabbis, to whom he made this remark, replied that 'Ben Stada was a
fool.' This verdict is more appropriate to the Jewish-Egyptian impostor
than to the much more dangerous Jeshu ha-Nōtzri. In later times the
two might easily be confused together. If there is anything in this
suggestion, the name Stada, the pronunciation of which is guaranteed by
the explanation 'Stath da,' might have some connexion with ἀνάστατος,
'seditious,' or at least with some cognate form from the root 'sta.' It should
be observed that R. Eliezer does not say that Ben Stada was put to death at
Lūd, and that according to Josephus the Egyptian himself escaped. The
execution of Ben Stada at Lūd is the result of identifying Ben Stada with
Jeshu ha-Nōtzri.

page a few lines higher up, given in the form Jeshua ben Pandiri. The passages (*e*) and (*f*) clearly prove the identity of Jeshu ben Pandira with Jeshu ha-Nōtzri.

For the identification of Ben Stada with Ben Pandira, which indeed would logically follow from the passages given above, we have the explicit statement.

b. Shabb. 104^b (see above, p. 35, No. (1)), "Ben Stada is Ben Pandira."

So far as the identification of the names is concerned the case is clear. Do these names denote the historical Jesus of Nazareth, the Founder of Christianity? The following passages supply the answer.

(*g*) b. Sanh. 107^b (see above, p. 51, No. (7)). "Jeshu ha-Nōtzri practised magic and deceived and led astray Israel."

(*h*) b. Sanh. 43^a (see above, p. 84, No. (22)), "It was different with Jeshu ha-Nōtzri, for he was near to the kingdom."

(*i*) *Ibid.* (see above, p. 90), "Jeshu [ha-Nōtzri] had five disciples."

(*j*) T. Ḥull. ii. 22, 23 (see above, p. 103, No. (28)), "There came in Jacob a man of Chephar Sama to cure him in the name of Jeshua ben Pandira."

(*k*) j. A. Zar. 40^d, 41^a (see above, p. 104, No. (30)). "He said, We will speak to thee in the name of Jeshu ben Pandira."

Taking all these passages together, we find that the person named in them was one who 'deceived and led astray Israel,' who was tried and executed for doing so, who had disciples, and in whose name those disciples performed, or sought to perform, cures of sick persons. Finally, since the person here named is called Jeshu ha-Nōtzri, the conclusion follows that he was either the historical Jesus of Nazareth, or else some otherwise totally unknown man of the same name and dwelling-place. There can be no question that the first of the two alternatives is the right one.

This conclusion is arrived at strictly from the evidence as given above, and takes no account of the *a priori* probability that a man, so important in Jewish history as Jesus, would be mentioned in the Talmud. That probability certainly strengthens the conclusion. Yet it is remarkable how very little the Talmud does say about Jesus, although there be no longer any room for doubt that he is referred to.

The conclusion here arrived at is sufficient to dispose of the arguments founded on chronological grounds, which are intended to show that there are in the Talmud two persons called Jesus, neither of whom is the historical Jesus of Nazareth. The earlier of these is the one mentioned in (7) above (p. 52 fol.) as the disciple, and therefore contemporary, of R. Jehoshua ben Perahjah, who lived a century before the Christian era. The second is the Ben Stada who was put to death at Lūd, and who was supposed to be contemporary with R. Aqiba, a century after that era began. It is quite possible that the compilers of the Talmud were not aware of the identity of these two; it is certain that chronology was not a science in which the Rabbis excelled, or one in which they laid stress upon accuracy.

Having now established the fact that the historical Jesus of Nazareth is referred to in the Talmud and

Midrash, I proceed to collect the scanty traditions therein contained, so as to show what was the extent of the Rabbinical knowledge or belief concerning him, and what were the probable sources of that knowledge.

Jesus, called ha-Nōtzri, Ben Stada, or Ben Pandira, was born out of wedlock (p. 43). His mother was called Miriam [Mary], and was a dresser of women's hair (pp. 35, 41). Her husband was Pappus ben Jehudah (p. 35). Her paramour was Pandira (p. 35). She is also said to have been descended from princes and rulers, and to have played the harlot with a carpenter (p. 48).

Jesus had been in Egypt and brought magic thence (pp. 35, 51). He was a magician (p. 51), and led astray and deceived Israel (*ibid.* and p. 83). He sinned and caused the multitude to sin (p. 51). He mocked at the words of the wise (*ibid.* and p. 68), and was excommunicated (p. 51). He was tainted with heresy (p. 57).

[He][1] called himself God, also the son of man, and said that he would go up to heaven (p. 62). [He][1] made himself to live by the name of God (p. 75).

He was tried in Lūd as a deceiver and as a teacher of apostasy (p. 79). Witnesses were concealed so as to hear his statements, and a lamp was lighted over him, that his face might be seen. He was brought to the Beth Din (p. 79).

He was executed in Lūd, on the eve of Pesaḥ, which was also the eve of Sabbath (pp. 79, 88). He was stoned (p. 79) and hung (p. 80), or crucified (p. 87). A herald proclaimed that he was to be stoned, and

[1] Jesus is not mentioned by name, but is evidently referred to. See the commentary on the passage.

invited evidence in his favour; but none was given (p. 83).

He [under the name of Balaam] was put to death by Pinḥas the robber [Pontius Pilatus] (p. 72), and at the time of his death was thirty-three years old (*ibid.*).

He was punished in Gehinnom, by means of boiling filth (p. 68).

He was a revolutionary (p. 83). He was near to the kingdom (p. 84).

He had five disciples (p. 90).

Under the name of Balaam he is excluded from the world to come (p. 65 fol.).

In the foregoing paragraphs we have, I believe, all that refers to Jesus in the Rabbinical literature of the first four centuries. The reasons for asserting the fact of this reference will be found in the commentary on the several passages.

It is remarkable that no mention is made of the alleged Messiahship of Jesus, even as a reason for putting him to death.

What are the sources of this tradition concerning Jesus? And, especially, do they imply a knowledge of the contents of a Gospel or Gospels? First let us investigate the authorities for the tradition, *i.c.* the various Rabbis who made the statements containing it, as presented in the passages successively translated in the earlier pages of this book.

It has been explained in the Introduction that the Talmud consists of two parts, Mishnah and Gemara, related to each other as text and commentary. The close of the Mishnah is usually dated at about A.D. 220. The Palestinian Gemara covers the period from the close of the Mishnah down to the middle or end of the fourth century; while the Babylonian Gemara was not completed till the end of the fifth, or possibly even the beginning of the sixth, century. Both the Gemaras, however, contain a great deal of material handed down from the period covered by the Mishnah. These two main periods, represented by the Mishnah and Gemaras, are known as the period of the Tannaim and of the Amoraim respectively. To the earlier period belong, not only the Mishnah, but the Tosephta, and the chiefly halachic Midrashim, Siphri, Siphra and Mechilta. There are no works holding a quite similar position in relation to the Gemaras; but while such Midrashim as Pesiqta, Pesiqta Rabbathi, Midrash Rabbah, are for the most part of much later date, even extending down to the eleventh or twelfth century, they also contain traditions from the period of the Amoraim and even of the Tannaim. The closing of the Mishnah thus marks a division in the Rabbinical literature which is of great importance. Many traditions recorded in the Amoraite collections may date from very early times. But traditions recorded in works of the Tannaite period have an additional warrant of authenticity.

Of the traditions concerning Jesus, the following are contained in the literature of the Tannaite period :—

(A.) Mishnah : [Jesus] born out of wedlock (p. 43).
    Balaam [Jesus] excluded from the world to come (p. 65).
(B.) Tosephta: Ben Stada [Jesus] a magician (p. 54). [Jesus] crucified (p. 87).
    Healing in the name of Jeshu ben Pandira (p. 103).

A word of heresy in the name of Jeshu ben
Pantiri (p. 138).

Ben Stada [Jesus] tried at Lūd (p. 79).

(C.) Baraithas (*i.e.* traditions of the Tannaite period,
and distinguished as such in the Gemaras):

Ben Stada [Jesus] brought magic from Egypt
(p. 35).

Ben Stada tried and hung at Lūd on the eve
of Pesaḥ (p. 80).

A herald announced that Jeshu ha-Nōtzri was
to be stoned, and invited evidence in his
favour; but none was given. He was hung
on the eve of Pesaḥ [and eve of Sabbath]
(p. 83).

Jeshu had five disciples (p. 90).

The remaining traditions are found in the Gemaras,
and to a very small extent in the later Midrashim.

Considering, for the present, the traditions of the
Tannaite period, it will be noticed that the Mishnah
does not contain the names Jeshu, or Ben Stada, or
Ben Pandira. Tosephta contains all three, but not
the form Jeshu ha-Nōtzri. Neither Siphri, Siphra, nor
Mechilta contain, so far as I know, any allusion to
Jesus. Tosephta further contains a covert reference
to Jesus in certain questions put to, and answered by,
R. Eliezer ben Horqenos (p. 46). These scarcely add
any details to the tradition, because they are so obscure
that their meaning is very uncertain. But they help
to carry back the Tradition to an early date; and not
only so, but they lend additional probability to the
suggestion that the Tradition concerning Jesus really
started with the aforesaid R. Eliezer. It was he who
referred to Ben Stada as a magician, and said that

he brought magic from Egypt (p. 35). It was he, also, who said that he had conversed with a disciple of Jeshu ben Pandira, who had repeated a saying which the latter had taught him. And the reader will be reminded in the following chapter that this same R. Eliezer was arrested on a charge of Minuth, which he ascribed to his intercourse with the disciple of Jesus just referred to ; also, that he was the author of two interpretations of texts bearing upon Minuth, which were often appealed to by later Rabbis. Now R. Eliezer was the disciple of R. Johanan ben Zaccai ; and the latter must certainly have seen and heard Jesus ; for he died, an old man, before A.D. 80, and his life was mainly spent in Jerusalem. We may, there- fore, take it as probable that R. Eliezer was the chief original authority for the Tradition about Jesus ; and, if this be so, then it becomes easier to understand why the series of questions (p. 46) referring to ' a certain person ' should have been addressed to R. Eliezer. The answers to these questions show a reluctance to speak openly of the person concerned, and a similar reluctance may be discerned in the Mishnah, which, as we have seen, does not mention Jesus by name.

If the Tradition concerning Jesus began with R. Eliezer, we may with much probability assign the next stage in its development to R. Aqiba. It is true that no recorded saying of his mentions Jesus. But R. Aqiba was a disciple of R. Eliezer ; and not only so, but when R. Eliezer was grieving over his having been arrested on the charge of Minuth (p. 137), R. Aqiba said to him (*ibid.*), " Rabbi, suffer me to say something of what thou hast taught me. . . .

Perhaps there has come Minuth into thy hand and it has pleased thee." Evidently R. Eliezer had told R. Aqiba something about Minuth, and more particularly about his encounter with Jacob the disciple of Jeshu ha-Nōtzri. It is further to be observed that Shim'on ben Azai, who discovered in Jerusalem the book of pedigrees (p. 43), was the intimate associate of R. Aqiba. Another disciple of R. Aqiba was R. Meir, who told the parable about the crucified King (p. 86).

Thus we have a well-marked line of descent of the Tradition concerning Jesus, coming down virtually to the end of the Tannaite period; for the Mishnah is chiefly based upon the work of R. Aqiba and R. Meir.

With this line of descent may be connected the remaining references to Jesus in the Tannaite period. R. Gamliel, who uttered the famous gibe against the Christian judge (p. 147), " The ass has come and trodden out the lamp," was the brother-in-law of R. Eliezer. And, although this story is not found in the Tannaite literature, but in that of the Amoraite period, it dates, if genuine, from the first century. R. Gamliel was the grandfather of R. Jehudah ha-Qadosh, who completed the Mishnah. Thus we have another line of descent from R. Eliezer down to Rabbi, who in his turn was the source from which nearly all the Amoraite tradition was derived.

Having now examined the Tradition concerning Jesus as contained in the Tannaite literature, I proceed to investigate that Tradition in the Gemaras. The Tradition at once divides into a Palestinian and a Babylonian form. At the head of each line stands

23

a disciple of Rabbi.   The Palestinian Tradition comes
for the most part through R. Johanan, directly or
indirectly.   The Babylonian Tradition was begun by
Rab, who founded the school at Sura.

The Palestinian Tradition, in the Amoraite period,
adds extremely little that is new concerning Jesus.
R. Abahu, a disciple of R. Johanan, uttered the
famous saying (p. 62), " If a man say, ' I am God,'
he is a liar," etc.   A saying by a Rabbi of uncertain
date, Reuben, is also recorded, " God has no son,"
etc. (p. 302).   Beyond these, we have only repetitions of the earlier statements about Ben Stada, and
healing in the name of Jeshu ben Pandira.   A second
instance of the latter is recorded in connexion with
R. Jehoshua ben Levi, a contemporary of R. Johanan
(p. 108).   But, on the whole, it would seem as if
the Palestinian Rabbis, in the Amoraite period,
ceased to take any interest in the Tradition concerning Jesus.   We shall see, however, that this is not
the case in regard to the development of the Christian
heresy.

When we turn to the Babylonian Gemara, we
find several additions to the Tradition concerning
Jesus.   And we are clearly right in placing R.
Hisda next after his teacher Rab in the line of
descent.   It was R. Hisda who tried to explain the
relation of Jesus to Stada and Pandira (p. 35).   His
explanation was wrong as regards the first, but right
as regards the second.   Also it was R. Hisda who
quoted from R. Jeremiah bar Abba the saying that
" Jeshu ha-Nōtzri burned his food in public " (p. 56).
We shall see, in the next chapter, that R. Hisda
uttered several sayings about Minuth.

The explanatory note concerning Ben Stada (p. 35) suggests another stage in the line of descent. R. Ḥisda's theory that Stada was the husband in the case is rejected, and the explanation is given, " the husband was Pappus ben Jehudah, the mother was Stada. The mother was Miriam, the dresser of women's hair, *as we say* in Pumbeditha, such a one hath gone aside from her husband." Evidently this tradition comes from Pumbeditha; and the college at this place was founded by R. Jehudah ben Jehezq'el, a disciple of Rab and contemporary with R. Ḥisda. The successor of R. Jehudah was R. Joseph bar Ḥija. Now this R. Joseph vouches for the story about Miriam, the dresser of women's hair, told by R. Bibi bar Abaji, his son-in-law (p. 41). I suggest that the remark above, " *as we say* in Pumbeditha," points to R. Joseph as the author of the explanation that Stada was the mother, and that while her real name was Miriam, the dresser of women's hair, Stada was a nickname derived from her unfaithfulness to her husband. The explanation of the name Stada may possibly be original to R. Joseph; but the name ' Miriam, the dresser of women's hair,'—Miriam megaddela nashaia—clearly is traditional, since it represents the name ' Miriam magdalaah,' *i.e.* Mary Magdalene. The line of tradition here accordingly is, Rabbi, Rab, R. Jehudah, R. Joseph.

Another addition is the statement of Ulla that Jesus was a revolutionary and that he was ' near to the kingdom ' (p. 83). Ulla was a Palestinian Rabbi, a disciple of R. Joḥanan; but he removed to Babylonia, where he was closely associated with R. Jehudah and with R. Ḥisda. It is possible that the

Jesus-Tradition may have reached the two Babylonian
teachers through Ulla, not through Rab.

A further trace of the descent of the Jesus-Tradition is to be seen in the saying of R. Papa (p. 47),
" She, who was descended from princes and rulers,
played the harlot with a carpenter." R. Papa received some of his teaching from Abaji, the disciple of
R. Joseph of Pumbeditha, already mentioned. The
remaining steps of the general Talmudic tradition,
including, of course, that relating to Jesus, are
R. Papa, R. Kahana, R. Ashi, the last being the
redactor of the Babylonian Gemara.

What remains of the Jesus-Tradition in the Gemara
is anonymous. Such are, the story of Jeshu ha-
Nōtzri and his excommunication by R. Jehoshua ben
Perahjah (p. 50); the story of Balaam and Jesus in
Hell (p. 67); the age of Balaam (p. 72). The story
about the birth of Jesus (p. 48) is also anonymous,
and later than the Gemara.

Outside the Gemara, very few references to Jesus
in the Amoraite period are found. R. Hija bar Abba
refers to the " son of the harlot " (p. 304) in Pesiqta r.
This Rabbi was contemporary with R. Johanan. R.
Abahu, another disciple of R. Johanan, uttered a
parable on the subject, ' God has no son ' (p. 303).
But these add nothing new to the Jesus-Tradition.

We have traced, so far as the evidence allows, the
line of descent of the Jesus-Tradition during the
period covered by the Mishnah and the Gemaras.
The question remains, What were the sources of this
Tradition ? Did the Rabbis, who made the several
statements concerning Jesus, base their assertions
upon oral information, derived ultimately from actual

recollection of the career of Jesus? Or did they, to any extent, obtain their knowledge from acquaintance with the written Gospel, in any of its forms? The latter question belongs partly to the following chapter, where the 'Books of the Minim' will be discussed; but it cannot be wholly omitted here.

If the summary of the Jesus-Tradition, given above (pp. 348-9) be examined, it will be found to contain little, if anything, which would imply the knowledge of a Gospel, or Gospels, on the part of the Rabbis. The general outline of the Tradition is sufficiently like the outline of the story in the Gospels to show that the same person is referred to; but the differences are hard to explain, if a knowledge of the Gospels be assumed. And since the Gospels themselves rest upon an oral tradition, it is more natural to suppose that some of that Christian tradition may have been known and repeated in Jewish circles than that the Rabbis should have read the written record of that tradition. In the beginning, the Jesus-Tradition was propagated by Jews amongst Jews; and while it was carefully preserved amongst the disciples of Jesus, it would not be wholly forgotten amongst those who were hostile to him, though there would be no inducement to them to remember it with accuracy. This applies to that part of the Tradition which related to the birth and parentage of Jesus. Of his public career, and of his trial and death, there would naturally be an independent Jewish tradition, however vague and defective it might be.

In regard to the birth and parentage of Jesus, the earliest tradition (p. 43) merely indicates that he was born out of wedlock. This is, obviously, only a coarse interpretation of the statement in the Christian tradition that Jesus was not the son of his mother's husband. There is a trace of this view of the origin of Jesus in the questions to R. Eliezer (p. 45), " What of a ' Mamzer' (bastard) as to his inheriting ? " Whether the name of ' Miriam megaddela ' (Mary Magdalene), as that of the mother of Jesus, passed into the Jewish tradition at this early stage I do not know. I am inclined to think that it did ; for, although it does not appear till the time of R. Joseph (p. 355), in the fourth century, yet he cannot have derived it from a Gospel, since the same Gospel which recorded the name would have shown that Mary of Magdala was not the mother of Jesus. If this be allowed, then the further detail, that the mother of Jesus mated with a carpenter (p. 47), may be explained in the same way, *i.e.* as an early tradition not recorded till a late date. The earliest tradition knows the name Ben Pandira as an epithet of Jesus ; but the explanation that Pandira was the name of the paramour of the mother of Jesus is not given till the time of R. Ḥisda (p. 354), in the third century. It is at least possible that the name Pandira, whatever it may have meant, was not originally intended to denote the father of Jesus, and that Ben Pandira was a descriptive epithet, like the name Boanerges, ' sons of thunder,' applied to James and John [Mark iii. 17]. In any case, the ascription to Jesus of the name Ben Pandira does not imply any acquaintance with a Gospel.

In regard to the tradition of the public career of Jesus, such acquaintance with a Gospel is even less to be assumed. The scanty and imperfect notices of the ministry and the death of Jesus, contained in the Rabbinical literature, are only what one would expect in reference to a person whose deeds and whose fate were of no immediate importance to the Rabbis, and whom they knew only as a renegade Jew, a troubler of Israel in former times. I think it is a mistake to suppose that the Rabbis took much interest in Jesus, or cared to know much about him. And for the mere fragments of tradition which, in connexion with legal questions, they recorded about him, no other foundation need be looked for than such oral communication as might have been made by those who saw him ; communications not intended as explicit teaching, but merely as casual remarks in conversation. In this way most if not all of the tradition concerning the public life and the execution of Jesus may be reasonably accounted for. The statements about Jesus in Hell (p. 67), and of his 'burning his food' (p. 56), and of his exclusion from the world to come (p. 65), are not to be regarded as parts of the tradition concerning him, but merely as haggadic inventions, based on the subject-matter of the tradition.

As to the historical value of the Jesus-Tradition in the Rabbinical literature, little need be said. It will have become evident, both from the consideration of the several passages in the earlier part of the book and from the analysis of them just made, that they add nothing new to the authentic history of Jesus, as contained in the Gospels. In general, though not in detail, they serve to confirm the Christian tradition, by giving independent, and indeed hostile, evidence that Jesus of Nazareth really existed, a fact which has by some been called in question. But if, beyond this, the Rabbinical Jesus-Tradition has no value for the history of Christianity, it does throw some light upon the attitude of Judaism, as represented by the Rabbis, towards Jesus. It shows how the violent hostility directed against him during his life left only the vague and careless memory of a deceiver and an apostate. Of the great personality of Jesus not a trace remains, no sign of recognition that the 'Sinner of Israel' had been a mighty man. His birth, which Christian devotion had transfigured into a miracle, Jewish contempt blackened into a disgrace; and his death, which has been made the central point of Christian theology, was dismissed as the mere execution of a pernicious criminal. Judaism went on its way, but little troubled in mind at the thought of the man whom it had cast out. And this is natural, because Rabbinical Judaism was in some respects so fundamentally different from the religion of Jesus that no real recognition of him, or assimilation of his teaching, was possible. This is by no means to say that Judaism stands condemned by its rejection of Jesus. It is merely to say that Rabbinical Judaism and the religion of Jesus stand at opposite poles of religious thought; they are mutually exclusive, but have equal right to exist; and each is proved, by the witness of history during nineteen centuries, to be capable of all the functions of a living religion.

CHAPTER II

THE MINIM

IN this final chapter I shall try to collect the general results to be obtained from the mass of evidence already presented, in the hope of being able to answer the questions, Who were the Minim? Why were they so called? What relation did they bear to the Gnostics? What is their place in the history of the Christian Church? In answering these questions, some repetition is unavoidable of what has been said in the earlier parts of this book, in relation to separate passages. In like manner, it was not practicable there to avoid provisional conclusions upon some points which can only be fully dealt with when the whole of the material has been collected. The very title of the book, *Christianity in Talmud and Midrash*, contains such a provisional conclusion, so far, at all events, as relates to the identification of the Minim with Christians. I wished the title to indicate the final result obtained (if my arguments are sound) from the evidence presented, not the process by which it was obtained. I trust I have sufficiently guarded myself against the charge of having begged the question that I set out to answer.

I proceed now to deal with the several problems already indicated which are suggested by the study of the Minim.

§. i. The Name Min (Minim, Minuth)

The word Min (מין), as the term applied to a heretic, is derived by Levy (N. H. W., iii. 104ᵃ) from an Arabic root, 'man,' meaning to lie, speak falsely. He also compares the Syriac, 'mania,' 'madness.' The Syriac word, however, is plainly borrowed from the Greek μανία, and throws no light upon the Hebrew word. I have no knowledge of Arabic; and if it be really necessary to go to that language for the etymology of the word מין, I cannot criticise Levy's hypothesis. But I suggest that it is not necessary to go beyond the limits of Hebrew, or, at all events, Aramaic. Levy's explanation implies a similarity in form and sound between two words derived from different roots. I would rather explain the word מין, denoting heretic, as a special use of the ordinary and familiar word מין, denoting 'sort' or 'kind.'

מין occurs frequently in the O.T., always in the adverbial phrase למינו, Gen. i. 2, or the cognate forms; here its meaning is 'kind,' 'species,' 'sort.' There is also found in the O.T. another word meaning 'kind,' 'species,' viz.:—the word זן (zan). It is found, Ps. cxliv. 13 and 2. Chron xvi. 14. It is the same as the Aramaic word זנא, which is used in the Targum to translate the word מין. Thus, in Gen. i. 2, למינו is rendered לזניה.

Now there is also in Hebrew the word זנה (Aram. זני), which means 'to commit fornication'; and

although the word זן, just mentioned, is probably
from the root זנן, it was believed to be connected
with the root זנה, as is shown by the punctuation,
זֵנִים not זַנִּים, 2 Chron. xvi. 14.   A curious illustration
of this supposed connexion is found in the Talmud,
b. B. Qamma 16ᵇ, in a comment upon the verse in
2 Chron.   The passage is as follows :—וישכבוהו במשכב אשר
מלא בשמים וזנים מאי בשמים וזנים רבי אלעזר אמר זיני זיני ר שמואל
בר נחמני אמר בשמים שכל המריח בהן בא לידי זימה: (In place of
זימה, the Aruch has זנות, which is probably the correct
reading, as it undoubtedly expresses the correct
meaning.)

*Translation.—They buried him in a bed that was
filled with spices and ' z'nim.'*   What are *spices and
z'nim*?   R. El'azar said, ' Different kinds [of spices].'
R. Shemuel bar Naḥmani said, ' Spices such that he
who smelt them was tempted to fornication.'

We have then the word זן, supposed to be connected with זנה ; and זן is equivalent to מין.   A
further step in the argument is that, according to
the well-known symbolism of the O.T., unfaithfulness towards the covenant-relation with the God of
Israel was represented under the figure of conjugal
infidelity.   The word זנה is used both in the literal
and in the figurative sense of ' being unfaithful.'
This usage is frequent in the O.T. ; in the Talmud
the literal meaning is much more common.   I
suggest that as מין = זן = ' kind,' ' species,' ' sort,' the
association of זן with זנה led to an extension of the
meaning of מין in the same direction ; and that
whereas זנה in the Talmud usually denotes literal
unfaithfulness, מין referred almost exclusively to
figurative unfaithfulness, *i.e.* some form of apostasy

from the national religion. That is unquestionably the connotation of מין, whatever the denotation may be. The theory worked out here is based on the suggestion of Friedmann in his note to Pesiqta 101ᵃ, quoted above, p. 304. If it is correct, then it explains why, in several of the passages which have been examined in the earlier part of the book, there is a secondary reference to fornication in the mention of the Minim and of Minuth. The interpretation of Prov. v. 8, *Keep thy way far from her*, and of Ecc. vii. 26, *the woman whose heart is snares and nets*, in reference to Minuth, lies ready to hand, if Minuth be spiritual unfaithfulness ; while, on the other hand, the way is open for the suggestion that Minuth led to actual immorality. This appears plainly in the story of R. Jonathan and the Minim (see above, p. 215). Further, this explanation of the term Min is in close agreement with the fact that those to whom the name was applied were of Jewish origin. None but a Jew could be guilty of unfaithfulness towards the covenant-relation between God and Israel. Hence, if the above etymology be correct, a Min must be an unfaithful Jew ; and, in examining the various instances where the term is used, we have found that in almost every case the Jewish origin of the Minim is either implied or not contradicted. In a few instances the term appears to be applied to Gentiles, in the sense of 'enemies of Judaism' (see above, pp. 248–9, and elsewhere).

Finally, if the explanation here given be correct, it accounts for the fact that the word מין in the Talmud is often used in its common and original meaning of 'sort' or 'kind' (see above, p. 161).

Other suggested derivations of the word are—

1st. That it is contracted from מאמין, a 'believer,' and denotes a 'believer in the doctrine of Two Powers.' This is to give to the word 'believer' a specialised meaning which is without warrant. No doubt the Minim did hold this particular belief; but that is no reason for calling them 'believers' *par excellence*. If the idea of 'belief' is introduced at all into the meaning of the word, then there would be more reason for approving the explanation that,

2nd. The word מין is composed of the initial letters of מאמין ישו נוצרי , *i.e.* 'believer [in] Jesus the Nazarene.' This is ingenious, but nothing more.

3rd. The derivation from the name Manes, the founder of the Manichæan system, is merely a guess based on some resemblance in form, and some supposed resemblance between the tenets of the Manichæans and those of the Minim. How the form Min is to be derived from Manes is not explained.

4th. A better derivation is that from the root מאן, to deny, cp. ביש from באש. This alone has any pretension to etymological soundness ; and I only reject it because the derivation given above seems to me to be etymologically no less sound, and more in accordance with the usage of the word, as shown in the various passages considered above.

§ ii. Who were the Minim

We have seen that the term 'Min' denotes an unfaithful Jew, one who was not loyal at heart to the principles of the Jewish religion, and who either in thought, word, or deed was false to the covenant between God and Israel. We have now to inquire whether the term was applied to all Jews tainted with heresy, or whether it was restricted to the adherents of one particular heresy and, if so, which heresy?

A passage has been given above (see p. 118 fol.) in which a severe censure is passed upon four classes of offenders, Minim, Meshummadim (apostates), Masoroth (betrayers), and Epiqurosin (T. Sanh. xiii. 4, 5). If Minim were a general term for all unfaithful Jews, there would have been no need of four descriptive names. And the construction of the sentence forbids us to assume that Minim is the *genus*, of which Meshummadim, Masoroth, and Epiqurosin are the *species*. All four seem to be placed on the same footing. The distinction between their several meanings seems to be as follows :—' Masoroth ' denotes ' delators,' political betrayers. ' Epiqurosin ' are free-thinkers, whether Jewish or Gentile. ' Meshummadim ' are those who wilfully transgress some part of the ceremonial law, and thereby proclaim their apostasy from the Jewish religion. The Minim are those who are false at heart, but who do not necessarily proclaim their apostasy. They are the more dangerous because more secret. They do not withdraw from the community of Israel, but have to be cast out. This is the end to be attained by the various devices for the detection of Minim, which we have met with in passages cited from the Talmud and Midrash. These are, the Formula against the Minim (p. 125 fol.), and the references to liturgical and ritual variations (pp. 199, 204). We do not find any such precautions taken against Meshummadim, Masoroth or even Epiqurosin. The result of such a policy of exclusion would be that the Minim would form communities of their own, and thus hold a position of independence as regards Jews ; but the possibility would always remain that Minim might be found in the Jewish synagogues. Hence, the Talmud speaks of the Minim as a definite and distinct body or sect, ' the Minim said, or did so-and-so.' And, in the curious story about R. Saphra (p. 266 fol.), it clearly appears that the Minim had a separate organisation of their own, while at the same time they regarded themselves as being so little different from Jews that they could ask for, and obtain, a Jewish Rabbi of unimpeachable orthodoxy to be their teacher.

The Minim, then, are unfaithful Jews condemned as such, but not admitting themselves to be such. Therefore the name applied to them was a term of abuse, not merely a descriptive epithet such as ' apostate,' ' betrayer,' or ' freethinker.' A Min might be an apostate, or a betrayer, and could hardly fail to be a freethinker ; but the real nature of his offence was rather that of a moral taint than an intellectual perversity. This is shown by the interpretation of Num. xv. 39, *Ye shall not walk after your heart*, as a definition of Minuth (see p. 195 fol.). This is to find in the prompting of selfish passion and lust, and not in the dictates of reason, the ground of departure from the true way in religion prescribed by authority. And it should be observed that this interpretation, which is contained in Siphri, § 115, p. 35ª, is the earliest indication of the meaning of the term Min. It is in close accordance with the etymology of the word, as already explained.

The question who were the persons called Minim

practically resolves itself into the choice between
Jewish Gnostics and Jewish Christians. That they
were Jews is beyond dispute. A Gentile is never
called a Min, unless in one or two instances through
ignorance or inadvertence (pp. 249, 332). A Gnostic
might, of course, be or claim to be a Christian, and
therefore the terms are not strictly exclusive; but the
Jewish Christian, generally speaking, was sufficiently
distinct from the Gnostic to make it possible, and
therefore necessary, to ascertain whether the Minim
are to be identified with the first or the second. To
the discussion of this important question I now proceed, and I shall examine first the arguments in
favour of the theory that the Minim are Gnostics.

The latest advocate of this view is Friedländer, in
the work already several times referred to, *Der vorchristliche jüdische Gnosticismus.* The conclusion
reached in this book is the definite statement (p. 68)
that the Minim are Gnostics of the Ophite sect, one
branch of which sect were further known as Cainites.
Friedländer rejects the theory commonly held, that
the Minim are Jewish Christians, as being based upon
a merely superficial study of the Rabbinical literature,
and fortifies his own theory with abundant citations.
With the first half of his work, in which he illustrates
the subject of Gnosticism from Philo and the early
Christian Fathers, I have nothing to do. For anything I know, his statements may be accurate, and
his conclusions sound. In the second portion he
deals with the evidences of Gnosticism in the
Rabbinical literature, and sets up his proof of the
identification of the Minim with the Gnostics.

The most ancient Gnosticism, he says, was concerned with the two main topics of Cosmology and Theosophy; and he has no difficulty in showing that such speculation was well known amongst the Rabbis of the first and second centuries. They referred to it under the names of ' Maaseh Bereshith ' and ' Maaseh Mercabah,' *i.e.* ' The Work of Creation,' and ' The Work of the Chariot,' the latter name being an allusion to the vision of Ezekiel. The study of these subjects is mentioned in the Mishnah, and the restrictions named under which alone it might be pursued. The text of the Mishnah and of the Gemara upon it are to be found in b. Ḥag. 11ᵇ, certainly a most instructive passage for the study of Jewish Gnosticism. Further, he describes the well-known case of Ben Zoma, a proficient in such studies, who appears to have lost his reason in consequence. He quotes from the Talmud a saying by R. El'azar of Mod'in [Aboth. iii. 15], " He who profanes the Sabbaths, and despises the set feasts, and makes void the covenant of Abraham our father, and gives interpretations of the Torah which are not according to the halachah, even though he have Torah and good works, he has no portion in the world to come." Then he says (p. 68), " When we look closer at this antinomian Gnosticism, as it filled Palestine with its noise in the time of Jesus, we are struck at the first glance by its relationship to Ophitism. If we examine more thoroughly the Talmudic passages bearing on the subject, we soon come to the conclusion that the heretics so often opposed by the Rabbis, the so-called Minim, belonged to the Ophite sect." That Friedländer is right in concluding that Gnosticism is referred to in the passages about the ' Chariot ' and

'Creation,' in the story of Ben Zoma, and the saying of R. El'azar of Mod'in, is probable enough. But if the Minim are the Gnostics in question, it is at least remarkable that the term Min is never used in connexion with those persons who are said to have pursued such studies. The long passage, b. Ḥag. 11ᵇ fol., which may be called the *locus classicus* for Gnosticism in the Talmud, makes no reference to Minim or Minuth.[1] Ben Zoma is never called a Min, or even said to have been in danger of becoming one. Ben Azai, who was another great student of theosophy, is in like manner never even remotely associated with Minuth; in fact, as we have seen above (p. 297), he was the author of a haggadah directed against the Minim. And, most striking of all, the arch-Gnostic of the Talmud, Elisha ben Abujah, known by the nickname of Aḥer, is never once called a Min. In the case of Ben Zoma and Ben Azai, their orthodoxy was never disputed; but Elisha ben Abujah did become an outcast from the community of Judaism, and if Min was the proper term to apply to him, as a Gnostic, it must surely have been once at least applied to him. The most that is said of him is that he used to read books of Minuth. And if it be said that this at once proves him to have been a Min, the answer is that he also read his Bible without on that account being an orthodox Jew. In any case the fact remains that he is nowhere in so many words said to have been a Min. When, therefore, Friedlander says that " Acher was the Min κατ' ἐξοχήν " (p. 110), the phrase is his own, not that of the Talmud.

---

[1] Except the statement that Elisha b. Abujah read books of Minuth.

Having then stated his thesis that the Minim are Gnostics, Friedländer proceeds to support it by citing passages where Minim are referred to; all of which he makes use being included in the collection we have already examined. On p. 71 fol. he gives the story of R. Eliezer who was arrested for Minuth (see above, p. 137 fol.). Then he says (p. 74), "We would ask, What is there in this passage which in the remotest degree points to Christianity? Nothing; absolutely nothing. Rather the other way. If our Talmudists had been able to read the Talmud with less conceit and more impartiality, they would never have made the mistake of imagining Christianity in this and similar passages." No one would guess from the foregoing extract that in the text of the Talmud, as Friedländer must have had it before him, the Min says to the Rabbi, כן למדני ישו הנוצרי, "*thus hath Jesus the Nazarene taught me.*" Friedländer has no right to find fault with the treatment of the Talmud by other scholars when he himself can be guilty of such an omission. To have given the passage in full would have damaged his theory, but it would have been more honest. Unfortunately, most of his readers will not be in a position to verify his references. The result of this correction is to show that, whatever Minuth may be, a notorious Min was, on his own showing, a Christian disciple. This fact does much to weaken the force of the arguments which Friedländer founds upon other references to Minim. Whatever likeness there may be between Minuth and Gnosticism, still the fact remains that in one instance, rightly called by Friedländer "sehr lehrreich," Minuth is expressly associated with Christianity.

On p. 80 he quotes the passage about the " Giljonim
and the books of the Minim" (b. Shabb. 116ᵃ; see
above, p. 160 fol.   I have translated from the version
in T. Shabb. xiii. 5, which, however, is almost the
same as that in the Gemara).   Friedländer asserts
that the Giljonim (properly margins of written
scrolls) are identical with the Diagramma of the
Ophite Gnostics; and his best argument is the
application of Isa. lvii. 8, *Behind the doors and the
posts thou hast set up thy memorial.* The Talmud,
however, does not say what was in the Giljonim,
except אזכרות, sacred names, so that the identification
of them with the Diagramma is at best only con-
jectural.   But Friedländer, in his translation of the
passage, again misleads his reader by manipulating
the text.   The Talmud says, comparing idolaters
with Minim, הללו מכירין וכופרין והללו אין מכירין וכופרין, *i.e.*
"These [viz. the Minim] acknowledge [God] and lie;
those [the idolaters] do not acknowledge [Him] and
lie."   Friedländer translates "denn diese, die Minim
nämlich, sind *Wissende* und leugnen; jene aber
leugnen aus Unwissenheit."   By using the word
'Wissende,' which he emphasises, Friedländer allows
it to be thought that the Talmud uses a word corresponding to 'Gnostic.'   If it did, that would be a
strong argument in support of his theory.   But the
Talmud does not say anything about 'knowing.'   The
word to express that would be ידעין.   The word
actually used is מכירין, 'acknowledge,' 'recognise.'
The Minim, being Jews, acknowledged the God of
Israel while they spoke falsely.   The idolaters, being
Gentiles, did not acknowledge him, and spoke falsely.
Here again it is not fair to the reader who may be

unable to consult the original text to deal with it as Friedländer does, nor does it increase one's respect for Friedländer himself as a reliable exponent of the Talmud. The text of the passage is indeed printed in a footnote; but the mistranslation is allowed to stand, and is repeated with emphasis on p. 82. As to the identification of the Giljonim with the Diagramma there is not sufficient evidence to decide one way or the other. Very possibly the Diagramma was included in the condemnation pronounced upon heretical writings in the present passage. But ' Giljonim ' does not mean ' tables,' ' tafeln,' as Friedländer says it does, p. 83.

On p. 100 fol. Friedländer deals in detail with the case of Elisha ben Abujah (Aḥer) and the story of the four men who entered Paradise. He has no difficulty in showing that all this refers to Gnosticism. But here again he makes changes which tell in favour of his theory. He suppresses words in the original text which contradict his interpretation of the passage b. Ḥag. 15ᵃ about Aḥer and Metatron, as has been shown (see above, p. 288). And, in his discussion of the doctrine of Metatron (p. 103 in Friedl.), he says, " Very instructive in regard to the position ascribed to Metatron in the haggadic literature of the first two Christian centuries, is the following dialogue, contained in the Talmud, between R. Idi and a Min," etc. The reference is to b. Sanh. 38ᵇ (see above, p. 286). Now R. Idi did not live in the second century, but in the fourth, a fact of which Friedländer ought to have been aware, and which makes the passage referred to useless as evidence in support of his theory.

On p. 108 (Friedl.) is another instance of misrepresentation of the text. The passage is quoted (Qoh. r. on vii. 26, see above, p. 219), in which R. Isi of Cæsarea expounded Ecc. vii. 26 in reference to Minuth. Six pairs of names are mentioned, of which the first in each pair represents those who "please God and escape" from Minuth, the second the "sinners who are caught." The first pair is ' R. Eliezer and Jacob of Chephar Neburaia.' Friedländer says that this is plainly meant to be Jacob of Chephar Sechanja. But Jacob of Ch. Neburaia was a well-known person, and possibly contemporary with R. Isi, who mentions him. The last pair, according to Friedländer, are " R. Elieser and R. Jehoshua, and (the sinner is) Elisha ben Abuja." Now the original text does not say this. It gives the last name simply as 'Elisha.' Even if this be the correct reading, the fact remains that nowhere else does 'Elisha' mean 'Elisha ben Abujah.[1] That man is always referred to either by his full name, or else by his nickname of Aḥer. It might be argued that in this instance Elisha does mean E. b. Abujah. But Friedländer does not argue it ; he simply takes it for granted, and allows his reader to suppose that he is supported by the original text.

Here then are no less than five instances in which Friedländer supports his theory by misrepresentations of the evidence, as contained in the original texts. A theory which rests upon such arguments cannot look for much favour. Previous Talmud scholars, who have held a different theory, and upon whose ignorance and superficiality Friedländer pours scorn,

---

[1] Except for brevity, when he has already been mentioned previously in the same passage. This is not the case here.

may have been mistaken in their opinion ; but at least they dealt fairly both with their text and with their readers, and did not descend to such methods as those here exposed.

Bereft of its false witnesses, the theory of Friedländer does not amount to much. Gnosticism, beyond a doubt, was known to the Talmudic Rabbis, and Elisha ben Abujah was the chief representative of it. In some instances the practices ascribed to the Minim are such as are associated with Gnostics, and especially Ophite Gnostics. And, if there were no other evidence, it would be reasonable enough to identify the Minim with the Gnostics. But, if we are at liberty to assume that what is true of one Min is true of all Minim (and Friedländer rests his whole argument upon this assumption), then the evidence connecting Minuth with Jewish Christianity is sufficient to disprove the alleged identity of the Minim with the Gnostics. Neither Friedländer nor anyone else would propose to identify the Jewish Christians with Gnostics, which is the only alternative. This much, however, may be conceded as a possibility, not as a certainty, that the Rabbis did not so sharply distinguish between Jewish Christians and Gnostics but that they occasionally attributed to the one what was really to the discredit of the other. In this way may be explained the unsavoury stories about the Minim, and the allegations against them of immoral conduct, of which we have met with several examples. Finally, there is to be reckoned in favour of Friedländer's theory the *a priori* probability that the Gnostics, rather than the Jewish Christians, would come into hostile relations with orthodox Jews. The

Gnostics gave much trouble to the Christian Church as well as to the Jewish. Whereas the Jewish Christians, if they adhered to the ceremonial law, as they are usually supposed to have done, and differed from the main body of Jews only in regard to the Messiahship of Jesus, might seem to be comparatively harmless. This is, indeed, the strongest argument in favour of Friedländer's theory; and it is to be regretted that he did not give more attention to it, instead of damaging his case by less respectable attempts at proof.

The view has usually been held that the Minim were, or included, Jewish Christians. That this is the right view seems to me to be put beyond dispute by the evidence of the passages in which the Minim are mentioned, at all events if we are at liberty to assume that what is said of Minim in one instance is true of Minim in general. In many of the passages examined there is nothing distinctive in what is said concerning the Minim, certainly nothing definitely Christian. But in a few of the passages a connexion between Minuth and Christianity is so definitely stated that it cannot be excluded from neutral passages except on the ground of an equally definite statement to the opposite effect. There is nowhere to be found, so far as I know, a definite statement connecting the Minim with some persons other than Christians.

The evidence for the connexion of Minim with Christians may be briefly summed up as follows:—

1st. In the passage already often referred to, b. A. Zar. 16ᵇ fol. (see above, p. 137), it is related how R. Eliezer was put on his trial for Minuth. He accounted for this, in conversation afterwards, by saying that he had once met 'one of the disciples of Jesus the Nazarene, by name Jacob of Chephar Sechanja,' who told him an exposition of a text which he said he had learnt from Jesus. In the version in T. Ḥull. ii. 24, it is said that this Jacob 'said a word of Minuth in the name of Jeshu ben Pantiri.' Also in b. A. Zar. 27ᵇ (see p. 104) this same 'Jacob of Chephar Sechanja' is called 'Jacob the Min,' and he is described as proposing to heal a sick man; according to the version T. Ḥull. ii. 22, 23, he wished to do this 'in the name of "Jeshua" ben Pandira.' This is the *locus classicus* for the identification of Minim with Christians.

2nd. In b. Shabb. 116ᵃ (see pp. 146, 156, 161) there are mentioned in close connexion the books of the Minim and the Evangelion.

3rd. Qoh. r. on i. 8 (see above, p. 211) gives the story of the Minim of Capernaum and their treatment of Ḥananjah, nephew of R. Jehoshua. The Rabbi says to his nephew, 'Since the ass of that wicked one has roused itself against thee,' etc. Here there is an unmistakable allusion to Jesus. The mention of Capernaum points in the same direction.

4th. The doctrine of Two Powers in Heaven is in many passages ascribed to the Minim (see above, p. 262 and elsewhere). In one place, Pesiqta r. xxi. p. 100ᵇ (see above, p. 304), is the phrase, 'If the son of the harlot saith to thee, there are two Gods,' etc. The 'son of the harlot' clearly indicates Jesus. The connexion of the doctrine of Two Powers in Heaven with Christianity is further shown by internal evidence, as the doctrine in question appears to rest upon the Christology of the Epistle to the Hebrews (see the discussion, p. 264 fol.).

The combined force of all these separate arguments seems to me to be very great, and to decide the question at issue in favour of the identification of Minim with Jewish Christians.

A remarkable confirmation of this view is found in a passage of Jerome (Ep. 89 ad Augustin : quoted by Gieseler, Ecc. Hist., i. 98 n. 4, Eng. Tr.), " Usque hodie per totas Orientis synagogas inter Judæos hæresis est, quæ dicitur Minæarum, et a Pharisæis nunc usque damnatur, quos vulgo Nazaræos nuncupant, qui credunt in Christum, filium Dei, natum de virgine Maria, et eum dicunt esse qui sub Pontio Pilato passus est et resurrexit ; in quem et nos credimus, sed, dum volunt et Judæi esse et Christiani, nec Judæi sunt nec Christiani." I have not till now referred to this interesting passage, because I wished to decide the question of the identity of the Minim from the evidence of the Rabbinical literature. Having done so, it is fair to call in this unimpeachable witness who can speak of the Minim out of his own personal knowledge. He says that they are a sect of the Jews who profess to be both Jews and Christians, and are, in fact, neither. This agrees exactly with what we have already ascertained, viz., that the Minim are secretly unfaithful Jews, claiming to be Christians, but yet remaining in communion with Jews.[1] Hence they were objects of suspicion and hatred to the Jews, while not acknowledged by

---

[1] Note that, according to Jerome, the Minim are to found 'per totas Orientis synagogas'; they needed, therefore, to be detected by such devices as the 'formula against the Minim.'

the great body of non-Jewish Christians. It is also interesting that Jerome says that the Minim are ' commonly called Nazaræi,' the equivalent of Notzri. This identification is not found expressly stated in the Talmud, though it is implied.[1] It is worth mentioning here that the term Ebionite (אביון), is nowhere used in the Rabbinical literature to designate heretics, whether Minim or any other.

The theory that the Minim are intended to designate Jewish Christians I regard as having been now conclusively proved. This may be otherwise expressed by saying that wherever the Talmud or the Midrash mentions Minim, the authors of the statements intend to refer to Jewish Christians. The possibility is still open that the Rabbis attributed to Minim opinions or actions which in fact were not held by Christians, or that they occasionally used the term Min as a name for enemies of Judaism, and applied it to Gentiles. These are exceptional cases, and do not affect the main argument.

It must, however, be admitted that the theory which identifies Minim with Jewish Christians is not free from difficulties, which would be serious if the evidence in favour of the theory were less decisive. It will have struck every reader who has gone through the long series of polemical discussions examined in the earlier part of the book, that the subjects of debate are not what we should have expected in the controversies of Jews with Christians. Most remarkable is the absence of all reference to the alleged Messiahship of Jesus. That Gentile

---

[1] The Notzrim are mentioned by R. Johanan (p. 171), and the Christian Sunday is called the Nazarene day (ibid.).

Christians should have ignored this might be understood ; but that neither Jews nor Jewish Christians
should have a word to say about it seems very
strange. Even in the passages where Jesus himself
is mentioned there is no allusion to his alleged
Messiahship, though it is perhaps implied in the
statement that he was a deceiver. And in the
passage in b. Sanh. 97–98, where a good deal is said
about the ' coming of the Son of David,' there is no
reference to the alleged fulfilment of the prophecy
in Jesus. I can only account for this by supposing
that the Minim were Jewish Christians whose Christology was developed beyond the point at which the
Messiahship was the chief distinction of Jesus. In
support of this view it is important to recall the
evidence of likeness between the doctrines of the
Minim and the Christology of the Epistle to the
Hebrews (see above, pp. 264, 272, 322, 340). The
identification of the Minim with Jewish Christians,
vouched for as it is by the explicit statements already
quoted, cannot claim the support of anything very
distinctive in the evidence furnished by the polemical
references. For the most part such evidence is
hardly more than neutral. It must be remembered,
however, that it was no part of the purpose of the
Talmud to supply a full description of the Minim.
They are only mentioned casually, where there was
opportunity or need for marking them off from the
faithful Jews.

I answer the question, then, ' Who were the
Minim ? ' by adopting the common view that they
were Jewish Christians, and add only these two
qualifications—first, that the name may occasionally

denote other heretics, but most often refers to Jewish Christians; second, that the Jewish Christians designated by the name Minim held a Christology similar to that of the Epistle to the Hebrews.[1]

§ iii. The Place of the Minim in History

This is perhaps a too ambitious title, seeing that the notices of the Minim are so fragmentary as we have found them to be. All that I can hope to do is to try and bring the scanty facts recorded about them into connexion with the history of their times, and particularly to inquire if any light can be obtained upon their relation to the Christian Church. I repeat here what I said in the preface, that I make no attempt to give a complete illustration of the subject from the side of the early Christian literature. If I can provide material that may be useful to students in that field, I shall be well content.

The first historical fact recorded in connexion with the Minim is the composition of the formula against them, known as the Birchath ha-Minim (see above, p. 125 fol.). This liturgical addition was introduced when R. Gamliel II. was president of the assembly at Jabneh, and it marks the first official recognition of the existence of the Minim. Why was it intro-

---

[1] This is virtually the same view as that of Grätz (G. d. J., iv. pp. 90-93, and especially Note ii. p. 433). I am the more glad to find myself in agreement with so distinguished a scholar, because I have worked out my case independently. His book presents the solution of the Minim-problem with admirable clearness, but with the brevity demanded by the other claims of his vast subject. There is therefore room for a discussion of the problem in minute detail such as I have attempted in this book.

duced at this time, and not earlier or later? The
factors which determine the date are three, viz., the
presidency of R. Gamliel, who ordered the formula;
the death of Shemuel ha-Qaton, who composed it,
and lived at least a year afterwards; and the destruction of the Temple and the desolation of
Jerusalem in A.D. 70. The first and second of these
factors are sufficient to fix the date, at all events
approximately. The third is necessary, however,
because it points to the reason why a formula against
the Minim was needed.

The chronology of the period immediately after
the fall of Jerusalem is extremely obscure in regard
to the lives of the leading Rabbis. R. Joḥanan ben
Zaccai made Jabneh the headquarters of Rabbinical
Judaism, having, according to tradition (b. Gitt. 56ª),
obtained from Vespasian the gift of that city 'with
its wise men.' Evidently there was an assembly of
some kind at Jabneh even before the capture of
Jerusalem. R. Joḥanan ben Zaccai presided for a
time at Jabneh, but probably not for more than two
or three years. He was not there when he died, for
it is said that his disciples after his death went to
Jabneh. He is said to have had a school (Beth ha-
midrash) at Berūr Ḥail (b. Sanh. 32ᵇ), and no doubt
that is where he died. After his death R. Gamliel
II., as chief of the descendants of Hillel, took the
lead, and was acknowledged apparently even by the
Roman government (M. Edu. vii. 7) as the official
head of the Jews. But when this took place, and
whether immediately after the death or retirement
of Joḥanan, cannot be determined. There is no
certain evidence which would warrant us in dating

the beginning of Gamliel's presidency much earlier
than A.D. 80.

The death of Shemuel ha-Qaton can hardly be
placed later than that year, if the reasons given above
(p. 129 fol.) are valid.

The bearing upon the question before us of the
destruction of the Temple is this, that to Jewish
Christians no less than to Jews the cessation of the
Temple services and all connected therewith was
an event of profound significance. As long as the
Temple yet stood, the Jewish Christians in Jerusalem
appear to have taken part in the ritual observances
equally with the non-Christian Jews, while at the
same time they formed a community to some extent
separate from the Jews. But when the Temple was
destroyed, and the ceremonial law thereby became
a dead letter, there was ground for a divergence of
opinion as to the real meaning of that event and
the practical lesson to be drawn from it. The Jews
maintained the validity *de jure* of the whole ceremonial law, though *de facto* its operation was sus-
pended. But it was equally possible to maintain
that *de jure* also the ceremonial law was abrogated,
and that henceforth its meaning was to be regarded
as symbolic instead of literal. That the Jewish
Christians as a whole took this view cannot be
shown, and is indeed unlikely. But that many of
them did so can hardly be doubted. For this is
precisely the link which connects the original Jewish
Christians with the Minim. If I am right in
ascribing to the Minim a theology akin to that set
forth in the Epistle to the Hebrews, then the inference lies ready to hand that it was the symbolic

interpretation of the ceremonial law which opened
the way for a Christology more highly developed
than that of the orginal Jewish Christians.   I do not
intend to say that this change of view was the result
of the teaching of the Epistle to the Hebrews.   I
would rather say that the epistle was the result of
the change, and that the real cause was the cessation of the ritual of the Temple.   The epistle, wherever it may have been written and to whom-
soever addressed, reflects the change by which the
original Jewish Christians became the Minim.   Grätz
(G. d. J., iv. p. 433) even holds that the Epistle to the
Hebrews is a sort of declaration of independence on
the part of the Minim, by which they marked their
severance from Judaism.   I would not go so far as
that ; because, as we have seen, the Minim did not
sever themselves from Judaism, but claimed to be
Jews no less than Christians.[1]   It was their secret,
not open, disloyalty to Judaism which made them
the object of distrust and fear on the part of the
Rabbis.   But that there is a very close connexion
between the Minim and the Epistle to the Hebrews
is beyond question ; and it is worth observing that
Harnack (Chronologie, p. 479), arguing on quite other

---

[1] In this connexion cp. Rev. ii. 9, *The blasphemy of them which say they*
are Jews, and they are not, but are a synagogue of Satan.   Also Rev. iii. 9,
where almost the same words occur.   Vischer, in his famous monograph, in
which he shows that the Apocalypse is a Jewish work edited by a Christian,
allows that cc. i.–iii. are of Christian origin.   No doubt for the most part
they are.   Yet it is hard to understand why a Christian should blame cther
Christians for saying that *they are Jews when they are not.*   Is it not possible
that in these phrases (and also in the references to Balaam ii. 14 and the
Nicolaitans ii. 6, 15), however they may have been interpreted by the
Christian editor, there is a trace of original Jewish hostility to the Minim ?
I can only suggest the question, and leave the solution of it to N.T. scholars.

lines, places the date of the Epistle between A.D.
65 and 95. We cannot, therefore, be far wrong in
assigning the formula against the Minim to the year
80, or thereabouts. The formula represents the
official condemnation by the Rabbis of the spurious
Judaism which was growing secretly in their
midst, and at the same time furnished a means of
detection.

The formula against the Minim was only one out
of several liturgical phrases which served as means
of detecting heresy. These have been examined
already (see above, p. 199 fol.). When these were
first associated with Minuth cannot be exactly determined. The Gemara which comments on the
Mishnah containing them throws no light on their
origin, and very little on their interpretation. This
of itself, however, implies a considerable antiquity ;
and although certainty on the point is not attainable,
it is at least a reasonable theory that they are due
to the same assembly at Jabneh which adopted the
formula against the Minim. We have also seen
(above, p. 197 fol.) that the book of Ecclesiastes
(Qoheleth) was by some deemed heretical, and that
on that account the Rabbis sought to withdraw it,
i.e. pronounce it uncanonical. The allegation of
heresy, Minuth, rests, it is true, only upon the
evidence of R. Benjamin b. Levi and R. Shemuel
b. Jitzḥaq, who both lived in the fourth century.
But the Mishnah (Jad. iii. 8) states expressly that
the question of withdrawing the book was debated
in the assembly at Jabneh, and that this took place
on the day when R. Gamliel was temporarily deposed
and R. El'azar b. Azariah elected Nasi in his stead.

25

The Mishnah does not give Minuth as the reason why the withdrawal of Ecclesiastes was proposed, nor is that assigned as the reason in b. Shabb. 30^b, where the proposal is referred to. On that account I do not venture positively to affirm that an alleged tendency to Minuth was one of the reasons. But at least the passage in the Mishnah (with the context before and after), does show that a considerable amount of attention was bestowed by the assembly at Jabneh on questions affecting Scripture; and it is certainly not improbable, still less impossible, that the existence of Minuth, which had led to the drawing up of the formula against the Minim should have been one of the causes which shaped the decisions of the Rabbis. The assertion that the debate on the book of Qoheleth, and on the other points mentioned, took place on the very day of the deposition of R. Gamliel can hardly be accepted literally, if only because no one day would suffice for such a varied discussion, to say nothing of the stormy scene which no doubt accompanied the deposition of R. Gamliel. May we not refer the decisions which are said to have been made 'on that day' to the time during which the degradation of R. Gamliel lasted? The year in which his deposition took place cannot be exactly determined, but was probably about A.D. 100.[1]

[1] I obtain the date suggested in the text from the following considerations. When R. Gamliel was deposed, R. Eliezer was already excommunicated, for his name does not occur amongst those present on the occasion (b. Ber. 27^b, 28^a) ; and, further, the report of what was done " on that day " was carried to him in Lūd, by one of his disciples (T. Jad. ii. 16). The excommunication of R. Eliezer took place probably in or about A.D. 95 (see above, p. 144 n.). R. Gamliel, shortly afterwards, made his journey to Rome, and

In the absence of more decisive evidence, it may be taken as fairly probable that the various regulations, liturgical and scriptural, concerning the Minim were made by the assembly at Jabneh, under the presidency of R. Gamliel, and thus dated from the end of the first century. The alternative is that they were made at Usha, where an assembly (Sanhedrin) was twice held. But very little is known of what was done at either of these assemblies, and that little does not refer to liturgical matters; there is, therefore, nothing beyond the bare possibility to warrant the theory that the regulations mentioned above were framed at Usha.

Of the practical effect of these detective formulæ nothing is known. No instance is recorded of any heretic having been discovered through their means. We can only assume that the general result was to widen the breach between Jews and Minim, and make it more difficult for the latter to remain in open association with the former. Yet, as we have seen (above, p. 378), according to Jerome the Minim were in his day to be found 'per totas Orientis synagogas.'

The consideration of the Formula against the Minim, and the liturgical variations connected therewith, leads naturally to the subject of the mutual relations between Jews and Minim. I go on, therefore, to inquire what general conclusions may be drawn from the evidence presented in the earlier part of the book upon that subject. In this con-

must have been absent at least some months. I do not know of any evidence for fixing the date of his deposition immediately after his return, and therefore give it only approximately as A.D. 100.

nexion the story of the arrest of R. Eliezer (see above, p. 137 fol.) is of great importance and deserving of further study. It will be remembered that R. Eliezer was arrested and tried on a charge of Minuth, and that after his acquittal he accounted for his having been accused on such a charge by recalling an encounter which he had once had with a Min, by name Jacob of Chephar Sechanja, a disciple of Jesus. The date of the arrest I have given as A.D. 109. That he was arrested for Minuth is, of course, the Jewish way of describing the affair. The Roman government knew nothing of Minim as such, but only of adherents of Jesus, as distinct from Jews, with whom they did not interfere. R. Eliezer evidently felt the charge of Minuth as a worse calamity than his arrest and trial. After his acquittal he went home in great trouble and refused to be comforted, a thing he certainly would not have done merely for having escaped with his life from a Roman tribunal. It was not merely that he had been tried for Minuth, but that, as he was reminded by the question of R. Aqiba, he had actually compromised himself by intercourse with a Min. The story shows that the existence of the Minim was recognised by the Jews as an actual source of danger to Judaism, and that the Minim, however much they desired to be regarded as Jews, were, as Christians, known as a distinct body of people, and were regarded as such not only by Jews but also by Gentiles. R. Eliezer himself, having suffered through Minuth, uttered many warnings on the subject. He interpreted Prov. v. 8, *Keep thy way far from her, and come not near the door of her*

house, in reference to Minuth. Also, probably,
Prov. ii. 19, *None that go to her return again ; and
If they return they do not attain the paths of life*
(see above, pp. 188–9). Also Ps. xiv. 1, *The fool
hath said in his heart there is no God* (p. 196 n.).
Also Ecc. vii. 26, *For she hath cast down many
wounded* (p. 138), and he used to say, "Ever let a
man flee from what is hateful, and from that which
resembles what is hateful." It should be remembered,
in this connexion, that R. Eliezer is the original
authority for the tradition concerning Jesus (p. 351).

This attitude of hostility towards, and dread of, the
Minim finds expression in the rule laid down in T.
Ḥull, ii. 20, 21, "Slaughtering by a Min is idolatry ;
their bread is Samaritan bread, their wine is wine
offered to idols, their fruits are not tithed, their books
are books of witchcraft, and their sons are bastards.
One does not sell to them or receive from them or take
from them or give to them. One does not teach their
sons trades, and does not obtain healing from them,
either healing of property or healing of lives" (above,
p. 177). This is not a halachah, an authoritative legal
decision, but it represents a consensus of opinion
amounting almost to a law. Therefore the instances
are mentioned in which it was not observed. Such
was the famous case of Ben Damah (above, p. 103),
which is recorded immediately after the passage just
quoted, in T. Ḥull. And it is followed by the case of
R. Eliezer's arrest. The rule laid down about having
no intercourse with the Minim may be fairly ascribed
to the Rabbis of Jabneh, possibly owing to the misfortune of R. Eliezer. In the case of Ben Damah,
the danger which was said to threaten him, if he let

himself be healed by Jacob the Min, was that he
would thereby transgress the words of the Wise,
i.e. the Rabbis. The reference is clearly to some
such rule as is here laid down.

Intercourse between Jews and Minim was thus
hindered as far as possible, but it could not be
altogether prevented. And one especial source of
danger was to be found in the books of the Minim,
lest they should find their way into the hands of Jews
and be read by them. So the rule just mentioned
says that the books of the Minim are books of
witchcraft. Another rule, contained in T. Jad. ii. 13,
states that 'the Rolls (or margins) and books of the
Minim do not defile the hands,' in other words, are
not to be regarded as sacred (see above, p. 160). It
would not have been necessary to make this rule unless such books contained sacred names and citations
of texts from the Hebrew scriptures. It can hardly
be doubted that amongst the books of the Minim
were included Gospels, but there is no definite statement on the point. The story of Imma Shalom,
R. Gamliel, and the Christian judge (p. 146) shows
that, perhaps as early as A.D. 72 or 73, texts were
known to the Jews which are now found in one of
the canonical Gospels. But the earliest authentic
use of the term Evangelion is to be found in the
witticism of R. Meir, the date of which is the middle
of the second century (p. 162). The only evidence
that the Gospels were actually known to the Jews is
the merely negative evidence of the strong prohibition
of the books of the Minim. The strongest denunciations of the books of the Minim are those of
R. Ishmael and R. Tarphon (p. 155), in the early

part of the second century. With this reprobation of the writings of the Minim may be associated the doubts as to the canonicity of the book of Ecclesiastes, on the ground that it contained words which led to Minuth. This probably was one of the grounds on which the proposed decanonization of the book was based ; but it is not distinctly stated to have been so until the fourth century (p. 197).

That the Jews, besides hating the Minim, could not afford to disregard them, is shown by the statement that certain proposed modifications of the liturgy were not carried out because of the 'carping' of the Minim, in other words, because they would give to the Minim an opportunity to deride the religious observances of the Jews (p. 308 fol.). With this may be connected the counsel of R. Aqiba (p. 316), 'Do not give occasion to the Minim to humble you.' The same words are also ascribed to R. José ben Ḥalaphta. What the precise bearing of the advice was I am unable to say, but it clearly points to a fear as well as a dislike of the Minim. The same is true of the story about the false witnesses and the new moon (p. 327 fol.).

The Rabbinical literature nowhere gives a complete account of the Minim. It relates many anecdotes about Minim, and also records dialogues between a Min and a Rabbi. Both classes of statement show the Minim in an unfavourable light ; but the former do so much more than the latter. The anecdotes about the Minim show them as grossly immoral in their lives, and also as practising magical arts. Examples of such allegations are found in the stories about the Minim of Capernaum (p. 211), and the

adventures of R. Jonathan (p. 215) and R. Jehudah
ben Naqosa (p. 218), of which Capernaum may have
been the scene.   Compare also the story of the
woman who desired to be received as a proselyte
(p. 188).   We have here an echo of the charges of
immorality against which the Christian Apologists
had to defend their co-religionists.   For the allegation
of magical powers the evidence is found in the stories
(pp. 112, 115), of ' signs and wonders ' done by Minim.
And with these must certainly be classed the stories
of attempts by Minim to heal sick persons in the
name of Jesus (pp. 103, 108).   The Talmud draws no
distinction between such deeds done by Minim and
similar deeds done by the Rabbis.   And it is noted
that R. Jehoshua ben Ḥananjah was more than a
match for the Minim in respect of power to do such
deeds.

When, however, we turn to the records of dialogues between Jews and Minim, we find no trace
of such repulsive characteristics.   The conversation
usually turns upon disputed interpretations of Scripture, often, but not always, with a hostile intention
on the part of the Min.   R. Eliezer, indeed, on his
own showing, was pleased with what Jacob the Min
said to him.   And in many of the dialogues which
have been presented in the earlier part of this book
there is hardly more than a civil exchange of opinion,
certainly nothing answering to the strong language
used against the Minim by R. Tarphon and R.
Ishmael.   There is, however, no real contradiction
between these two representations of the Minim.
The one indicates what the Rabbis thought of the
Minim, the other what they said to them.   And it

may be further remarked that relations between Jews and Minim were probably most hostile at the end of the first century and the beginning of the second, and that gradually they became more friendly as the Minim proved to be less dangerous and less powerful. For, in the first century, even at the close of it, when the official condemnation of the Minim was made, it was not evident to the Jews that the development of the Christian Church would proceed on Gentile lines, and would leave the Minim, *i.e.* the Jewish Christians, behind. The Jewish dread of Minuth was really dread of the Christian heresy; and as it gradually appeared that the Minim did not represent the strength of the Christian movement, the danger of Minuth became less; because there was obviously less danger to Judaism from a mainly Gentile Christianity than from a Jewish form of it, connected at so many points with pure Judaism. Of Gentile Christianity the Rabbinical literature takes scarcely any notice at all. We have met, indeed, with a polemical reference to Christian Rome (p. 210) by R. Aḥa, who lived in or after the time of Constantine the Great. Beyond this one instance, I do not know of any further allusion to Gentile Christianity.[1] The references to the 'kingdom being turned to Minuth' (p. 207) only indicates the hos-

---

[1] There are a few cases, noted as they occurred, where the Min was probably a Gentile, not a Jew; but nothing turns on the Christianity of the Min in such cases. He is merely an opponent of the Jews. When it is said (p. 179) that there are no Minim among the Gentiles, that means that a Gentile could not be a Min, although he might be a Christian. It does not imply that Minim were never to be found in Gentile countries. At least, if that were implied, it is not true, for we have met with Minim in Rome (p. 228), Alexandria (p. 221), and probably Antioch (p. 283).

tility to Minuth already mentioned. The increase of that deadly heresy is not stated as a fact, but noted as one of the signs of the future advent of the Messiah.

It is in accordance with this view of the diminishing hostility between Jews and Minim that the curious story about R. Saphra and the Minim of Cæsarea (p. 266) becomes intelligible. There we find that R. Abahu, an unimpeachable Jew, recommended R. Saphra, another unimpeachable Jew, to the Minim as their teacher, and that they accepted him as such. Even if, as Bacher suggests, R. Saphra was engaged not as a teacher but as an accountant, the fact would still remain that a Jew entered the service of the Minim upon the recommendation of another Jew. That would have been impossible in the first century, or even the second. R. Abahu himself had frequent intercourse with the Minim. The case of Jacob of Chephar Neburaia (p. 334 fol.) also goes to show the diminished hostility of relations between Jews and Minim in the fourth century. And the general conclusion may be drawn that the Minim, or Nazarenes, were by that time recognized to be a comparatively harmless body, though possibly numerous. They had no share in the vitality either of Judaism or Christianity, being rejected by the adherents of both religions. As Jerome says (p. 378), "They profess to be both Jews and Christians, while in fact they are neither Jews nor Christians." They had no inherent power of progress, and appear to have gradually died out.

Of a history of the Minim, or Nazarenes, there can be no question, since the data are far too incom-

plete. From the collection of passages, examined in
the earlier part of this book, we gain a number of
passing glances at them, and learn a few facts, some
of great importance, some of little or none. They
are represented as a kind of spurious Jews, vainly
claiming fellowship with the true Judaism, and rejected because of their connexion with Christianity.
They were in Judaism, but not of it. They fre-
quented the synagogues, where suspicion of them
found expression in liturgical devices for their detection, and in the noting of various phrases and
gestures which were thought to betray their heresy.
In their theology, so far as it can be ascertained,
they departed from the strict monotheism of Judaism,
and held the doctrine of the relation between God
and Christ which is set forth in the Epistle to the
Hebrews. Apparently they did not go any further
along the line subsequently followed by Christian
theology. There is, so far as I know, only the
slightest trace of any reference to the doctrine of
the Trinity to be found in the Rabbinical allusions
to Minuth.[1] The Talmud knows of Gnostics and
Gnosticism ; but it does not identify these with
Minim and Minuth, although it is possible that the
line between them was not always clearly marked.
In the early days of the separation of Christianity
from Judaism, the Minim were hated and feared.

---

[1] See above, p. 256, where the Minim ask R. Simlai to explain the threefold designation, ' God, God, the Lord.' This can hardly be other than an
allusion to the three Persons of the Trinity ; but it is remarkable that there
is no further allusion. The question most frequently debated was that of
Two Powers or One. If the Jewish doctrine of the Divine Unity were to
be maintained, it mattered nothing whether the alternative was a doctrine of
Two Powers or of three, or of several.

This hostility gradually diminished ; and, in any case, it was chiefly in Palestine that the existence of Minuth was felt to be a danger.   In the Babylonian schools there was hardly more than a vague knowledge of what Minuth was and why it was dangerous.

I have now reached the end of my task, which was to present, in as full detail as possible, all the references which I could find in the Rabbinical literature of the first four centuries to the origin and development of Christianity.   Looking back on the miscellaneous collection of extracts which we have examined, it is interesting to observe how the two main groups into which it is divided have but slight connexion with each other.   One group contains the evidence for the Jesus-Tradition, the other the notices of the Minim.   These two groups stand apart not merely because they have been dealt with separately, but by reason of the curious fact that in the passages which mention Minim and Minuth there is seldom any direct mention of Jesus.   There is only enough to justify the identification of Minim with some form of Christians.   In other words, the Jesus-Tradition was apparently handed down within the Rabbinical schools mainly as a tradition, and received little or no additions from the intercourse between Jews and Minim, of which so many instances have been given.

The general result of the whole study in which we have been engaged is to show, in two ways, how Judaism released itself from what it considered to be the danger of Christianity.   It preserved only a careless and contemptuous tradition about Jesus, and resolutely resisted all attempts on the part of his

Jewish-born disciples to come to terms with Jewish belief and practice. Judaism fought the enemy within her gates; of the rival outside, growing in power with every century, she took no notice. She went on her way, and on the line she chose for herself worked out her own salvation through centuries of noble and most tragic history. In like manner, though on other lines, Christianity went on its way and forgot its Jewish origin. In the land of its birth, and amongst the people who furnished the first disciples, Christianity was represented by a discredited and dwindling sect, claiming kinship with Jews and Christians, and disowned by both.

In the hope that this study of an obscure field of history may be of service to scholars, in spite of the scantiness of the harvest which has been gathered, and that it may awaken in perhaps one or two readers something of the same deep interest which it has given to me during my labours upon it, I finish this book; and, in parting from it, take regretful leave of what has been to me a friend and companion through many years.

APPENDIX

**CONTAINING THE ORIGINAL TEXTS TRANSLATED
AND COMMENTED ON IN THE COURSE OF
THE WORK**

TEXTS OF PASSAGES TRANSLATED IN THE
FOREGOING PAGES.

(1) p. 35.

b. Shabb. 104[b]:— המסרט על בשרו: תניא אמר להן רבי אליעזר
לחכמים והלא בן סטדא הוציא כספים ממצרים בסריטה שעל בשרו
אמרו לו שוטה היה ואין מביאין ראיה מן השוטים [בן סטדא בן
פנדירא הוא אמר ר' חסדא בעל סטדא בועל פנדירא בעל פפוס בן
יהודה הוא אמו סטדא אמו מרים מגדלא נשיא הואי כדאמרינן
בפומבדיתא סטת דא מבעלה]:

The passage enclosed in [ ], which occurs also in b. Sanh. 67[a],
is not found in the modern Editions; it is supplied from Rabbinowicz, Diqduqé Sopherim, on the authority of the Munich and
Oxford Mss, and the older Editions.

---

(2) p. 41.

b. Hagg. 4[b] רב יוסף כי מטי להאי קרא בכי ויש נספה בלא
משפט אמר מי איכא דאזיל בלא זמניה אין כי הא דרב ביבי בר
אביי הוה שכיח גביה מלאך המות אמר ליה לשלוחיה זיל אייתי
לי מרים מדגלא שיער נשייא אזל אייתי ליה מרים מגדלא דרדקי
אמר ליה אנא מרים מגדלא שיער נשייא אמרי לך אמר ליה אי הכי
אהדרה אמר ליה הואיל ואייתיתה ליהוי למניינא:

(2a) ibid. Tosaphoth on same passage: הוה שכיח גביה מלאך
המות המספר מה שאירע לו כבר דהאי עובדא דמרים מגדלא נשייא
זבית שני היה דהיתה אמו של פלוני כדאיתא בשבת (דף קד):

26*

(3) p. 43.

M. Jeb. IV. 13:— אמר רבי שמעון בן עזאי מצאתי מגלת
יוחסין בירושלים וכתוב בה איש פלוני ממזר מאשת איש לקיים
דברי ר׳ יהושע :

———

(4) p. 45.

b. Joma 66ᵇ שאלי את ר׳ אליעזר פלוני מהו לעולם הבא א״ל לא
שאלתוני אלא על פלוני מהו להציל רועה כבשה מן הארי אמר להם
לא שאלתוני אלא על הכבשה מהו להציל הרועה מן הארי אמרלהם
לא שאלתוני אלא על הרועה ממזר מה הוא לירש מהו ליבם מהו
לסוד את ביתו מהו לסוד את קברו לא מפני שהפליגן בדברים אלא
מפני שלא אמר דבר שלא שמע מפי רבו מעולם וגר׳:

(5) p. 47.

b. Sanh. 106ᵃ:— אמר ר׳ יוחנן בתחלה נביא ולבסוף קוסם אמר ר׳
פפא היינו דאמרי אינשי מסגני ושליטי הואי אייזן לגברי נגרי:

———

(6) p. 48.

b. Kallah 51ᵃ עז פנים רבי אליעזר אומר ממזר רבי יהושע
אומר בן הנדה רבי עקיבא אומר ממזר ובן הנדה: פעם אחת היו
זקנים יושבים בשער ועברו לפביהם שני תינוקות אחד כסה את
ראשו ואחד גילה את ראשו זה שגילה את ראשו רבי אליעזר אומר
ממזר רבי יהושע אומר בן הנדה רבי עקיבא אומר ממזר ובן הנדה
אמרו לו לרבי עקיבא היאך מלאך לבך לעבור על דברי חביריך·
אמר להן אני אקיימנו· הלך אצל אמו של תינוק וראה שהיתה יושבת
ומוכרת קטניות בשוק· אמר לה בתי אם את אומרת לי דבר שאני
שואלך אני מביאך לחיי עולם הבא אמרה לו השבע לי·· היה רבי
עקיבא נשבע בשפתיו ומבטל בלבו אמר לה בנך זה מה טיבו אמרה
לו כשנכנסתי לחופה נדה הייתי ופירש ממני בעלי ובא עלי שושביני
והיה לי בן זה נמצא התינוק ממזר ובך הנדה· אמרו גדול היה
רבי עקיבא כשהכחיש את רבותיו· באותה שעה אמרו ברוך ה׳ אלהי
ישראל אשר גילה סודו לרבי עקיבא:

———

(7) p. 50.

b. Sanh. 107ᵇ תנו רבנן לעולם תהא שמאל דוחה וימין מקרבת
לא כאלישע שדחפו לגחזי בשתי ידים ולא כרבי יהושע בן פרחיה
שדחפו לישו (הנוצרי) בשתי ידים גחזי דכתיב ...... ר' יהושע
בן פרחיה מאי היא כדקטלינהו ינאי מלכא לרבנן אזל רבי יהושע
בן פרחיה [וישו] לאלכסנדריא של מצרים כי הוא שלמא שלח ליה
שמעון בן שטח מיני [ירושלם] עיר הקודש ליכי אלכסנדריא
שלמצרים [אחותי] בעלי שרוי בתוכך ואנכי יושבת שוממה· קם
אתא ואתרמי [ליה] (ב)ההוא אושפיזא עבדו ליה יקרא טובא אמר
כמה יפה אכסניא זו אמר ליה (ישו) רבי עיניה טרוטות אמר ליה
רשע בכך אתה עוסק אפיק ארבע מאות שיפורי ושמתיה אתא
לקמיה כמה זימנין אמר ליה קבלן לא הוה קא משגח ביה יומא
חד הוה קא קרי קרית שמע אתא לקמיה סבר לקבולי אחוי ליה
בידיה הוא סבר מידחא דחי ליה אזל זקף לבינתא והשתחוה לה
אמר ליה הדר בך אמר ליה כך מקובלני ממך כל החוטא ומחטיא
את הרבים אין מספיקין בידו לעשות תשובה ואמר מר ישו הנוצרי
כישף והדיח את ישראל:

(8) p. 54.

T. Shabb. XI. 15. המסרט על בשרו ר' אליעזר מחייב וחכמים
פוטרין אמר להם ר' אליעזר והלא בן סטדא לא למד אלא בכך אמרו
לו מפני שוטה אחד נאבד את כל הפיקחין:

(9) p. 56.

b. Sanh. 103ᵃ דאמר ר' חסדא אמר ר' ירמיה בר אבא מאי
דכתיב לא תאונה אליך רעה ונגע לא יקרב באהלך .... ד"א
לא תאונה אליך רעה שלא יבעתוך חלומות רעים והרהורים רעים
ונגע לא יקרב באהלך שלא יהא לך בן או תלמיד שמקדיח תבשילו
ברבים כגון ישו הנוצרי:

(10) p. 62.

j. Taan. 65ᵇ:— אמר ר' אבהו אם יאמר לך אדם אל אני מכזב
הוא בן אדם אני סופו לתחות בו שאני עולה לשמים ההוא אומר
ולא יקימנה:

(11) p. 63.

רבי אלעזר הקפר אומר נתן האלהים כח 766, § .Jalq. Shim
בקולו והיה עולה מסוף העולם ועד סופו בשביל שהיה צופה וראה
האומות שמשתחוים לשמש ולירח ולכוכבים ולעץ ולאבן וצפה וראה
שיש אדם בן אשה שעתיד לעמוד שמבקש לעשות עצמו אלוה ולהטעות
כל העולם כולו לפיכך נתן כח בקולו שישמעו כל אומות העולם וכן
היה אומר תנו דעתיכם שלא לטעות אחרי אותו האיש שנ' לא איש
אל ויכזב ואם אומר שהוא אל הוא מכזב והוא עתיד להטעית
ולומר שהוא מסתלק ובא לקיצים אמר ולא יעשה ראה מה כתיב
וישא משלו ויאמר אוי מי יהיה משומו אל אמר בלעם אוי מי
יהיה מאותה אומה ששמעת אחרי אותו האיש שעשה עצמו אלוה :

(12) p. 64.

שלשה מלכים וארבע הדיוטות אין להם חלק —: M. Sanh. X. 2
ארבע .... לעולם הבא שלשה מלכים ירבעם אחאב ומנשה
הדיוטות בלעם ודואג ואחיתופל וגחזי :

(13) p. 67.

אונקלוס בר קלוניקוס בר אחתיה דטיטוס .57ᵃ .b. Gitt. 56ᵇ
הוה בעי לאיגיורי אזל אסקיה לטיטוס בנגידא אמר ליה מאן
השיב בההוא עלמא אמר ליה ישראל מהו לאידבוקי בהו אמר ליה
מילייהו נפישין ולא מצית לקיומינהו זיל איגרי בהו בההוא עלמא
והוית רישא דכתיב היו צריה לראש וגו' כל המיצר לישראל נעשה
ראש אמר ליה דיניה דההוא גברא במאי א"ל במאי דפסיק אנפשיה
כל יומא מכנשי ליה לקוטמיה ודייני ליה וקלו ליה ומבדרי אשב
ימי אזל אסקיה לבלעם בנגידא אמר ליה מאן חשיב בההוא עלמא
א"ל ישראל מהו לאידבוקי בהו א"ל לא תדרוש שלומם וטובתם כל
הימים א"ל דיניה דההוא גברא במאי א"ל בשכבת זרע רותחת אזל
אסקיה בנגידא לפושע* ישראל א"ל מאן חשיב בההוא עלמא א"ל
ישראל מהו לאדבוקי בהו א"ל טובתם דרוש רעתם לא תדרוש כל הנוגע
בהן כאילו נוגע בבבת עינו א"ל דיניה דההוא גברא במאי א"ל בצואה
רותחת דאמר מר כל המלעיג על דברי חכמים נידון בצוה רותחת
תא חזי מה בין פושעי ישראל לנביאי אומות העולם עובדי ע"ז:

* So the older Editions; the moderns read פושעי. The קונטרס reads רשעי.

(14) p. 70. n.

b. Sanh. 106ᵇ :— א"ל מר בריה דרבינא לבריה בכולהו לא
תפיש למדרש לבר מבלעם הרשע דכמה דמשכחת ביה דרוש ביה:

_____

(15) p. 72.

b. Sanh. 106ᵇ א"ל ההוא מינא לרבי חנינא מי שמיע לך בלעם
בר כמה הוה א"ל מיכתב לא כתיב אלא מדכתיב אנשי דמים ומרמה
לא יחצו ימיהם בר תלתין ותלת שנין או בר תלתין וארבע א"ל
שפיר קאמרת לדידי הזי לי פנקסיה דבלעם והוה כתיב ביה בר
תלתין ותלת שנין בלעם חגירא כד קטיל יתיה פנחס ליסטאה:

_____

(16) p. 75.

b. Sanh. 106ᵃ :— וישא משלו ויאמר אוי מי יהיה משמו אל
[אמר רשב"ל אוי מי שמחיה עצמו בשם אל]

The passage in brackets was struck out by the Censor,
but is vouched for by Rabbinowicz, on the authority of Mss.
and the older Editions.

(17) p. 76.

b. B. Bathr. 14ᵇ :— משה כתב ספרו ופרשת בלעם:

This is repeated, in almost the same words, in j. Sotah. 20ᵈ.

_____

(18) p. 77.

j. Ber. I. 8. (3ᶜ) דרב מתנה ורב שמואל בר נחמן אמר תרוייהון
אמרין בדין הוה שיהו קורין עשרה דברות בכל יום ומפני מה אין
קורין אותן מפני טענת המינין שלא יהו אומ' אלו לבד' ניתנו
למשה בסיני: ר' שמואל בר נחמן בשם רבי יהודה בר זבודא בדין
היה שיהו קורין פרשת בלק ובלעם בכל יום ומפני מה אין קרין
אותם שלא לחטרי' על הציבור · ר' הונה אמ' מפני שכתיב שכיבה
וקומה ר' יוסא בי ר' בון אמר מפני שכתיב בהן יציה ומצבית א"ר
אלעזר מפני שכתובה בתורה בנביאים ובכתובים:

_____

(19) p. 78.

T. Sanh. X. 11. כל חייבי מיתות שבתורה אין ¹ מכמינין עליהן
חוץ מן המסית כיצד ² עושין לו ³ מוסרין לו שני תלמידי חכמים

בבית הפנימי והוא יושב בבית החיצון ומדליקין לו את הנר כדי
שיהו רואין אותו ושומעין את קולו וכן עשו [4] לבן סטדא בלוד
נימנו עליו שני תלמידי חכמים [5] וסקלוהו:

[1] ממיתיך (Cod. Erfurt)   [2] om. (C. Erfurt)   [3] בונסתין (Cod. Wien)
[4] לבית סטדא (C. Wien.) לאיש אחד (ed. Venice 1522)   [5] add והביאהו
לבית דין (Cod. Wien)

(20) p. 79.

המסית זה ההדיוט כו' הא חכם (.j. Sanh. VII. 16. p. 25[c. d]
לא מכיון שהוא מסית אין זה חכם מכיון שהוא ניסית אין זה
חכם כיצד עושין לו להעדים עליו מכמינין עליו שני עדים בבי'
הפנימי ומושיבין אותו בבית ההיצון ומדליקין את הנר על גביו כדי
שיהיו רואין אותו ושומעין את קולו כך עשו לבן סוטד' בלוד
והכמינו עליו שני תלמידי החכמים והביאוהו לב"ד וסקלוהו:

[The same passage is found j. Jeb. 15[d] with no material
variation.]

———

(21) p. 79.

דתניא ושאר כל חייבי מיתות שבתורה אין (b. Sanh. 67[a]
מכמינין עליהן חוץ מזו כיצד עושין לו מדליקין לו את הנר בבית
הפנימי ומושיבין לו עדים בבית ההיצון כדי שיהו הן ראין אותו
ושומעין את קולו והוא אינו רואה אותן והלה אומר לו אמור מה
שאמרת לי ביחוד והוא אומר לו והלה אומר היאך נניח את
אלהינו שבשמים ונעבוד עבודת כוכבים אם חוזר בו מוטב ואם
אמר כך היא חובתינו וכך יפה לנו העדים ששומעין מבחוץ מביאן
אותו לבית דין וסוקלין אותו וכן עשו לבן סטדא בלוד ותלאוהו
בערב פסח: בן סטדא וגו':

(22) p. 83.

והתניא [1] בערב הפסח תלאוהו לישו [2] והכרוז (b. Sanh. 43[a]:—
יוצא לפניו מ' יום [3] יוצא ליסקל על שכיסך והיסית והידיח את
ישראל כל מי שיודע לו זכות יבא וילמד עליו ולא מצאו לו זכות
ותלאוהו [1] בערב פסח [אמר עולא] ותסברא [3] בר הפוכי [4] זכות הוא
מסית הוא ורחמנא אמר לא תחמול ולא תכסה עליו שאני ישו
[2] דקרוב למלכות הוה:

[1] בערב שבת ובערב פסח (Cod. Flor)   [2] הנוצרי (Cod. Monac.) add
[3] ישו הנוצרי (Cod. Mon.) add   [4] ליה (Cod. Monac.) add

(23) p. 86.

M. Sanh. VI. 4.:— כל הנסקלין נתלין דברי רבי אליעזר וחכמים
אומרים אינו נתלה אלא המגדף והעובד כו"ם:

---

(24) p. 86.

T. Sanh. IX. 7:— היה ר' מאיר אומ' מה תלמ' לומר כי קללת
אלהים תלוי לשני אחים תאומים דומין זה לזה אחד מלך על כל
העולם כולו ואחד יצא לליסטייא לאחר זמן נתפס זה שיצא לליסטייא
והיו צולבין אותו על הצלוב והיה כל עובר ושב אר' דומה שהמלך
צלוב לכך נאמר כי קללת אלהים תלוי:

---

(25) p. 90.

b. Sanh. 43ª ת"ר חמשה תלמידים היו לו לישו מתאי נקאי
נצר ובוני ותודה אתייה למתי אמר להו מתי יהרג הכתיב מתי
אבוא ואראה פני אלקים אמרו לו אין מתי יהרג דכתיב מתי ימות
ואבד שמו אתיוה לנקאי אמר להו נקאי יהרג הכתיב ונקי וצדיק
אל תהרג אמרו לו אין נקאי יהרג דכתיב במסתרים יהרג נקי אתיוה
לנצר אמר להו נצר יהרג דכתיב ונצר משורשיו יפרה אמרו ליה
אין נצר יהרג דכתיב ואתה השלכת מקברך כנצר נתעב אתיוה
לבוני אמר להו בוני יהרג הכתיב בני בכורי ישראל אמרו לו אין
בוני יהרג דכתי' הנה אנכי הרג את בנך בכורך אתיוה לתודה אמר
להו תודה יהרג הכתיב מזמור לתודה א"ל אין תודה יהרג דכתיב
זובח תודה יכבדני:

(26) p. 95.

Abarbanel, מעייני הישועה, on Dan. VII. 8.:— ראה גם ראה
איך פירשו אותו הקרן אחרי זעירא על בן נצר שהוא ישוע הנוצרי
ורצו בענינו כפי המשך הכתוב מלכות הרשעה שהיא אדום כי
היא אומתו וגו'

---

(27) p. 97.

b. Sotah 47ª:— תנו רבנן לעולם תהא שמאל דוחה וימין
מקרבת לא כאלישע שדחפו לגחזי בשתי ידיו ולא כיהושע בן
פרחיה שדחפו לישו הנוצרי בשתי ידיו אלישע מאי היא דכתיב

ויאמר נעמן הואל קח ככרים וכתיב ויאמר אליו לא לבי הלך
כאשר הפך איש מעל מרכבתו לקראתך העת לקחת את הכסף
ולקחת בגדים וזיתים וכרמים וצאן ובקר ועבדים ושפחות ומי
שקיל כולי האי כסף ובגדים הוא דשקיל אמר ר' יצחק באותה
שעה היה אלישע עוסק בשמונה שרצים אמר לו רשע הגיע עת
ליטול שכר שמנה שרצים וצרעת נעמן תדבק בך ובזרעך לעולם
וארבעה אנשים היו מצורעים אמר רבי יוחנן זה גחזי ושלשה
בניו וילך אלישע דמשק למה הלך אמר ר' יוחנן שהלך להחזירו
לגחזי בתשובה ולא חזר אמר לו הזור בך אמר לו כך מקובלני
ממך כל מי שחטא והחטיא את הרבים אין מספיקין בידו לעשות
תשובה מאי עבד איכא דאמרי אבן שאבת תלה לו לחטאת ירבעם
והעמידו בין שמים לארץ ואיכא דאמרי שם הקק לה אפומה
והיתה אומרת אנכי ולא יהיה לך ואיכא דאמרי רבנן דחה מקמיה
דכתיב ויאמרו בני הנביאים אל אלישע הנה נא המקום אשר אנחנו
יושבים שם לפניך צר ממנו מכלל דעד האידנא לא הוה דחיק:
יהושע בן פרחיה וגר':

[Part of this passage occurs in b. Sanh. 107^b and forms
the beginning of the extract given as (7) p. 49 above. To
give the text of the version in Sanh. is needless, as it contains
nothing of any importance beyond what is contained in the
much fuller version in Sotah now before us.]

(28) p. 103.

T. Ḥull II. 22, 23.:— מעשה בר' אלעזר בן דמה שנשכו נחש
ובא יעקב איש כפר סמא לרפאותו משום ישוע בן פנדירא ולא
הניחו ר' ישמעאל אמר לו אי אתה רשאי בן דמה אמר לו אני
אביא לך ראיה שירפאני ולא הספיק להביא ראיה עד שמת אמר ר'
ישמעאל אשריך בן דמה שיצאת בשלום ולא פירצת גזירן של
חכמים שכל הפורץ גדירן של חכמים לסוף פורענות בא עליו שנ':
פורץ גדר ישכנו נחש:

(29) p. 103.

j. Shabb. 14^d:— Almost word for word the same as (28),
then follows ולא נחש נשכו אלא שלא ישכנו נחש לעתיד לבוא
ומה הוה ליה למימר אשר יעשה אותם וחי בהם:

(30) p. 104.

j. A. Zar. 40ᵈ, 41ᵃ:— Same as (29) except that after the words

לרפותו .... רבא :— is added: אמר לו נימר לך בשם ישו בן פנדרא

---

(31) p. 104.

b. A. Zar. 27ᵇ:— לא ישא ויתן אדם עם המינין ואין מתרפאין
מהן אפילו לחיי שעה מעשה בבן דמא בן אחותו של ר' ישמעאל
שהכישו נחש ובא יעקב מינא איש כפר סכניא לרפאותו ולא
הניחו ר' ישמעאל וא"כ ר' ישמעאל אחי הנח לו וארפא ממנו ואני
אביא מקרא מן התורה שהוא מותר ולא הספיק לגמור את הדבר
עד שיוצא נשמתו ומת קרא עליו ר' ישמעאל אשריך בן דמא שגופך
טהור ויצתה נשמתך בטהרה ולא עברת על דברי חביריך שהיו
אומרים ופורץ גדר ישכנו נחש שאני מינות דמשכא דאתי למימשך
בתרייהו :

(32) p. 108.

j. Shabb. 14ᵈ:— בר בריה הוה ליה בלע אתא חד בר נש
ולחש ליה מן שמיה דישו פנדירא ואינשם כד נפיק א"ל מאי
לחשתה ליה א"ל מילה פלן א"ל נוח היה ליה אלו הוה מיית
ולא כן והות ליה כן כשגג' שיוצא מלפני השליט :

(33) p. 109.

b. A. Zar. 28ᵃ:— והא רבי אבהו דאדם חשוב הוה ורמא ליה
יעקב מינאה סמא אשקיה ואי לא רבי אמי ורבי אסי דלחכי'הו
לשקיה פסקיה לשקיה :

---

(34) p. 112.

j. Sanh. 25ᵈ:— דלמא ר' לעזר ור' יהושע ור' עקיבא עלון
למסחי בהדין דימוסין דטיברי'' · חמתון חד מינייי · אמר מה דמר
ותפשיתון כיפ' · א"ר לעזר לר' יהושע מה יהושע בן חנניה חמי
מה דאת עבד · מי נפיק אהן מינייא אמר ר' יהושע מה דמר
ותפש יתיה תרעה : והוה כל מאן דעליל הוה יהיב ליה הד
מרתוקה וכל מאן דנפיק הוה יהיב ליה בנתיקה · אמר לון שרון
מה דעבדתון אמרין ליה שרי ואנן שריי · שרון אילון ואילין מן
דנפקון א"ר יהושע להההוא מינייא הא מה דאת חכם · אמר ניחות

לימא מן דנחתון לימא אמר ההוא מיניייא מה דאמר ואיתבזע ימא
אמר לון ולא כן עבד משה רבכון בים' · אמרין ליה לית את מודה
לן דהליך משה רבן בגויה · אמר לון אין · אמרין ליה והלוך
בגויה · הלך בגויה גזר ר' יהושע על שרה דימא ובלעיה:

(35) p. 115.

א"ר יהושע בן חנניה יכיל אנא נסיב קריין
ואבטיחין ועביד לון איילין וטבין והידנון עבידין איילין וטבין:
א"ר ינאי מהלך הוינא בחדא אסרטא דציפורי וחזית חד מיניי
נסיב צרור וזרק ליה לרומא והוה נחת ומתעביד עגל · ולא כן א"ר
לעזר בשם ר' יוסי בר זמרא אם מתכנסין הן כל באי העולם אינן
יכולין לבראות יתוש אחד ולזרוק בו נשמה · נימר לא נסבה הוא
מיניייא חד צרור וזרקיה לרומא ואיתעביד עגל אלא לסריח קרא
וגנב ליה עגל מן בקוותא אייתי לים · א"ר חיננא בירבי חנניה
מטייל הוינא באילין גופתא דציפורין וחמית חד מיניי נסך חדא
גולגלא וזרקיה לרומא והיא נחתא ומתעבדא עגל · אתית ואמרית
לאבא · אמר לי אין אכלת מינה מעשה הוא ואי לא אחיזת עינים הוא:

(36) p. 118.

פושעי ישראל בגופן ופושעי אומות
העולם בגופן יורדין לגיהנם ונידונין בה שנים עשר חודש ולאחר
שנים עשר חודש נפשותן כלה וגופן נשרף וגיהנם פולטתו ונעשין
אפר והרוח זורה אותן ומפזרתן תחת כפות רגלי הצדיקים שנ'
ועשיתם רשעים כי יהיו אפר תחת כפות רגלי צדיקים ליום אני
עושה אמר י"י צבאות: אבל המינין והמשומדין והמסורות ואפיקורוסין
ושכפרו בתורה ושפורשין מדרכי ציבור ושכפרו בתחיית המתים
וכל מי שחטא והחטיא את הרבים כגון ירבעם ואחאב ושנתנו
חיתיתם בארץ החיים ושפשטו ידיהם בזבול גיהנם נינעלת בפניהם
ונידונין בה לדורי דורות שנ' ויצאו וראו בפגרי האנשים הפושעים
בי כי תולעתם לא תמות ואשם לא תכבה והיו דראון לכל בשר
שאול בלה ודין אינן בלין שנ' וצורם לבלות שאול מי גרם כהן
שפשטו ידיהם בזבול שנ' מזבול לו ואין זבול אלא בית המקדש שנ'
בנה בניתי בית זבול לך מכון לשבתך עולמים:

The above occurs in b. R. ha. Sh. 17ᵃ almost in the same words.

(37) p. 125.

j. Ber. 9ᶜ:— שמואל הקטון עבר קומי תיבותא ואשגר מכניע
זדים בסופה שרי משקיק עליהון אמרין ליה לא שיערו חכמים כך:

———

(38) p. 125.

b. Ber. 28ᵇ. 29ᵃ:— ת"ר שמעון הפקולי הסדיר י"ח ברכות
לפני רבן גמליאל על הסדר ביבנה אמר להם ר"ג לחכמים כלום
יש אדם שיודע לתקן ברכת המינים עמד שמואל הקטון ותקנה
לשנה אחרת שכחה והשקיק בה שתים ושלוש שעות ולא העלוהו
אמאי לא העלוהו והאמר רב יהודה אמר רב טעה בכל ברכות
כלן אין מעלין אותו בברכת המינים מעלין אותו חיישינן שמא
מין הוא שאני שמואל הקטון דאיהו תקנה וניחוש דילמא הדר ביה:

———

(39) p. 128.

T. Sotah. XIII. 4.:— אך הוא אומר בשעת מיתתו שמעון
וישמעאל לחרבא וחברוהי לקטלא ושאר עמא לביזא ועקן סגיאין
יהוון אחרי דנא ובלשון ארמית אמרן:

(40) p. 129.

j. Sotah 24ᵇ, Same as (39) except that after the words
ולא ידעי מה אמר, there follows :ובלשון ארמית אמרן

(41) p. 129.   b Sotah 48ᵇ, same as (39).

(42) p. 129.   b Sanh. 11ᵃ same as (39).

(43) p. 136.

T. Ber. III. 25:— שמונה עשרה ברכות שאמרו חכמים כנגד
שמונה עשרה אזכרות שבהבי לה' בני אלים כולל של מינים בשל
פרושים ושל גרים בשל זקנים ושל דויד בשל ירושלם ואם אמרו
אלו לעצמן יצא:

———

(44) p. 136.

j. Ber. IV. 3. (8ᵃ):— א"ר הונה אם יאמר לך אדם שבע עשרה
אינון אמור לו של מינין כבר קבעו חכמים ביבנה התיב ר"א בי
רבי יוסי קומי רבי יוסי והכתיב אל הכבוד הרעים א"ל והתני

כולל של מינים ושל פושעים במכניע זדים ושל זקנים ושל גרים
במבטח לצדיקים ושל דוד בבונה ירושלם:

(45) p. 137.

T. Ḥull. II. 24.:— מעשה בר׳ אליעזר שנתפס על דברי מינות
והעלו אותו לבמה לדון לבמה אמר לו אותו הגמון זקן כמותך יעסוק
בדברים הללו אמר לו נאמן עלי דיין כסבור אותו הגמון שלא אמר
אלא לו ולא נתכוין אלא נגד אביו שבשמים אמר לו הואיל והאמנתני
עליך אף אני כך אמרתי אפשר שהסיבו הללו טועים בדברים הללו
דימוס הרי אתה פטור וכשנפטר מן הבימה היה מצטער שנתפס
על דברי מינות נכנסות למידיו לנחמו ולו קבל נכנס ר׳ עקיבא ואמר
לו ר׳ אומר לפניך דבר שמא אין אתה מיצר אמר לו אמור אמר
לו שמא אחד מן המינין אמר לך דבר של מינות והנאך אמר השמים
הזכרתני פעם אחת הייתי מהלך באיסתרטיא של ציפורי מצאתי
יעקב איש כפר סכנין ואמר דבר של מינות משום ישוע בן פנטירי
והנאני ונתפסתי על דברי מינות שעברתי על דברי תורה הרחק
מעליה דרכך ואל תקרב אל פתח ביתה כי רבים חללים הפילה
וגו׳ שהיה ר׳ אליעזר אומר לעולם יהא אדם בורח מן הכיעור ומן
הדומה לכיעור:

(46) p. 138.

ת״ר כשנתפס ר״א למינות העלוהו לגרדום: b. A. Zar. 16ᵇ. 17ᵃ
לידון אמר לו אותו הגמון זקן שכמותך יעסוק בדברים בטלים
הללו אמר לו נאמן עלי הדיין כסבור אותו הגמון עליו הוא אומר
והוא לא אמר אלא כנגד אביו שבשמים אמר לו הואיל והאמנתי
עליך דימוס פטור אתה כשבא׳ לביתי נכנסו תלמידיו אצלו לנחמו
ולא קיבל עליו תנחומין אמר לו ר״ע רבי תרשיני לומר דבר אחד
ממה שלימדתני אמר לו אמור אמר לו רבי שמא מינות בא לידך
והנאך ועליו נתפסת [למינות] אמר לו עקיבא הזכרתני פעם אחת
הייתי מהלך בשוק העליון של ציפורי ומצאתי [אדם] אחד [מתלמידי
ישו הנוצרי] ויעקוב איש כפר סכניא שמו אמר לי כתוב בתורתכם
לא תביא אתנן זונה וגו׳ מהו לעשות הימנו בהכ״ס לכ״ג ולא
אמרתי לו כלום אמר לי כך לימדני [ישו הנוצרי] מאתנן זונה
קבצה ועד אתנן זונה ישובו ממקום הטנופה באו למקום הטנופה ילכו

והנאני הדבר על ידי זה נתפסתי למינות ועברתי על מה שכתוב בתורה
הרחק מעליה דרכך זו מינות ואל תקרב אל פתח ביתה זו רשות:
[ ] add. cod. Monac. teste Rabbnowicz.

(47) p. 139.

Qoh. r. on I. 8. p. 4ᵃ:— כתוב בתורתכם לא תביא אתנן זונה
ומחיר כלב מה הן אמרתי לו אסורין אמר לי לקרבן אסורין לאבדן
מותר אמרתי לו וא"כ מה יעשה בהם אמר לי יעשה בהן בתי
מרחצאות ובתי כסאות אמרתי לו יפה אמרת ונתעלמה ממני הלכה
לשעה כיון שראה שחודיתי לדבריו אמר לי [hiatus in printed text]
מצואה באו ולצואה יצאו שנ' כי מאתנן זונה קבצה ועד אתנן
זונה ישובו יעשו כורסוון לרבים ועל אותו הדבר נתפשתי לשם
מינות וגו':

_____

(48) p. 146.

b. Shabb. 116ᵃˑᵇ: אימא שלום דביתהו דרבי אליעזר אחתיה
דרבן גמליאל הואי הוה ההוא פילוסופא בשבבותיה דהוה שקיל
שמא דלא מקבל שוחדא בעו לאחוכי ביה אעיילא ליה שרגא דדהבא
ואזול לקמיה אמרה ליה בעינא דניפלגי לי בנכסי דבי נשי אמר
להו פלוגו א"ל כתיב לן במקום ברא ברתא לא תירות א"ל מן יומא
דגליתון מארעכון איתנטלית אורייתא דמשה ואיתיהיבת אורייתא
דעון גליון* וכתיב ביה ברא וברתא כחדא ירתון למחר הדר עייל
ליה איהו חמרא לובא אמר להו שפילית לסיפיה דספרא וכתיב ביה
אנא לא למיפחת מן אורייתא דמשה אתיתי ולא לאוספי על אורייתא
דמשה אתיתי וכתיב ביה במקום ברא ברתא לא תירות אמרה ליה
נהור נהוריך כשרגא א"ל רבן גמליאל אתא חמרא ובטש לשרגא:
* Cod. Oxford, Rabbinowicz.

(49) p. 155.

T. Shabb. XIII. 5. הגליונים וספרי מינין אין מצילין אותן
אלא נשרפין הן במקומן הן ואזכרותיהן ר' יוסי הגלילי אומ' בחול
קודר את האזכרות וגונז ושורף את השאר אמר ר' טרפון אקפח
את בניי שאם יבואו לידי שאני שורף הן ואזכרותיהן שאלו הרודף
רודף אחריי נכנסתי לבית עבודה זרה ואיני נכנס לבתיהן שעובדי

עבודה זרה אין מכירין אותו וכופרין בו והללו מכירין אותו וכופרין
בו ועליהם הכתוב אומר ואחר הדלת והמזוזה שמת זכרונך אמר ר'
ישמעאל ומה אם לעשות שלום בין איש לאשתו אמר המקום שמי
הנכתב בקדושה ימחה על המים ספרי מינין שמטילין איבה וקנאה
ותחרות בין ישראל לאביהם שבשמים על אחת כמה וכמה [2] שימחו
הן ואזכרותיהן ואליהם הכתוב אומר הלוא משנאיך יי' אשנא
ובתקוממיך אתקוטט תכלית שנאה שנאתים לאו' היו לי וכשם
שאין מצילין אותן מפני הדליקה כך אין מצילין אותן לא מפני
המפלות ולא מפני המים ולא מכל דבר המאבדון :

[1] Cod. Vienna, and b Shabb. 116ᵃ.   [2] Cod. Vienna.

(50) p. 156.   j. Shabb. 15ᶜ almost the same words.

(51) p. 156.   b. Shabb. 116ᵃ almost the same words.

---

(52) p. 157.

b. Gittin 45ᵇ:— אמר ליה רב בודיא לרב אשי יתר על כדי
דמיהן הוא דאין לוקחין הא בכדי דמיהן לוקחין שמע מנה ס"ת
שנמצא ביד עובד כוכבים קורין בו דילמא לגנוז אמר רב נחמן
נקטינן ספר תורה שכתבו מין ישרף כתבו עובד כוכבים יגנז נמצא
ביד מין יגנז נמצא ביד עובד כוכבים אמרי לה יגנז ואמרי לה
קורין בו ספר תורה שכתבו עובד כוכבים תני חדא ישרף ותניא
אידך יגנז ותניא אידך קורין בו לא קשיא וגו' :

---

(53) p. 160.

T. Jadaïm II 13:— הגליונים וספרי מינין אינן מטמאות
את הידים ספרי בן סירא וכל ספרים שנכתבו מכאן ואילך אינן
מטמאין את הידים

---

(54) p. 161.

b. Shabb. 116ᵃ:— בעי מיניה רב יוסף בר חנין מר' אבהו
הני ספרי דבי אבידן מצילין אותן מפני הדליקה או אין מצילין
אין ולאו ורפיא בידיה רב לא אזיל לבי אבידן וכל שכן לבי נצרפי
שמואל לבי נצרפי לא אזיל לבי אבידן אזיל אמרו ליה [1] לרב מ"ט
לא אתית לבי אבידן אמר להו דקלא פלניא איכא באורחא וקשיא לי

²לִיעֲקָרְיָה דוכתיה קשי לי מר בר יוסֵ אמר מינייהו אבא ולא
מסתפינא מינייהו זימנא הדא אזיל בעו לסכֵיניה רבי מאיר קרֵ־
ליה און גליון ר׳ יוחנן קרֵ ליה עון גליון:

(55) p. 165.

א"ל קיסר לֵר׳ יהושע בן חנניה מ"ט לא —
אתית לבי אבידן א"ל טור תלג סחרוֹנֵי גלידין כלביהי לא נבחין
טהנֵוֹהֵי לא טוחנין:

(56) p. 165.

א"ל מ"ט לא אתית לבי אבידן אמר להו —
זקן הייתי ומתיירא אני שמא תרמסוני ברגליכם:

(57) p. 165.

איזו היא אשרה סתם אמר רב כל —
שכומרים שומרין אותה ואין טועמין מפירותיה ושמואל אמר כגון
דאמרי הני תמרי לשיכרא דבי נצרפי דשתו ליה ביום אידם:

(58) p. 171.

דאמר רב תחליפא בר אבדימי אמר (ib. 7ᵇ):—
שמואל יום נוצרי לדברי רבי ישמעאל לעולם אסור:

(59) p. 171.

בערב שבת לא היו מתענין מפני כבוד השבת :—
ק"ו בשבת עצמה באחד בשבת מ"ט לא אמר ר׳ יוחנן מפני הנוצרים:

(60) p. 173.

הגויים והרועים בהמה דקה ומגדליה לא —
מעלין ולא מורידין המינין והמשומדים והמסורות מורידין ולא
מעלין :

(61) p. 173.

תני רבי אבהו קמֵי׳ דרבי יוחנן העובדי
כוכבים ורועי בהמה דקה לא מעלין ולא מורידין אבל המינין
והמסורות והמומרים היו מורידין ולא מעלין א"ל אני שנה לכל

אבידת אחיך לרבות את המומר ואת אמרת היו מורידין סמי מכאן
מומר ולישני ליה כאן במומר אוכל נבילות לתיאבון כאן במומר
אוכל נבילות להכעיס קסבר אוכל נבילות להכעיס מין הוא איתמר
מומר פליגי רב אחא ורבינא חד אמר לתיאבון מומר להכעיס מין
חיי וחד אמר אפילו להכעיס נמי מומר אלא איזהו מין זה העובד
אלילי כוכבים מיתיבי אכל פרעוש אחד או יתוש אחד הרי זה
מומר והא הכא דלהכעיס היא וקתני מומר התם בעי למיטעב
טעמא דאיסירא:

(62) p. 177.

T. Hull. 11. 20. 21: בשר שנמצא ביד גוי מותר בהנאה ביד
המין אסור בהנאה היוצא מבית ע"ז הרי זה בשר זבחי מתים מפני
שאמרו שחיטת המין ע"ז פתן פת כותי רייכב יין נסך יפירותיהן
טבלין וספריהן ספרי קוסמין יבניהן ממזרין: אין מוכרין להן ואין
לוקחין מהן ואין נושאין מהן ואין נותנין להן ואין למדין את
בניהן אומנית ואין מתרפאין מהן לא ריפוי ממון ולא ריפוי נפשות:

[Note. Here follow the stories of Elazar ben Dama who
wished to be healed by Jacob of Chephar Sama, a Min, and
of R. Eliezer's arrest on the charge of Minuth; see above
nos 28. 45.]

(63) p. 178.

b. Hull. 13ᵇ: — אמר מר שחיטת עובד כוכבים נבלה ייהיש
שמא מין הוא אמר רב נחמן אמר רבה בר אביה אין מיניין באומות
עוברי כוכבים והא קאחזינן דאיכא אימא אין רוב עובדי כוכבים
מינין סבר לה כי הא דאמר ר' חייא בר אבא א"ר יוחנן נכרים
שבחוצה לארץ לעובדי עבודת כוכבים הן אלא מנהג אבותיהן
בידיהן אמר רב יוסף בר מניומי אמר רב נחמן אין מיניין באומית
עובדי כוכבים למאי אילימא לשחיטה השחא שחיטת מין דישראל
אמרת אסירא דעובד כוכבים מבעיא אלא למורידין השחא דישראל
מורידין דעובד כוכבים מבעיא:

(64) p. 181.

j. Sanh. 29ᶜ: — א"ר יוחנן לא גלו ישראל עד שנעשו עשרים
וארבע כיתות של מינים: מה טעמא בן אדם אני שולח אני איתך אל

בני ישראל אל גוים המורדים אשר מרדו בי · אל גוי המורד אין
כתיב כאן אלא גוים המורדים אשר מרדו בי המה ואבותיהם
פשעו בי עד היום הזה:

(65) p. 182.

b. A. Zar. 17ª: — הרחק מעליה דרכך זו מינות ואל תקרב
אל פתח ביתה זו הרשות ואיכא דאמרי הרחק מעליה דרכך זו
מינות והרשות ואל תקרב אל פתח ביתה זו זונה וכמה אמר רב
חסדא ארבע אמות ורבנן האי מאתנן זכה מאי דרשי ביה כדרב
חסדא דאמר רבחסדא כל זונה שנשכרת לבסוף היא שוכרת שנאמר
ובתתך אתנן ואתנן לא נתן לך ותהי להפך ופליגא דרב פדת דא"ר
פדת לא אסרה תורה אלא קריבה של גלוי עריות בלבד שנא' איש
איש אל כל שאר בשרו לא תקרבו לגלות ערוה עולא כי הוה אתי
מבי רב הוה מנשק להו לאחתיה אבי ידייהו ואמרי לה אבי הדייהו
ופליגא דידיה אדידיה דאמר עולא קריבה בעלמא אסור משום לך
לך אמרין נזירא סחור סחור לכרמא לא תקרב לעלוקה שתי בנות
הב הב מאי הב הב אמר מר עוקבא קול שתי בנות שצועקות
מגיהנם ואומרות בעולם הזה הבא הבא ומאן נינהו מינות
והרשות איכא דאמרי אמר רב חסדא אמר מר עוקבא קול גיהנב
צועקת ואומרת הביאו לי שתי בנות שצועקות ואומרית בעולם הזה
הבא הבא כל באיה לא ישיבון ולא ישיגו אורחות חיים וכי מאחר
שלא שבו היכן ישיגו ה"ק ואב ישיבו לא ישיגו אורחות חיים
למימרא דכל הפירש ממינית מיית יהא ההיא דאתאי לקמיה דרב
חסדא ואמרה ליה קלה שבקלות עשתה בנה הקטן מבנה הגדול
ואמר לה רב חסדא טרחו לה בזוודתא ולא מתה מדקאמרה קלה
שבקלות עשתה ממינית נמי הויא בה ההוא דלא הדרא שפיר
ומש"ה לא מתה איכא דאמרי ממינות אין מעבירה לא יהא ההיא
דאתאי קמיה דרב חסדא וא"ל ר"ה זוידו לה זוודתא ומתה
מדקאמרה קלה שבקלות ממינית מכל דמינית נמי הויא בה ומעבירה לא
והתניא אמרו עליו על ר"א בן דורדאיא .... הניה
ראשו בין ברכיו וגעה בבכיה עד שיצתה נשמתו יצתה בת קול
ואמרה ר"א בן דורדאיא מזומן לחיי העולם הבא והא חכא בעבירה
הוא ומית התם נמי כיון דאביק בה טובא כמינית דמיא בכה רבי

ואמר יש קונה עולמו בכמה שנים ויש קונה עולמו בשעה אחת
ואמר רבי לא דיין לבעלי תשובה שמקבלין אותן אלא שקורין
אותן רבי וגר':

(66) p. 188.

Qoh. r. I. 8.:— מעשה באשה אחת שבאת אצל ר' אליעזר
להתגייר אמרה לו רבי קרבני אמר לה פרטי את מעשיך אמרה
בני הקטון מבני הגדול נזף בה הלכה אצל ר' יהושע וקבלה אמרו
לו תלמידיו ר' אליעזר מרחק ואתה מקרב אמר להם כיון שנתנה
דעתה להתגייר אינה חיה לעולם דכתיב כל באיה לא ישובון ואב
ישובו לא ישיגו אורחות חיים:

(67) p. 191.

Shem. r. XIX. 4. p. 36d:— שאין ישראל המהולים יורדים
לגיהנם אמר ר' ברכיה כדי שלא יהיו המינים ורשעי ישראל אומרים
הואיל ואנו מהולין אין אני יורדין לגיהנם מה הק"בה עושה
משלח מלאך ומושך ערלתן והם יורדין לגיהנם שנאמר שלח ידיו
בשלומיו חלל בריתו וכיון שגיהנם רואה לערלה תלויה בהם
פיותחת פיה ולוחכת אותם הוי ופערה פיה בלי חוק:

(68) p. 192.

Bamm. r. XVIII. 17. p. 75d:— א"ר אלעזר עצת מינות היה
בהן למה היו דומין לבית שהוא מלא תבן והיה בבית חורין
והיה התבן נכנס בהם לאחר ימים התחיל אותו התבן שהיה בתוך
אותן החורין יוצא ידעו הכל כי היה אותו הבית של תבן כך
דואג ואחיתופל לא היו בהן מצות מתחלה אע"פ שנעשו בני תורה
היו כתחלתן הוי כי רעית במגורים בקרבם:

(69) p. 193.

j. Sanh. 27d האפיקורוס· רבי יוחנן ורבי לעזר חד אמר כהן
דאמר אהן ספרא וחרנה אמר כהן דאמר אילין רבנין רבי אלעזר ור'
שמואל בר נחמן חד אמר לכיפה של אבנים כיון שנתרועעה אחת
מהן נתרועעו כולן וחרנ' אמר לבית שהוא מלא תבן אף על גב
דאת מעב' ליה מיניה אהן מוצא דבגוייה הוא מרעיע בתליא:

APPENDIX

(70) p. 195.

Siphri. § 115. p. 35ª:— ולא תתורו אחרי לבבכם זו מינות
כענין שנאמר ומוצא אני מר ממות את האשה אשר היא מצוד'
וחרמים לבה אסורים ידיה והמלך ישמח באלהים:

---

(71) p. 196.

Siphri. § 320. p. 137ᵇ:— בגוי נבל אכעיסם אלו המינין וכן
הוא אומר אמר נבל בלבו אין אלהים:

---

(72) p. 196.

Vajiqr. r. § 28. 1. p. 40ᶜ· ᵈ:— אמר ר' בנימין בן לוי בקשו
לגנוז ספר קהלת שמצאו בו דברים שהם נוטים לצד מינות אמרו
כך היה ראוי שלמה לומר שמח בחור בילדותך ויטיבך לבך בימי
בחורותיך משה אמר ולא תתורו אחרי לבבכם ואחרי עיניכם ושלמה
אמר והלך בדרכי לבך ובמראה עיניך אלא הותרה רצועה לית דין
ולית דיין כיון שאמר ודע כי על כל אלה יביאך האלהים במשפט
אמרו יפה אמר שלמה אמר ר' שמואל בר נחמני בקשו לגנוז ספר
קהלת שמצאו בו דברים שהם נוטים לצד מינות אמרו כך היה
שלמה צריך לומר מה יתרון לאדם יכול אף בעמלה של תורה
במשמע הזרו ואמרו אילו אמר בכל עמל ושתק היינו אומרים אף
בעמלה של תורה במשמע הוא הא אינו אומר אלא בכל עמלו
בעמלו הוא שאינו מועיל אבל בעמלו של תורה מועיל:

---

(73) p. 198.

b. Sanh. 38ᵇ:— אמר רב יהודה אמר רב אדם הראשון מין
היה שנאמר ויקרא ה' אלהים אל האדם ויאמר לו איכה אן נטה
לבך וגו':

---

(74) p. 199.

M. Meg. IV. 8. 9 cf. M. Ber. V. 3:— האומר איני עובר לפני
התיבה בצבועין אף בלבנים לא יעבור בסנדל איני עובר אף יחף
לא יעבור והעושה תפלתו עגולה סכנה ואין בה מצוה נתנה על
מצחו או על פס ידו הרי זו דרך המינות ציפן זהב ונתנה על בית
אונקלי שלו הרי זו דרך החיצונים:

האומר יברכוך טובים הרי זו דרך המינות על קן צפור יגיעו רהמיך
ועל טוב יזכר שמך מודים מודים משתקין אותו וגו':

---

(75) p. 204.

j. Ber. 9ᶜ (v. 4):— רבי אחא ורבי יודה בן פזי יתבון בחד
כנישתא אתי עבר חד קומי תיבותא ואשגר חד ברכה· אתון ושייליון
לרבי סומון אמר לו רבי סימון בשם רבי יהושע בן לוי שלי· ציבור
שהשגיר שתים שלש ברכות אין מחזירין אותו· אשכח תניי ופליג·
לכל אין מחזירין אותו חוץ ממי שלא אמר מחיה המתים ומכניע
זדים ובונה ירושלם· אני אומר מין הוא:

---

(76) p. 207.

M. Sotah. IX. 15:— בעקבות ...... רבי אליעזר הגדול אומר
משיחא חוצפא יסגא .... והמלכות תהפך למינות וגי':

---

(77) p. 210.

j. Nedar. 38ᵃ:— רבי אחא בשם רבי הונא עתיד עשו הרשע
לעטוף טליתו ולישב עם הצדיקים בגן עדן לעתיד לבוא והקדוש
ברוך הוא גוררו ומוציאו משם מה טעמא אם תגביה כנשר ואם
בין כוכבים שים קנך משם אורידך נאם יי'· ואין כוכבים אלא
צדיקים כמה דאת אמר ומצדיקי הרבים ככוכבים לעולם ועד:

---

(78) p. 211.

Qoh. r. on I 8. p. 4ᵇ:— חנינא בן אחי ר' יהושע אזל להדיה
כפר נחום ועבדון ליה מינאי מלה ועלון יתיה רכיב חמרא בשבתא
אזל לגביה יהושע חביביה ויהב עלוי משח ואיתסי א"ל כיון דאיתער
בך חמרא דההוא רשיעא לית את יכיל שרי בארעא דישראל נחת
ליה מן תמן לבבל ודמך תמן בשלמיה:

(79) p. 215.

Qoh. r. on I. 8 (p. 4ᵇ):— ר' יונתן ערק חד מן תלמידוי לגביהון·
אזל ואשכחיה עבד בן אפטופניות· שלחון מינים בתריה כד אמרין
ליה ולא כך כתיב גורלך תפיל בתוכנו כיס אחד יהיה לכולנו והוה
פרח ואינון פרחין בתריה· אמרין ליה רבי איתא גמיל חסדא

לחדא כלתא הלך ומצאן עסוקים בריבה אחת אמר לון בן ארחיהון
דיהודאי עבדין׳ אמרין ליה ולא כן כתיב בתורה גורלך תפיל בתוכנו
כיס וגו׳׳ וההוה פרח ואינון פרחין בתריה עד דמטא לתרע וטרד
באפיהון׳ אמרין ר׳ יונתן אזיל גלוג לאמך דלא הפכת ולא איסתכלת
בן דאילו הפכת ואיסתכלת בן יותר מן מה דהוינן פרחין בתרך
הוית פריה בתרן :

(80) p. 218.

Qoh. r. on I. 8: — ר׳ יהודה בן נקוסא היו המינין מתעשקים
עמו היו שואלים אותו ומשיב ומשיב שואלין אותו ומשיב׳ אמר לון על
מגן אתון מגיבין אתון נעביד ביניגן דכל בר נש דנצח חבריה
יהא פצע מוחיה דהבריה בקורנס והוא נצח לון ופצע מוחיהון עד
דאיתהמלאון פיצעין פיצעין׳ וכיון דאתא אמרין ליה תלמידוי רבי
סייעוך מן השמים ונצחת אמר לון ועל מגן לכו והתהפללו על אותו
האיש ועל אותה החמת שהיתה מלאה אבנים טובים ומרגליות אבל
עכשיו מלאה פחמין :

(81) p. 219.

Qoh. r. VII. 26 p. 21ᵈ: — ר׳ איסי דקיסרין פתר קרייה במינות
טוב זה ר׳ אלעזר וחוטא זה יעקוב איש כפר נבוריא ד״א טוב זה
אלעזר בן דמא וחוטא זה יעקוב איש כפר סאמא ד״א טוב זה
חנניא בן אחי ר׳ יהושע וחוטא אלו בני כפר נחום ד״א טוב זה
יהודה בן נקוסא וחוטא אלו המיניב ד״א טוב זה ר׳ נתן וחוטא זה
תלמידו ד״א טוב זה ר׳ אליעזר ור׳ והושע וחוטא זה אלישע :

(82) p. 221.

b. Hagg. 5ᵇ: — ואנכי הסתר אסתיר פני ביום ההוא אמר רבא
אמר הק״בה אף על פי שהסתרתי פני מהם בחלום אדבר בו רב
יוסף אמר ידו נטויה עלינו שנא׳ ובצל ידי כסיתיך ר׳ יהושע בן
חנניה הוה קאי בי קיסר אחוי ליה ההוא מינא עמא דאהדרינהו
מריה לאפיה מיניה אחוי ליה ידו נטויה עלינו אמר ליה קיסר לר׳
יהושע מאי אחוי לך עמא דאהדרינהו מריה לאפיה מיניה ואנא
מחוינא ליה ידו נטויה עלינו אמרו ליה לההוא מינא מאי אחוית
ליה עמא דאהדרינהו מריה (לפיה) מיניה ומאי אחוי לך לא ידענא

אמרו גברא דלא ידע מאי מהוי ליה במחוג יהוי קמי מלכא
אפקוהו וקטלוהו כי קא ניחא נפשיה דרבי יהושע בן חנניה אמרו
ליה רבנן מאי תיהוי עלן קמי מינאי אמר להם אבדה עצה מבנים
נסרחה חכמתם כיון שאבדה עצה מבנים נסרחה חכמתם של אומיה
העולם:

(83) p. 226.

א"ל ההוא מינא לרבי יהושע בן חנניה :— b. Erub. 101ª.
הדקאה דכתיב בכר טובם כחדק אמר ליה שטיא שפיל לסיפיה דקרא
דכתיב ישר ממסוכה ואלא מאי טובם כחדק כשם שהדקים הללו
מגינין על הפירבה כך טובים שבנו מגינין עלינו דבר אחר טובב
כחדק שמהדקין את הרשעים לגיהנם שנא' קומי ודושי בת ציון כי
קרנך אשיב ברזל ופרסותיך אשים נחושה והדיקות עמים רבים וגו':

(84) p. 228.

מעשה ברבן גמליאל ור' יהושע :— Shem. r. XXX. 9. p. 53ᶜ·ᵈ.
ור"א בן עזריה ור' עקיבא שהלכו לרומי ודרשו שם אין דרכיו
של הק"בה כבשר ודם שהוא גוזר גזירה והוא אומר לאחרים לעשות
והוא אינו עושה כלום והק"בה אינו כן היה שם מין אחד אחר
שיצאו אמר להם אין דבריכם אלא כזב לא אמרתם אלהיב אומר
ועושה למה אינו משמר את השבת אמרו לו רשע שבעולם אין
אדב רשאי לטלטל בתוך חצירו בשבת א"ל הן אמרו לו העליונים
והתחתונים חצירו של הק"בה שנאמר מלא כל הארץ כבודו ואפילי
אדב עובר עבירה אינו מטלטל מלא קימתי א"ל הן אמרו לו כתיב
הלא את השמים ואת הארץ מלא אני:

(85) p. 231.

שאלו מינין את רבן גמליאל מניין שהקדוש :— b. Sanh. 90ᵇ.
ברוך הוא מחיה מתים אמר להם מן התורה ומן הנביאים ומן
הכתובים ולא קיבלו ממנו מן התורה דכתיב ויאמר ה' אל משה
הנך שוכב עם אבותיך וקם אמרו לו ודילמא וקם העם הזה וזנה
בין הנביאים דכתיב יהיו מתיך נבלתי יקומון הקיצו ורננו שוכבי
עפר כי טל אורות טלך וארץ רפאים תפיל ודילמא מתיב שהחיה
יחזקאל מן הכתובים דכתיב וחכך כיין הטוב הולך לדודי למישריב
דובב שפתי ישנים ודילמא רחושי מרחשת שפוותיה בעלמא:

APPENDIX · 423

(86) p. 235.

b. Jebam. 102ᵇ:— אמר ליה ההוא מינא לר"ג עמא דחלץ
ליה מריה מיניה דכתיב בצאנם ובבקרם ילכו לבקש את ה' ולא
ימצאו חלץ מהם אמר ליה שוטה מי כתיב חלץ להם חלץ מהם
כתיב ואילו יבמה דחלצו לה אחין מידי משמא אית ביה:

(87) p. 237.

b. Ber. 10ᵃ:— אמר לה ההוא מינא לברוריא כתיב רני עקרה
לא ילדה משום דלא ילדה רני אמרה ליה שטיא שפיל לסיפיה
דקרא דכתיב כי רבים בני שוממה מבני בעולה אמר ה' אלא מאי
עקרה לא ילדה רני כנסת ישראל שדומה לאשה עקרה שלא ילדה
בנים לגיהנם כותייכו:

(88) p. 239.

b. Hull 87ᵃ:— א"ל ההוא מינא לרבי מי שיצר הרים לא ברא
רוח ומי שברא רוח לא יצר הרים דכתיב כי הנה יוצר הרים ובורא
רוח אמר ליה שוטה שפיל לסיפיה דקרא ה' צבאות שמו אמר ליה
נקוט לי זימנא תלתא יומי ומהדרנא לך תיובתא יתיב רבי תלת
יומין בתעניתא כי הוה קא בעי מיברך אמרו ליה מינא קאי אבבא
אמר ויתנו בברותי רוש וגו' אמר לו רבי בשורות טובות אני אומר
לך לא מצא תשובה אויבך ונפל מן הגג ומת אמר לו רצונך שתסעוד
אצלי אמר לו הן לאחר שאכלו ושתו א"ל כוס של ברכה אתה
שותה או ארבעים זהובים אתה נוטל אמר לו כוס של ברכה אני
שותה יצתה בת קול ואמרה כוס של ברכה ישוה ארבעים זהובים
אמר ר' יצחק עדיין ישנה לאותה משפחה בין גדולי רומי יקורין
אותה משפחת בר לויאנוס:

(89) p. 245.

b. Sanh. 38ᵇ:— אמר ליה ההוא מינא לר' ישמעאל בר' יוסי
כתיב וה' המטיר על סדום ועל עמרה גפרית ואש מאת ה' מאתו
מיבעי ליה א"ל ההוא כובס שבקיה אנא מהדרנא ליה דכתיב ויאמר
למך לנשיו עדה וצלה שמען קולי נשי למך נשיי יבעי ליה אלא
משתעי קרא הכי הכא נמי משתעי קרא הכי א"ל מנא לך הא
מפירקיה דר"מ שמיע לי:

(90) p. 247.

b. Pesaḥ. 87[b]:— אמר ר׳ הושעיא מאי דכתיב צדקת פרזונו
בישראל צדקה עשה הק״בה בישראל שפזרן לבין האומות והייני
דא״ל ההוא מינא לרבי חנינא אנן מעלינן מיניייכו כתיב בבי
כי ששת חדשים ישב שם וגו׳ ואלו אנן איתייכו גבן כמה שני
ולא קעבדינן לכו מידי אמר לו רצונך יטפל לך תלמיד אחד נטפל
ליה ר׳ הושעיא א״ל משום דלא ידעיתו היכי תעבדו תכלינן כולהו
ליתנהו גבייכו מאי דאיכא גבייכו קרי לכו מלכותא קטיעתא אמר
ליה גפא דרומי בהא נחתינן ובהא סלקינן:

(91) p. 250.

b. Joma 56[b]. 57[a]:— אמר ליה ההוא מינא לר׳ חנינא השתא ברי
טמאין אתון דכתיב טומאתה בשוליה אמר ליה תא חזי מה כתיב
בהו השוכן אתם בתוך טומאתב אפילו בזמן שהן טמאין שכינה
שרויה ביניהן:

(92) p. 251.

b. Gitt. 57[a]:— אמר ההוא מינא לרבי חנינא שקורי משקריתו
אמר ליה ארץ צבי כתיב בה מה צבי זה אין עורו מחזיק את
בשרו אף ארץ ישראל בזמן שיושבין עליה רווחא ובזמן שאין
יושבין עליה גמדא:

(93) p. 253.

Ber. r. § 82. p. 155[b]:— ותמת רחל ותקבר סמוך למיתה קבורה
בדרך אפרת היא בית לחם רבי ינאי ורבי יונתן הוו יתבין אתא
ההוא מינא שאלינהו מאי דכתיב בלכתך היום מעמדי וגו׳ והלא
בצלצח בגבול בנימין וקבורת רחל בגבול יהודה דכתיב ותקבר בדרך
אפרתה וכתיב בית לחם אפרתה א״ר ינאי אסוך חרפתי א״ל הכי
אמר בלכתך היום מעמדי עם קבורת רחל ומצאת ב׳ אנשים בגבול
בנימין בצלצח ואית דאמרי בלכתך היום מעמדי בגבול בנימין
בצלצח ומצאת ב׳ אנשים עם קבורת רחל והאי דווקא:

(94) p. 255.

j. Ber. 12[d]. 13[a]:— המינין שאלו את ר׳ שמלאי כמה אלוהות
בראו את העולם אמר להן ולי אתם שואלין לכו ושאלו את אדם

הראשון שנ׳ כי שאול׳ נא לימים ראשונים וגו׳ אשר ברא אלהים
אדם על הארץ אין כתיב כאן אלא למן היום אשר ברא אלהים אדם
על הארץ אמרו ליה והכתיב בראשית ברא אלהים אמר להן וכי
בראו כתיב אין כתיב אלא ברא אמר ר׳ שמלאי כל מקום שפקרו
המינין תשובה בצידן חזרו ושאלו אותו מה אהן דכתיב נעשה אדם
בצלמינו כדמותינו אמר להן ויבראו את האדם בצלמם אין כתיב כאן
אלא ויברא אלהים את האדם בצלמו אמרו לו תלמידיו לאלו דחיתה
בקנה לנו מה אתה משיב אמר להן לשעבר אדם נברא מן העפר
וחוה נבראת מן האדם מאדם [מכאן?] ואילך בצלמינו כדמותינו
א״א לאיש בלא האשה וא״א האשה בלא האיש א״א לשניהן בלא
שכינה וחזרן ושאלו אותו מה ההן דכתיב אל אלהים ה׳ אל אלהים
ה׳ הוא יודע אמר להן הם יודעים אין כתיב כאן אלא הוא יודע
כתיב אמרו לו תלמידיו ר׳ לאלו דחית בקנה לנו מה אתה משיב
אמר להן שלושתן שב אחד כאינש דאמר בסיליויוס קיסר אגושתוס
חזרו ושאלו אותו מהו דכתיב אל אלהים ה׳ דיבר ויקרא ארץ
אמר להן וכי דיברו ויקראו כתיב כאן אין כתיב אלא דיבר ויקרא
אמרו לו תלמידיו רבי לאלו דחית בקנה ולנו מה אתה משיב אמר
להן שלשתן שב אחד כאינש דאמר אומנין בניין ארכיטקטון חזרו
ושאלו אותו מהו דכתיב כי אלהים קדושים הוא אמר להן קדושים
המה אין כתיב כאן אלא הוא אל קנא הוא אל קנא הוא אמרו לו תלמידיו
רבי לאלו דחית בקנה ולנו מה אתה משיב אמר רבי יצחק קדוש
בכל מיני קדושה דאמר ר׳ יודן בשם רבי אחא הק״בה דרכו בקדושה
דיבורו בקדושה וישובו בקדושה השיפת זרועו בקדושה אלהים
נירא ואדיר בקדושה דרכו בקדושה אלהים בקודש דרכך הילוכו
בקדושה הליכו׳ אלי מלכי בקודש מושבו בקדושה אלהים ישב על
כסא קדשו דיבורו בקדושה אלהים דיבר חשיפת זרועו בקדושה
השף ה׳ את זרוע קדשו. נורא ואדיר בקדושה מי כמוכה נאדר
בקודש חזרו ושאלו אותו מהו אהן דכתיב מי גוי גדול אשר
לו אלהים קרובים אליו אמר להן כה׳ אלהינו בכל קראינו אליהם
אין כתיב כאן אלא בכל קראינו אליו אמרו לו תלמידיו רבי
לאלו דחית בקנה לנו מה אתה משיב אמר להן קרוב בכל מיני
קריבות:

(95) p. 265, 304.

אמר ר׳ חייא בר אבא אם —: Pesiqta. r. XXI. p. 100[b]. 101[a]
יאמר לך ברא דזניתא תרין אלהים אינון אימר ליה אנא הוא דימא
אנא הוא דסיני .... ד״א אמר ר׳ חייא בר אבא אב יאמר לך ברא
דזניתא תרין אלהים אינון אימא ליה פנים בפנים דברו אין כתיב
כאן אלא דבר ה׳ עמכם:

----

(96) p. 266.

משתבח להו ר׳ אבהו למיני ברב ספרא דאדם —: b. A. Zar. 4[a]
גדול הוא שבקו ליה מיכסא דתליסר שנין יומא חד אשכחוהו אמרו
ליה כתיב רק אתכם ידעתי מכל משפחות האדמה על כן אפקיד
עליכם את כל עונותיכם מאן דאית ליה סיסיא ברחמיה מסיק ליה
אישתיק ולא אמר להו ולא מידי רמו ליה סודרא בצואריה וקא
מצערו ליה אתא רבי אבהו אשכחינהו אמר להו אמאי מצעריתו
ליה אמרו ליה ולא אמרת לן דאדם גדול הוא ולא ידע למימר לן
פירושא דהאי פסוקא אמר להו אימר דאמרי לכו בתנאי בקראי מי
אמרי לכו אמרו ליה מ״ש אתון דידעיתון אמר להו אנן דשכיחינן
גביכון רמינן אנפשין ומעיינן אינהו לא מעייני אמרו ליה לימא
לן את אמר להו אמשול לכם משל למה הדבר דומה לאדם שנושה
משני בנ״א אחד אוהבו ואחד שונאו אוהבו נפרע ממנו מעט מעט
שונאו נפרע ממנו בבת אחת:

----

(97) p. 270.

אפיקורוסין שאלו לרבי אבהו אמרו —: Ber. r. XXV. 1. p. 55[c]
לו אין אנו מוצאין מיתה לחנוך אמר להם למה לו נאמרה
כאן לקיחה ונאמרה להלן כי היום ה׳ לוקח את אדונך מעל ראשך
אמר להם אם ללקיחה אתם דורשים נאמר כאן לקיחה ונאמר להלן
הנני לוקח ממך את מחמד עיניך א״ר תנחומא יפה השיבן רבי
אבהו:

----

(98) p. 272.

אמר לו ההוא מינא לר׳ אבהו כתיב מזמור —: b. Ber. 10[a]
לדוד בברחו מפני אבשלום בנו וכתיב לדוד מכתם בברחו מפני
שאול במערה הי מעשה הוה ברישא מכדי מעשה שאול הוה ברישא

לכתוב ברישא אמר ליה אתון דלא דרשיתון סמוכין קשיא לכו אנן
דדרשינן סמוכים לא קשיא לן:

(99) p. 274.

b. Shabb. 152^b:— א"ל ההוא מינא לר"אבהו אמריתו נשמתן
של צדיקים גנוזות תחת כסא הכבוד אוב טמיא היכא אסקיה
לשמואל בנגידא א"ל התם בתוך שנים עשר חדש הוה דתניא כל
י"ב חדש גופו קיים ונשמתו עולה ויורדת לאחר י"ב הדש הגוף
בטל ונשמתו עולה ושוב אינה יורדת:

(100) p. 275.

b. Sanh. 39^a:— א"ל ההוא מינא לרבי אבהו אלהיכם גחכן
הוא דקאמר ליה ליחזקאל שכב על צדך השמאלי וכתיב ושכבת על
צדך הימיני אתא ההוא תלמידא א"ל מ"ט דשביעתא א"ל השתא
אמינא לכו מילתא דשויא לתרוייכו אמר הק"בה לישראל זרעו שש
והשמיטו שבע כדי שתדעו שהארץ שלי היא והן לא עשו כן אלא
חטאו וגלו מנהגו של עולם מלך בשר ודם שסרחה עליו מדינה
אם אכזרי הוא הורג את כולן אם רחמן הוא רחמן חצים אם רחמן
מלא רחמים הוא מייסר הגדולים שבהן ביסורין אף כך הק"בה
מייסר את יחזקאל כדי למרק עונותיהם של ישראל

א"ל ההוא מינא לרבי אבהו אלהיכם כהן הוא דכתיב ויקחו לי
תרומה כי קבריה למשה במאי טביל וכי תימא במיא והכתיב מי
מדד בשעלו מים א"ל בנורא טביל דכתיב כי הנה ה' באש יבא ומי
סלקא טבילותא בנורא א"ל אדרבה עיקר טבילותא בנורא הוא
דכתיב וכל אשר לא יבא באש תעבירו במים:

(101) p. 276.

b. Sanh. 99^a:— והיינו דא"ל ההוא מינא לרבי אבהו אימתי
אתי משיח א"ל לכי חפי להו חשוכא להנהו אינשי א"ל מילט קא
לייטת לי א"ל קרא כתיב כי הנה החושך יכסה ארץ וערפל לאומים
ועליך יזרח ה' וכבודו עליך יראה:

(102) p. 277.

b. Succ. 48^b:— א"ל ההוא מינא דשמיה ששון לר' אבהו
עתידיתו דתמלו לי מים לעלמא דאתי דכתיב ושאבתם מים בששון

א"ל אי הוה כתיב לששון כדקאמרת השתא דכתיב בששון משכיה
דההוא גברא משויגן ליה גודא ומלינן ביה מיא:

(103) p. 278.

b. Sanh. 91ᵃ:— א"ל ההוא מינא כו' אמי אמריתי דשכבי חיי
והא הוי עפרא ועפרא מי קא חיי א"ל אמשול לך משל למה הדבר
דומה למלך בשר ודם שאמר לעבדייו לכו ובנו לי פלטרין גדולים במקום
שאין מים ועפר הלכו ובנו איתי לימים נפלו אמר להם חזרו ובנו
אותו במקום שיש עפר ומים אמרו לו אין אני יכולין בעם עליהב
ואמר להן במקום שאין מים ועפר בניתם עכשיין שיש מים ועפר
על אחת במה וכמה ואם אי אתה מאמין צא לבקעה וראה עכבר
שהיום חציו בשר וחציו אדמה למחר השריץ ונעשה כולו בשר
שמא תאמר לזמן מרובה עלה להר וראה שהיום אין בו אלא חלוזן
אחד למחר ירדו גשמים ונתמלא כולו הלוזינות:

(104) p. 281.

b. Sanh. 91ᵃ:— א"ל ההיא מינא לגביהא בן פסיסא ווי לכון
חייביא דאמריתון מיתי חיין דחיין מיתי דמיתי חיין א"ל ווי לכון
חייביא דאמריתון מיתי לא חיין דלא הוו חיי חיי דהוי חיי לא כ"ש
א"ל חייביא קרית לי אי קאימנא בעיטנא בך ופשיטנא לעקמותך
מינך א"ל אם אתה עושה כן רופא אומן תקרא ושכר הרבה תטול:

(105) p. 282.

b. Sanh. 39ᵃ:— אמר ליה קיסר כו' תנחומא תא ליהוי כולן
לעמא חד אמר לחיי אנן דמחלינן לא מצינן מיהוי כוותייכו אתון
מחליתו והוו כוותן א"ל מימר שפיר קאמרת מיהו כל דזכי למלכא
לשדיוה לביבר שדיוה לביבר ולא אכלוה א"ל ההוא מינא האי דלא
אכלוה משום דלא כפין הוא שדיוה ליה לדידיה ואכלוה:

The same story is told in Jalq. Shim. on Zeph III. 9, with
no essential variation.

(106) p. 285.

b. Sanh. 38ᵇ:— אמר רב נחמן האי מאן מאן דידע לאהדורי למיניס
כרב ¹אידית ליהדר ואי לא לא ליהדר אמר ההוא מינא לרב ¹אידית
כתיב ואל משה אמר עלה אל ה' עלה אלי מיבעי ליה א"ל זהו

מטטרון ששמו כשם רבו דכתיב כי שמי בקרבו אי חכי ² נפלחו
ליה כתיב אל תמר בו אל תמירני בו אם כן לא ישא לפשעכם למה
לי א"ל הימנותא ³ בידן דאפילו בפרוונקא נמי לא ¹ קבילניה דכתיב
ויאמר אליו אם אין פניך הולכים וגו':

¹ אידר Cod. Monac. apud. Rabbez. ² פלחו idem. ³ בידך idem. ⁴ קבליניה idem.

The above is contained also in Jalq. Shim., Mishpat. § 359.

(107) p. 287.

b. Hagg. 15ᵃ:— חזא מיטטרון דאיתיהבא ליה רשותא למיתב
למיכתב זכוותא דישראל אמר גמירא דלמעלה לא הוי לא ישיבה
ולא תחרות ולא עורף ולא עיפוי שמא חס ושלום ב' רשויות הן
אפקוהו למיטטרון ומחיוהו שיתין פולסי דנורא:

----

(108) p. 290.

b. Sanh. 39ᵃ:— אמר ליה ההיא מינא לרבי אבינא כתיב מי
כעמך כישראל גוי אחד בארץ מאי רבותייהו אתון נמי ערביתו
בהדן דכתיב כל הגוים כאין נגדו אמר ליה מדידכו אסחידו עלן
דכתיב ובגוים לא יתחשב:

(109) p. 291.

M. Sanh. IV. 5.: ושלא יהו .... לפיכך נברא אדם יחיד'
מיינין אימרים הרבה רשויות בשמים:

----

(110) p. 292.

T. Sanh. VIII. 7.: אדם נברא באחרונה ולמה נברא באחרונה
שלא יהו המינין אומרים שותף היה עמו במעשה:

(111) p. 293.

b. Sanh. 38ᵇ:— תנן התם ר"א אומר הוי שקוד ללמוד תורה
ודע מה שתשיב לאפיקורוס אמר ר' יוחנן לא שנו אלא אפיקורוס
של עובדי כוכבים אבל אפיקורוס ישראל כ"ש דפקר טפי א"ר יוחנן
כל מקום שפקרו המינים תשובתן בצידן נעשה אדם בצלמנו ויברא
אלהים את האדם בצלמו הבה נרדה ונבלה שם שפתם וירד ה' לראות
את העיר ואת המגדל כי שם נגלו אליו האלהים לאל העונה אותי

ביום צרתי כי מי גוי גדול אשר לו אלהים קרובים אליו כה'
אלהינו בכל קראנו אליו ומי כעמך כישראל גוי אחד בארץ אשר
הלכו אלהים לפדות לו לעם עד די כרסוון רמיו ועתיק יומין יתיב
הנך למה לי כדרבי יוחנן דא"ר יוחנן אין הקדוש ברוך הוא עושה
דבר אא"כ נמלך בפמליא של מעלה שנאמר בגזירת עירין פתגמא
ובמאמר קדישין שאילתא התינח כולהי עד די כורסוון רמיו מאי איכא
למימר אחד לו ואחד לדוד דתניא אחד לו ואחד לדוד דברי ר'
עקיבא א"ל ר' יוסי עקיבא עד מתי אתה עושה שכינה חול אלא
אחד לדין ואחד לצדקה קבלה מיניה או לא קבלה מיניה ת"ש
דתניא אחד לדין ואחד לצדקה דברי ר' עקיבא א"ל ר' אלעזר בן
עזריא עקיבא מה לך אצל הגדה כלך אצל נגעים ואהלות אלא אחד
לכסא ואחד לשרפרף כסא לישב עליו ושרפרף להדום רגליו:

(112) p. 297.

Siphri § 143. p. 54ª:— שמעון בן עזאי אותר בוא וראה בכל
הקרבנות שבתורה לא נאמר בהם לא אלהים ולא אלהיך ולא שדי וצבאות
אלא יו"ד ה"א שם מיוחד שלא ליתן פתחון פה למינים לרדות:

(113) p. 297.

b. Menaḥ. 110ª:— תניא אמר ר' שמעון בן עזאי בוא וראה
מה כתיב בפרשת קרבנות שלא נאמר בהם לא אל ולא אלהים
אלא ה' שלא ליתן פתחון פה לבעל דין לחלוק:

(114) p. 297.

Siphra 4ᶜ: Same in substance as (112), but ascribed to
R. José [ben Ḥalaphta] instead of to R. Shim'on ben Azai.

The saying is also found in Jalq. Shim. § 604.

(115) p. 299.

Echah. r. I. 1. p. 10ª:— לא גלו ישראל עד שכפרו ביחידו
של עולם ובמילה שנתנה לעשרים דורות בעשרת הדברות ובחמשה.
ספרי תורה:

(116) p. 299.

Siphri § 329. p. 139ᵇ:— ראו עתה כי אני אני הוא זאת
תשובה לאומרים אין רשות בשמים האומר שתי רשויות בשמים

משיבין אותו ואומרים לו ואין אלהים עמדי או שמא אין יכול
להחיות ולא להמית לא להרע ולא להטיב ת"ל אני אמית ואחיה
ואומר כה אמר ה' מלך ישראל וגואלו ה' צבאות אני ראשון ואני
אחרון ומבלעדי אין אלהים:

(117) p. 300.

ואומר חזה הוית עד די — Mechilta Jithro § 5. p. 66b:—
כרסון רמיו ואומר מהר דינור נגד ונפק מן קדמוהי וגו' שלא יתן
פתחון פה לאומות העולם לומר שתי רשויות הן אלא אנכי יי'
אלהיך אני על הים אני על היבשה אני לשעבר אני לעתיד לבא אני
לעולם הזה אני לע"הב שנאמר ראו עתה כי אני אני הוא עד זקנה
אני הוא כה אמר יי' מלך ישראל וגואלו יי' צבאות אני ראשון ואני
אחרון ואומר מי פעל ועשה קורא הדורות מראש אני יי' אני ראשון
ר' נתן אומר מכאן תשובה למינין שאומרים שתי רשויות הן
שכשעמד הק"בה ואמר אנכי יי' אלהיך מי עמד ומיחה כנגדו:

(118) p. 301.

רבי שמואל בר נחמן בשם רבי — Ber. r. VIII. 8. p. 22d:—
יונתן אמר בשעה שהיה משה כותב את התורה היה כותב מעשה
כל יום ויום כיון שהגיע לפסוק הזה שנאמר ויאמר אלהים נעשה
אדם בצלמנו כדמותנו אמר לפניו רבון העולם מה אתה נותן פתחון
פה למינים אתמהא אמר לו כתוב והרוצה לטעות יטעה:

(119) p. 302.

דמי לבר אלהין אמר ראובן באותה שעה ירד — j. Shabb. 8d:—
מלאך וסטרי להוא רשע על פיו א"ל תקין מיליך ובר אית ליה
חזר ומר בריך אלההון די שדרך מישך ועבד נגו די שלח בריה
לית כתיב כאן אלא די שלח מלאכיה ושיזיב לעבדוהי די התרחיצו
עלוהי:

(120) p. 303.

ד"א אנכי ה' אלהיך א"ר אבהו — Shem. r. XXIX. 5. p. 51b:—
משל למלך בשר ודם מולך ויש לו אב או אח אמר הק"בה אני
איני כן אני ראשון שאין לי אב ואני אחרון שאין לי בן ומבלעדי
אין אלהים שאין לי אח:

28

(121) p. 304.

Pesiq. r. XXI. p. 100[b]: same as (95) above.

(122) p. 306.

Debar. r. II. 33. p. 104[c]:—עם שונים אל תתערב עם אלו שאומרים
יש אלוה שני אל תתערב א"ר יהודה בר סימון והיה בכל הארץ
נאם ה' פי שנים בה יכרתו ויגועו הפיות שאומרים שתי רשויות הן
יכרתו ויגועו ומי עתיד להיות קיים והשלישית יוותר בה אלו
ישראל שנקראו שלישין שהם משולשין כהנים לוים וישראלים שהן
מג' אבות אברהם יצחק ויעקוב ד"א שהן מקלסין להק"בה בג'
קדושות קדוש קדוש קדוש אמר ר' אחא כעס הק"בה על שלמה
כשאמר הפסוק הזה א"ל דבר של קידש שמא היית אומרו בלשון
נוטריקון ועם שונים אל תתערב מיד חזר ופירש את הדבר יש אחד
ואין שני גם בן ואח אין לו אין לו אח ולא בן אלא שמע ישראל
ה' אלהינו ה' אחד :

──────

(123) p. 308.

j. Ber. 3[c]:—וקראו עשרת הדברות שמע והיה אם שמוע
ויאמר ר' אמי בשם ר"ל זאת אומרת שאין הברכות מעכבות א"ר בא
אין מן הדא לית ש"מ כלום שעשרת הדברות הן הן גופה של שמע
דרב מתנה ור' שמואל בר נחמן אמר תרוייהון אמרין בדין הוה שיהו
קורין עשרת הדברות בכל יום ומפני מה אין קורין אותו מפני
טענת המינין שלא יהו אומרים אלו לבד נתנו לו למשה בסיני :

──────

(124) p. 308.

b. Ber. 12[a]:—וקורין עשרת הדברות שמע והיה אם שמוע
ויאמר אמת ויציב ועבודה וברכת כהנים· א"ר יהודה אמר שמואל
אף בגבולין בקשו לקרות כן אלא שכבר בטלום מפני תרעומת
המינין תניא נמי הכי ר' נתן אומר בגבולין בקשו לקרות כן אלא
שכבר בטלום מפני תרעומת המינין רבה בב"ח* סבר למקבעינהו
בסורא א"ל רב חסדא כבר בטלום מפני תרעומת המינין אמימר סבר
למקבעינהו בנהרדעא א"ל רב אשי כבר בטלום מפני תרעומת
המינין :

* בר רב הונא Rabbcz.

──────

(125) p. 309.

b. Pesaḥ. 56ᵃ:— ת"ר כיצד היו כורכין את שמע אומרים
שמע ישראל ה' אלהינו ה' אחד ולא היו מפסיקין דברי רבי מאיר
רבי יהודה אומר מפסיקין היו אלא שלא היו אומרים ברוך שם
כבוד מלכותו לעולם ועד ואנן מאי טעמא אמרינן ליה כדדריש ר'
שמעון בן לקיש דאמר רשב"ל ויקרא יעקב אל בניו ויאמר האספו
ואגידה לכם ביקש יעקב לגלות לבניו קץ הימין ונסתלקה ממנו
שכינה אמר שמא חס ושלום יש במטתי פסול כאברהם שיצא ממנו
ישמעאל ואבי יצחק שיצא ממנו עשו אמרו לו בניו שמע ישראל ה'
אלהינו ה' אחד אמרו כשם שאין שאין בלבך אלא אחד כך אין בלבנו
אלא אחד באותה שעה פתח יעקב אבינו ואמר ברוך שם כבוד
מלכותו לעולם ועד אמרי רבנן היכי נעביד נאמרוהו לא אמרו
משה רבינו לא נאמרוהו אמרו יעקב התקינו שיהו אומרים אותו
בחשאי אמר רבי יצחק אמרי דבי רבי אמי משל לבת מלך
שהריחה ציקי קדירה אם תאמר יש לה גנאי לא תאמר יש לה
צער התחילו עבדיה להביא בחשאי אמר רבי אבהו התקינו שיהו
אומרים אותו בקול רם מפני תרעומת המינין ובנהרדעא דליכא
מינין עד השתא אמרי לה בחשאי:

(126) p. 313.

M. Ber. IX. 5:— כל חותמי ברכות שהיו במקדש היו אומרים
מן העולם משקלקלו המינין ואמרו אין עולם אלא אחד התקינו
שיהו אומרים מן העולם ועד העולם והתקינו שיהא אדם שואל את
שלום חברו בשם שנאמר והנה בא בעז וגו':

(127) p. 315.

Shem. r. XLIV. 6. p. 73ᶜ· ᵈ:— ד"א זכור לאברהם למה הזכיר
ג' אבות א"ר לוי אמר משה רבון העולם חיים הם המתים א"ל
משה נעשית מין וגו':

(128) p. 315.

T. Meg. IV. 37:— מיכן היה ר' שמעון בן אלעזר אומר אין
היחיד רשאי להשיב על הקלקלה שבתשובה שהשיבו *משה לאחרון
משם פרשו מינין:

* Cod. Vienn. למשה אחרון.

28*

(129) p. 316.

b. Meg. 25ᵇ:— תניא ר"ש בן אלעזר אומר לעולם יהא אדם

זהיר בתשובותיו שמתוך תשובה שהשיבו אהרון למשה פקרו *המינין

שנאמר ואשליכהו באש ויצא העגל הזה:

* So the Mss.; text has מערערים.

----

(130) p. 316.

T. Par. III. 3:— אמרו לפני ר' עקיבא משום ר' ישמעאל

כוסות של אבן היו תלויות בקרני שוורים כיון ששוורים שחי־

לשחות נתמלאו הכוסות אמר להם אל תתנו מקום למינין לרדד

אחריכם:

(131) p. 319.

Ber. r. XLVIII. 6. p. 97ᵇ· ᶜ:— א"ר יונתן כל חנופה שנאמר

במקרא במינות הכתוב מדבר ובנין אב שבכולן פחדו בציון חטאים

אחזה רעדה חנפים:

——————

(132) p. 320.

Shem. r. XIII. 3. p. 24ᵈ:— ד"א כי אני הכבדתי את לבו·

א"ר יוחנן מכאן פתחון פה למינין לומר לא היתה ממנו שיעשה

תשובה שנא' כי הכבדתי את לבו א"ל ר"ש בן לקיש יסתם פיהם

של מינים אלא אם ללצים הוא יליץ שהק"בה מתרה בו באדם

פעם ראשונה שניה ושלישית ואינו חוזר בו והוא נועל לבו מן

התשובה כדי לפרוע ממנו מה שחטא אף כך פרעה הרשע כיון

ששיגר הק"בה ה' פעמים ולא השגיח על דבריו א"ל הק"בה אתה

הקשית ערפך והכבדת את לבך חריני מוסיף לך טומאה על

טומאתך:

(133) p. 323.

Jalqut Shimoni. on Ps. LX. 9 [Hebr.; 7. Engl.]:— ד"א לי

גלעד א"ר שמעון בן *[לוי] אם יאמרו לך המינין שאין הק"בה

מחיה מתים אמור להם הרי אליהו מתושבי גלעד מעיד שההחייתי

על ידו. ולי מנשה אם יאמרו לך שאין הק"בה מקבל תשובה

אמור להם הרי מנשה מעיד שקבלתי אותו בתשובה שנאמר ויתפלל

* Bacher corrects לוי into לקיש. A. d. P. A. I. 372. n.

אל ה' ויעתר לו וישמע תפלתו. ואפרים מעט ראשי ואם יאמרו
לך שאין הק"בה פוקד עקרות [אמור להם] הרי אלקמה שכתוב בו
בן תוחו בן צוף אפרתי מעיד שפקדתי לחנה. יהודה מחוקקי
ואם יאמרו שאין הק"בה מציל מן האש הרי חנניה וחבריו
מעידים שהציל אותם מן האש שנאמר ויהיבהם מבני יהודה
דניאל חנניה:

(134) p. 325.

ר' שמעון בן מנסיא אומר שתה ᴵמים — Siphri § 48. p. 84ᵃ:
מבורך שתה ממים של בוראך ואל תשתה עכורים ותמשך עם
דברי מינים:

(135) p. 325.

אשיב נקם לצרי אלו כותיים שנאמר — Siphri § 331. p. 140ᵃ:
וישמעו צרי יהודה ובנימין כי בני הגולה בונים ההיכל וגו' ולמשנאי
אשלם אלו המינים וכן הוא אומר הלא משנאיך ה' אשנא ובתקוממיך
אתקוטט תכלית שנאה שנאתים לאויבים היו לי:

(136) p. 326.

ואמר רב חנן בר רבא אמר רב אמיה — B. Bathr. 91ᵃ:
דאברהם אמתלאי בת כרנבו אמיה דהמן אמתלאי בת עורבתי
וסימניך טמא טמא טהור טהור אמיה דדוד נצבת בת עדאל [שמה]
אמיה דשמשון צללפונית ואחתיה נשיין למאי נפקא מינה לתשובת
המינין:

(137) p. 327.

אם אינן מכירין אותו משלחין אחר — M. R. ha-Sh. II. 1.:
עמו להעידו בראשונה היו מקבלין עדות החדש מכל אדם משקלקלו
המינין התקינו שלא יהו מקבלין אלא מן המכירין:

(138) p. 329.

בראשונה היו מקבלין עדות החרש מכל — b. R. ha-Sh. 22ᵇ:
אדם וכו' תנו רבנן מה קלקול הבייתוסין פעם אחת וכו':

---

(139) p. 338.

אמר רבי זכריה משום רבי ישמעאל ביקש — b. Nedar. 32ᵇ:
הק"בה להוציא כהונה משם שנאמר והוא כהן לאל עליון כיון

שהקדים ברכת אברהם לברכת המקום הוציאה מאברהם שנאמר
ויברכהו ויאמר ברוך אברם לאל עליון קונה שמים וארץ וברוך
אל עליון אמר לו אברהם וכי מקדימין ברכת עבד לברכת קונו
מיד נתנה לאברהם שנאמר נאם ה' לאדני שב לימיני עד אשית
אויביך הדום לרגליך ובתריה כתיב נשבע ה' ולא ינחם אתה כהן
לעולם על דברתי מלכי צדק על דיבורו של מלכי צדק והיינו דכתיב
והוא כהן לאל עליון הוא כהן ואין זרעו כהן:

INDICES

29

I.—INDEX OF SUBJECTS

II.—INDEX OF PERSONS

Rabbis of the Tannaite period (see p. 350), are distinguished thus (T.), those of the Amoraite period thus (A.) after the name.

Harnack, A., 384.
Hija bar Abba (A.), 6, 179, 306, 356.
Hillel (T.), 2, 6 n., 57 f., 135.
Hisda (A.), 37, 57, 60 n., 124, 187 f., 308, 354-5.
Hitzig, 39 n.
Hoshaia (A.), 247 f.
Huna (A.), 77, 186, 210.

Idi (A.), 286 f.
Imma Shalom, 146 f.
Ishmael ben Elisha (T.), 29, 103 f., 129 f., 156 f., 172, 339.
—— ben José (T.), 245.
Isi of Cæsarea (A.), 215, 219 f., 334.

Jacob of Chephar Sama (Sechanja), 106 f., 138 f.
—— the Min, 109, 111.
Jannai (A.), 115, 253, 258.
—— the King, 52.
Jehoshua ben Hananjah (T.), 43 f., 48, 115 f., 117, 153, 165, 188, 211 f., 221 f., 226 f., 280.
—— ben Levi (A.), 108, 332, 354.
—— ben Perahjah, 38, 52 f., 97, 347.
Jehudah II. (Nesiah) (A.), 109.
—— ben Jehesq'el (A.), 126, 223, 227, 308, 355.
—— ben Naqosa (T.), 218 f.
—— ben Tabbai, 52.
—— bar Zebuda (A.), 77.
—— ha-Qadosh (Rabbi) (T.), 17, 128, 184, 208, 218, 223, 240 f., 297, 353.
Jeremiah bar Abba (A.), 56 f.
Jerome, 378.
Jesus, 9, 37-96 passim, 102, 117, 143, 150, 214, 224 n., 234, 305, 330, 344-60 passim; see also heads of sections in Division I. A.
Jitzhaq (A.), 100, 159 n., 209, 240, 244, 246, 261, 310.

Johanan (A.), 20 n., 28, 47, 68, 73, 75, 98, 108, 110, 120, 149, 162, 172, 174-5, 179, 180, 186, 193, 216, 279, 315, 321, 354.
—— ben Zaccai (T.), 43, 84, 142 n., 352, 382.
Jonathan ben El'azar (A.), 216 f., 254 f., 301, 319.
José bar Būn (A.), 77.
—— ben Halaphta (T.), 136, 245, 317.
—— ben Joezer, 2.
—— ben Johanan, 2.
—— ben Zimra (A.), 115.
José ha-Galili (T.), 155, 296.
Joseph, father of Jesus, 48.
—— bar Hija (A.), 42 f., 355, 358.
—— bar Hanin (A.), 162.
—— bar Jehoshua ben Levi (A.), 19.
—— bar Minjomi (A.), 179.
Josephus, Flavius, 345 n.
Joshua, 2.
Jost, J. M., 61 n., 96, 130, 166.
Judah ben Pazi (A.), 205 f., 307.
Judan (A.), 257.
Judas Iscariot, 71, 75.
Julian the Apostate, 283 f.
Justin Martyr, 85 n., 156 n., 171.

Kahana (A.), 333, 356.
Keim Th., 31, 53 n., 82, 95.

Laible, H., 35-94 passim.
Levi (A.), 315.
Levy, J., 47, 95, 113, 166, 362.
Livianos, see Bar Livianos.

Mar bar Joseph (A.), 162.
—— bar Rabina (A.), 70 n.
—— Uqba (A.), 183, 186.
Marx, G. A., 3 n., 77.
Mathnah (A.), 77, 308.
Matthai, disciple of Jesus, 92 f.

III.—INDEX OF PLACES

IV.—INDEX OF O.T. PASSAGES REFERRED TO

V.—INDEX OF N.T. PASSAGES REFERRED TO

VI.—INDEX OF RABBINICAL PASSAGES REFERRED TO

Texts transcribed and translated in full are indicated thus (*).

1. MISHNAH

2. TOSEPHTA